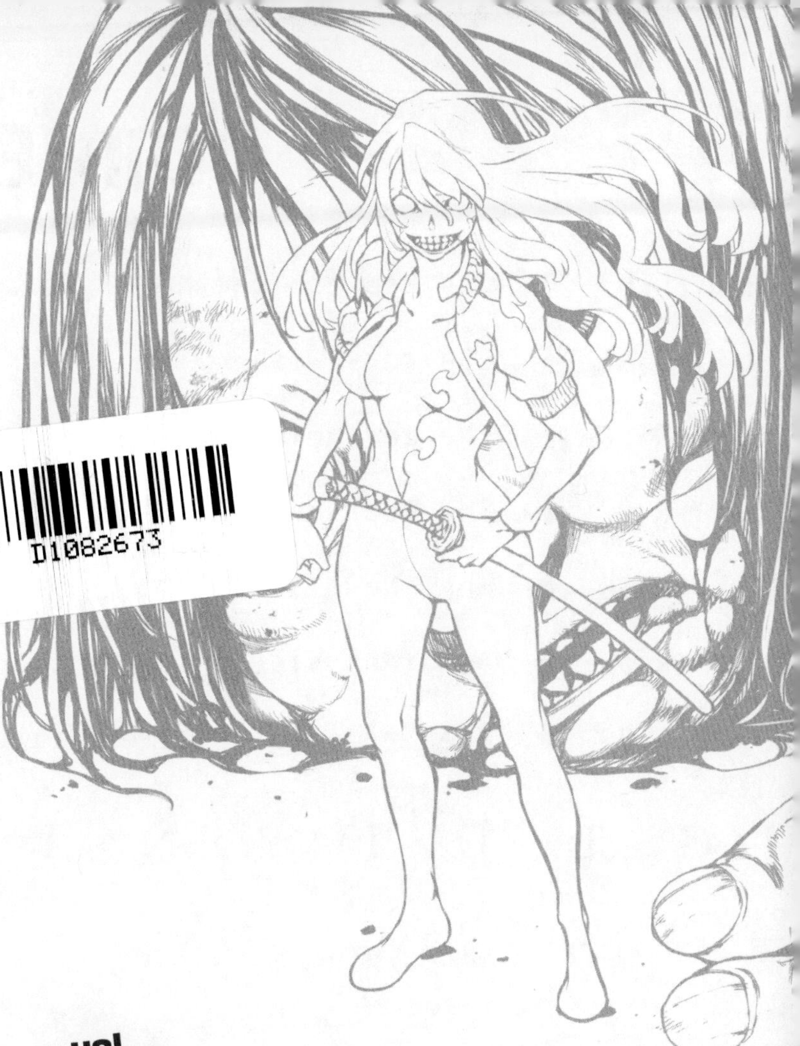

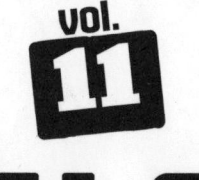

vol.
11

GLEIPNIR

SUN TAKEDA

CONTENTS

G L E I P N I R

CHAPTER 64

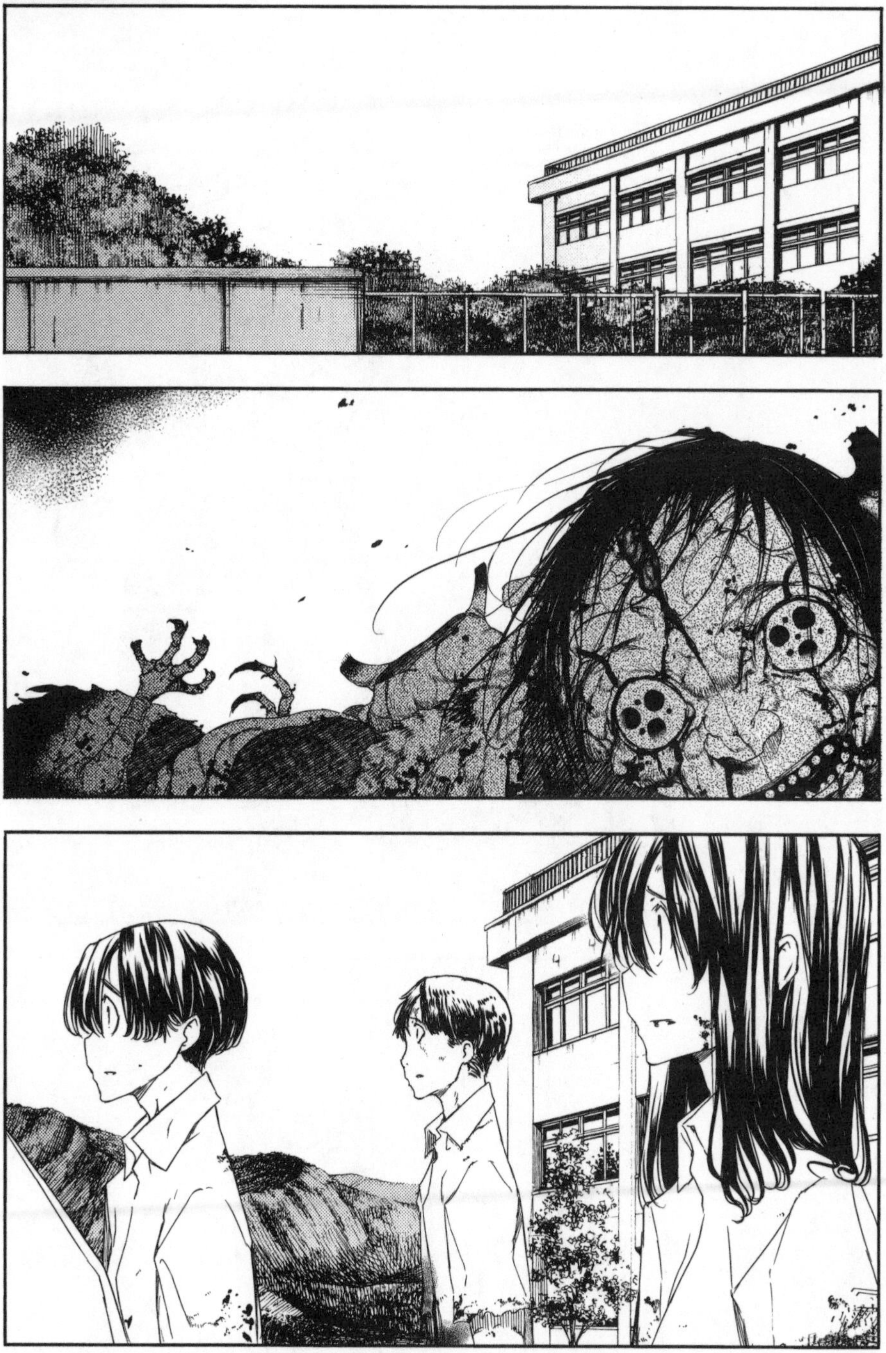

CHAPTER 64 ✚ OUR HEARTS TOGETHER

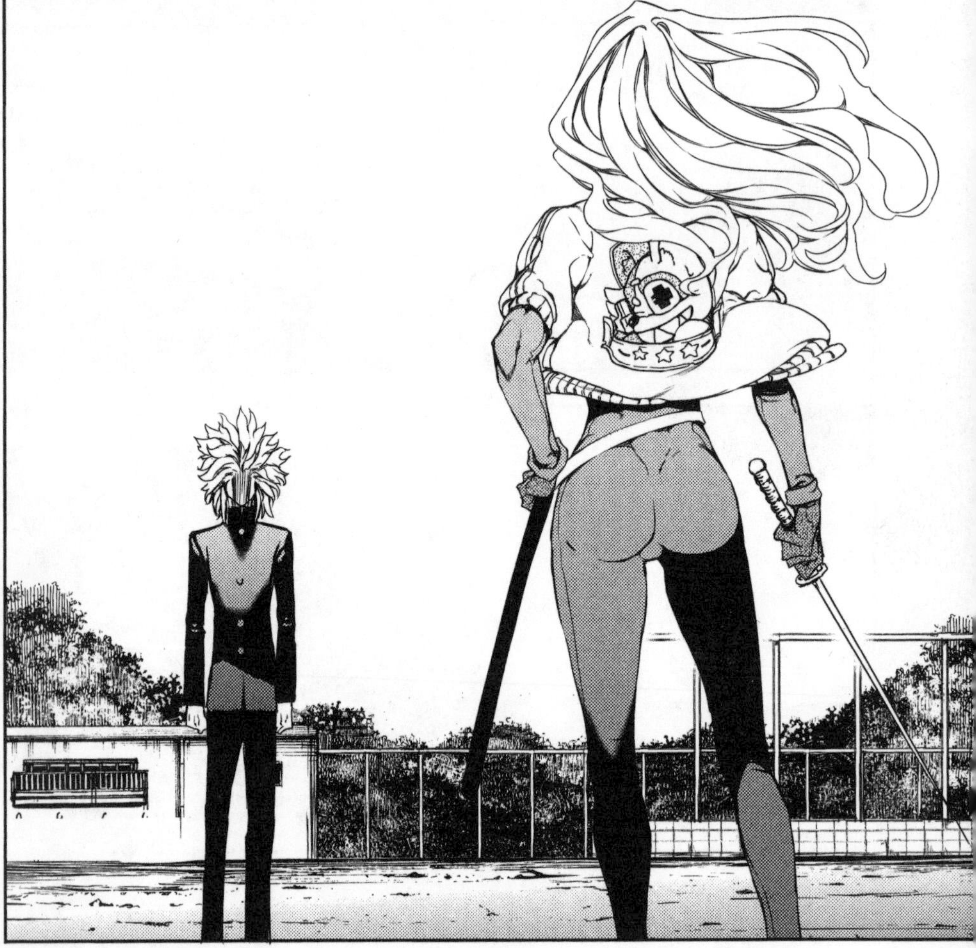

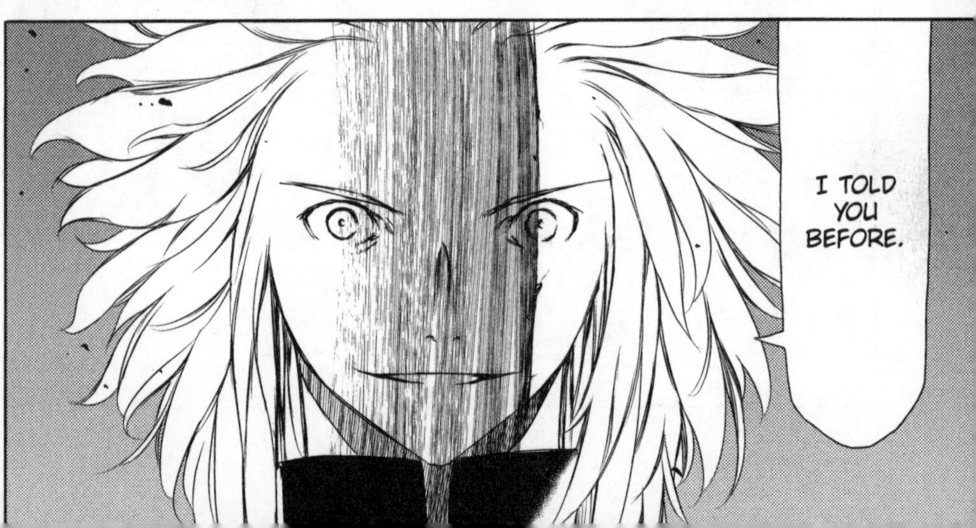
I TOLD YOU BEFORE.

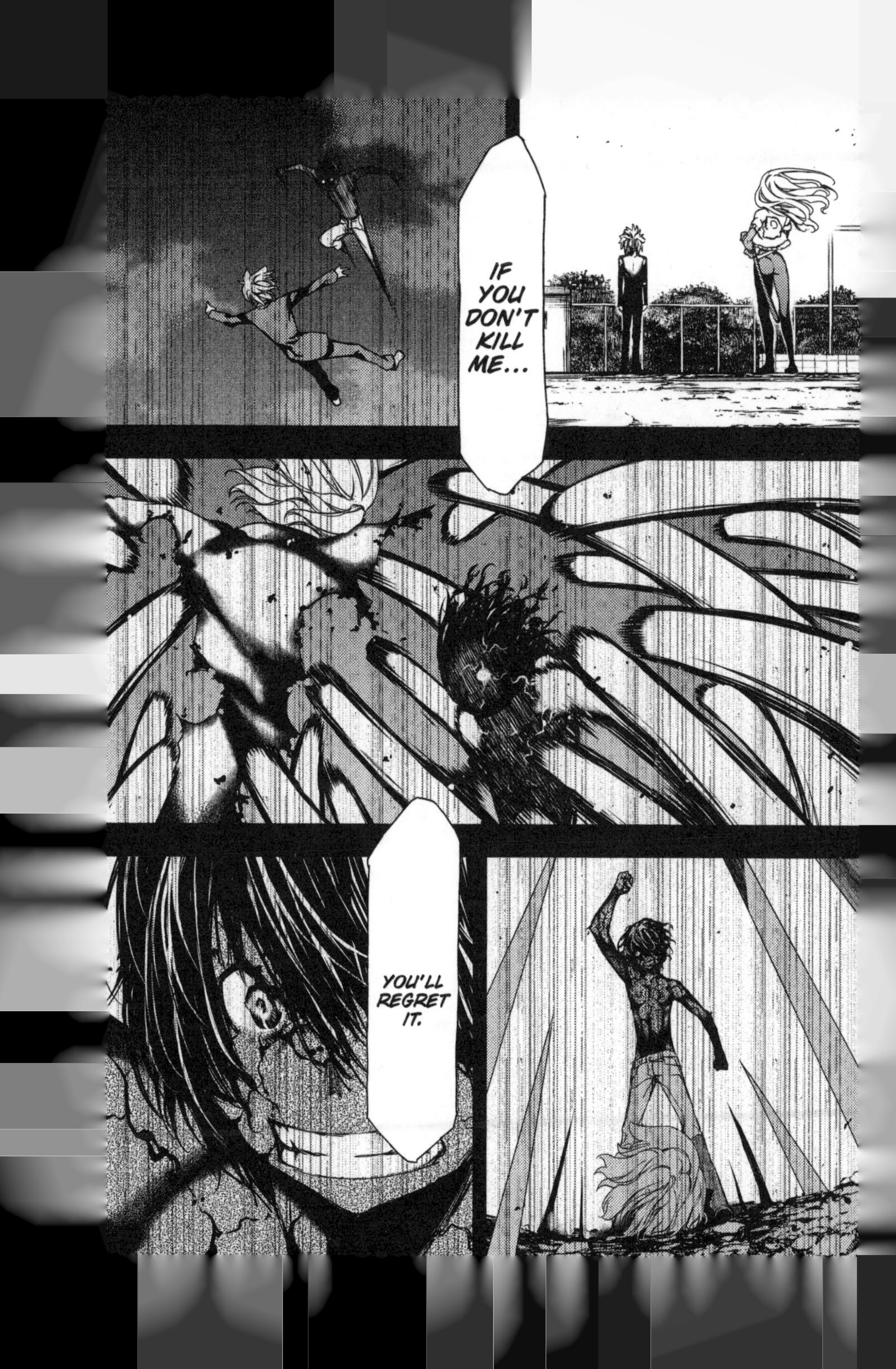
IF YOU DON'T KILL ME...
YOU'LL REGRET IT.

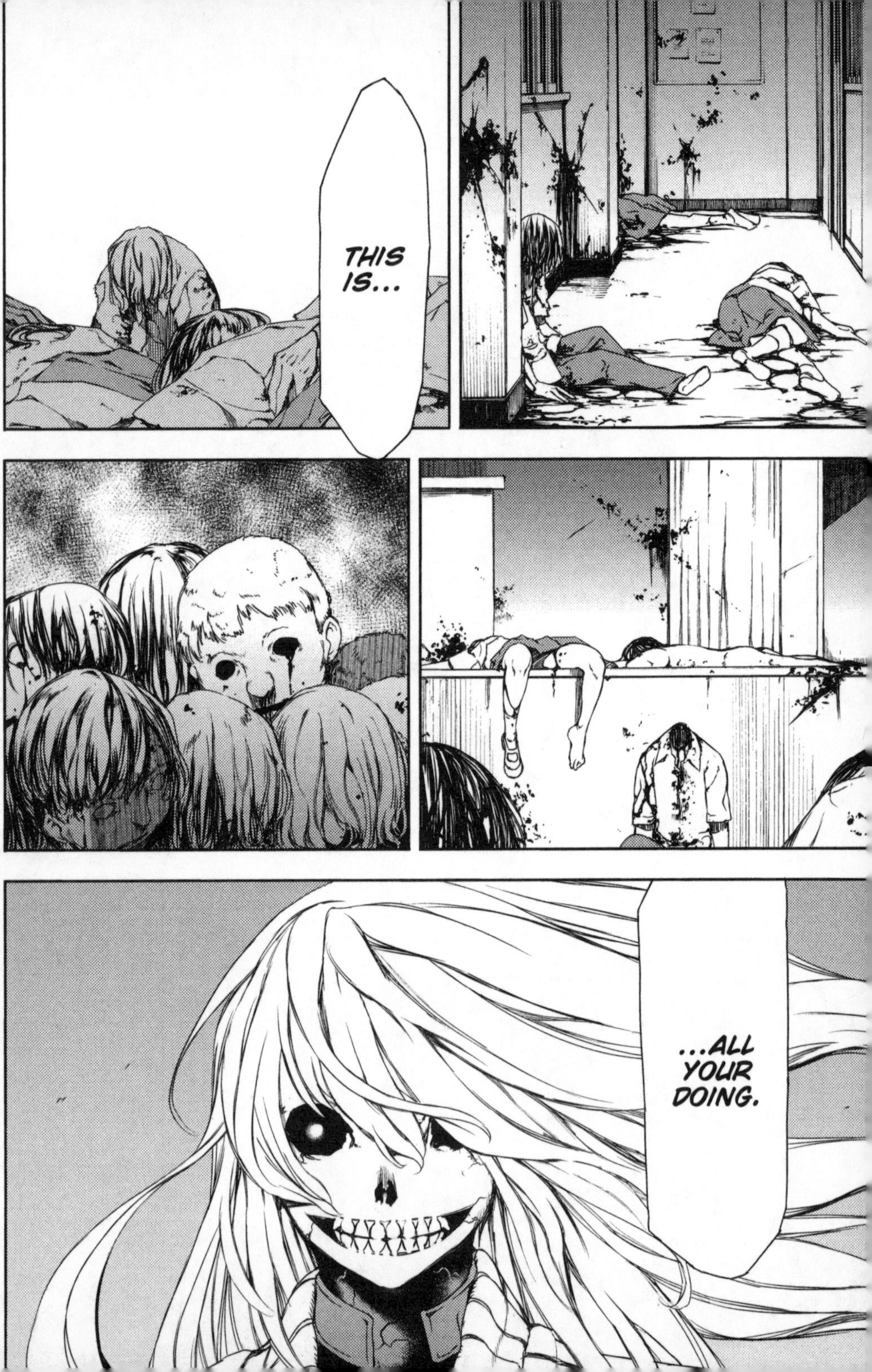
THIS IS...
...ALL YOUR DOING.

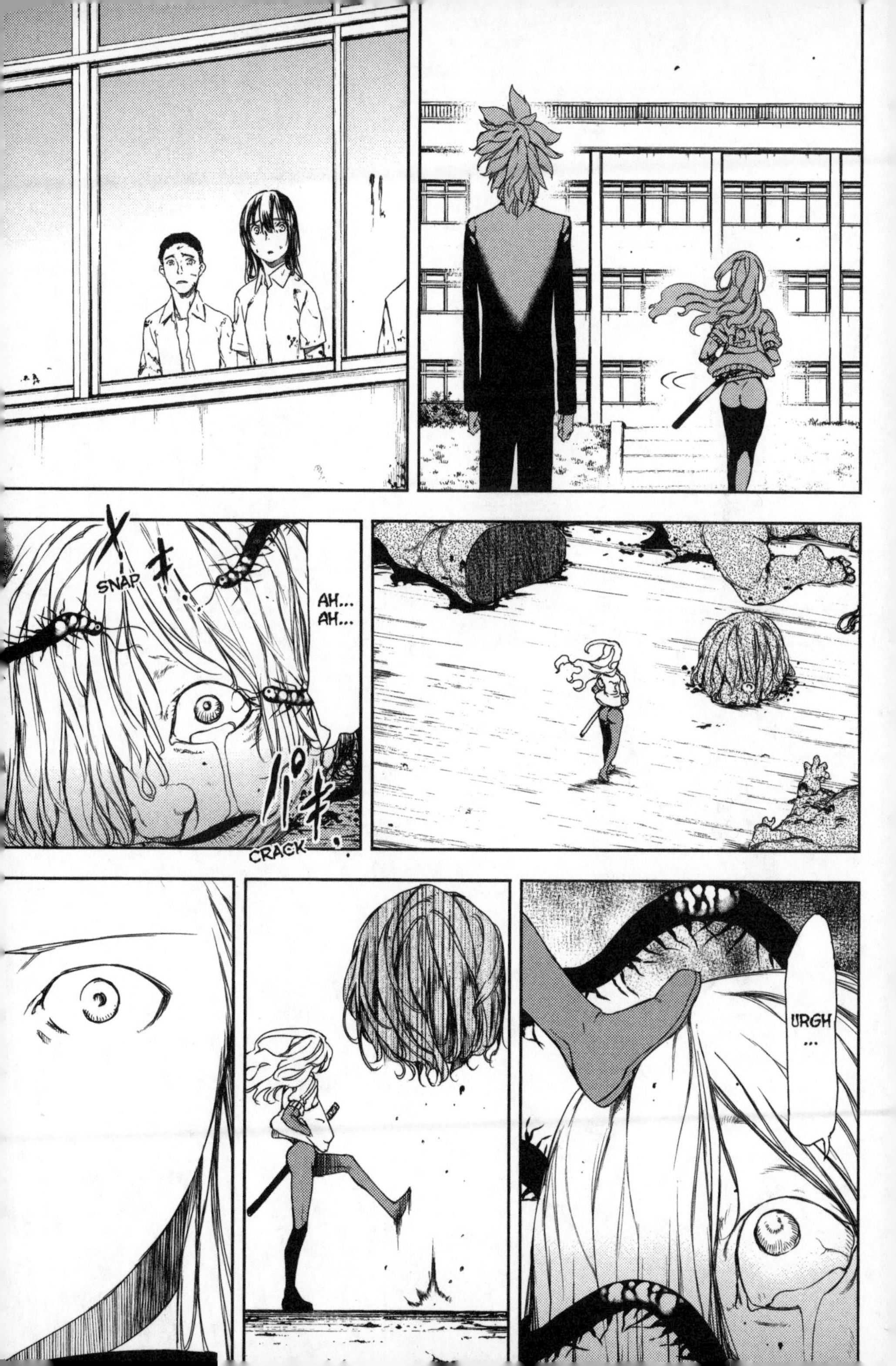
AH... AH...
SNAP
CRACK
URGH ...

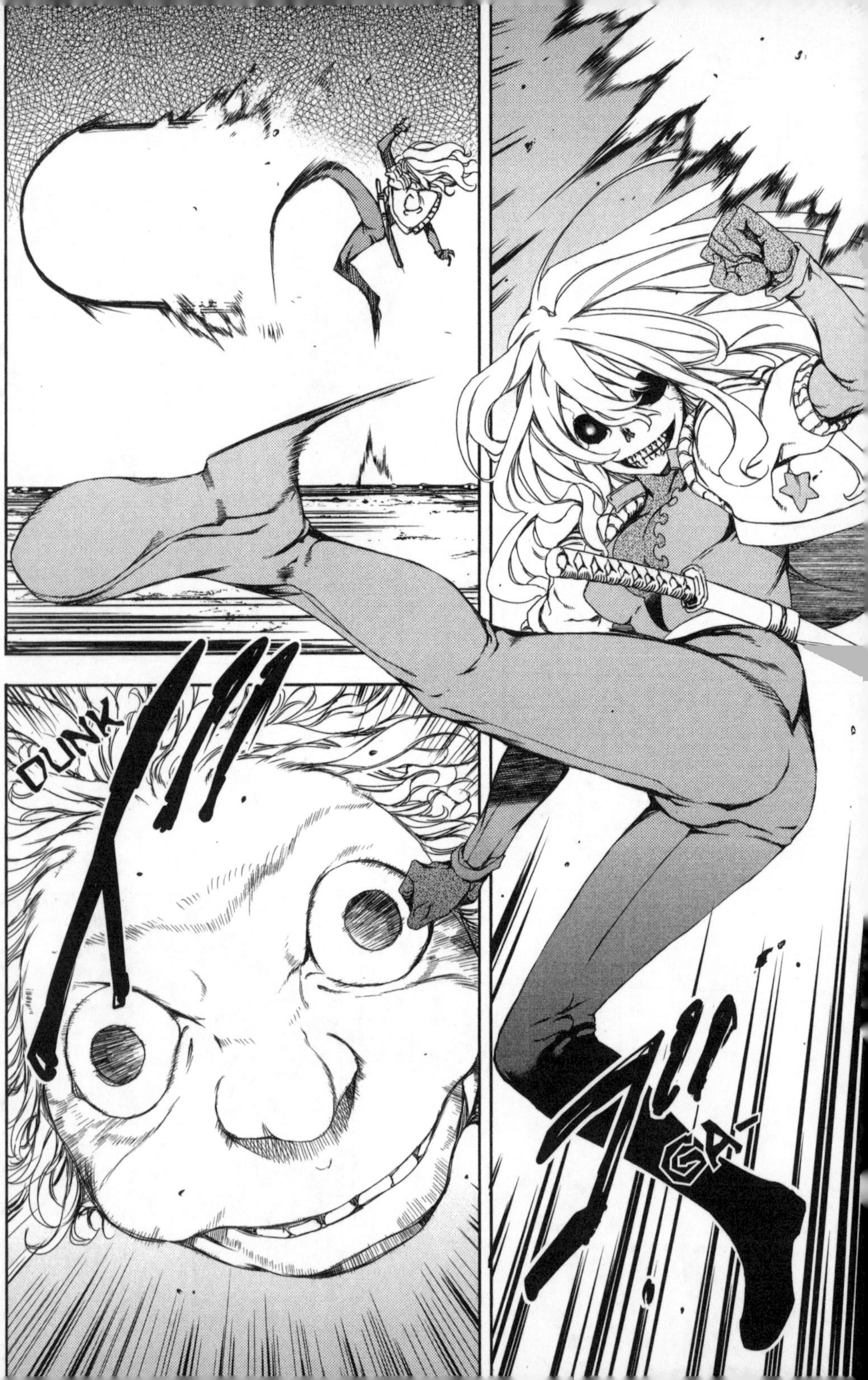
DUNK
GA

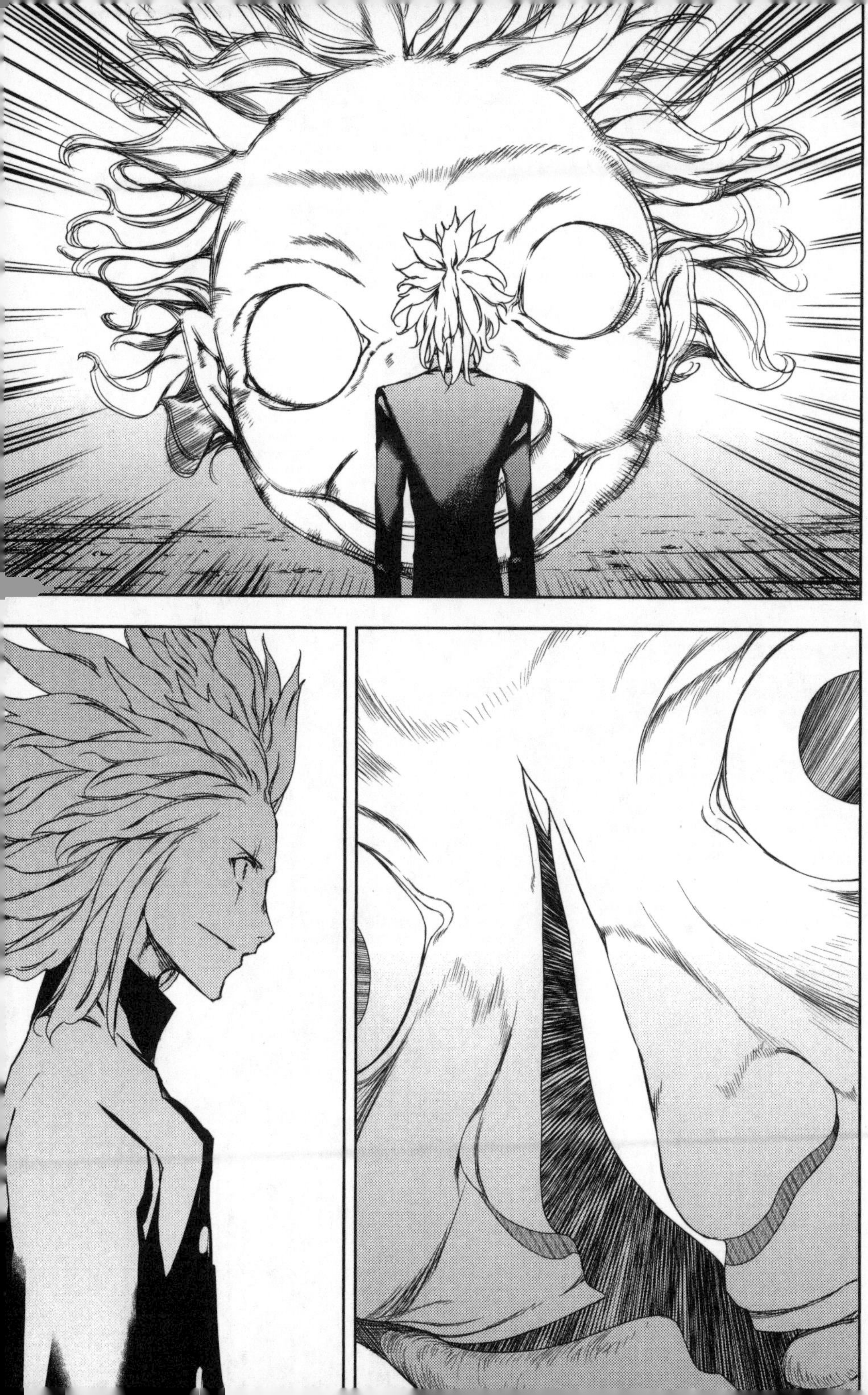

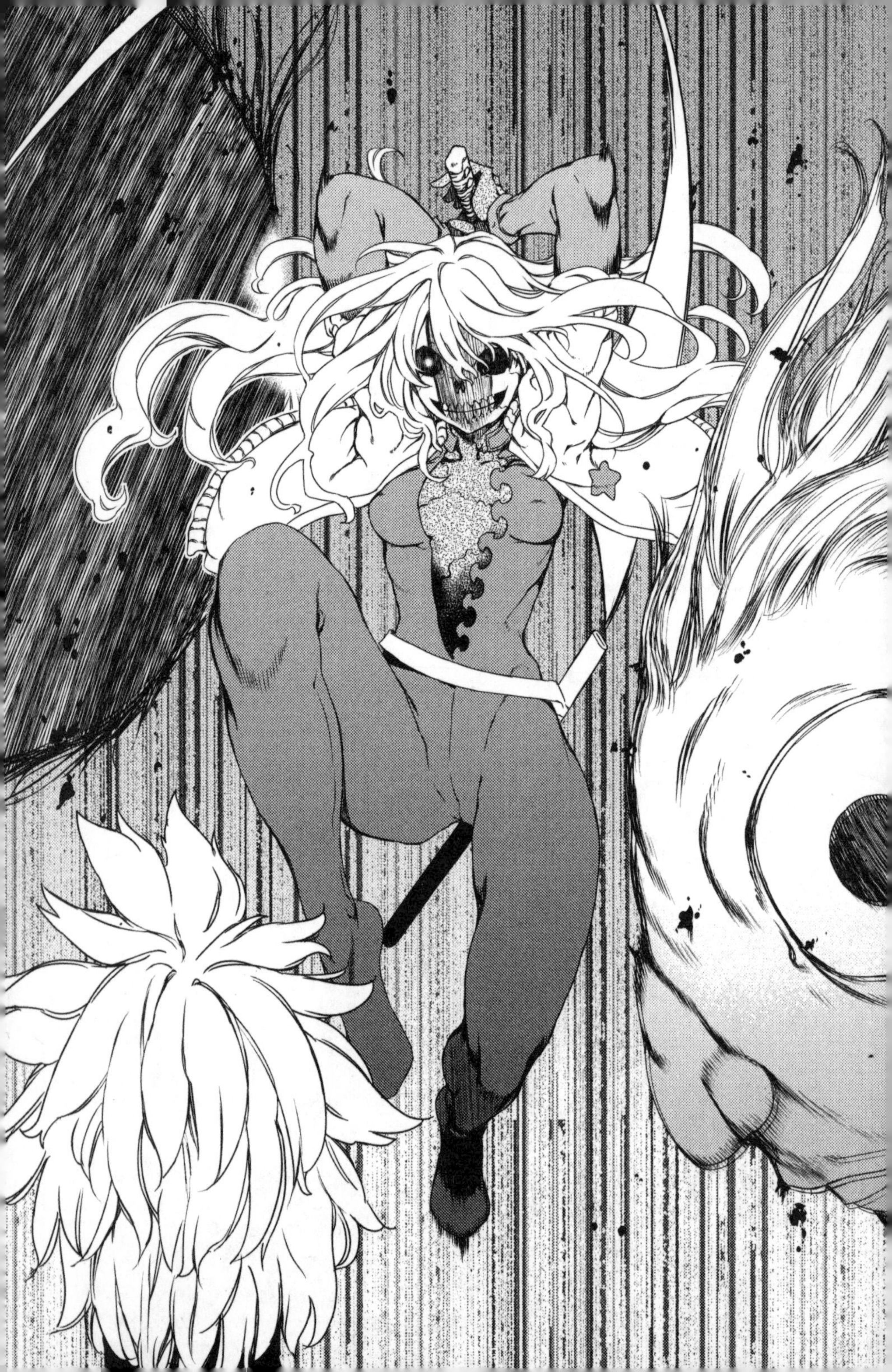

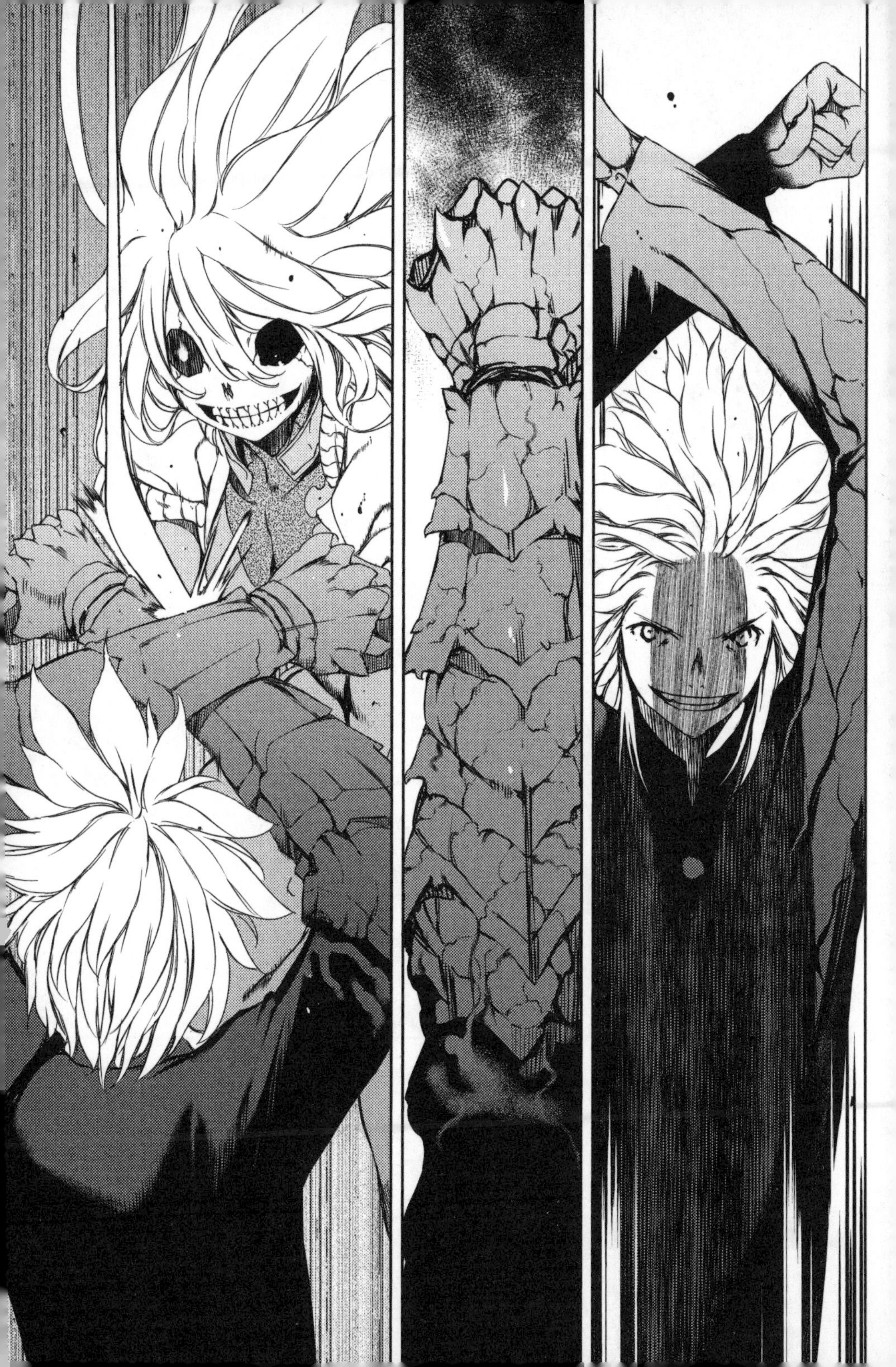

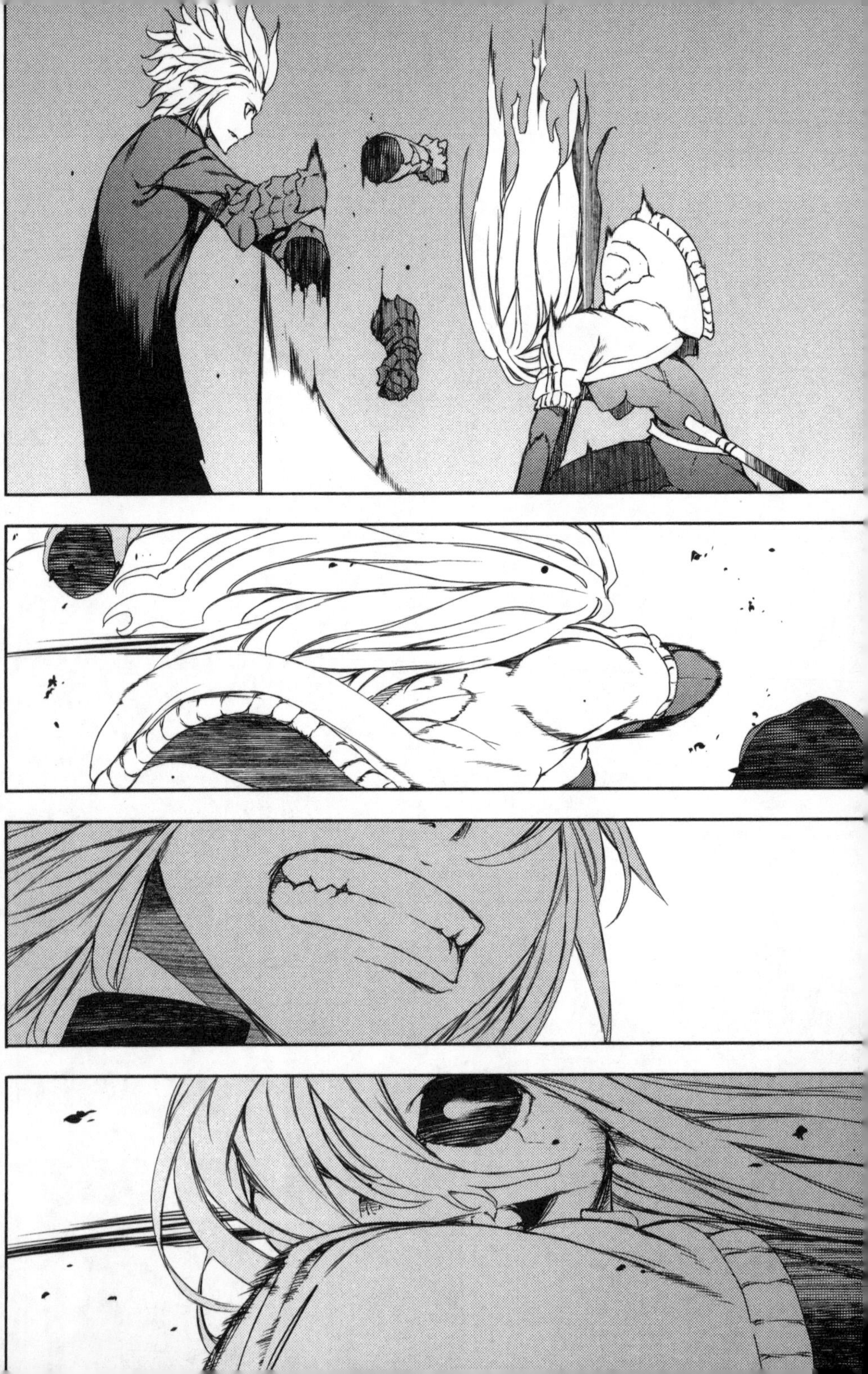

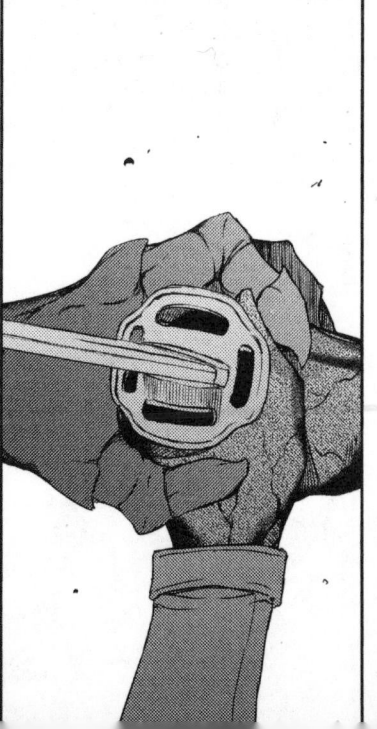

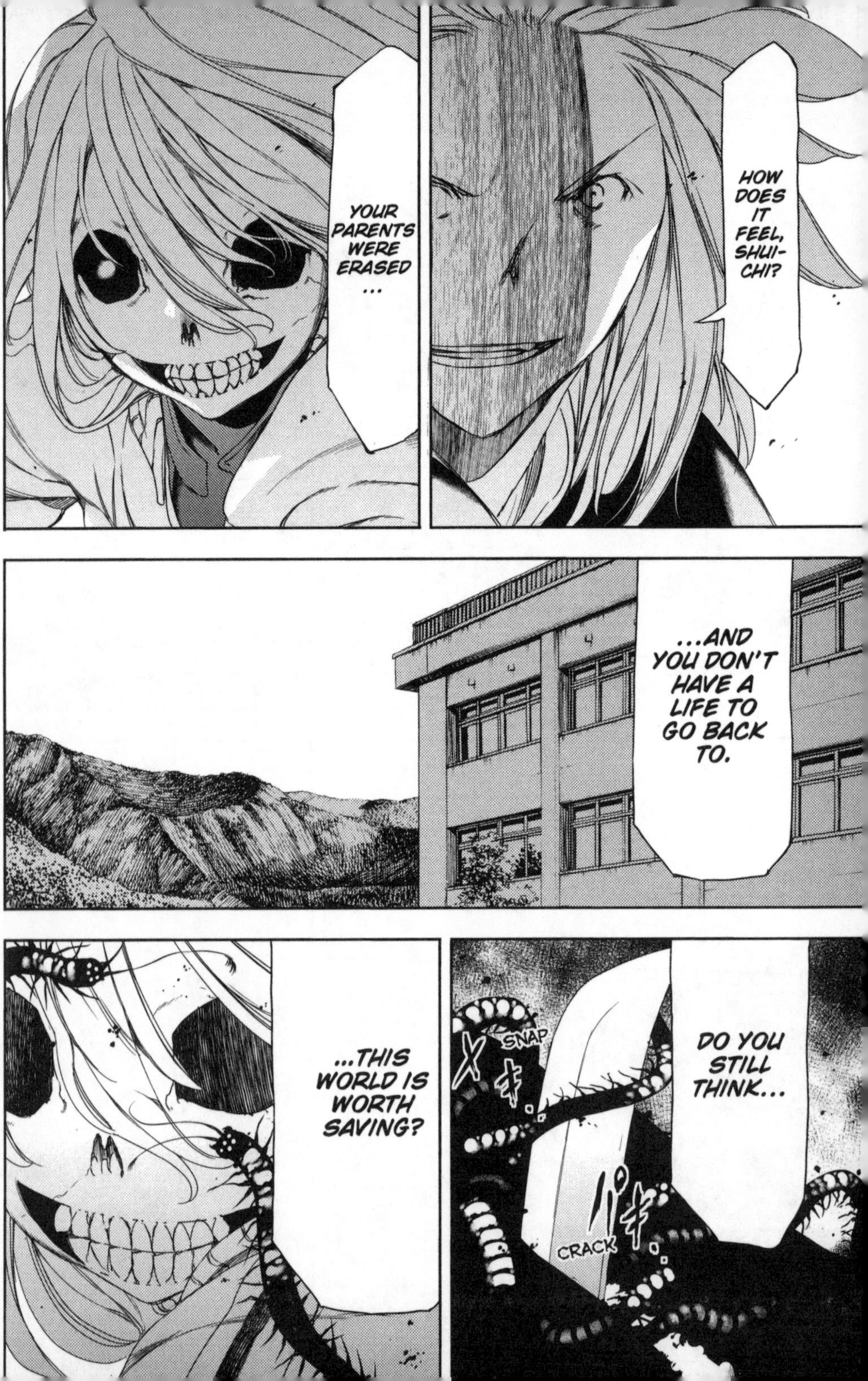
HOW DOES IT FEEL, SHUICHI?
YOUR PARENTS WERE ERASED ...
...AND YOU DON'T HAVE A LIFE TO GO BACK TO.
DO YOU STILL THINK...
SNAP
CRACK
...THIS WORLD IS WORTH SAVING?

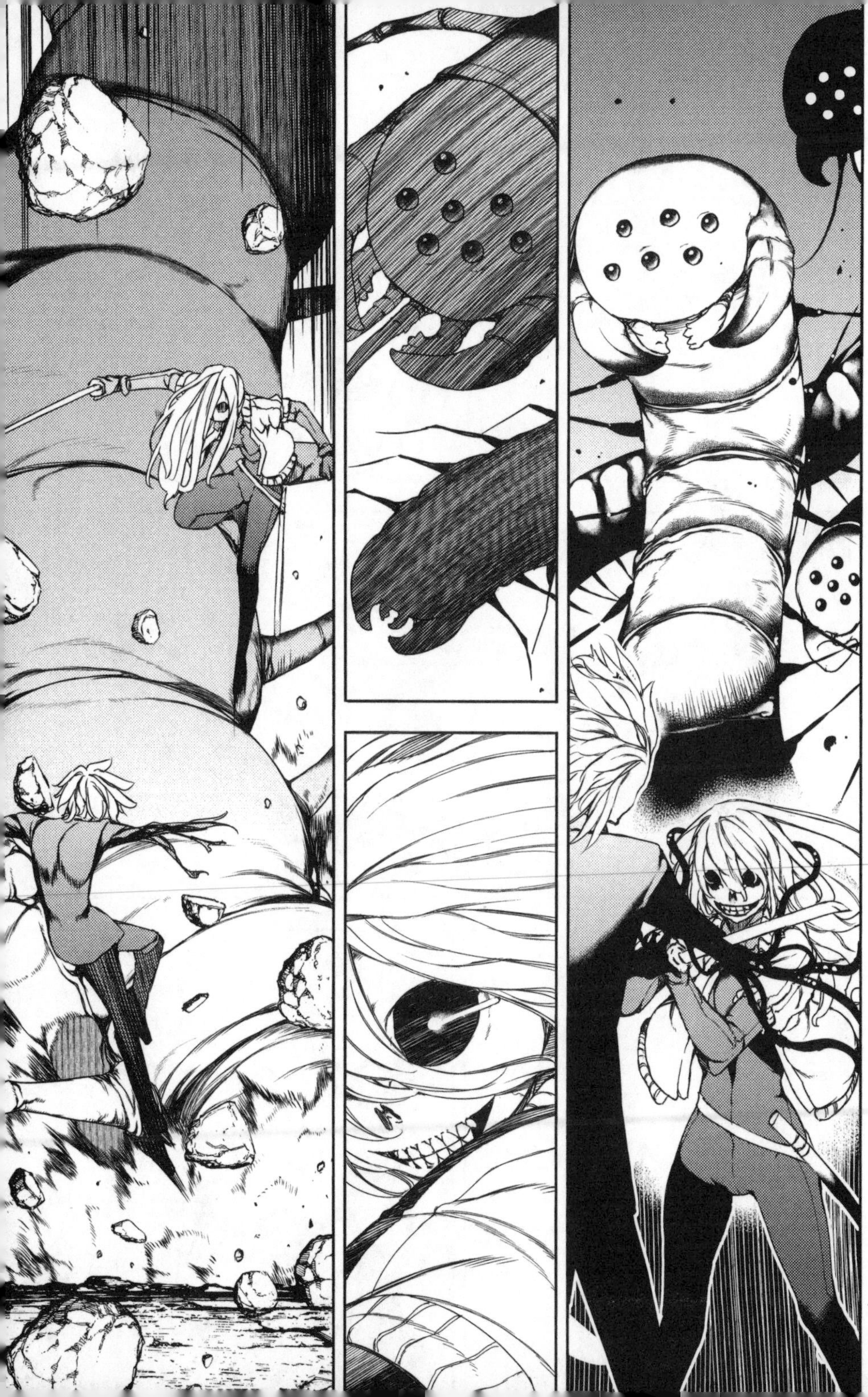

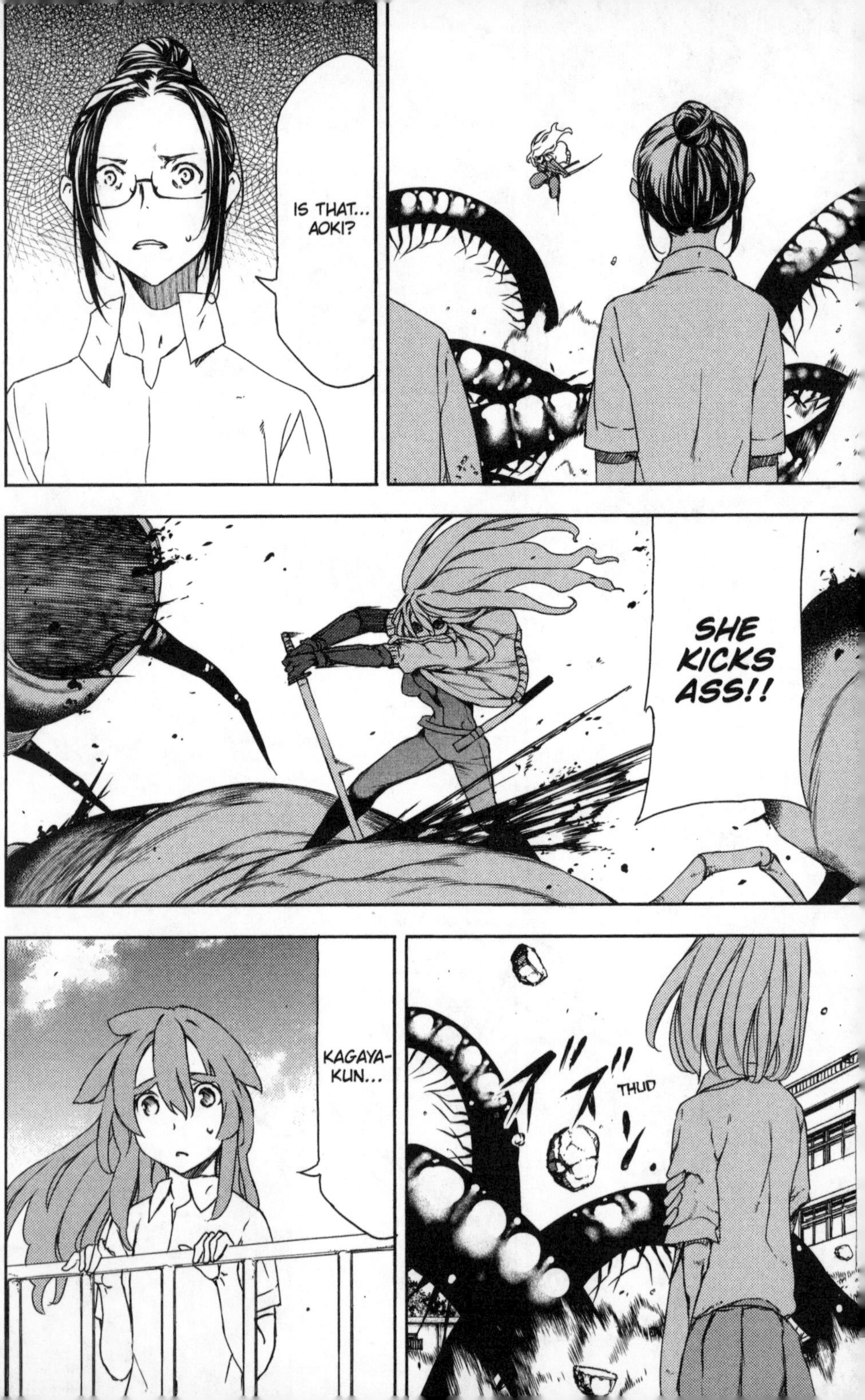
IS THAT... AOKI?
SHE KICKS ASS!!
THUD
KAGAYA-KUN...

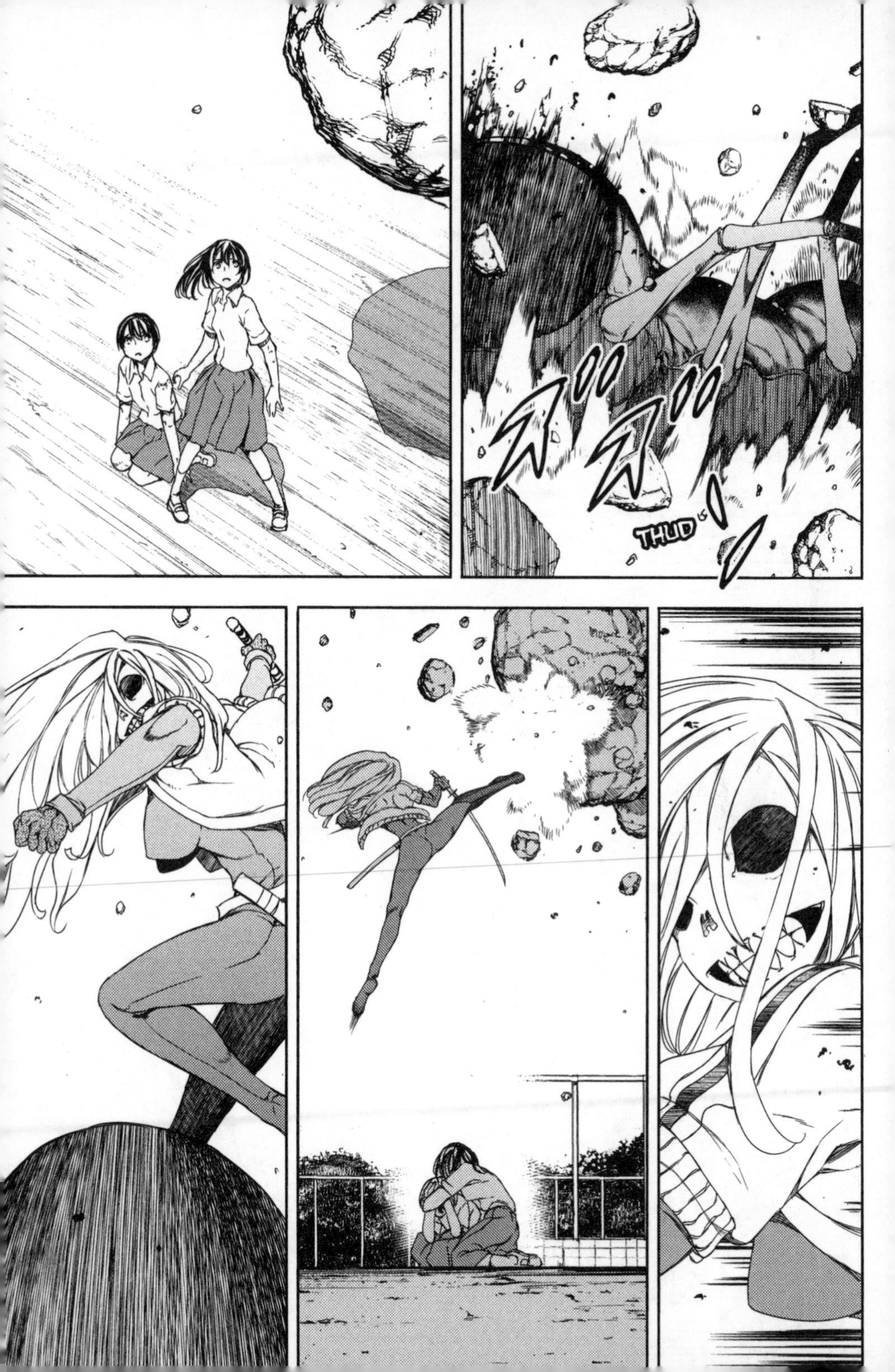
THUD

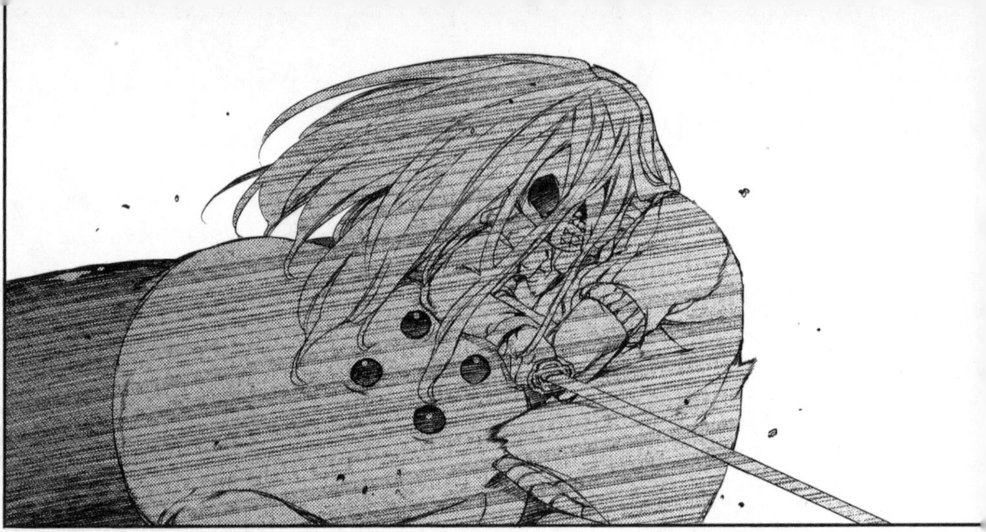
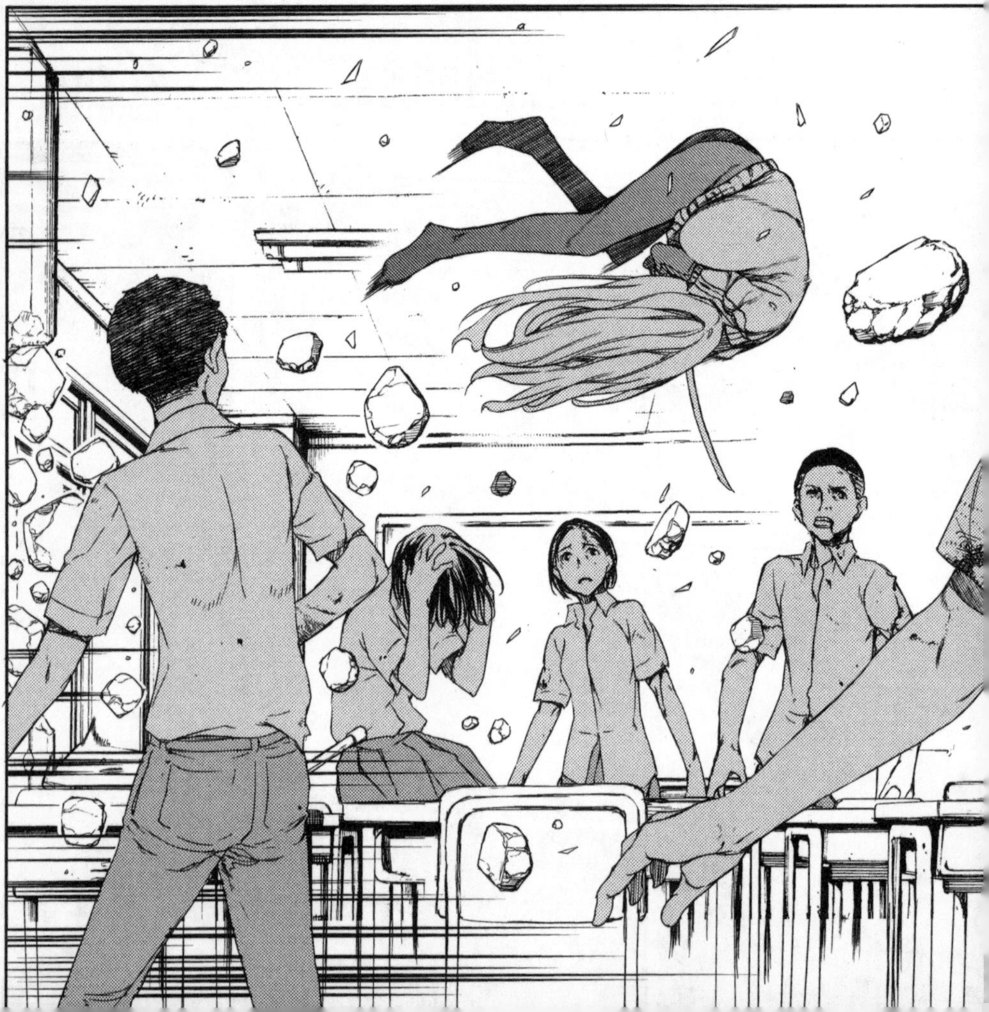

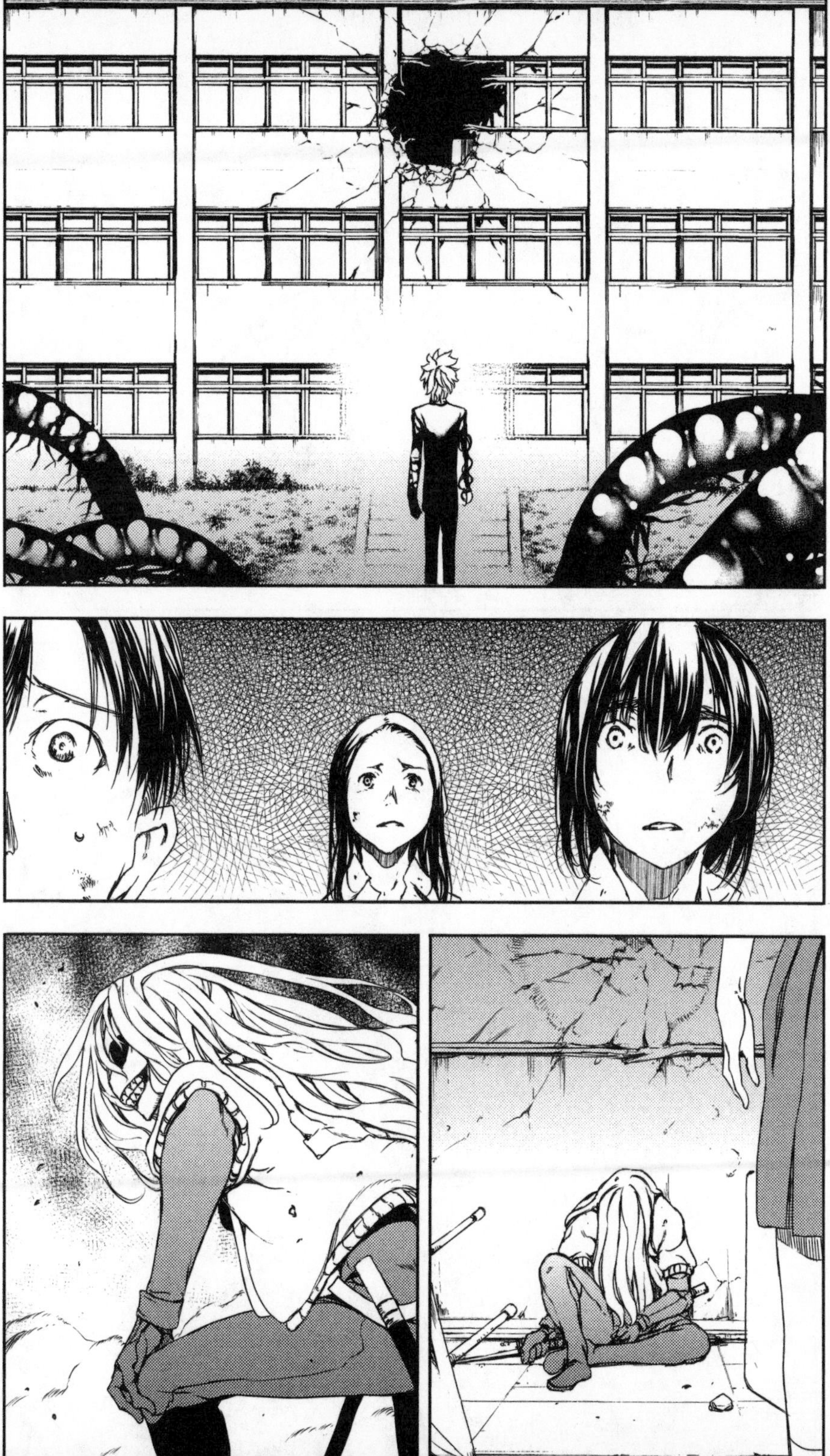

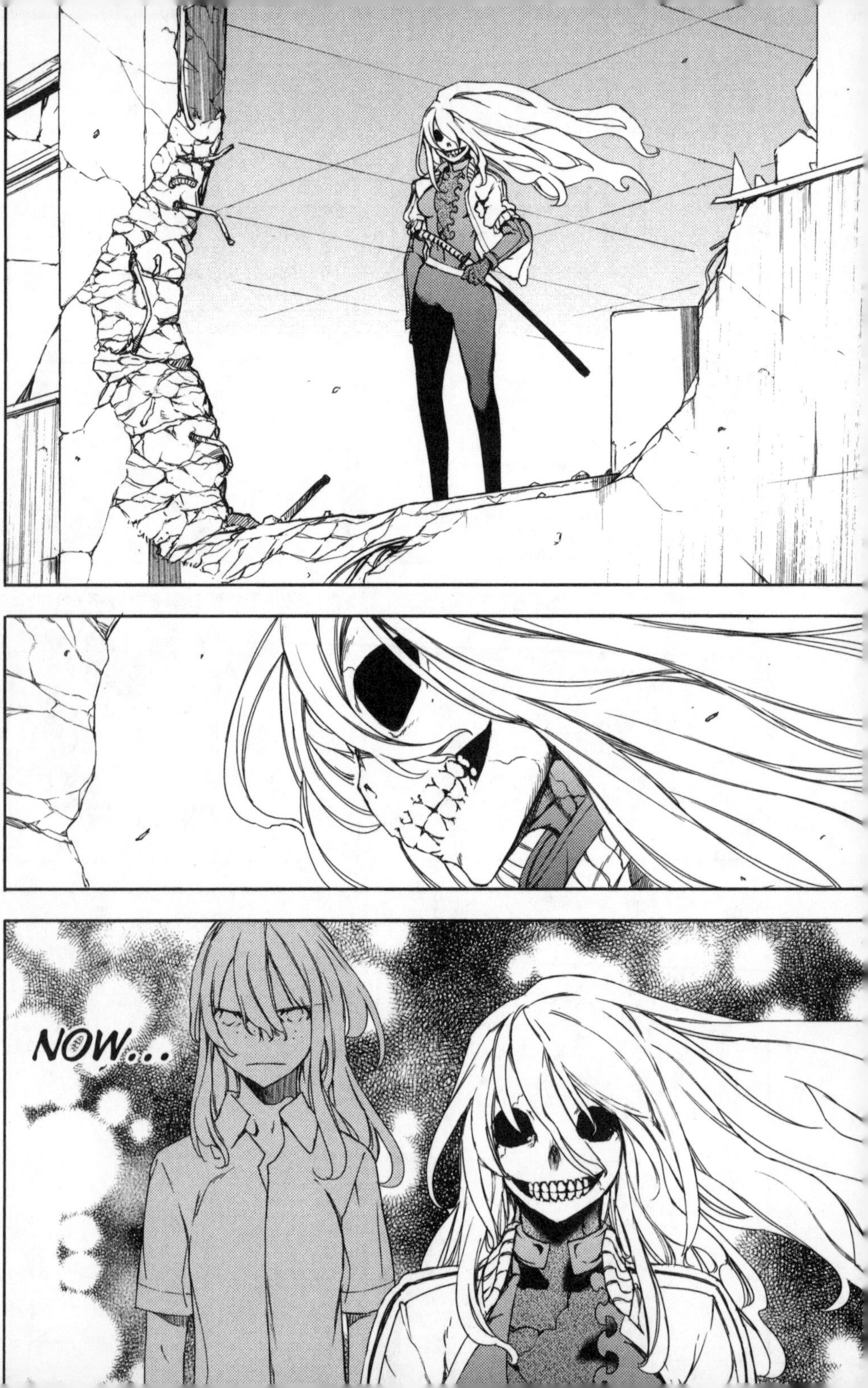
NOW...

...I CAN SENSE EXACTLY HOW SHUICHI FEELS.

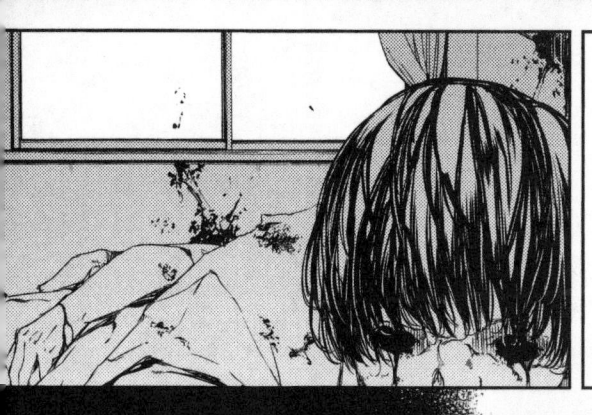

RAGE...

BUT THERE'S MORE TO IT THAN THAT...

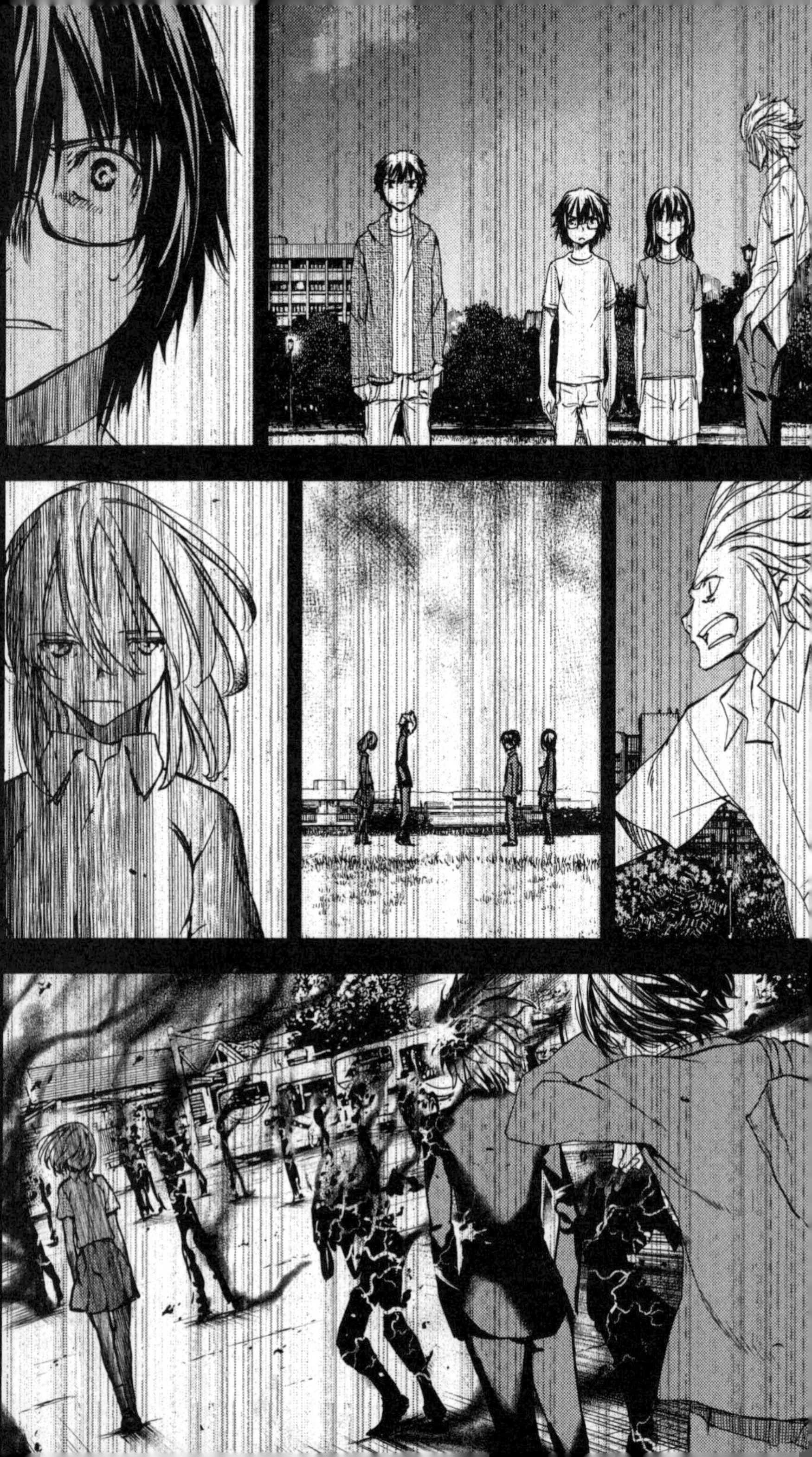

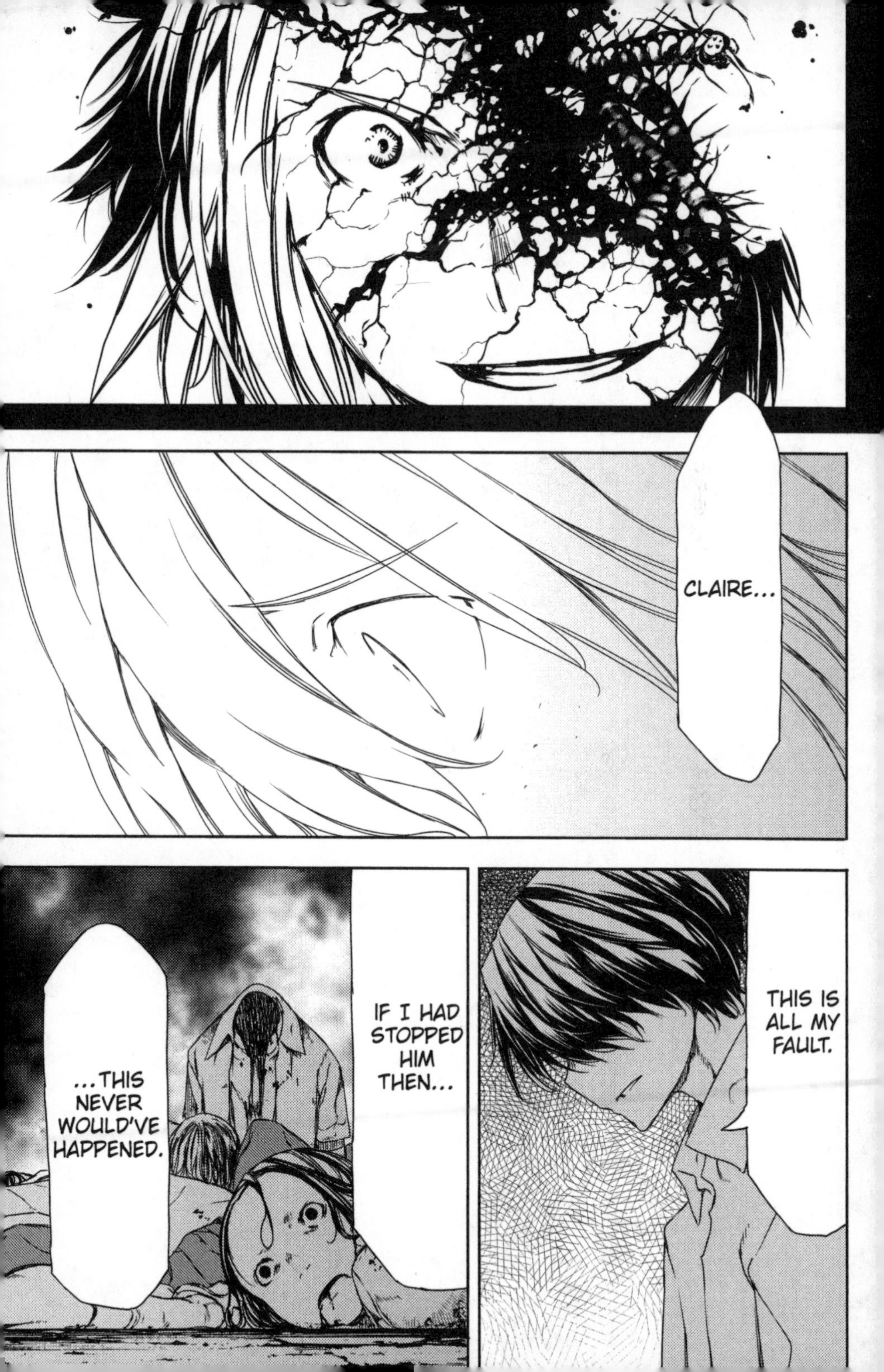
CLAIRE...
THIS IS ALL MY FAULT.
IF I HAD STOPPED HIM THEN...
...THIS NEVER WOULD'VE HAPPENED.

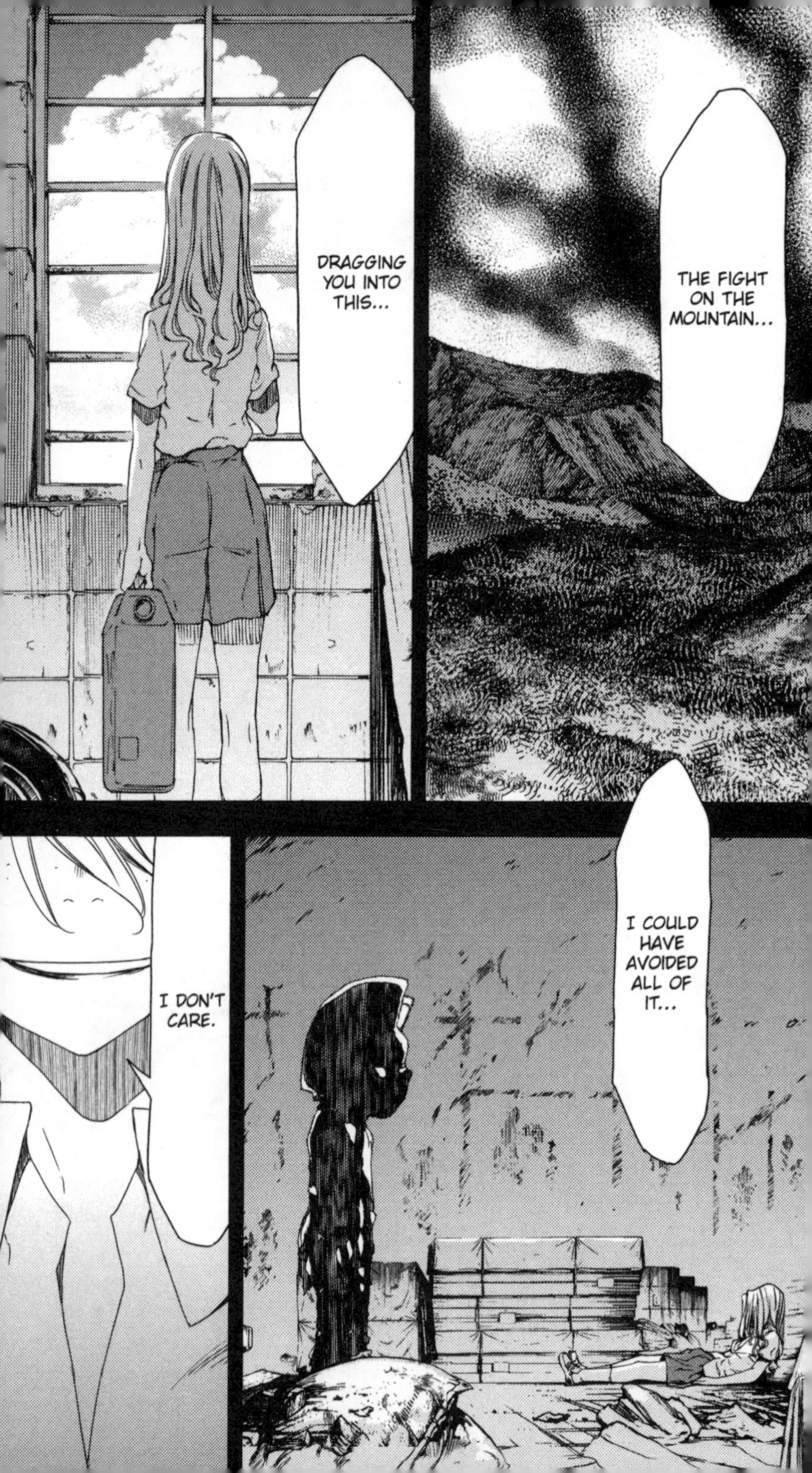
THE FIGHT ON THE MOUNTAIN...
DRAGGING YOU INTO THIS...
I COULD HAVE AVOIDED ALL OF IT...
I DON'T CARE.

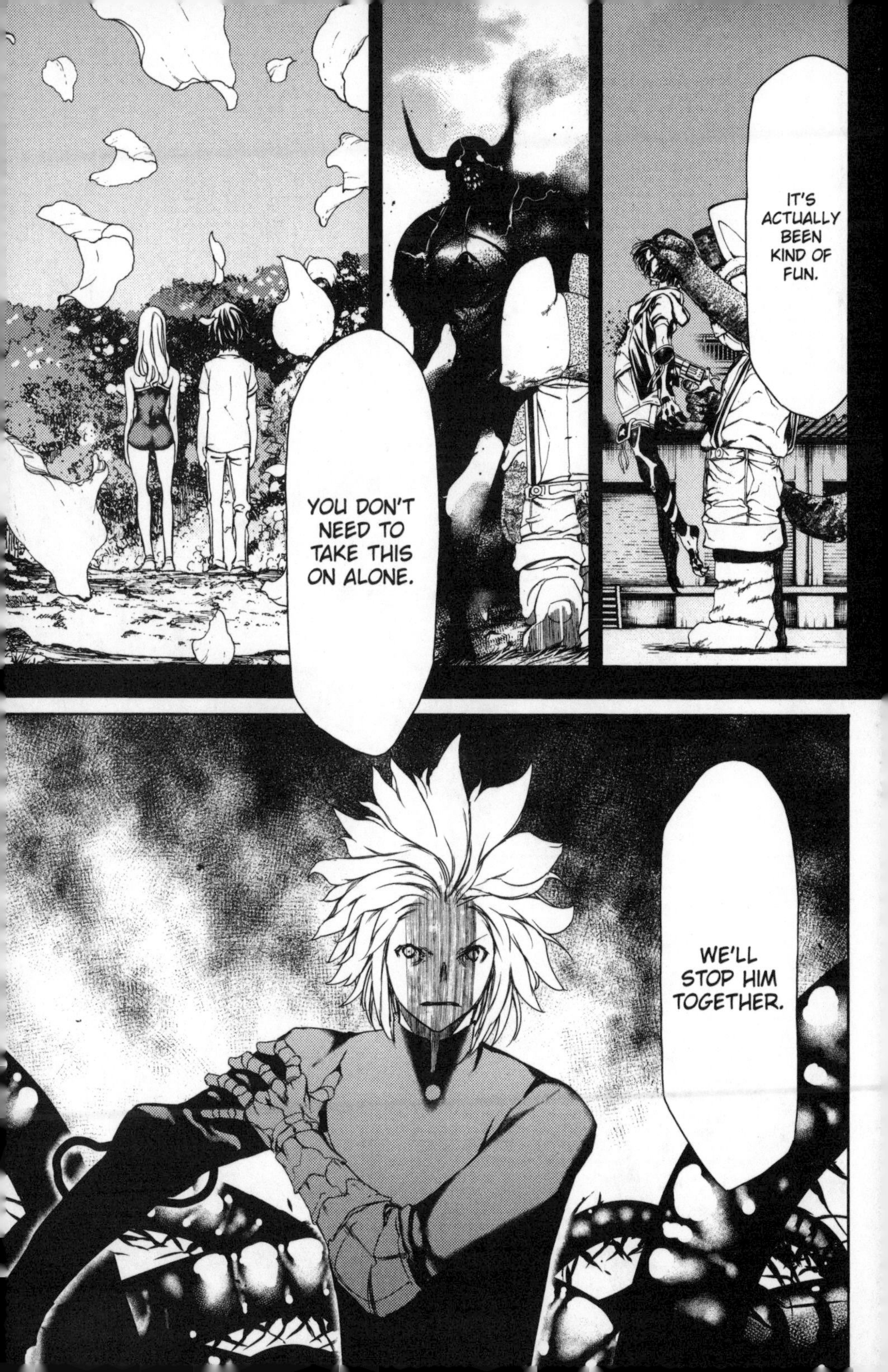
IT'S ACTUALLY BEEN KIND OF FUN.
YOU DON'T NEED TO TAKE THIS ON ALONE.
WE'LL STOP HIM TOGETHER.

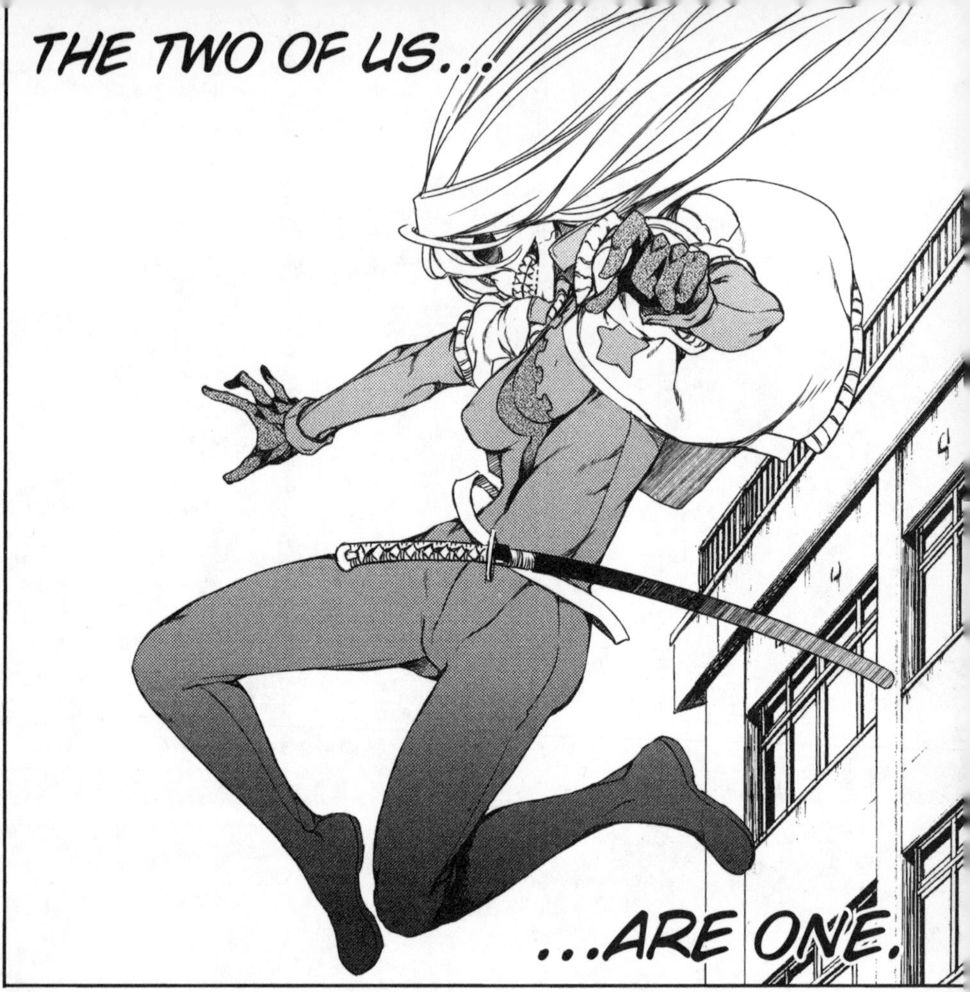
THE TWO OF US...
...ARE ONE.
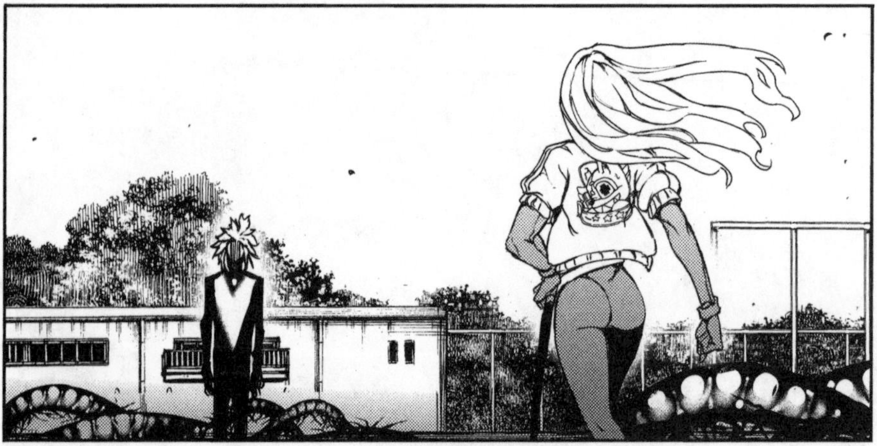

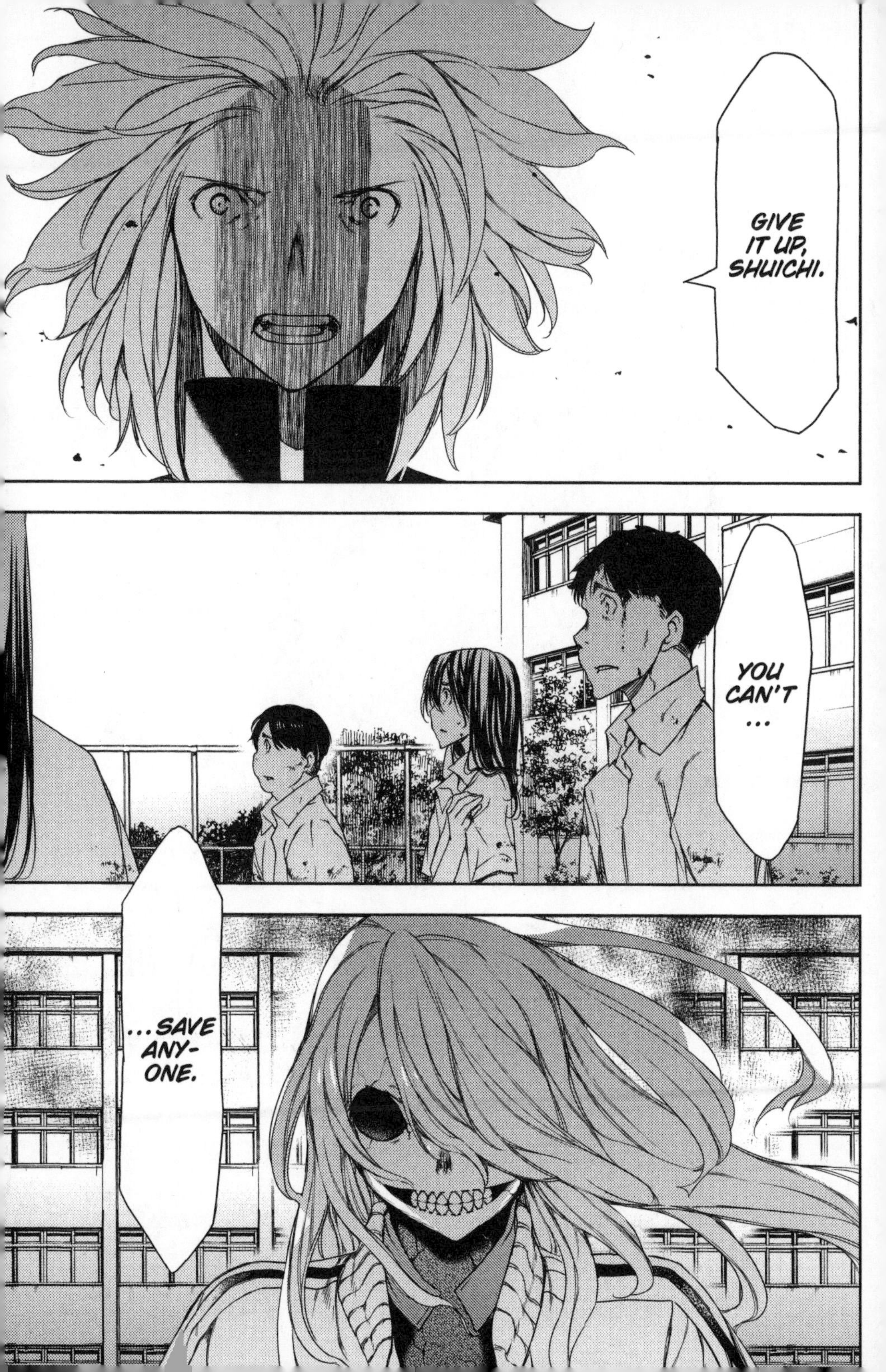
GIVE IT UP, SHUICHI.
YOU CAN'T ...
...SAVE ANY-ONE.

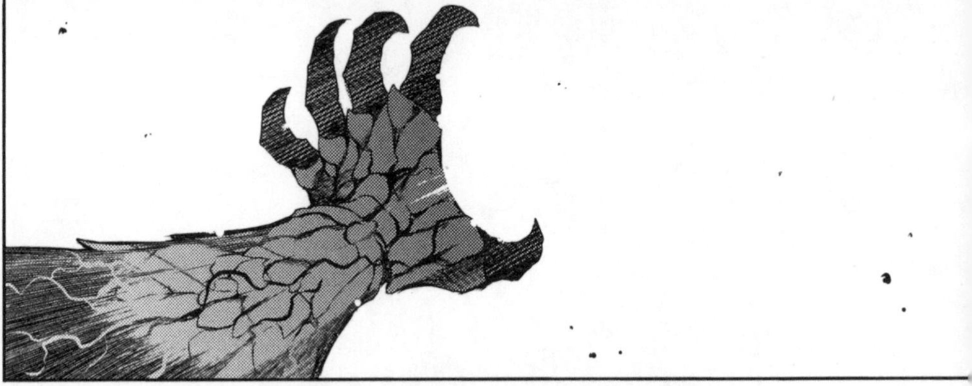
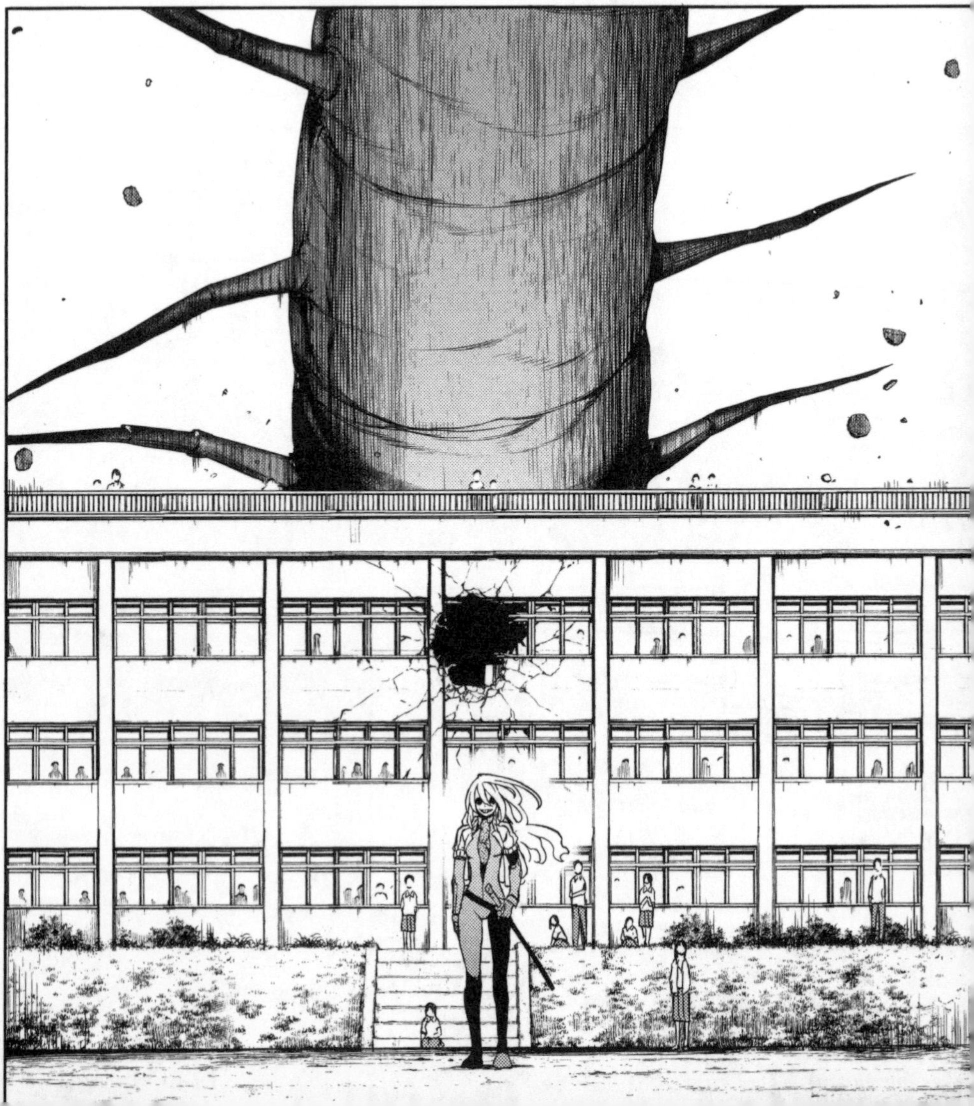

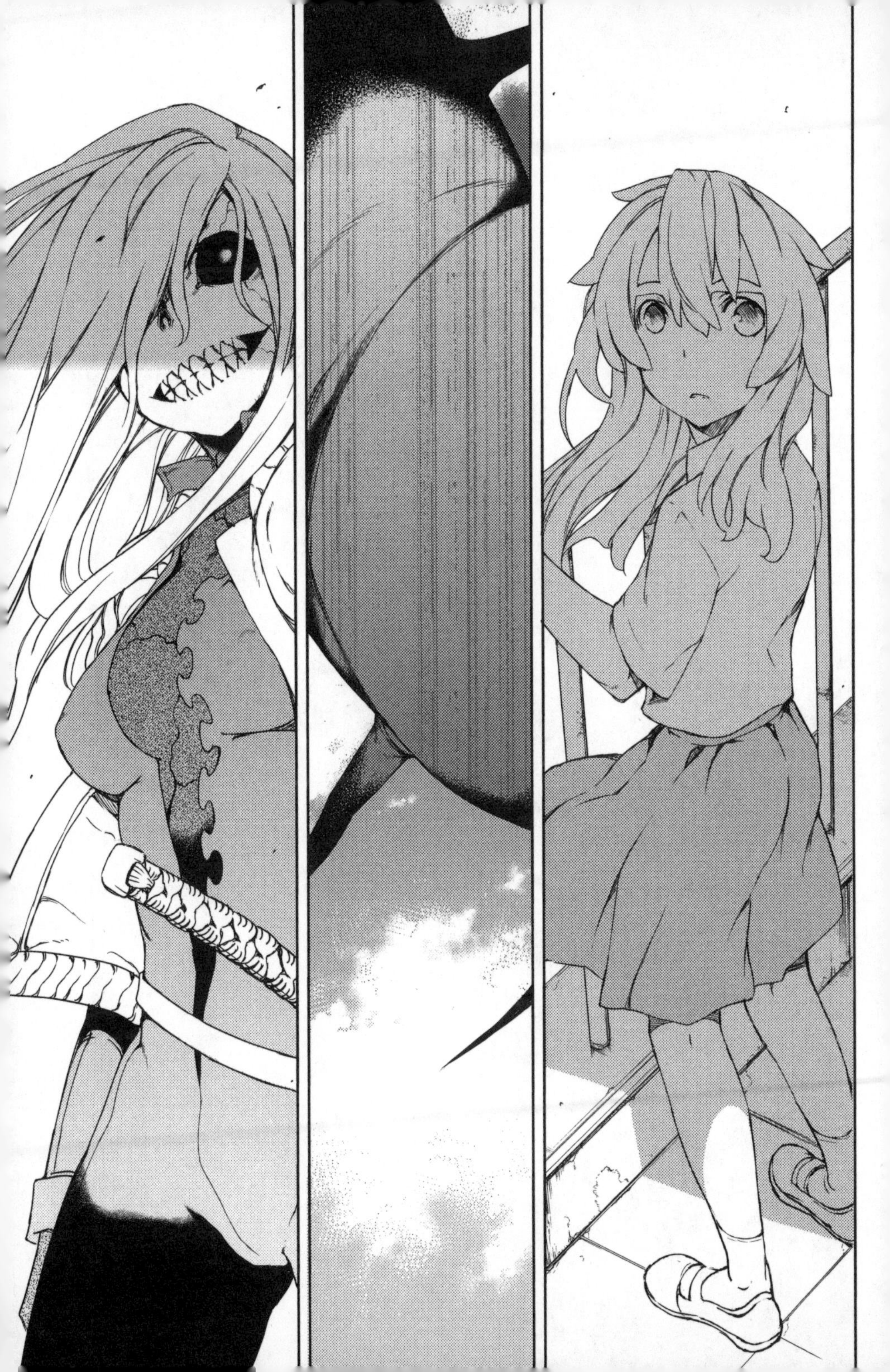

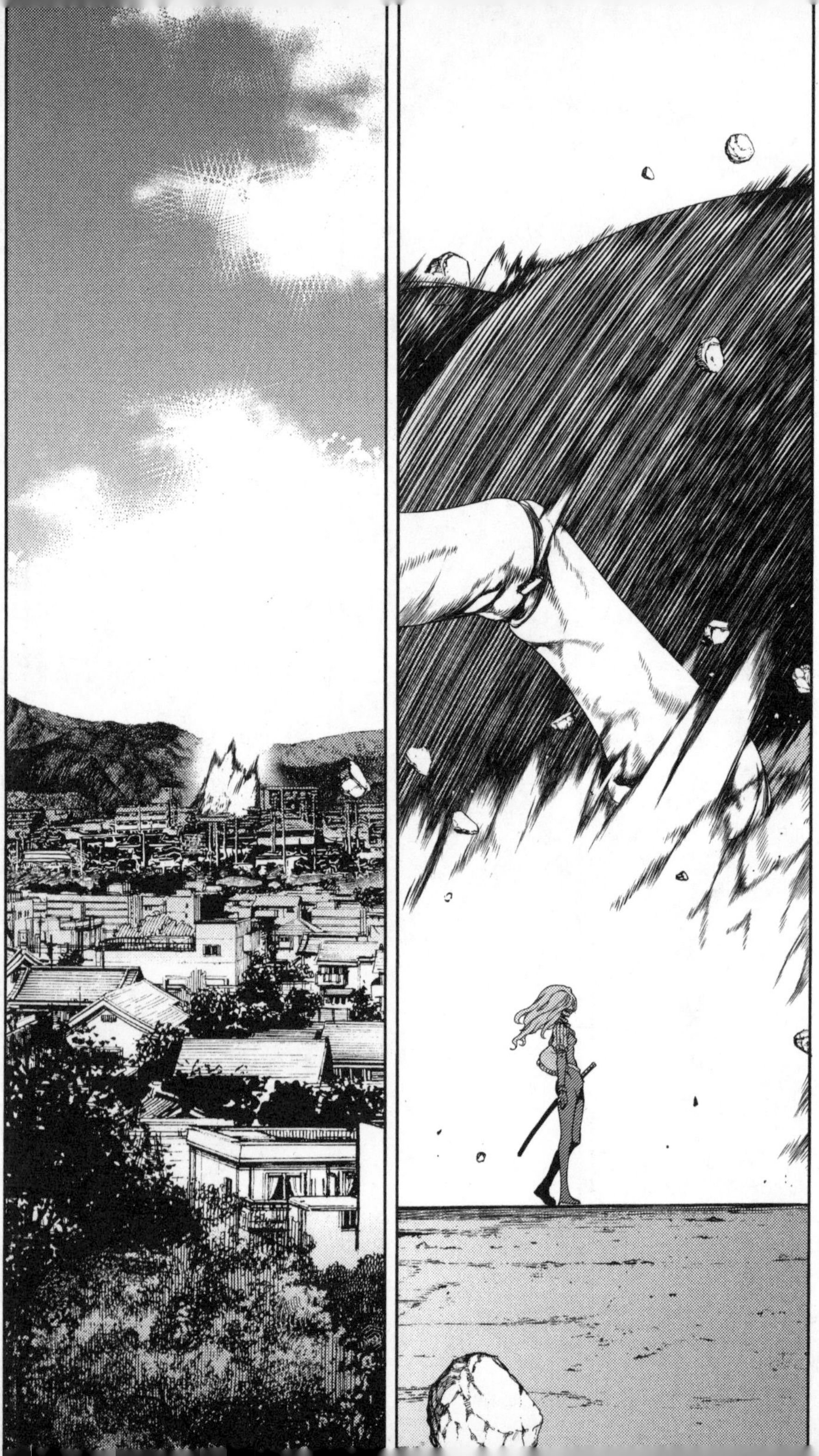

CHAPTER 65 ✚ CLAIRE'S WISH

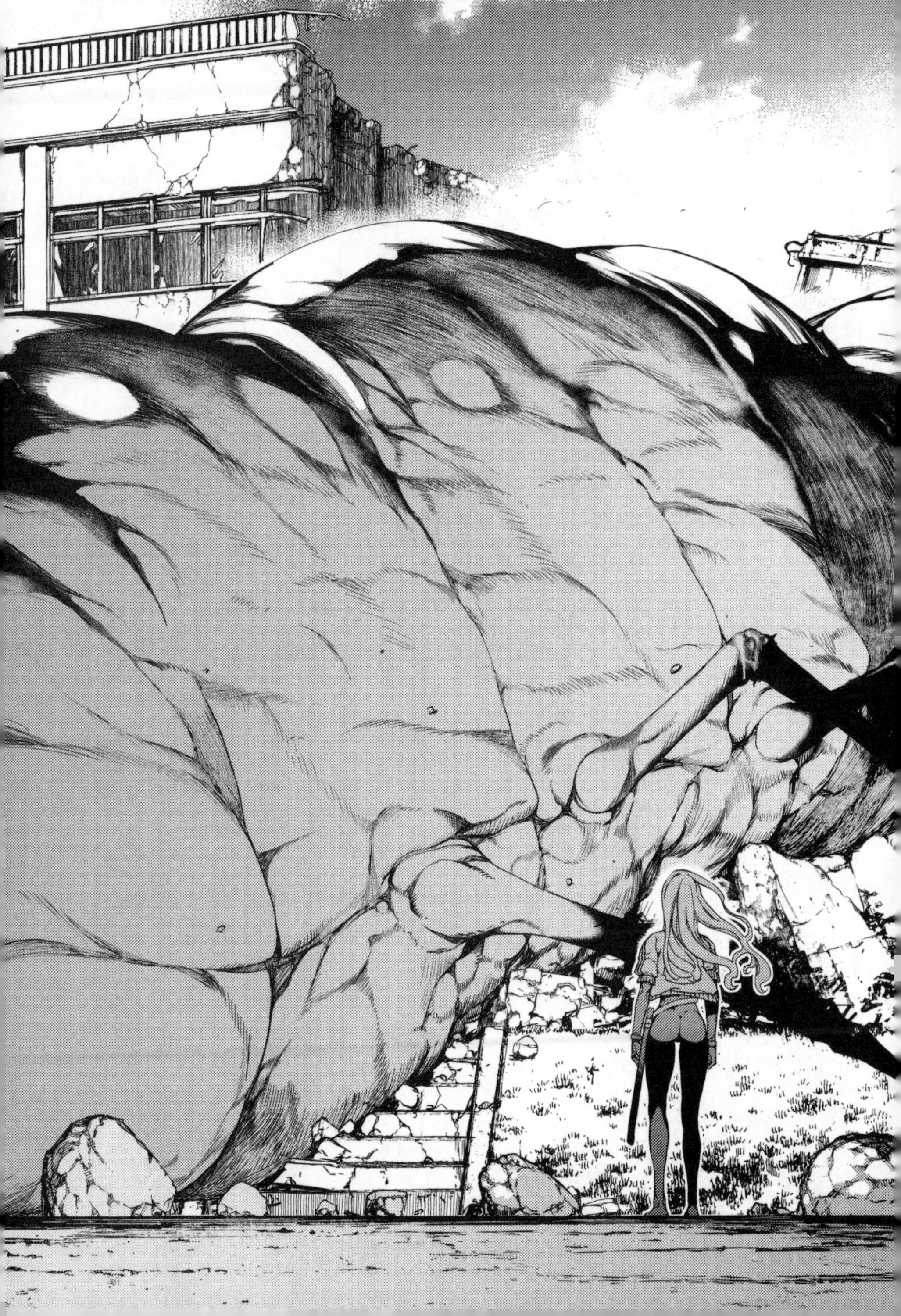

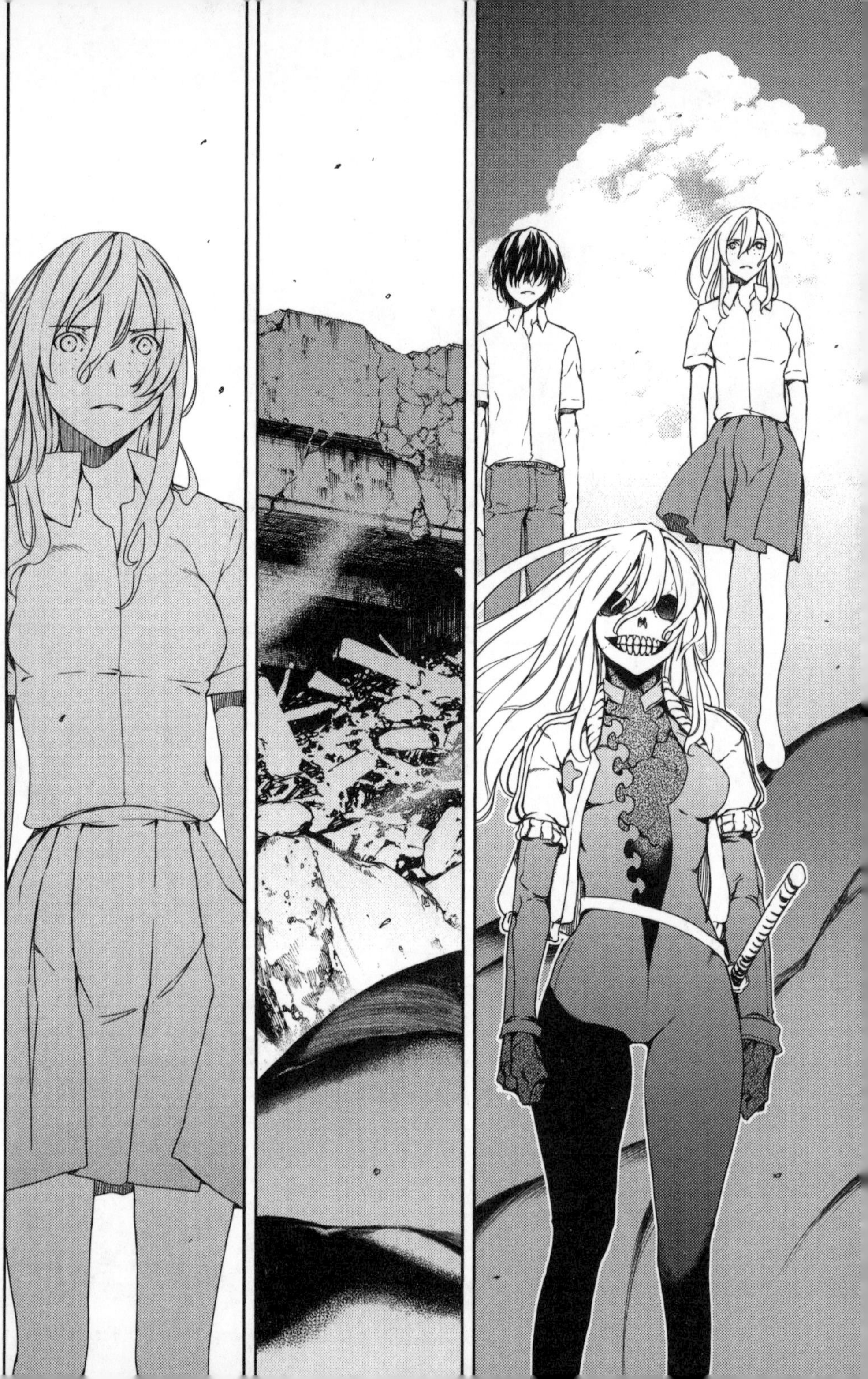

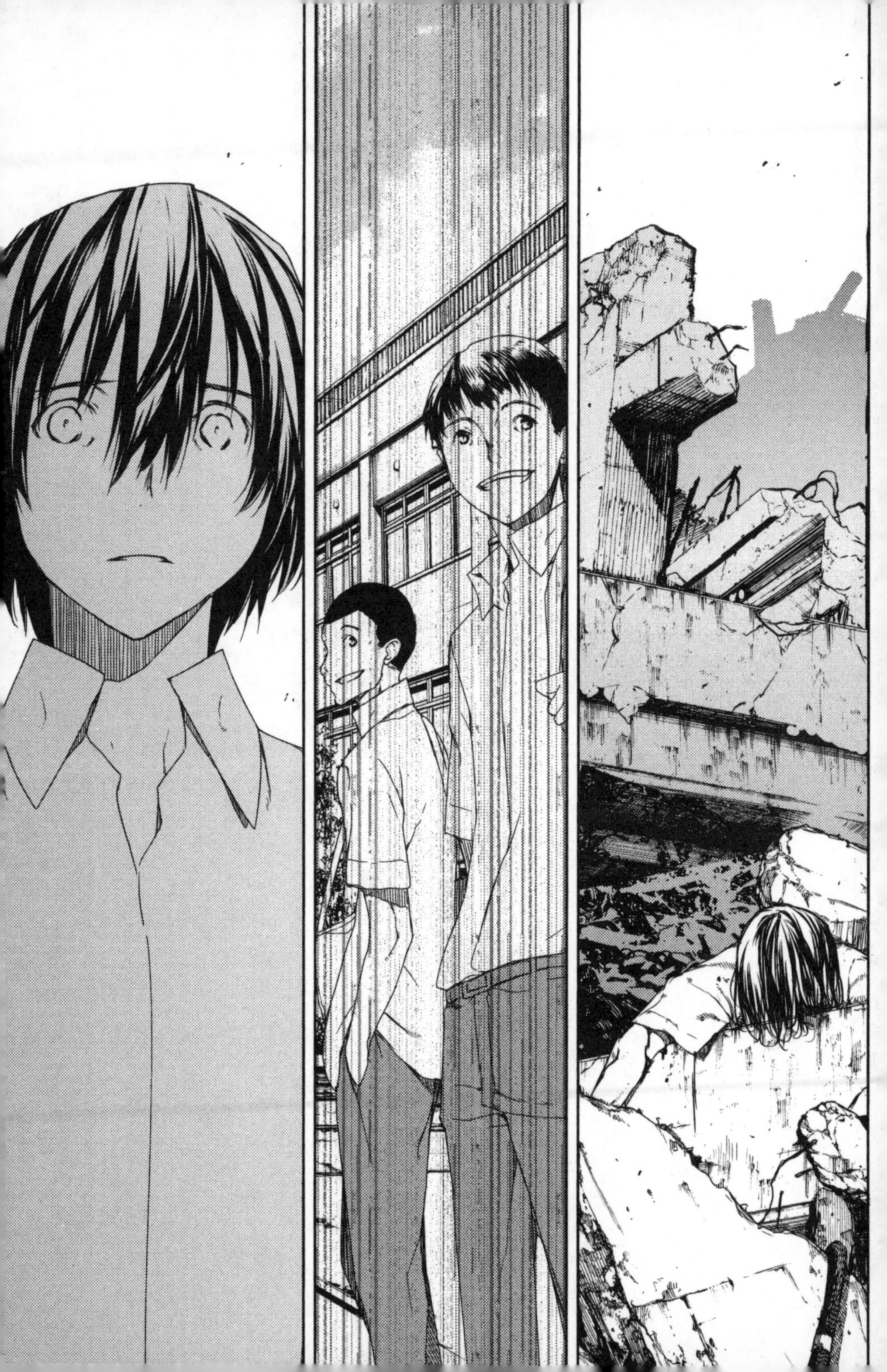

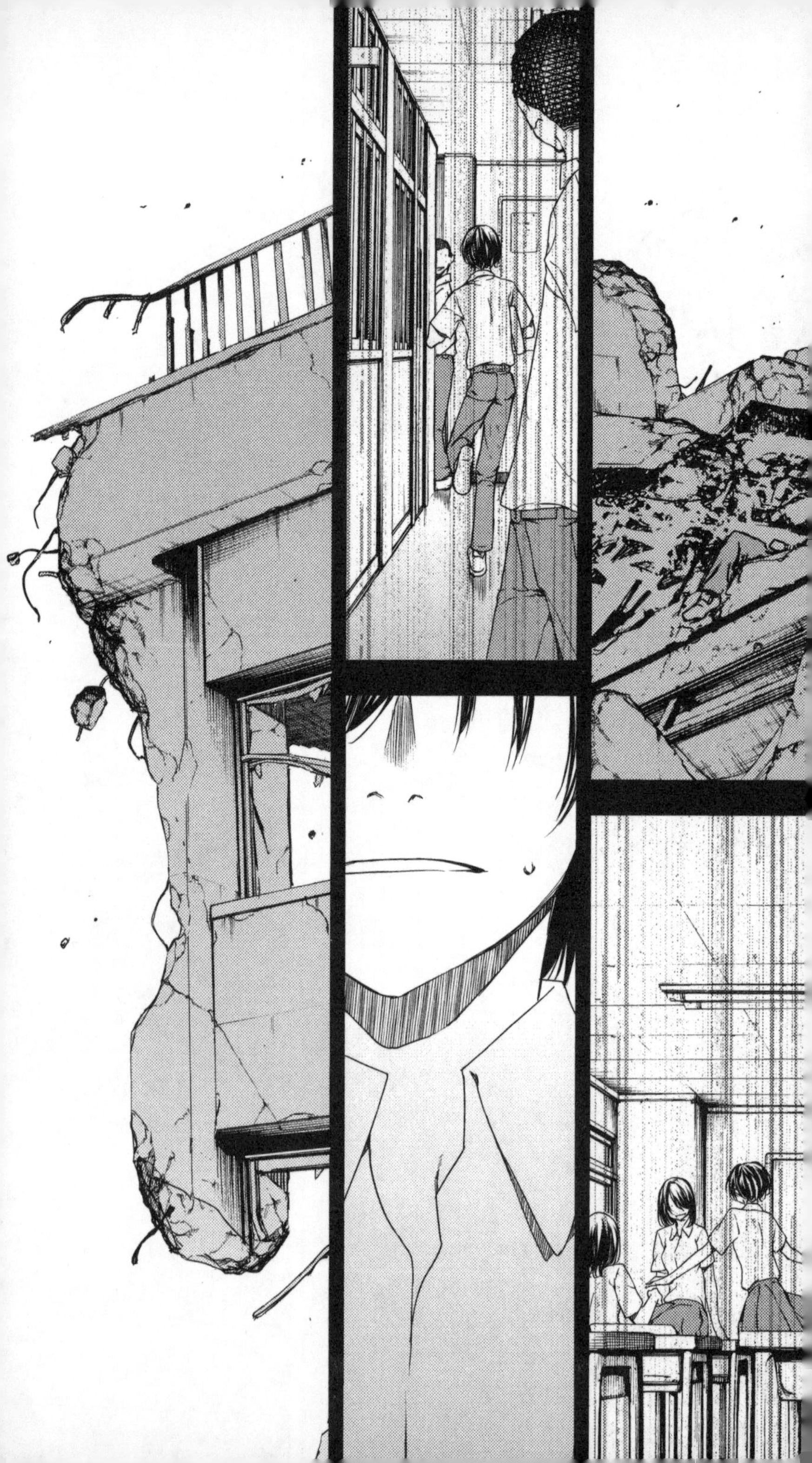

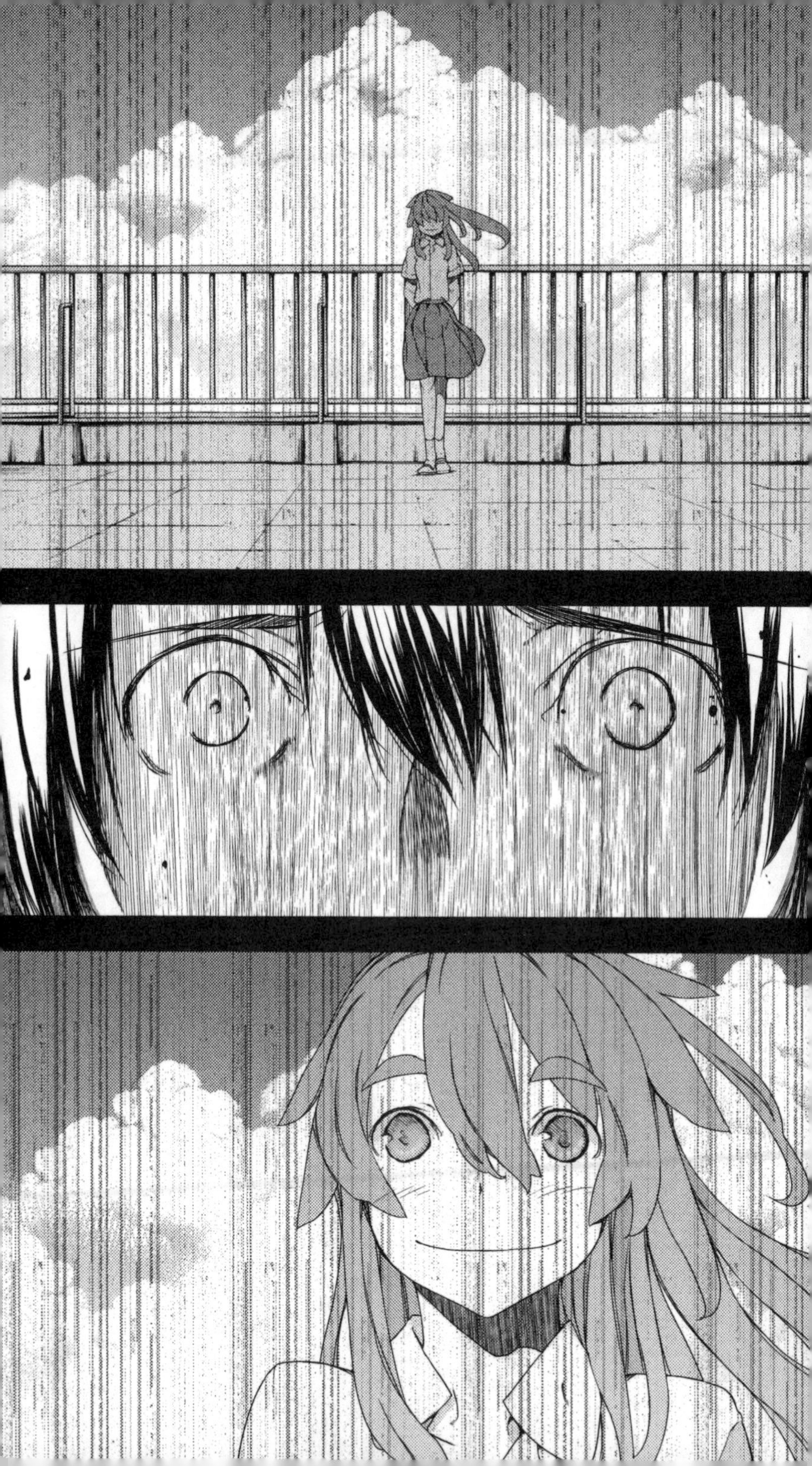

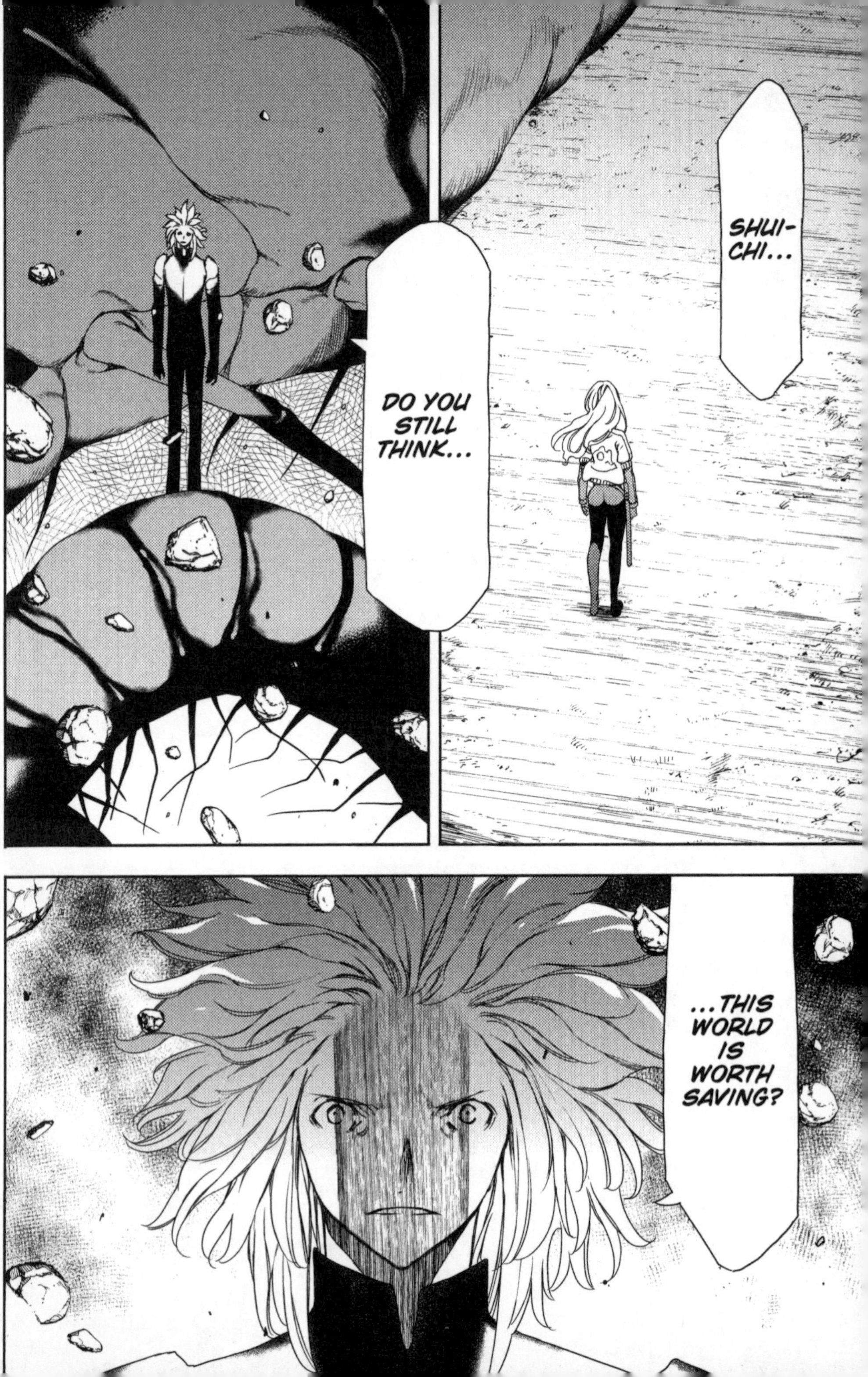
SHUI-CHI...
DO YOU STILL THINK...
...THIS WORLD IS WORTH SAVING?

WHAT
THE
HELL...

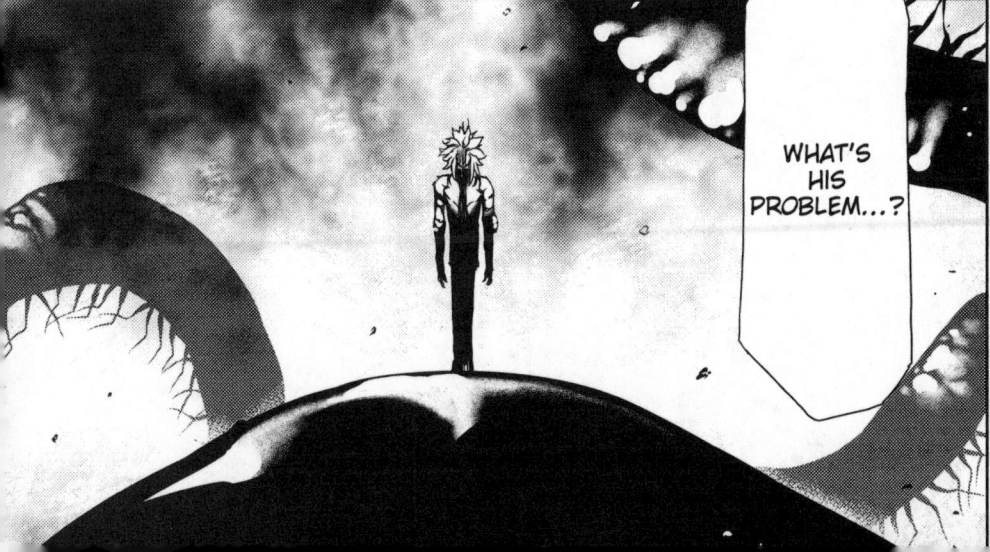

WHAT'S
HIS
PROBLEM...?

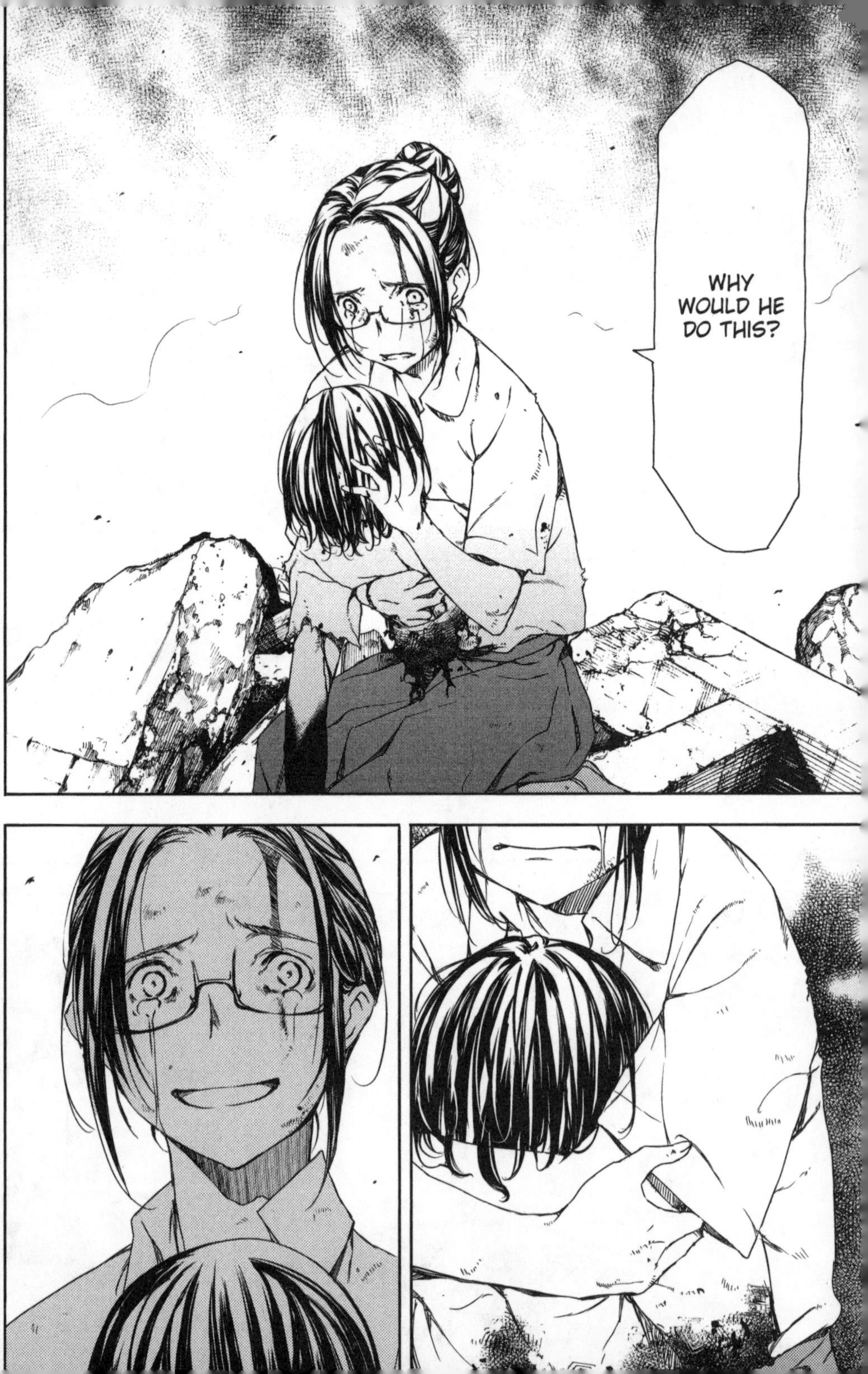
WHY WOULD HE DO THIS?

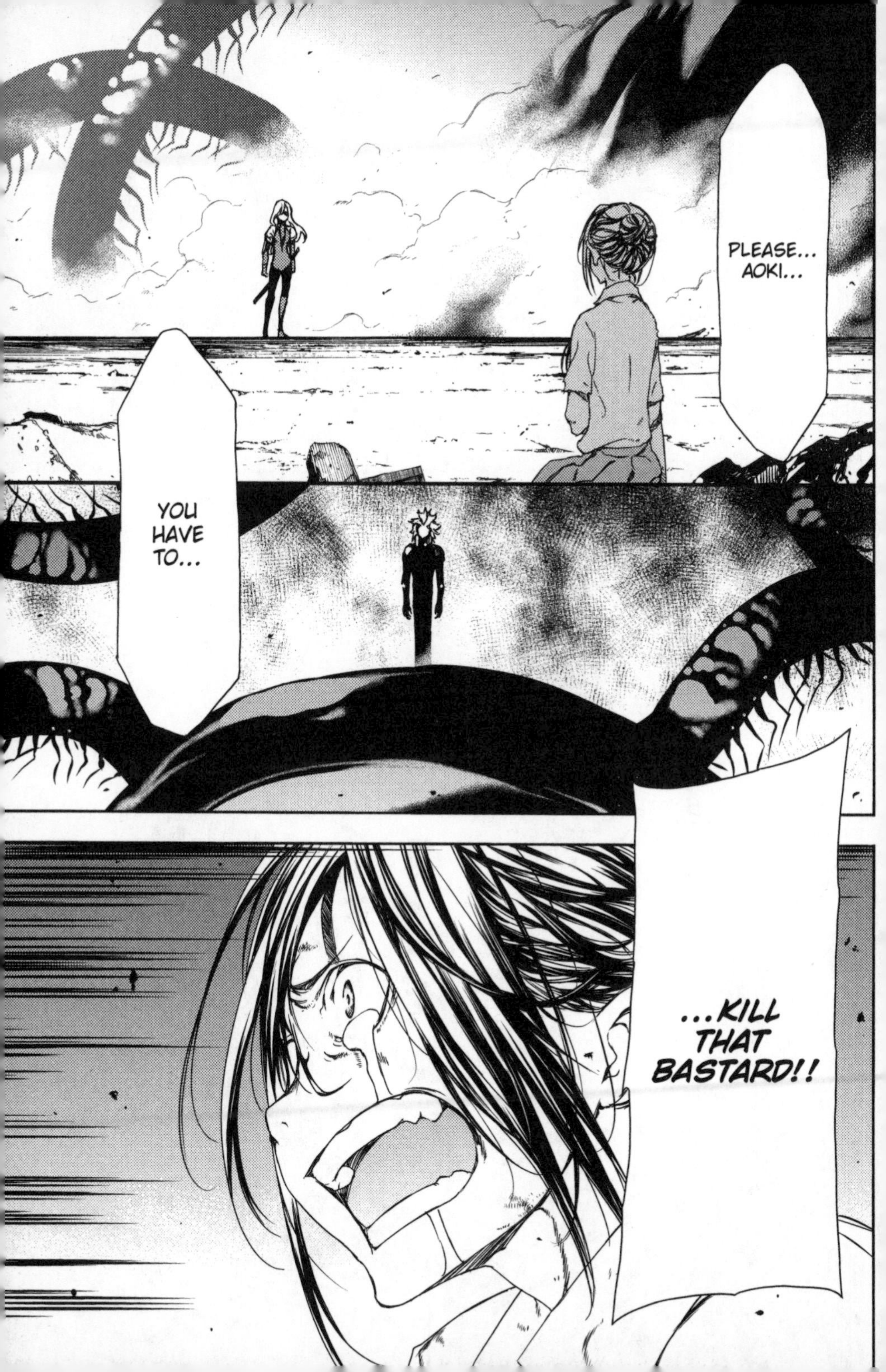
PLEASE... AOKI...
YOU HAVE TO...
...KILL THAT BASTARD!!

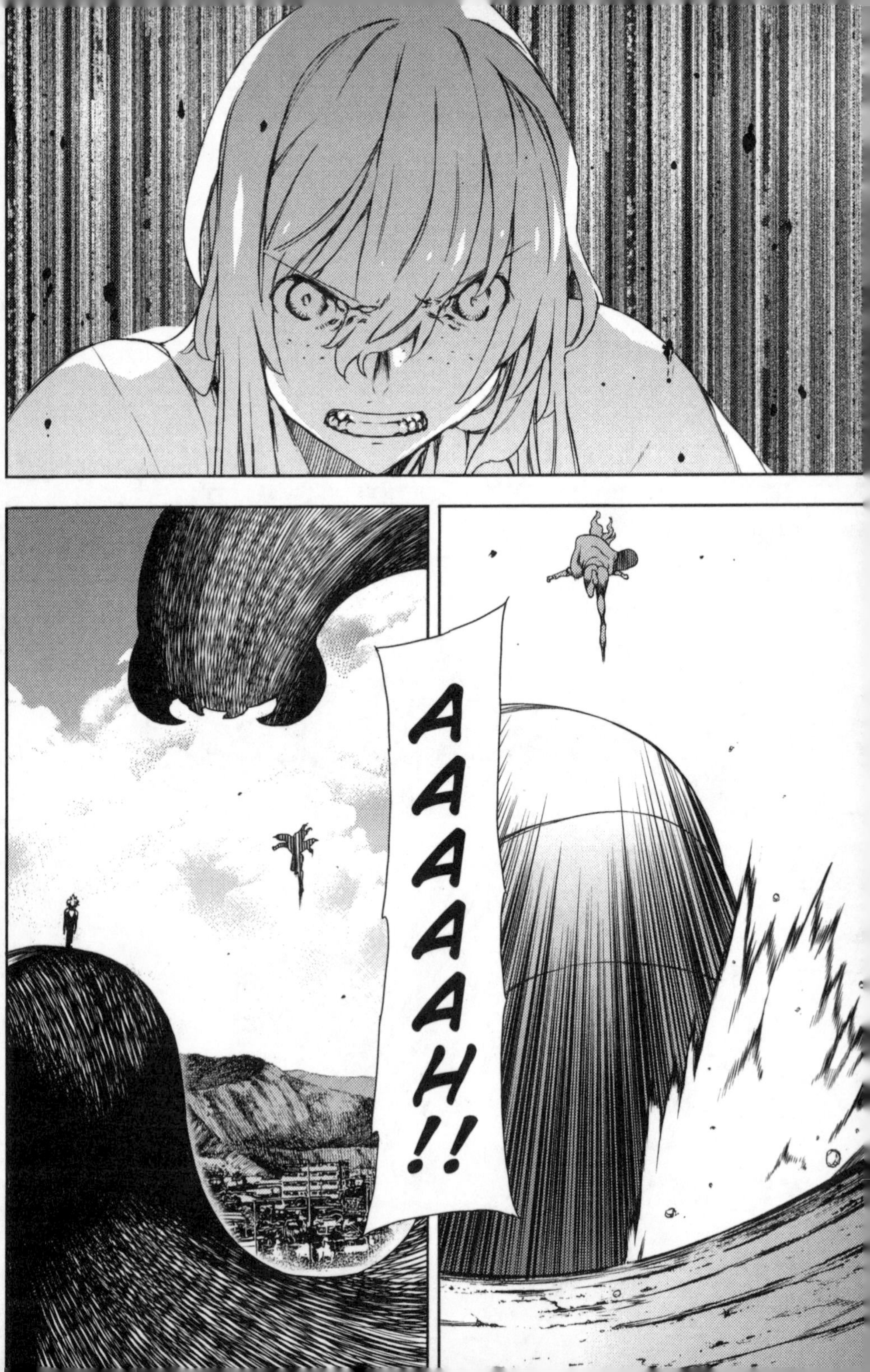
AAAAAH!!

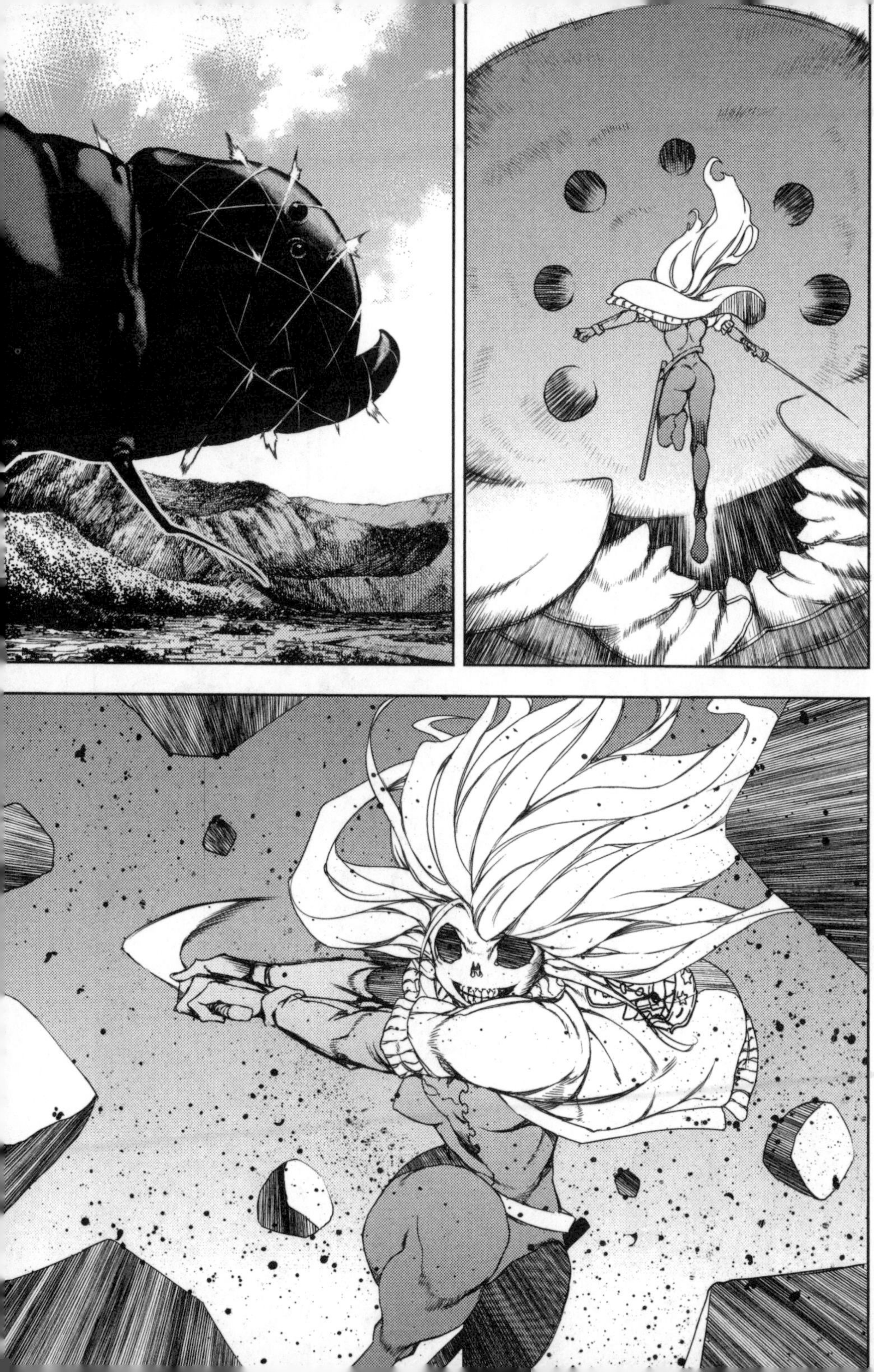

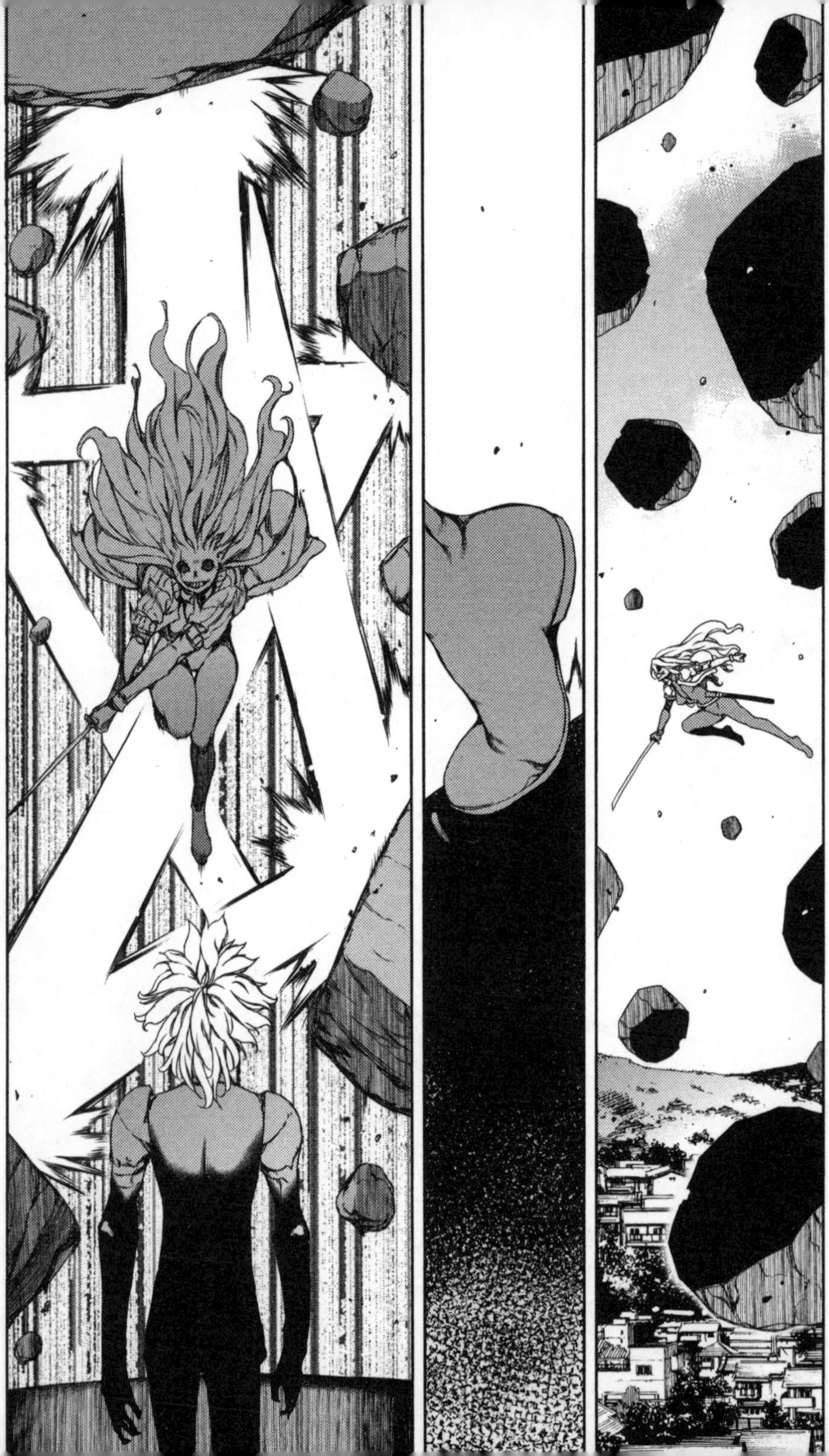

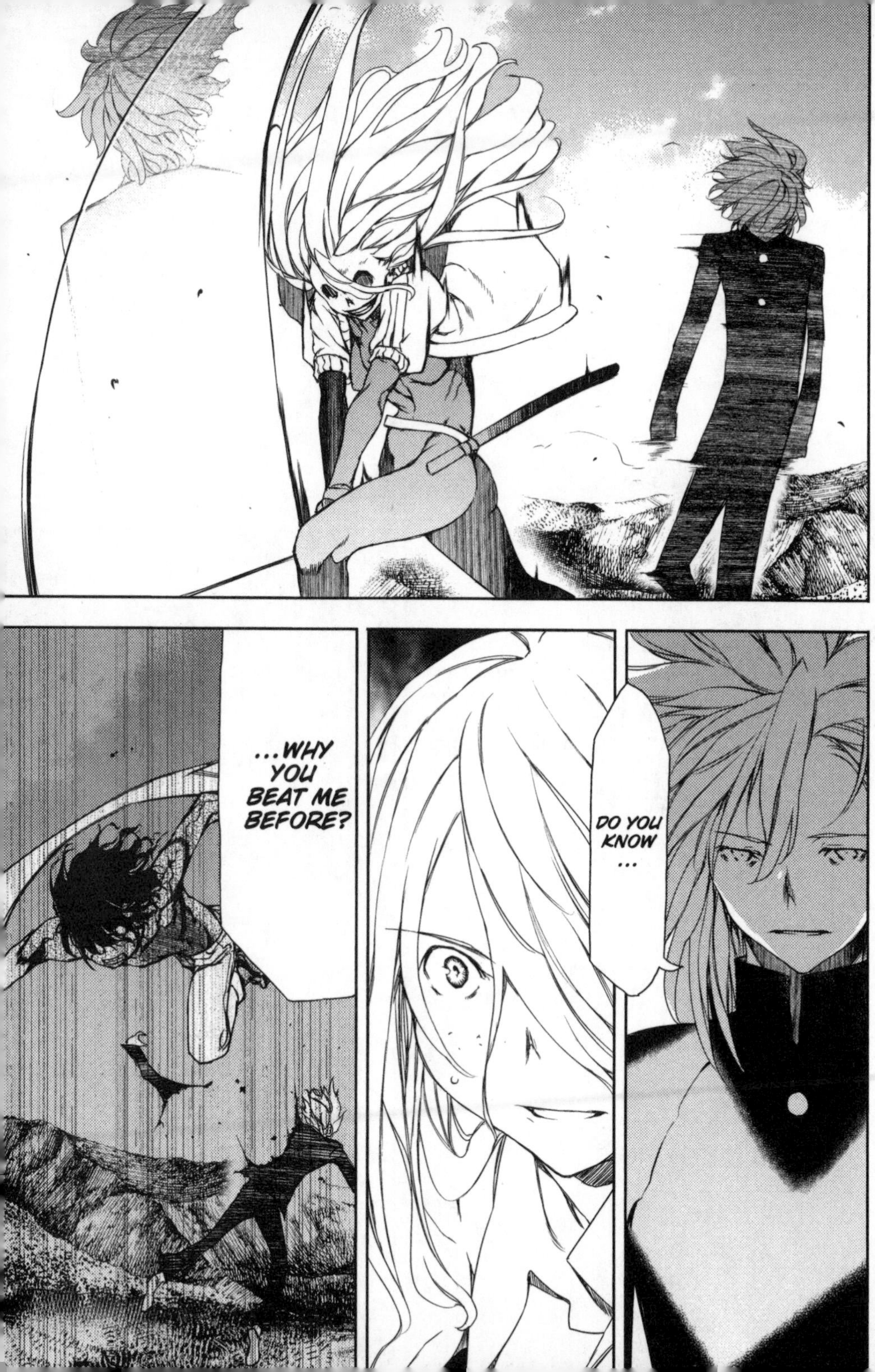
DO YOU KNOW ...
...WHY YOU BEAT ME BEFORE?

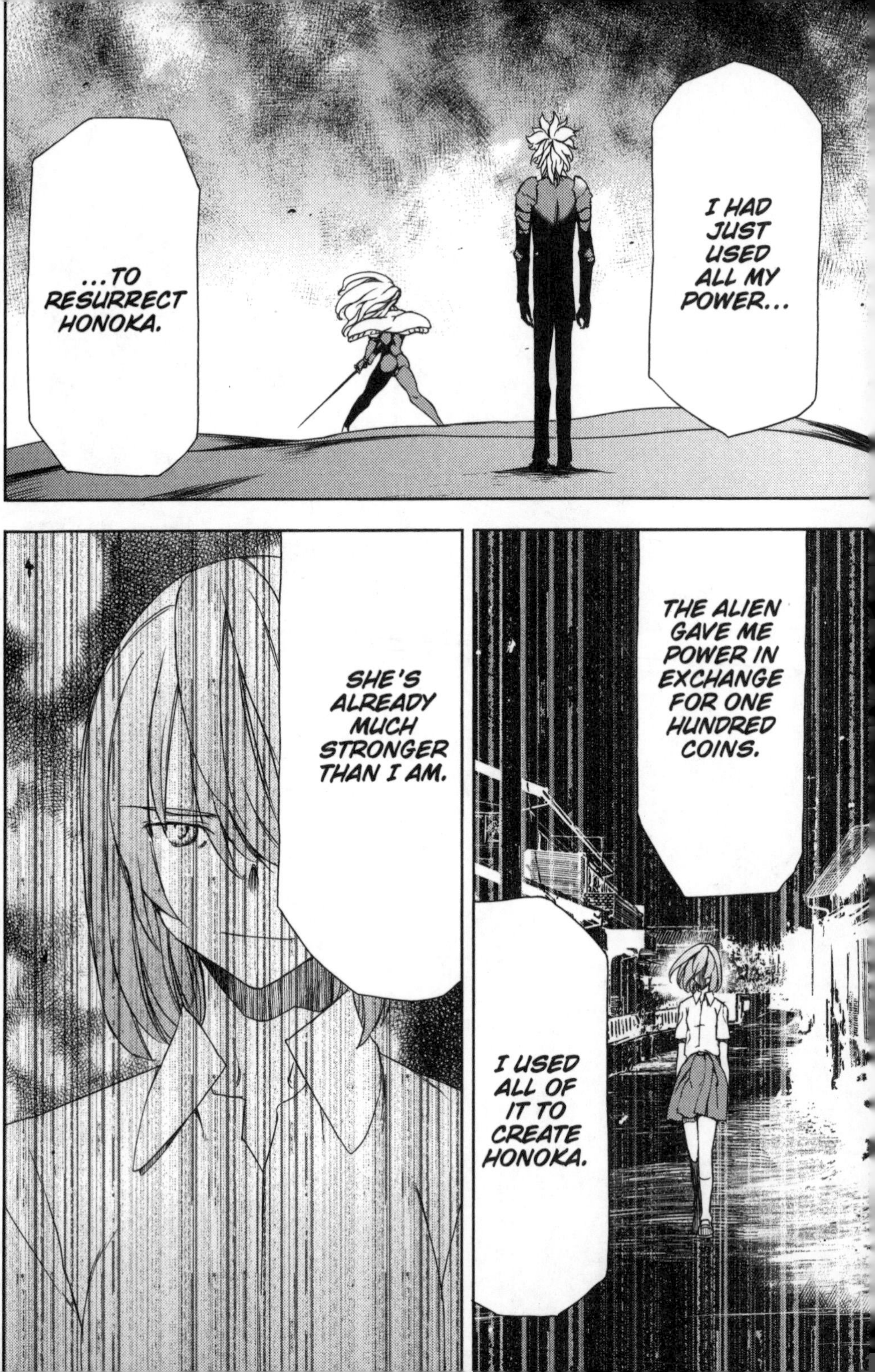
I HAD JUST USED ALL MY POWER...
...TO RESURRECT HONOKA.
THE ALIEN GAVE ME POWER IN EXCHANGE FOR ONE HUNDRED COINS.
I USED ALL OF IT TO CREATE HONOKA.
SHE'S ALREADY MUCH STRONGER THAN I AM.

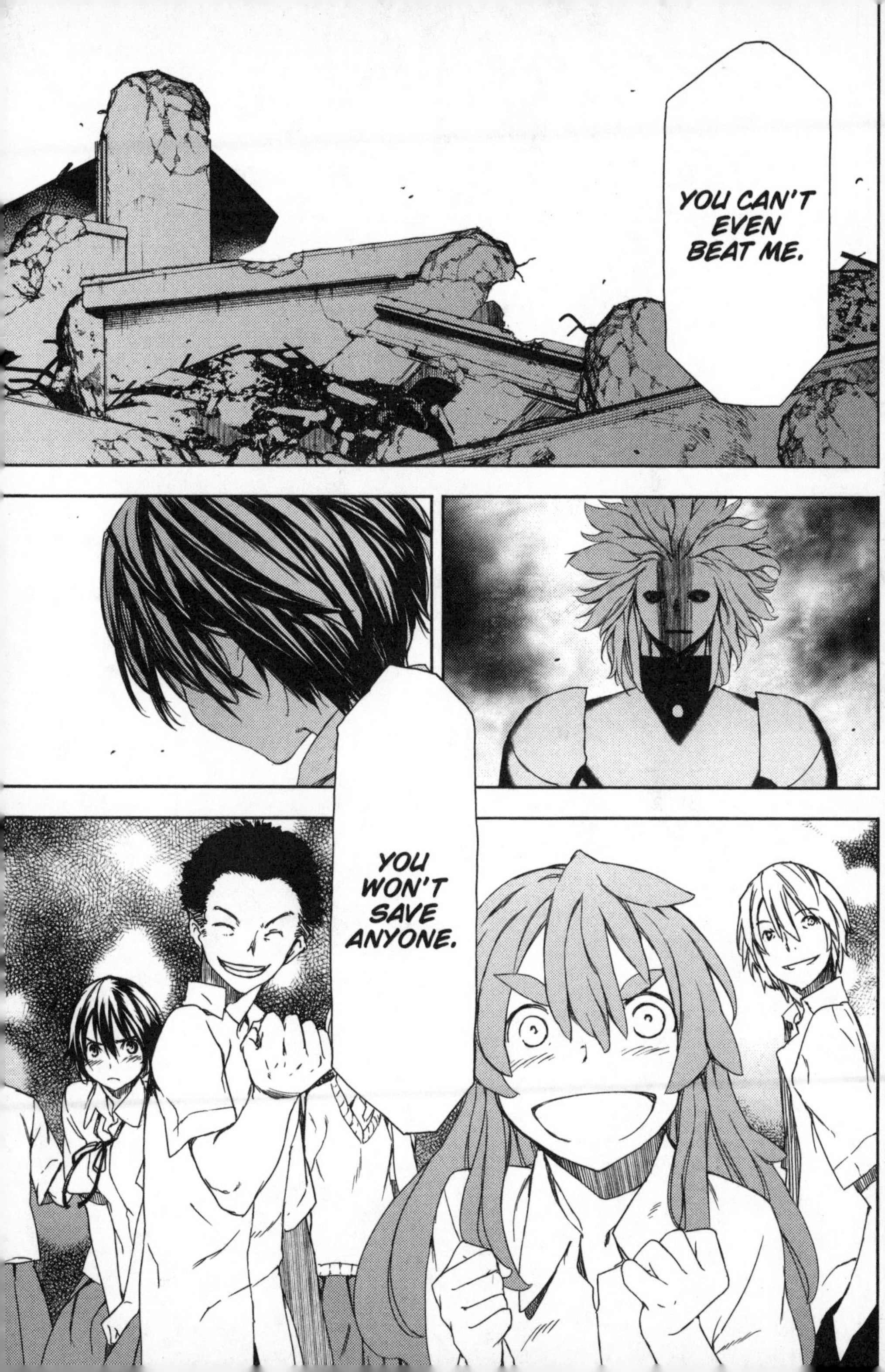
YOU CAN'T EVEN BEAT ME.
YOU WON'T SAVE ANYONE.

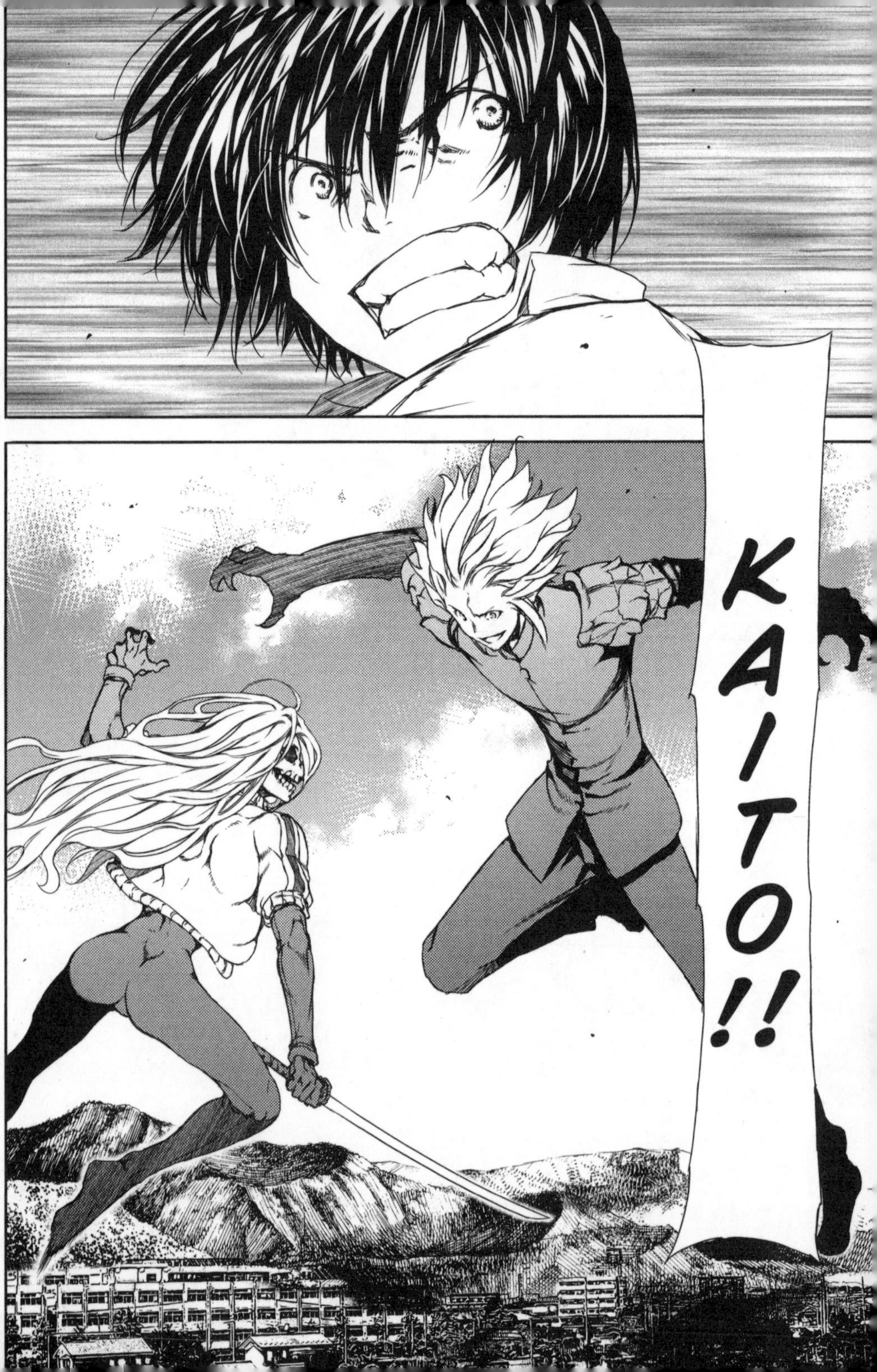
KAITO!!

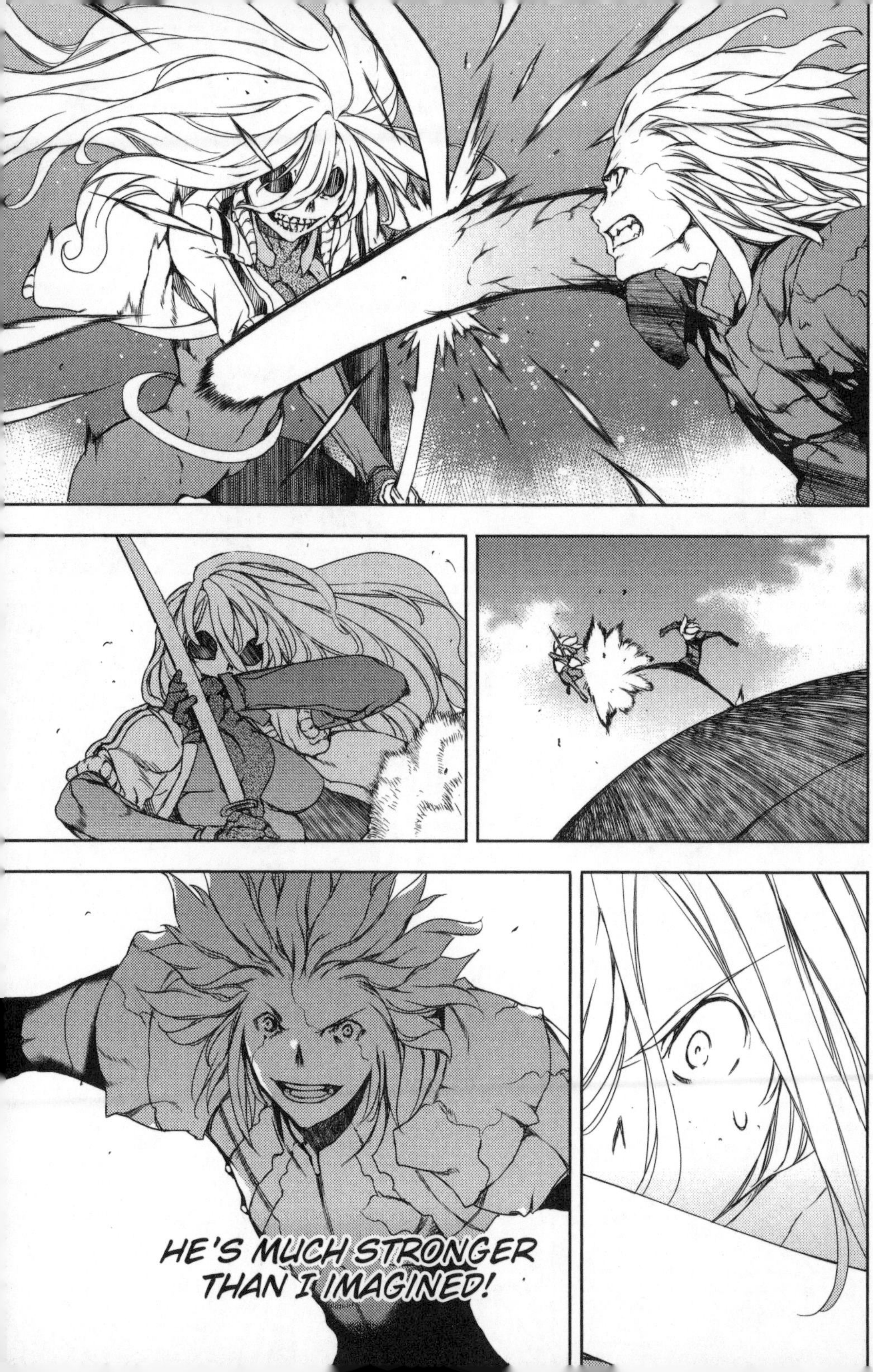
HE'S MUCH STRONGER
THAN I IMAGINED!

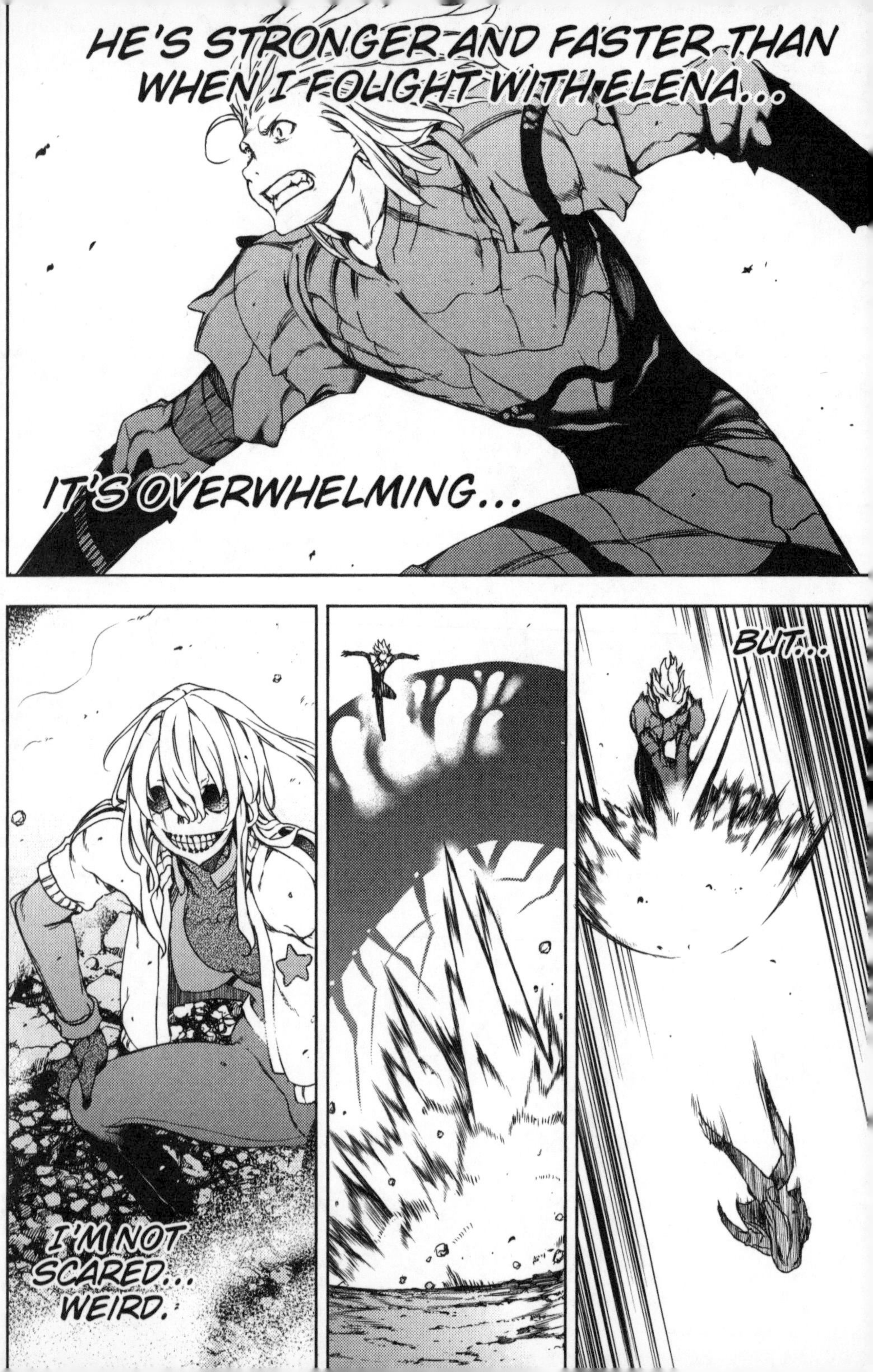
HE'S STRONGER AND FASTER THAN WHEN I FOUGHT WITH ELENA...
IT'S OVERWHELMING...
BUT...
I'M NOT SCARED... WEIRD.

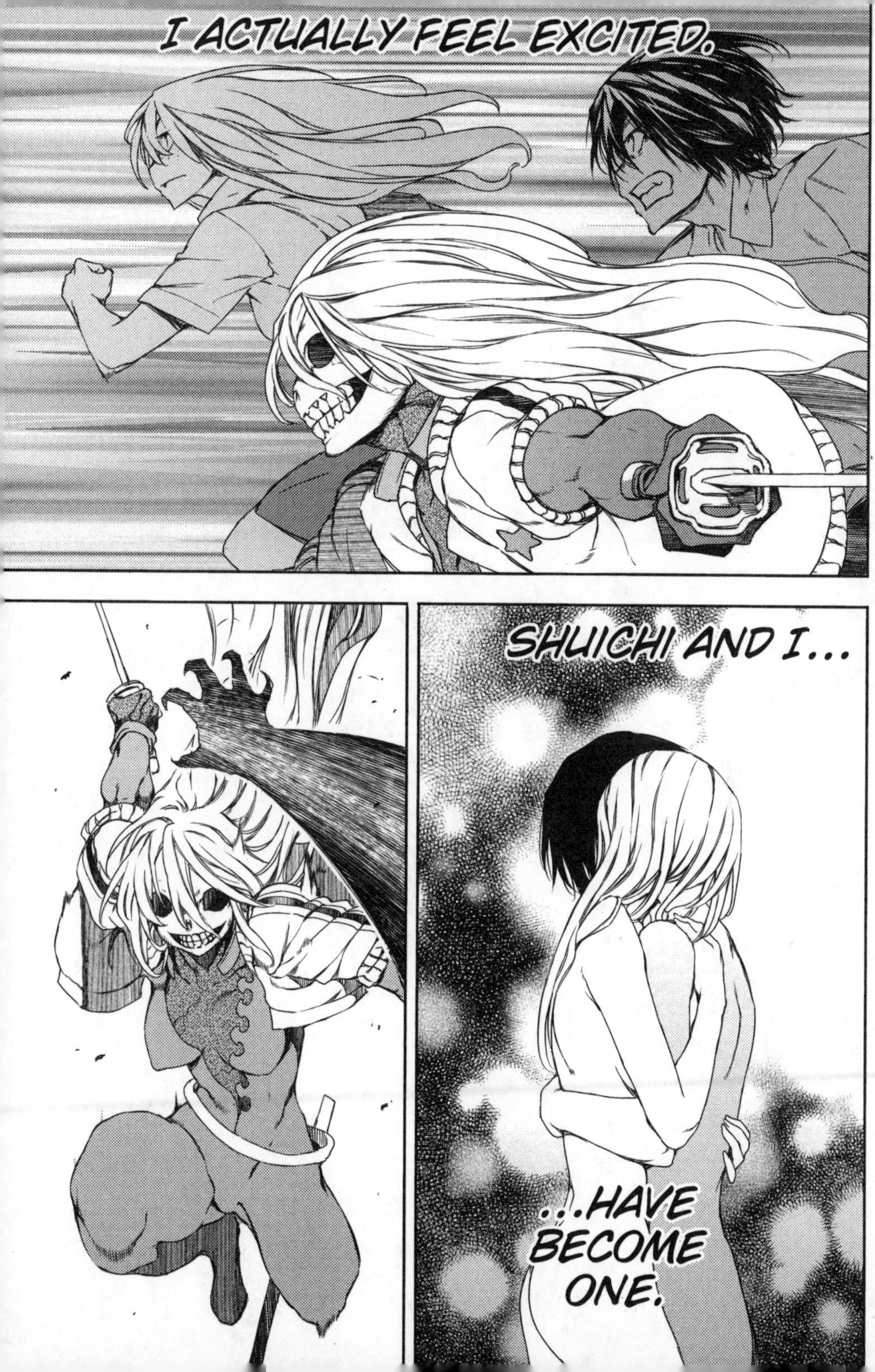
I ACTUALLY FEEL EXCITED.
SHUICHI AND I...
...HAVE BECOME ONE.

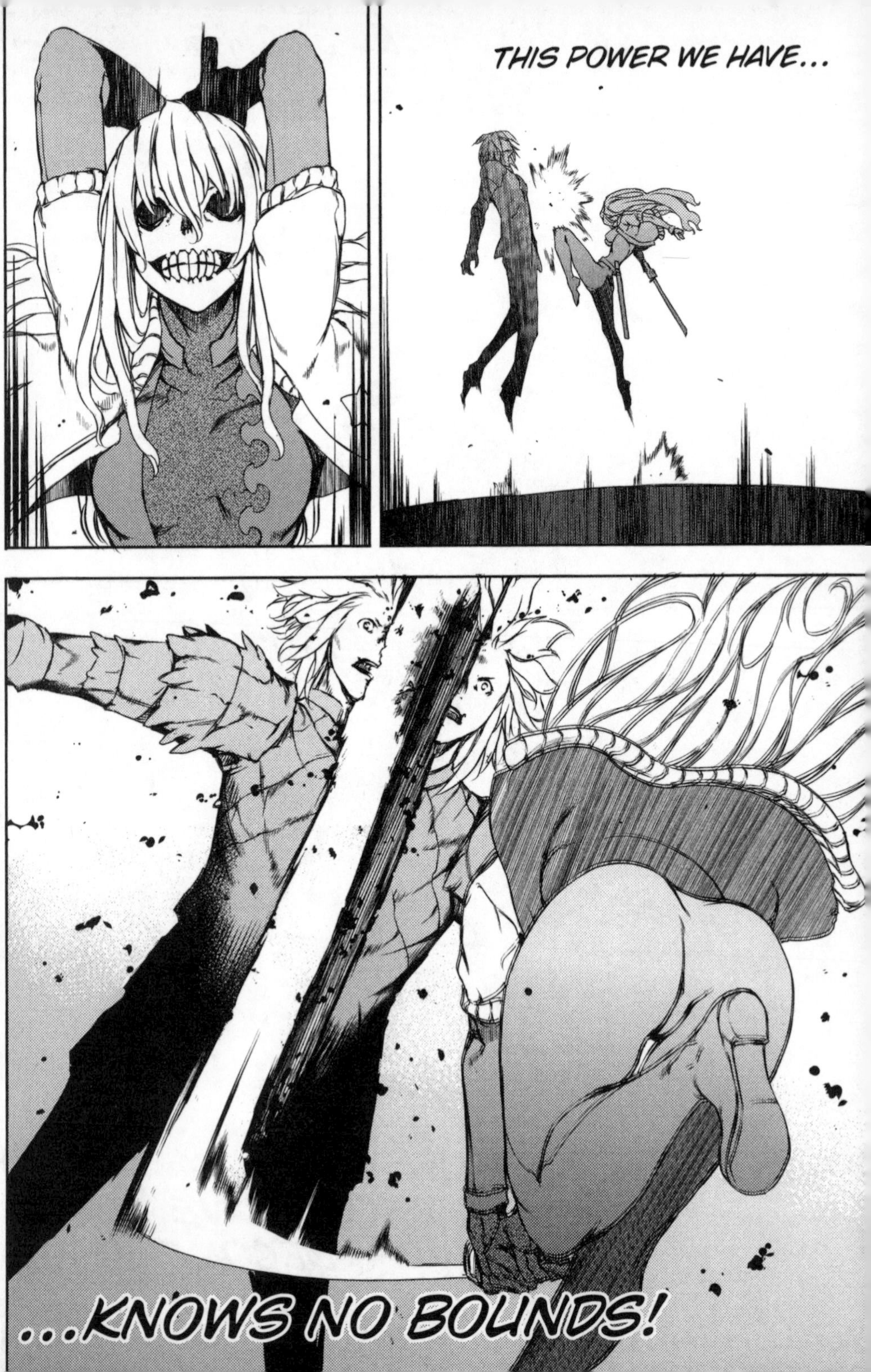
THIS POWER WE HAVE...
...KNOWS NO BOUNDS!

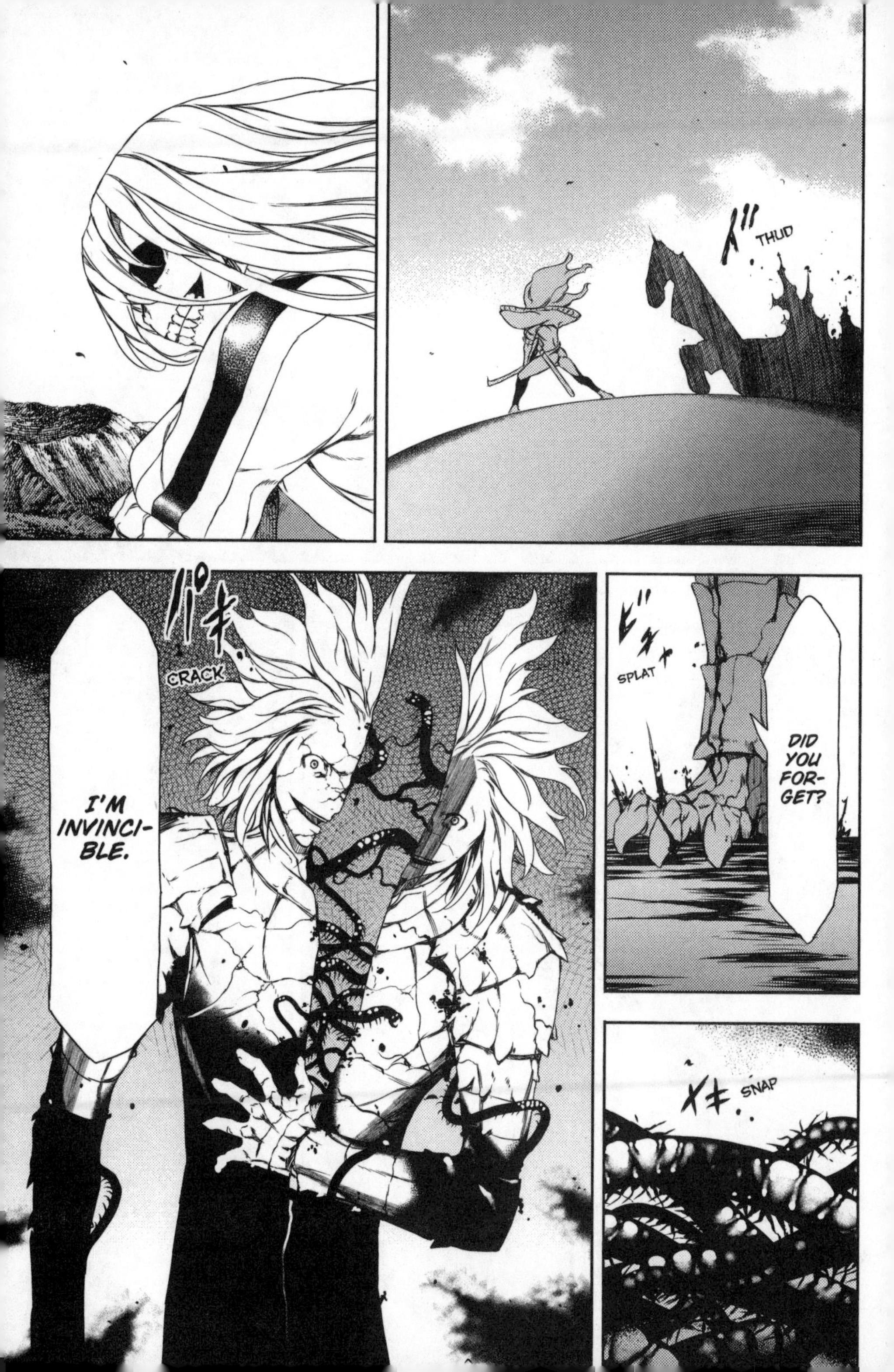
THUD
SPLAT
DID YOU FOR-GET?
CRACK
I'M INVINCI-BLE.
SNAP

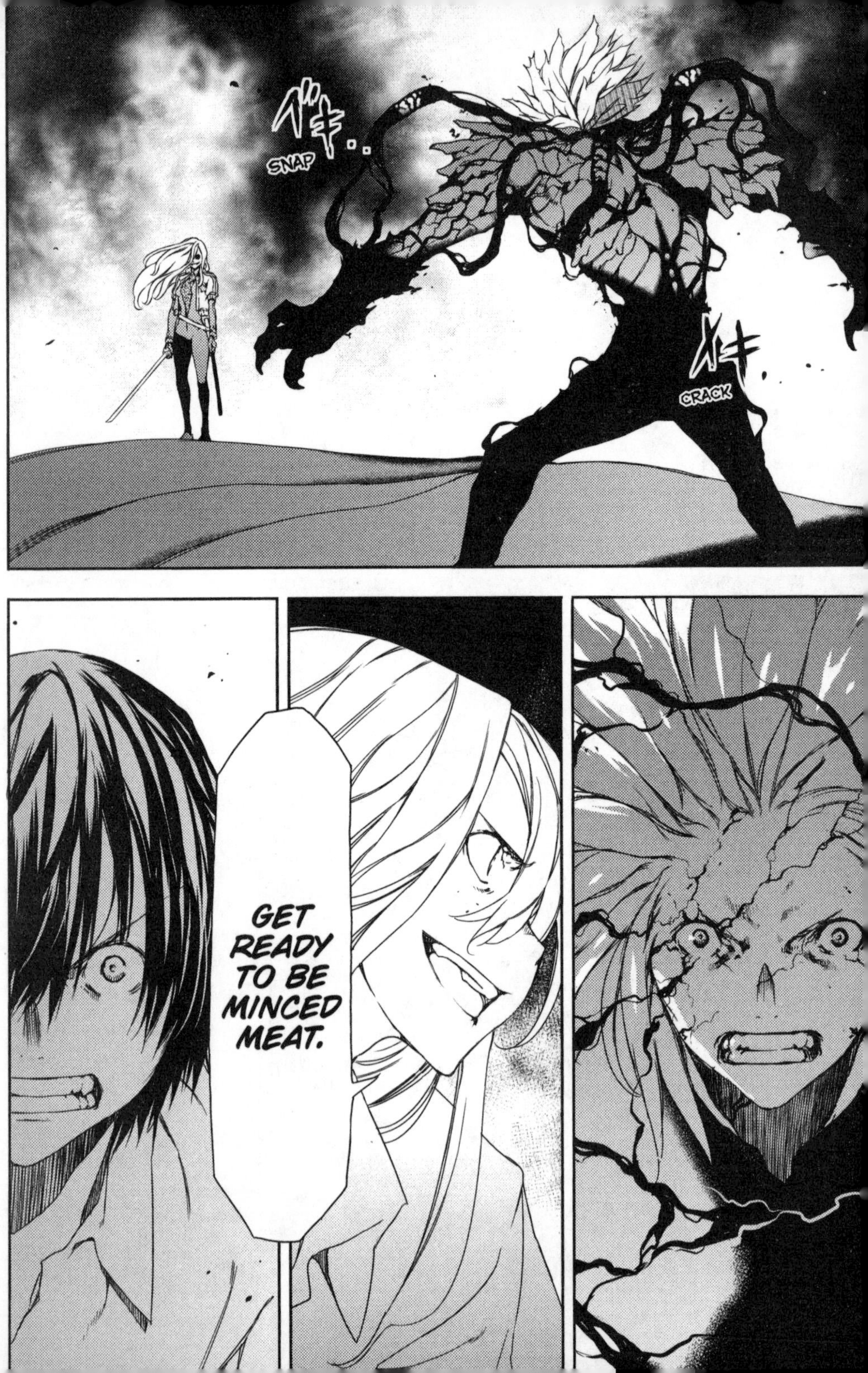
SNAP
CRACK
GET READY TO BE MINCED MEAT.

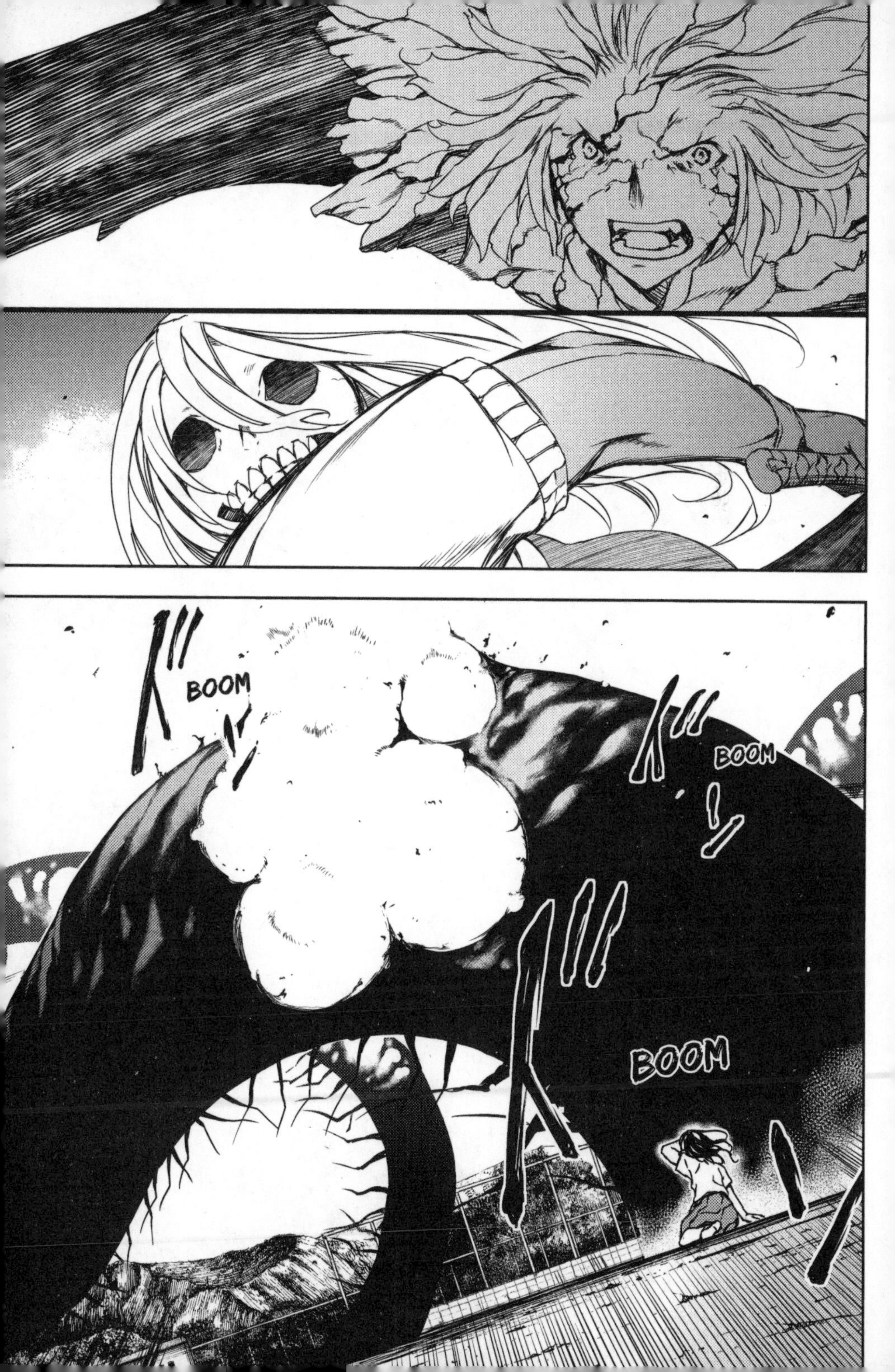
BOOM
BOOM
BOOM

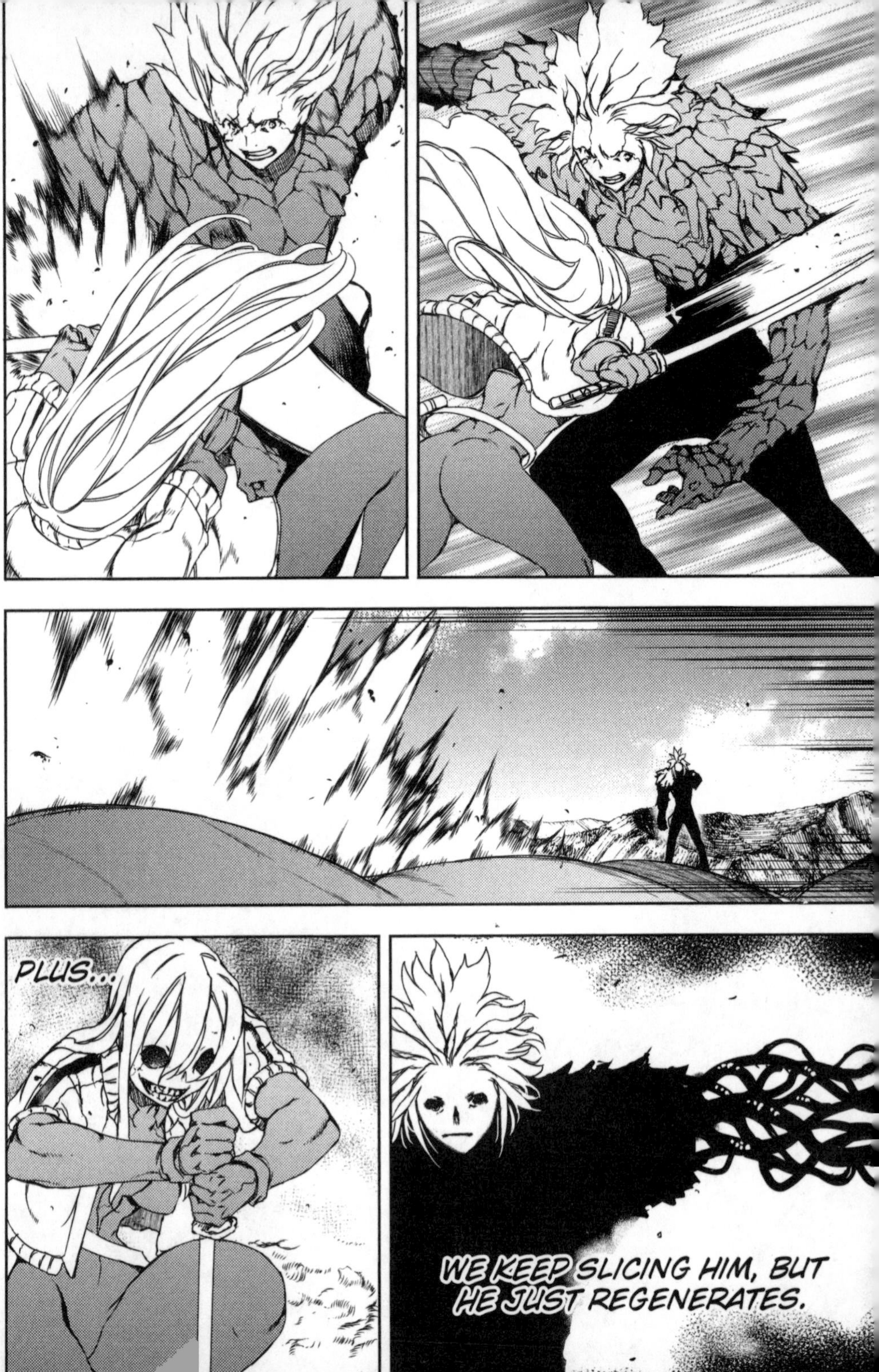
PLUS...
WE KEEP SLICING HIM, BUT HE JUST REGENERATES.

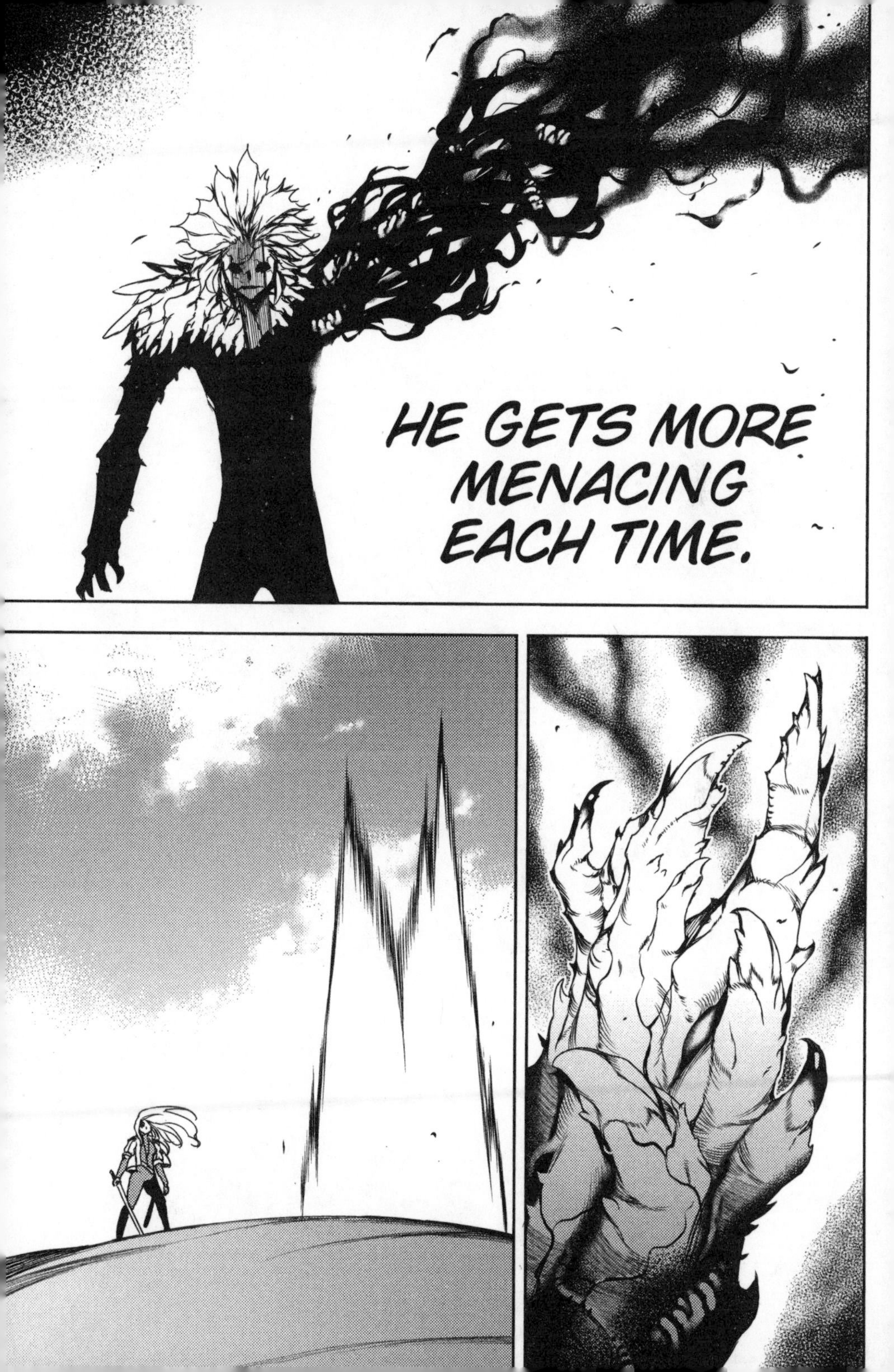
HE GETS MORE MENACING EACH TIME.

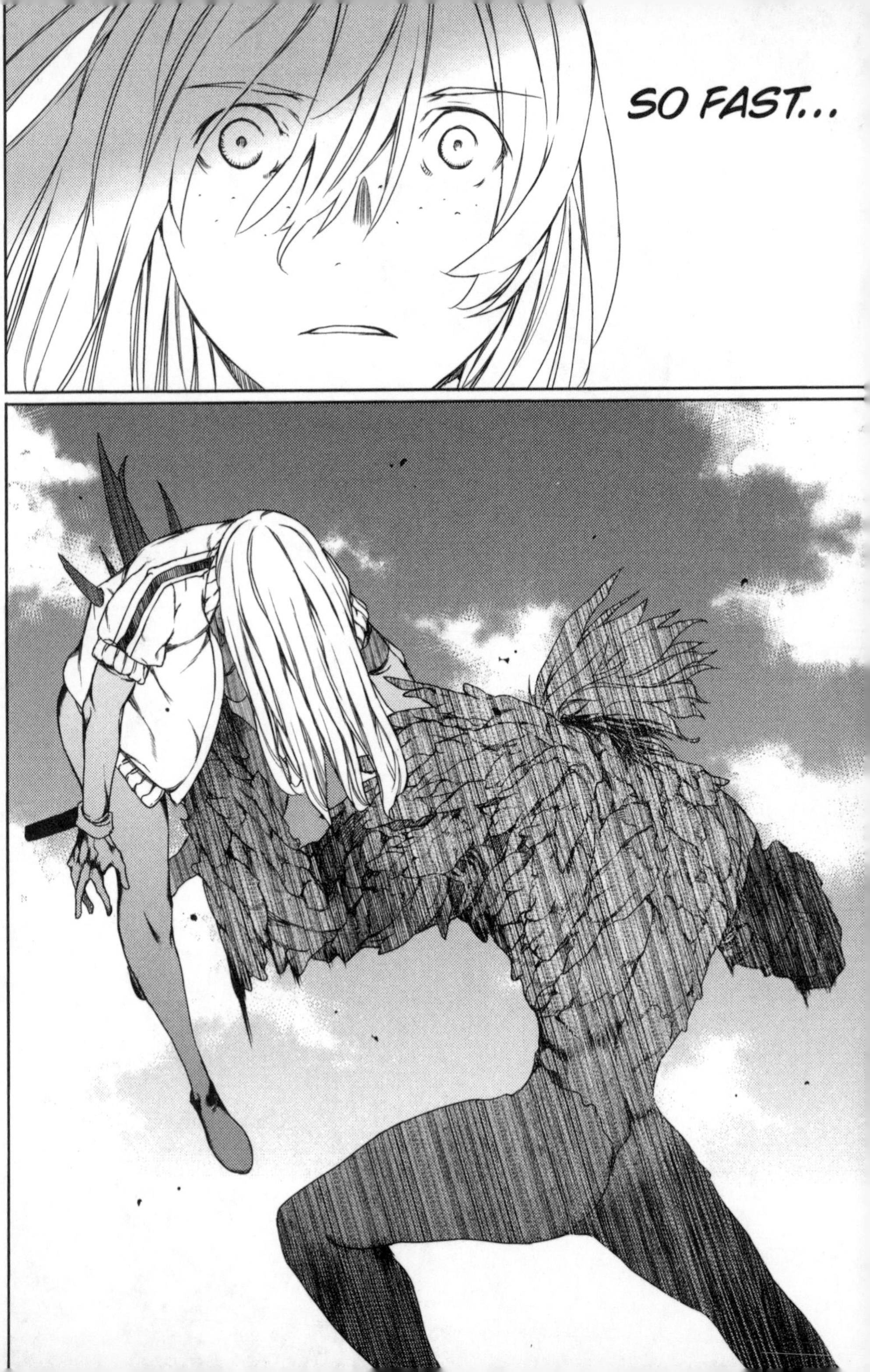
SO FAST...

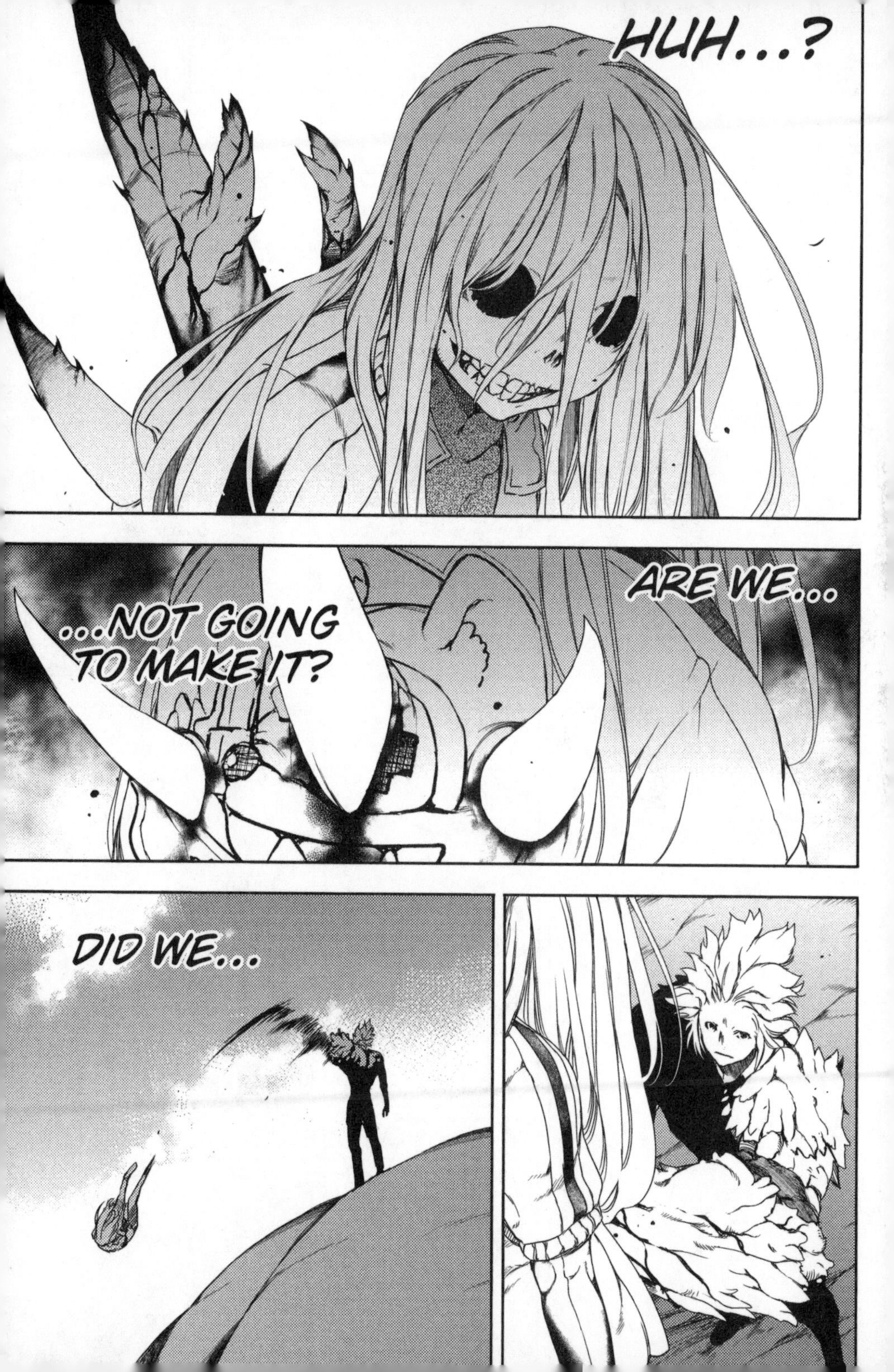
HUH...?
ARE WE...
...NOT GOING TO MAKE IT?
DID WE...

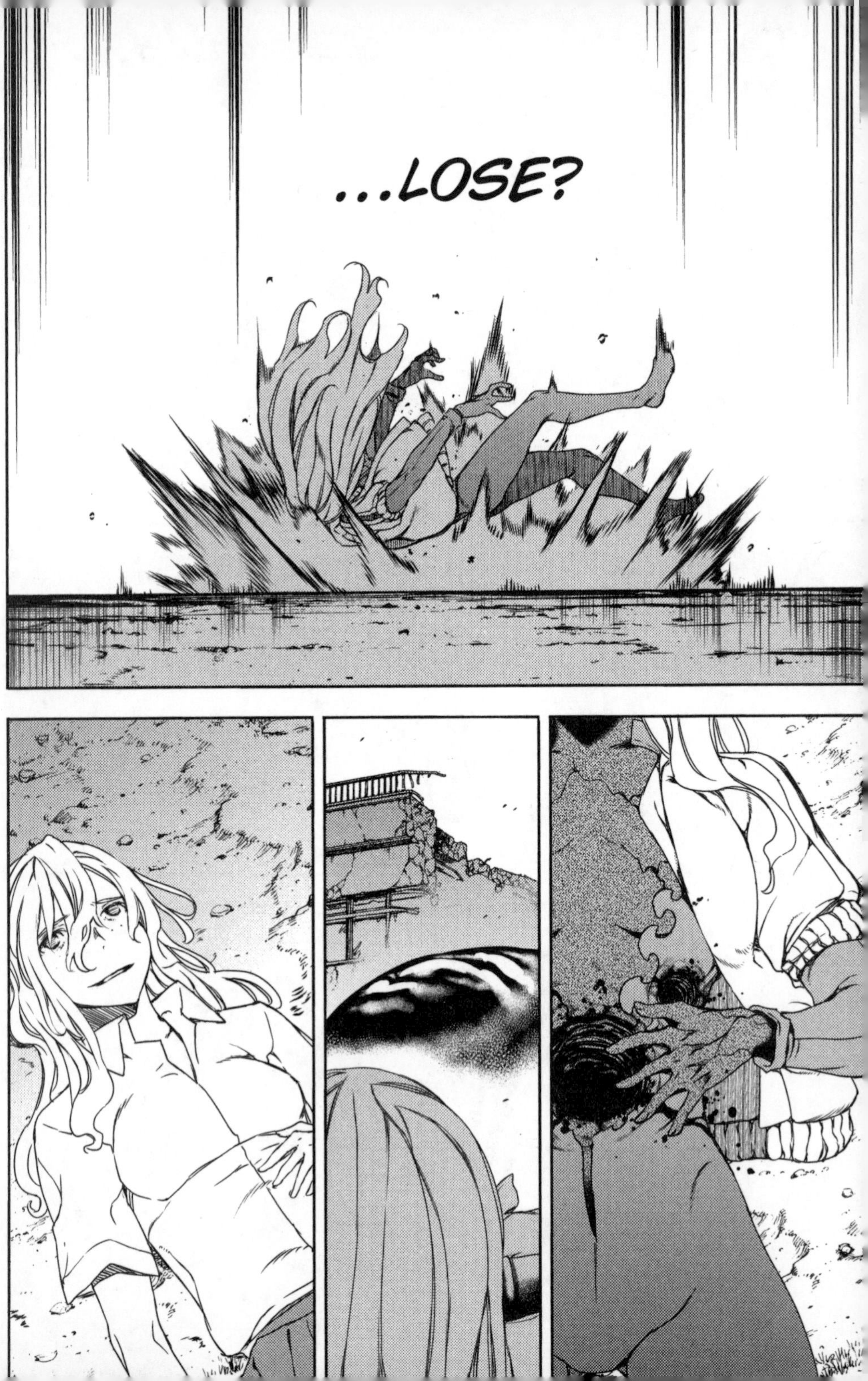
...LOSE?

OH WELL...

CLAIRE
...

AS LONG AS I CAN
DIE WITH SHUICHI...

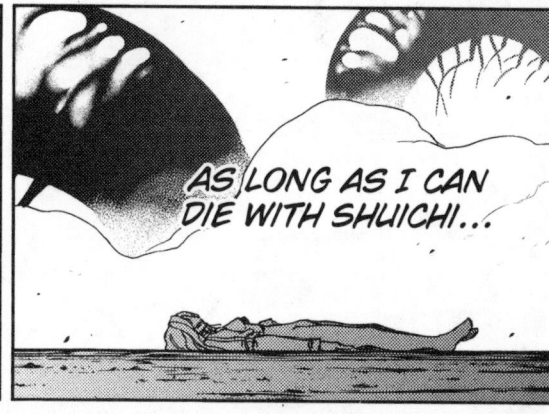

I'M
UNDOING
OUR
TRANS-
FORMA-
TION.

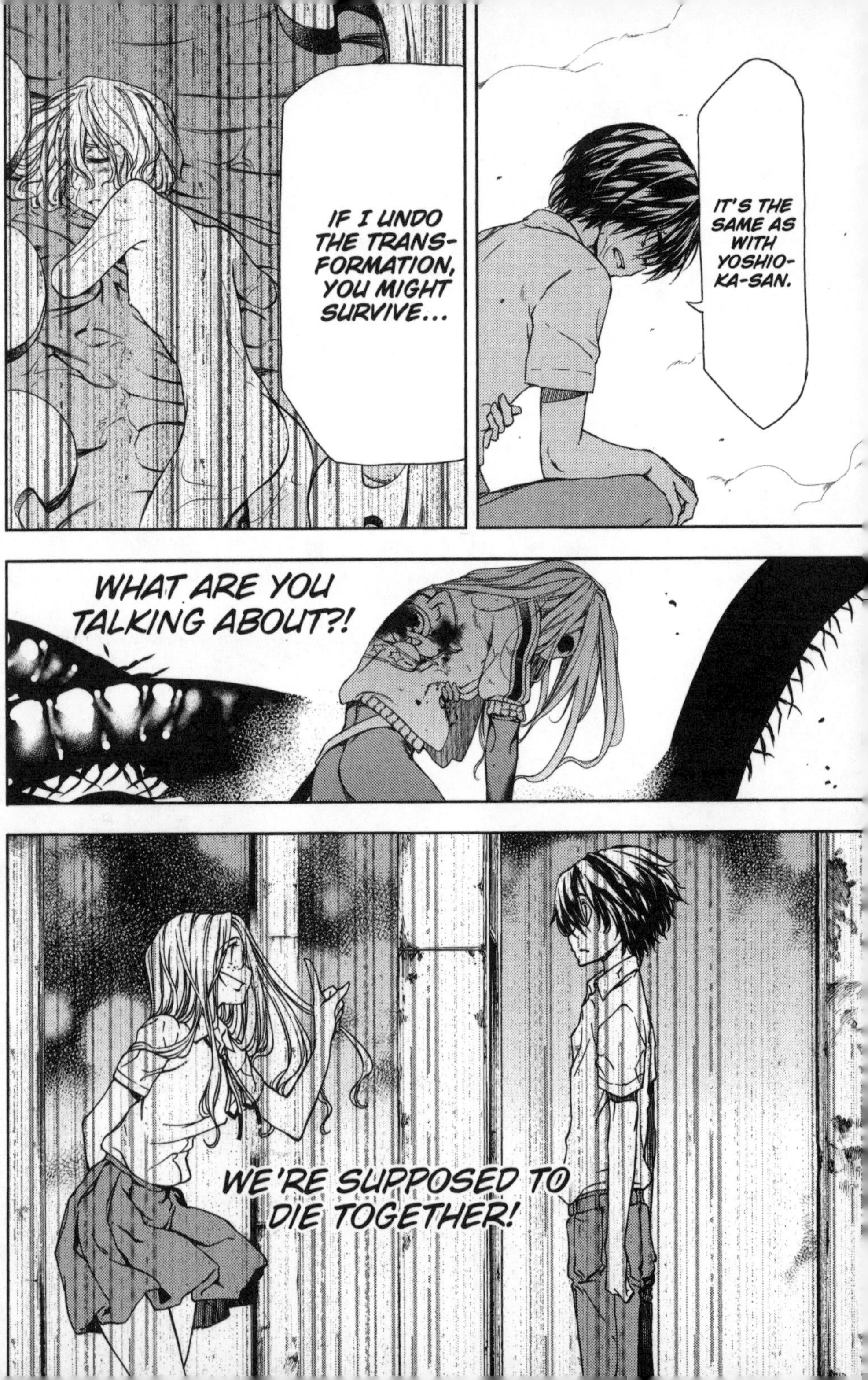
IT'S THE SAME AS WITH YOSHIOKA-SAN.
IF I UNDO THE TRANSFORMATION, YOU MIGHT SURVIVE...
WHAT ARE YOU TALKING ABOUT?!
WE'RE SUPPOSED TO DIE TOGETHER!

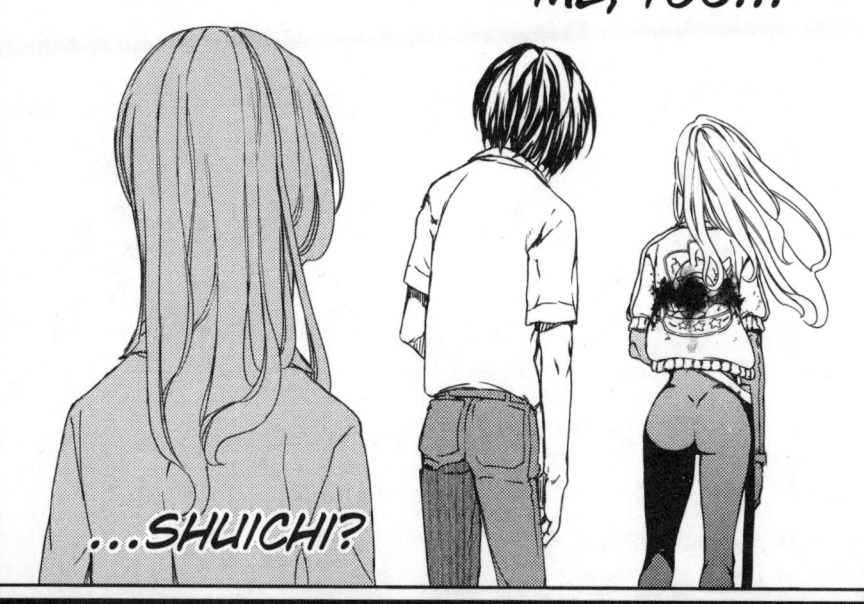

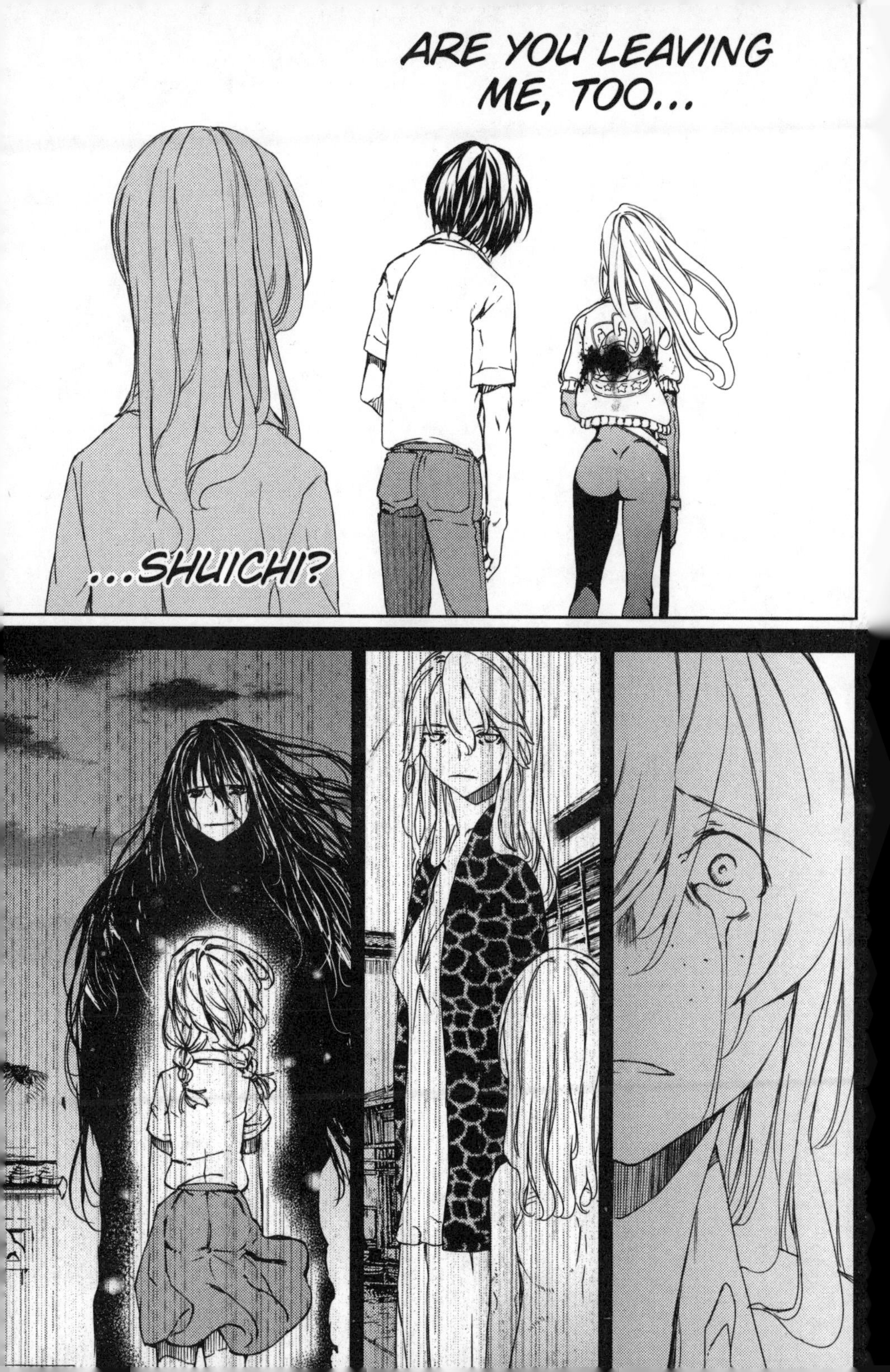
ARE YOU LEAVING ME, TOO...
...SHUICHI?

I DON'T WANT TO
BE ALONE...

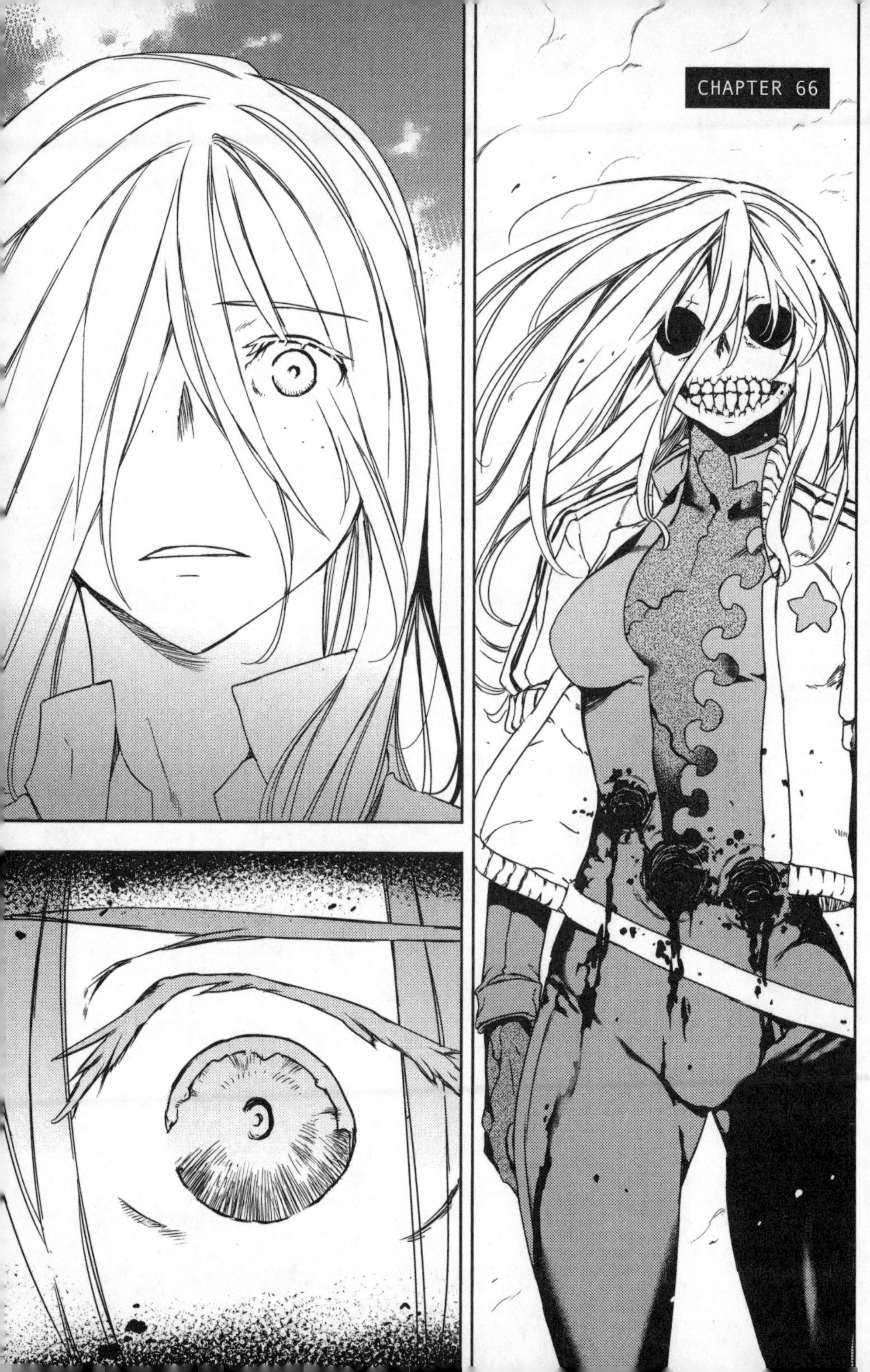
CHAPTER 66

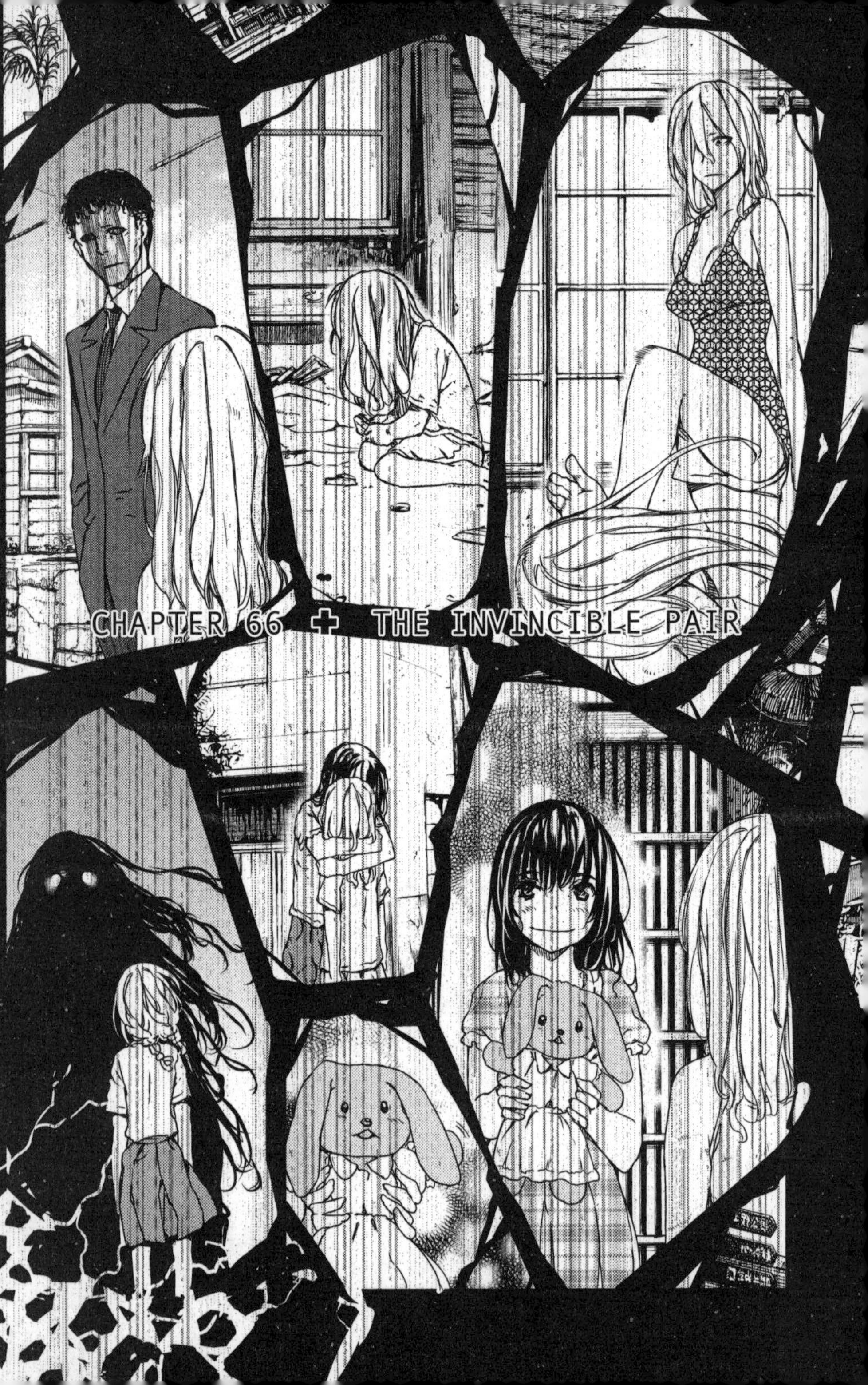
CHAPTER 66 ✚ THE INVINCIBLE PAIR

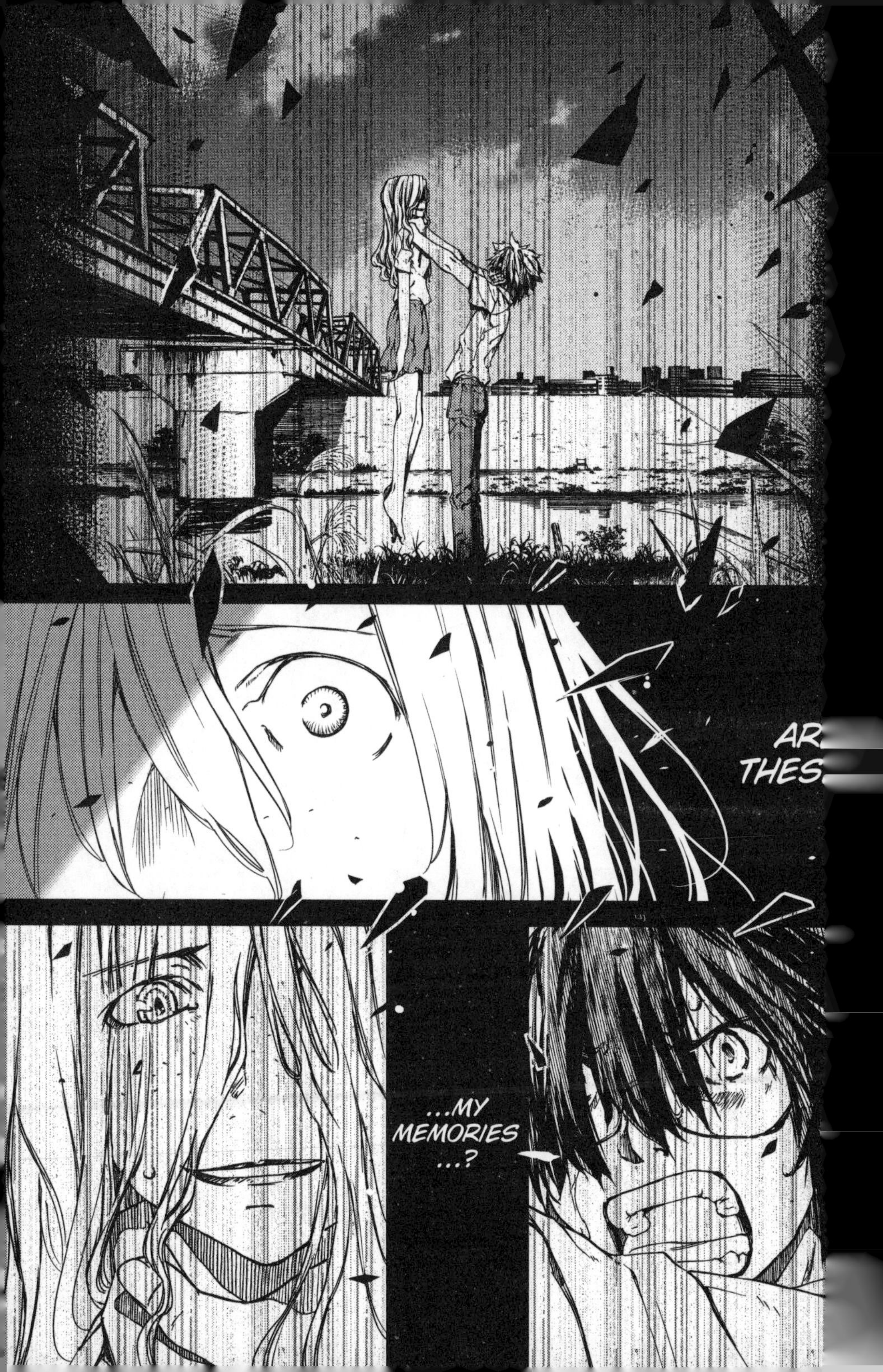
AR
THES
...MY MEMORIES ...?

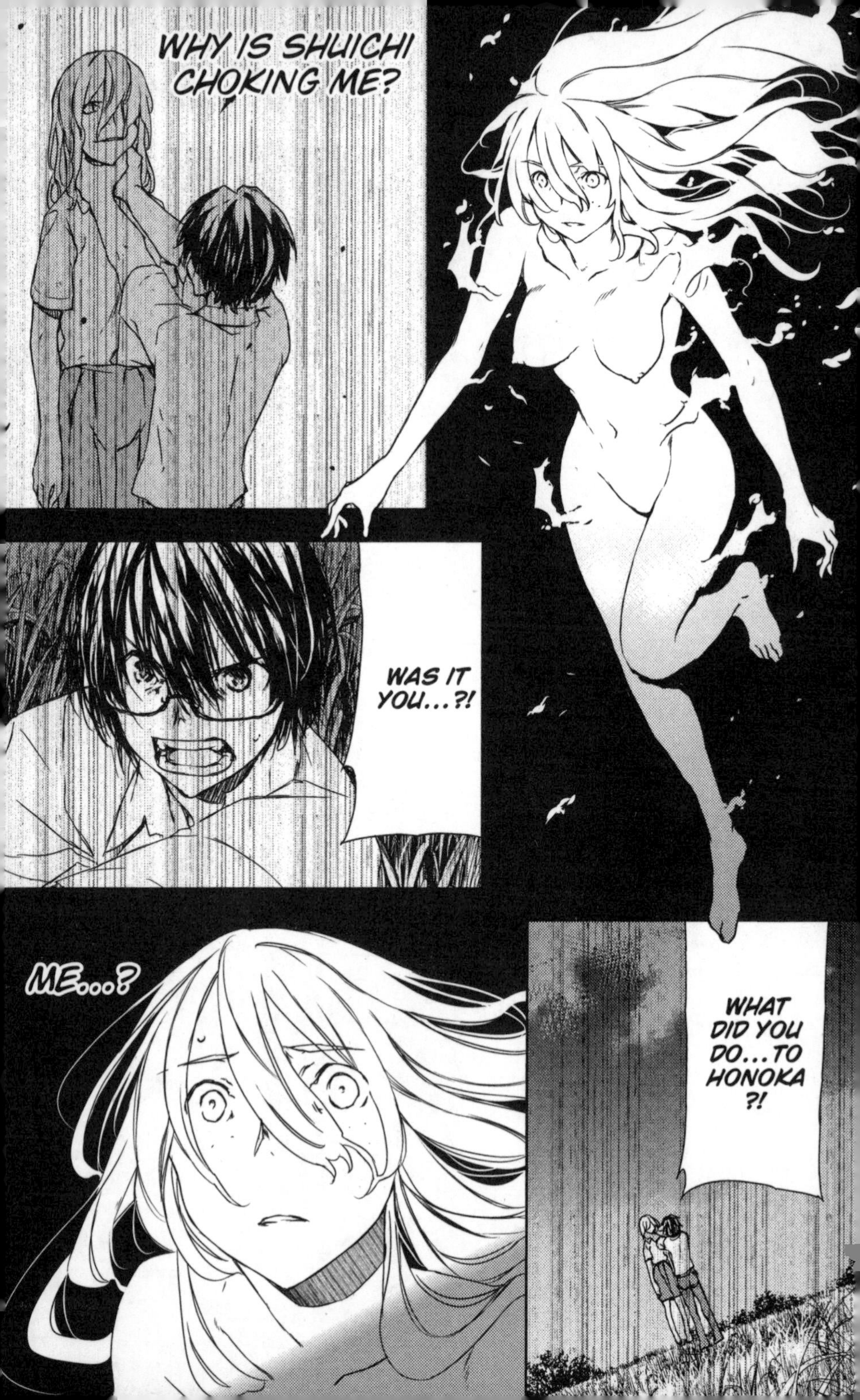
WHY IS SHUICHI CHOKING ME?
WAS IT YOU...?!
WHAT DID YOU DO...TO HONOKA ?!
ME...?

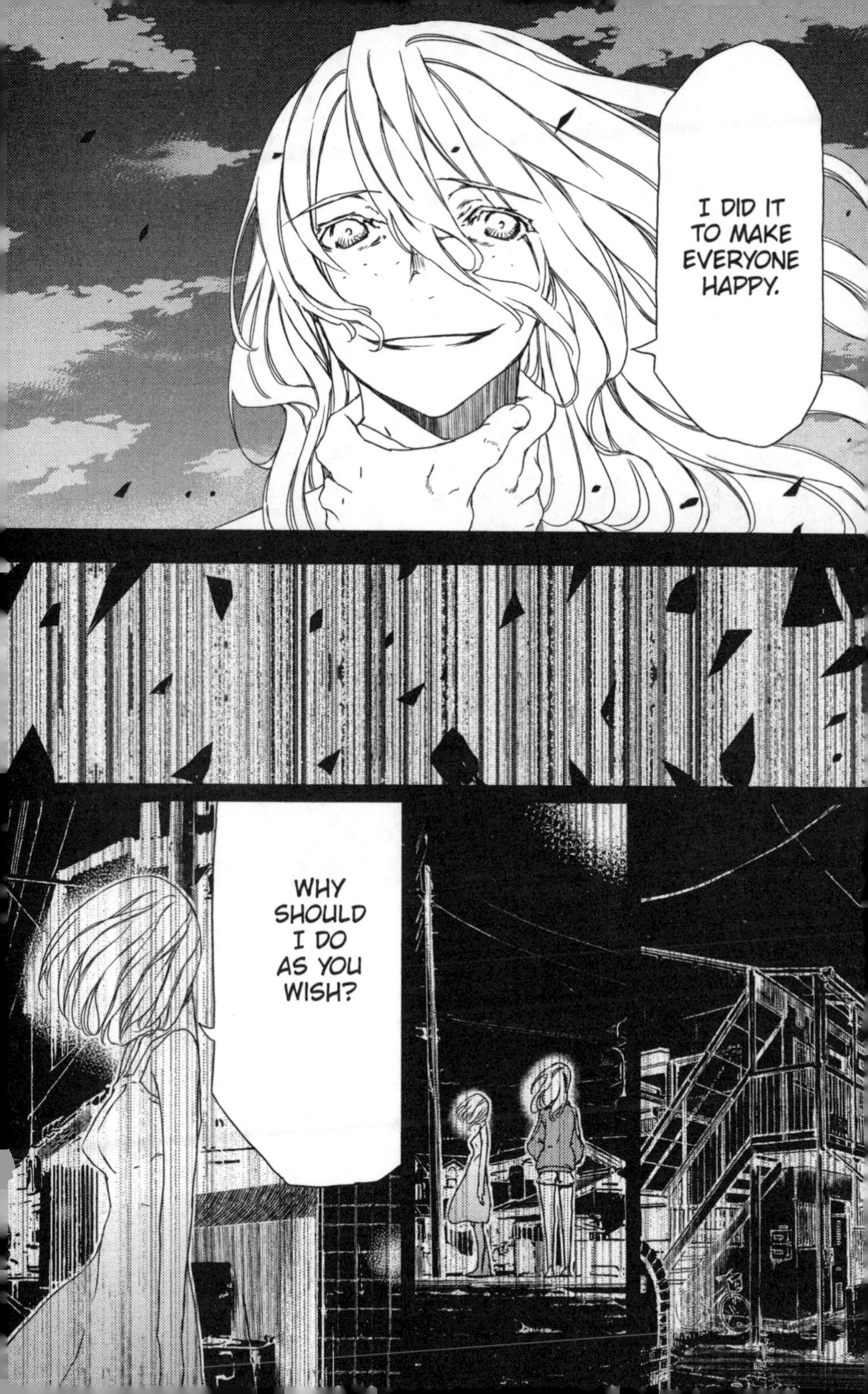
I DID IT TO MAKE EVERYONE HAPPY.
WHY SHOULD I DO AS YOU WISH?

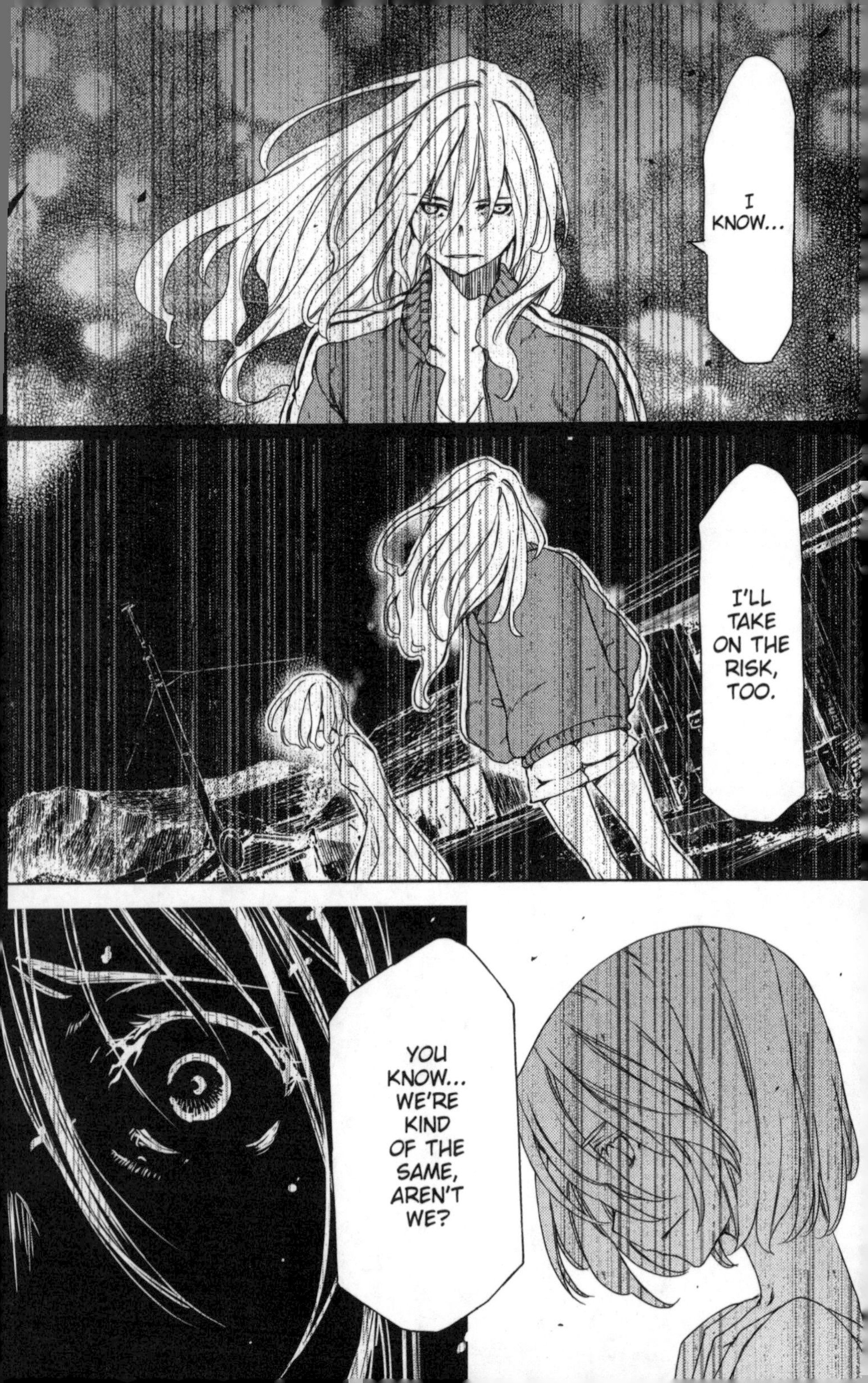
I KNOW...
I'LL TAKE ON THE RISK, TOO.
YOU KNOW... WE'RE KIND OF THE SAME, AREN'T WE?

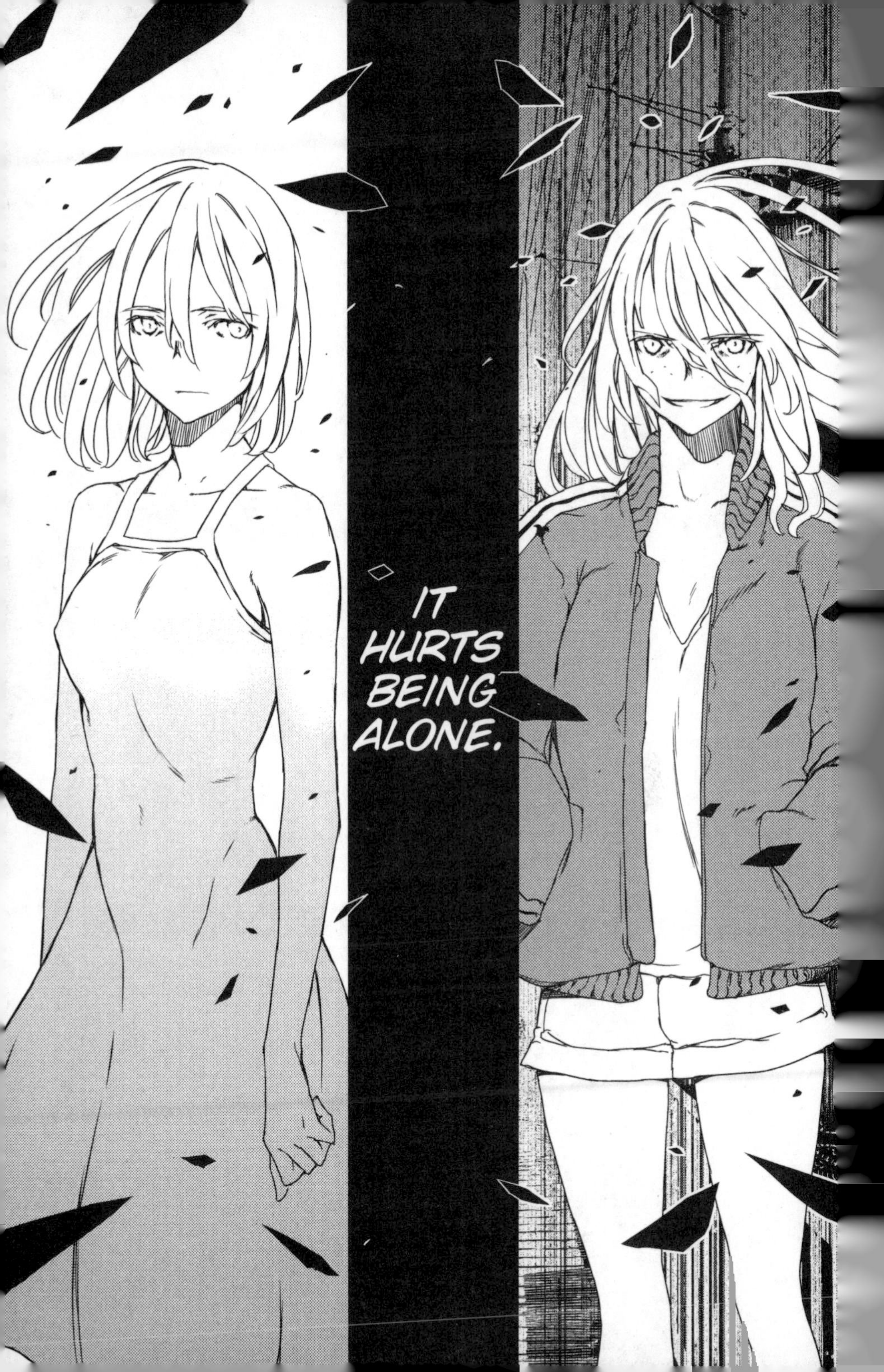
IT HURTS BEING ALONE.

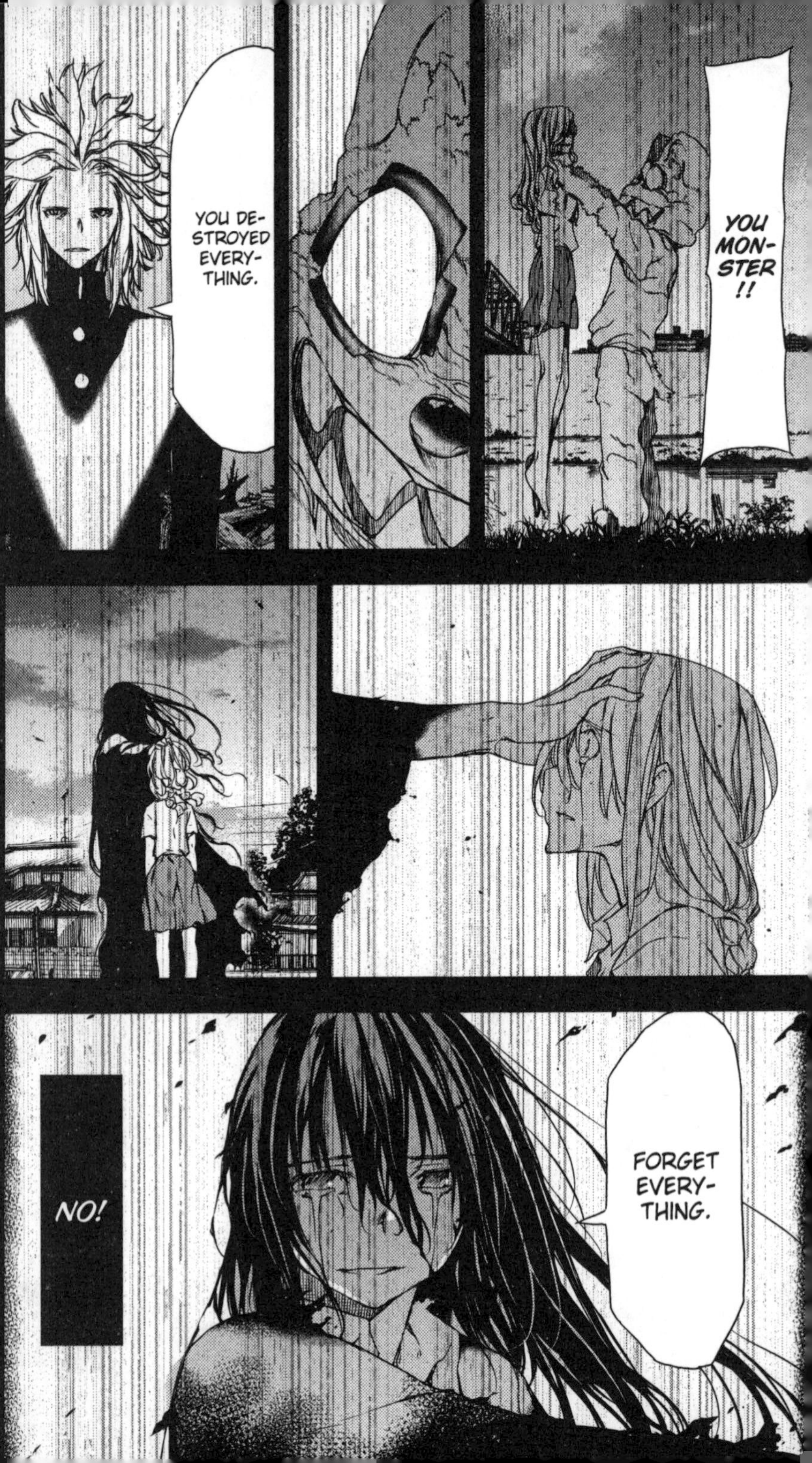
YOU MON-STER!!
YOU DE-STROYED EVERY-THING.
FORGET EVERY-THING.
NO!

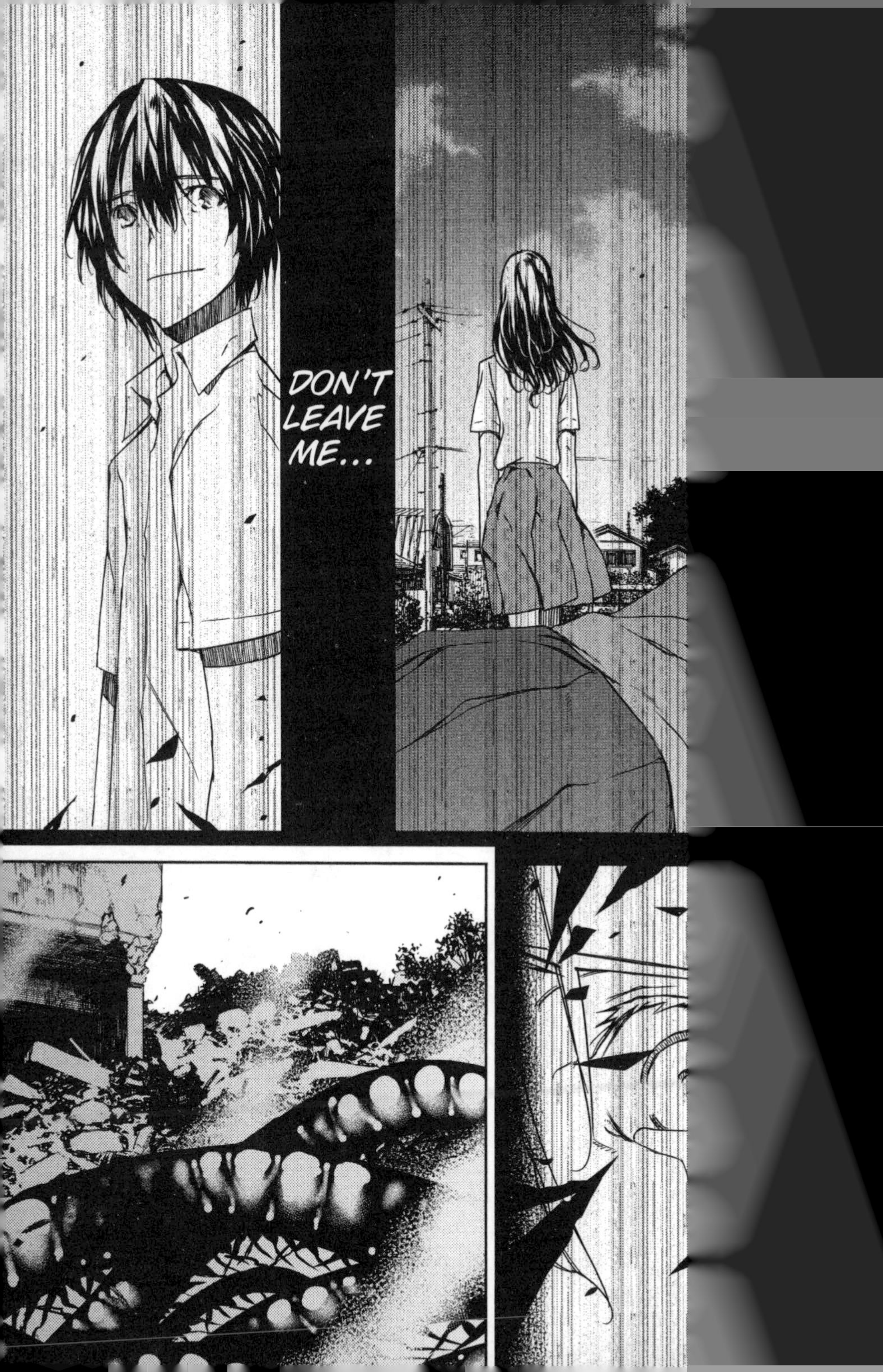
DON'T
LEAVE
ME...

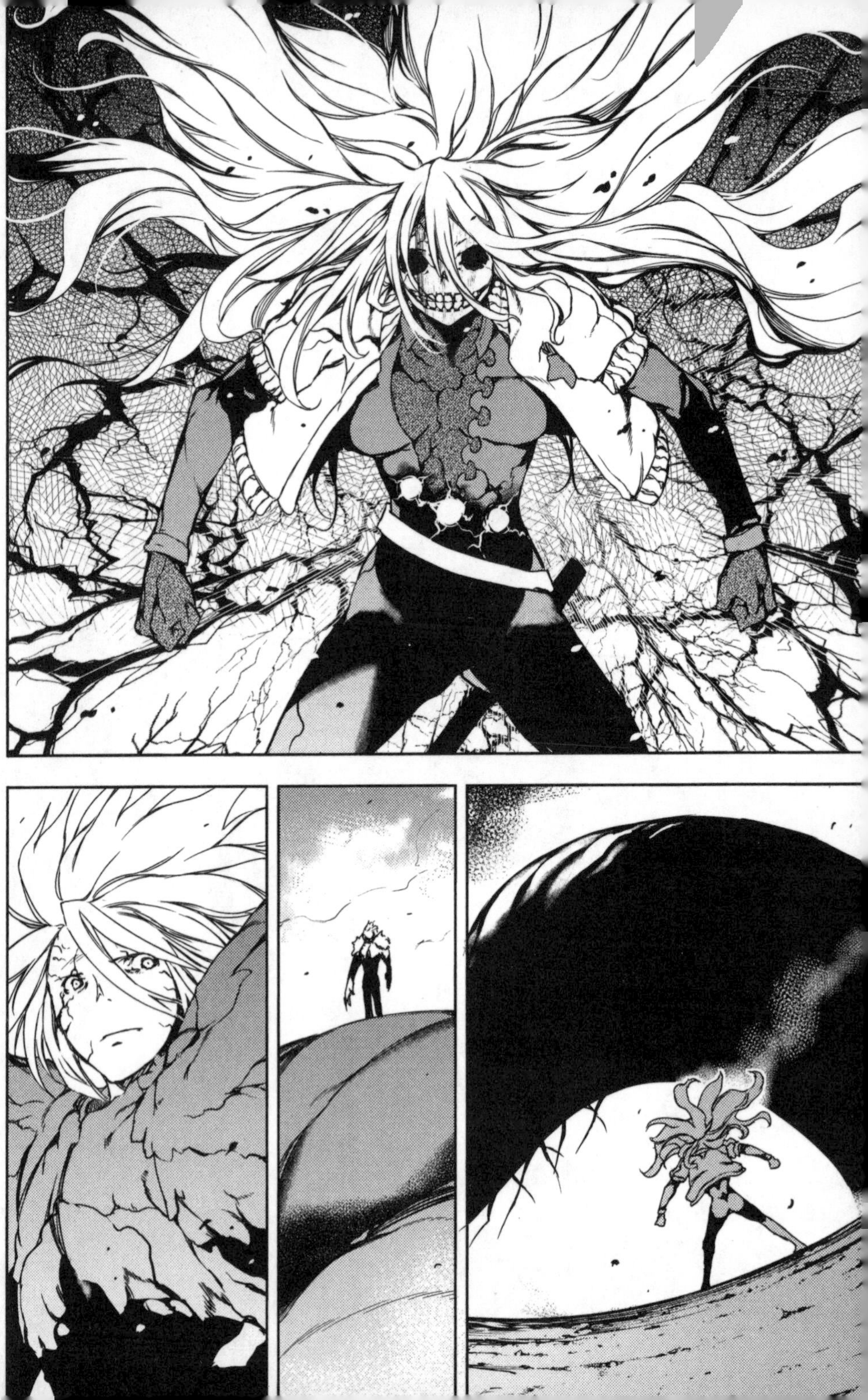

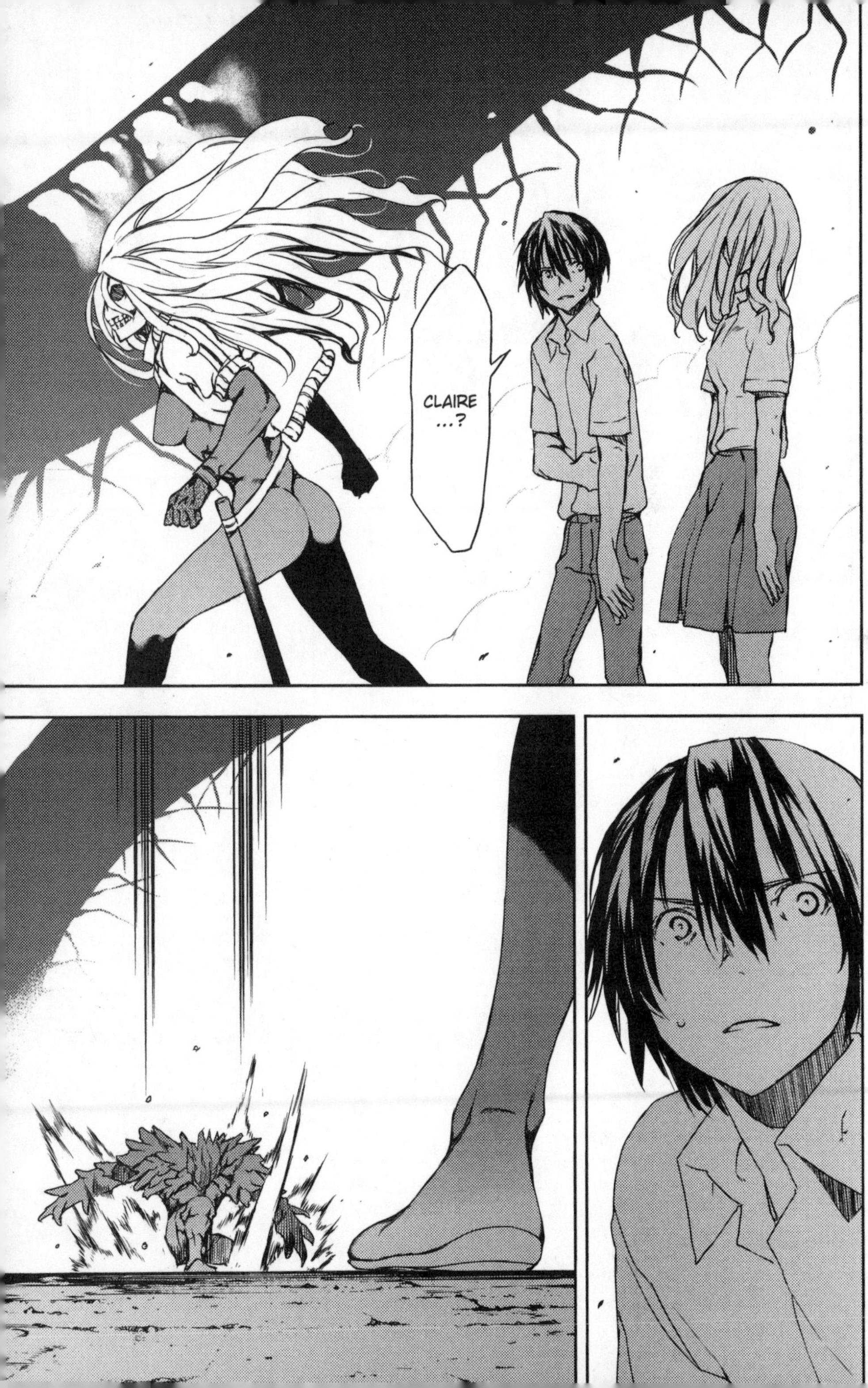
CLAIRE ...?

WHAT HAPPENED?

I CAN'T TELL WHAT SHE'S THINKING...

NO...

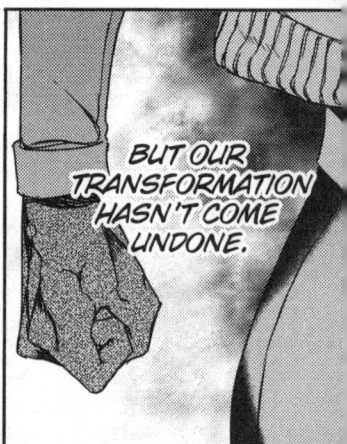

BUT OUR TRANSFORMATION HASN'T COME UNDONE.

I CAN'T UNDO IT!

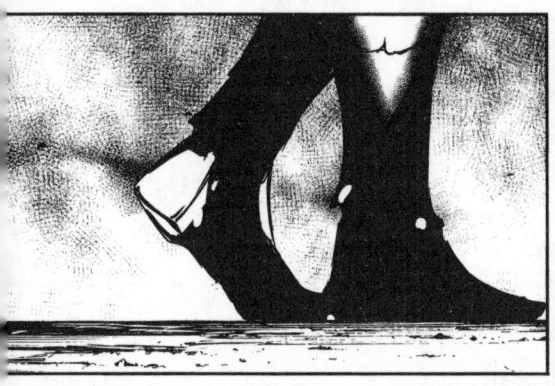

THE ONLY THING TO DO IS FIGHT!

IF I LOSE NOW...

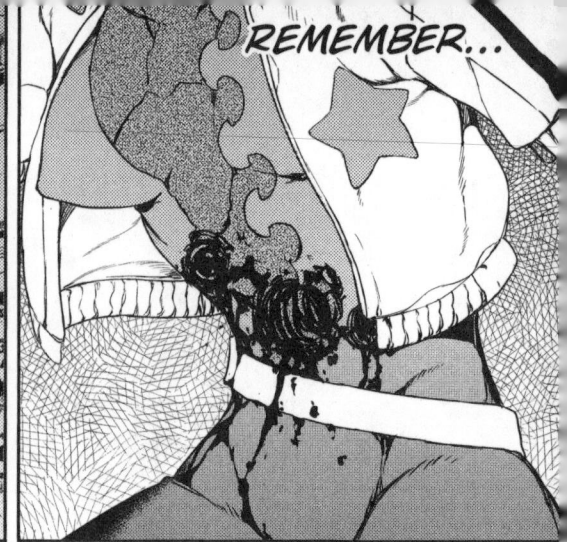

REMEMBER...

A LOT OF PEOPLE...

...WILL DIE.

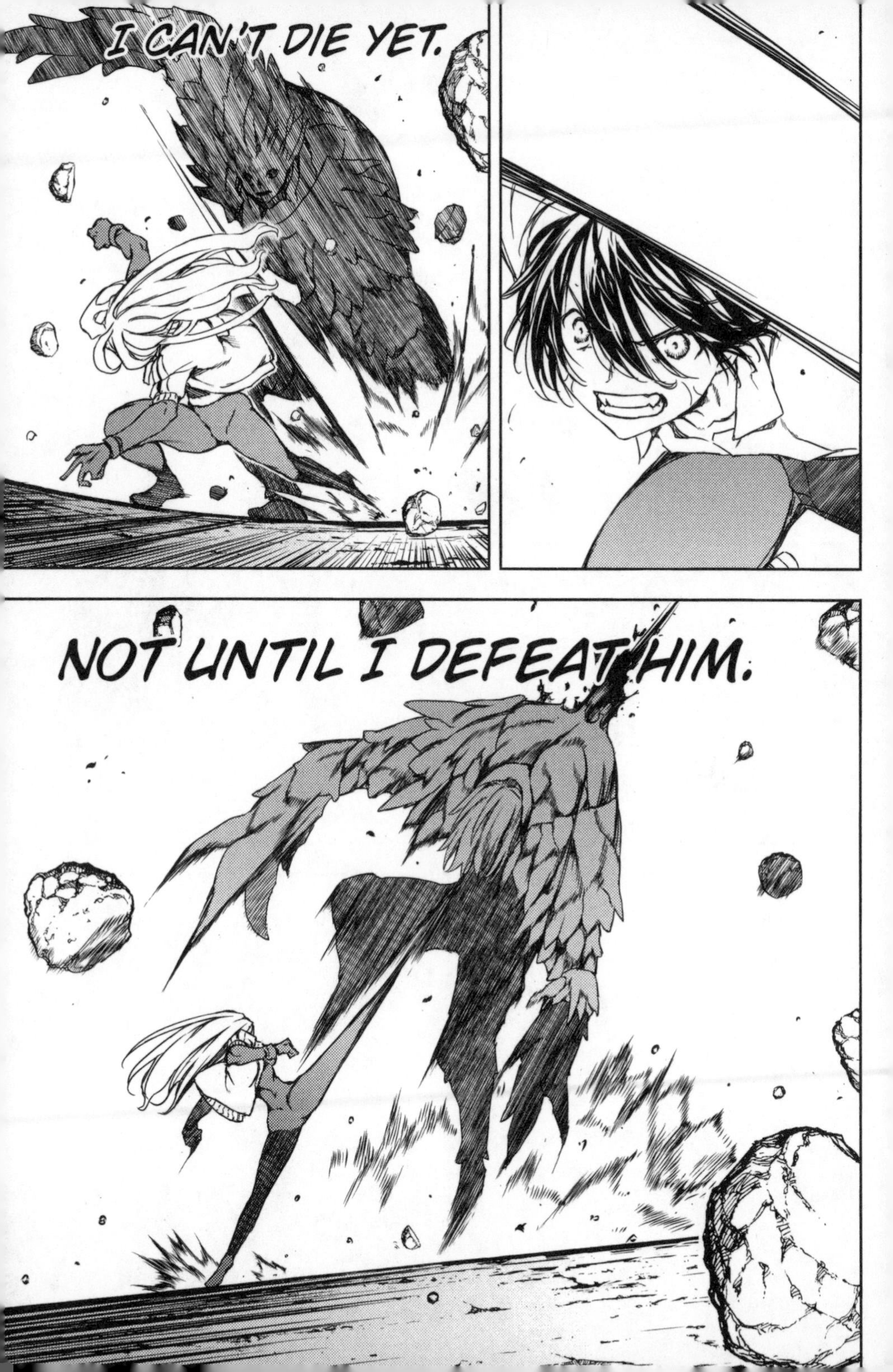
I CAN'T DIE YET.
NOT UNTIL I DEFEAT HIM.

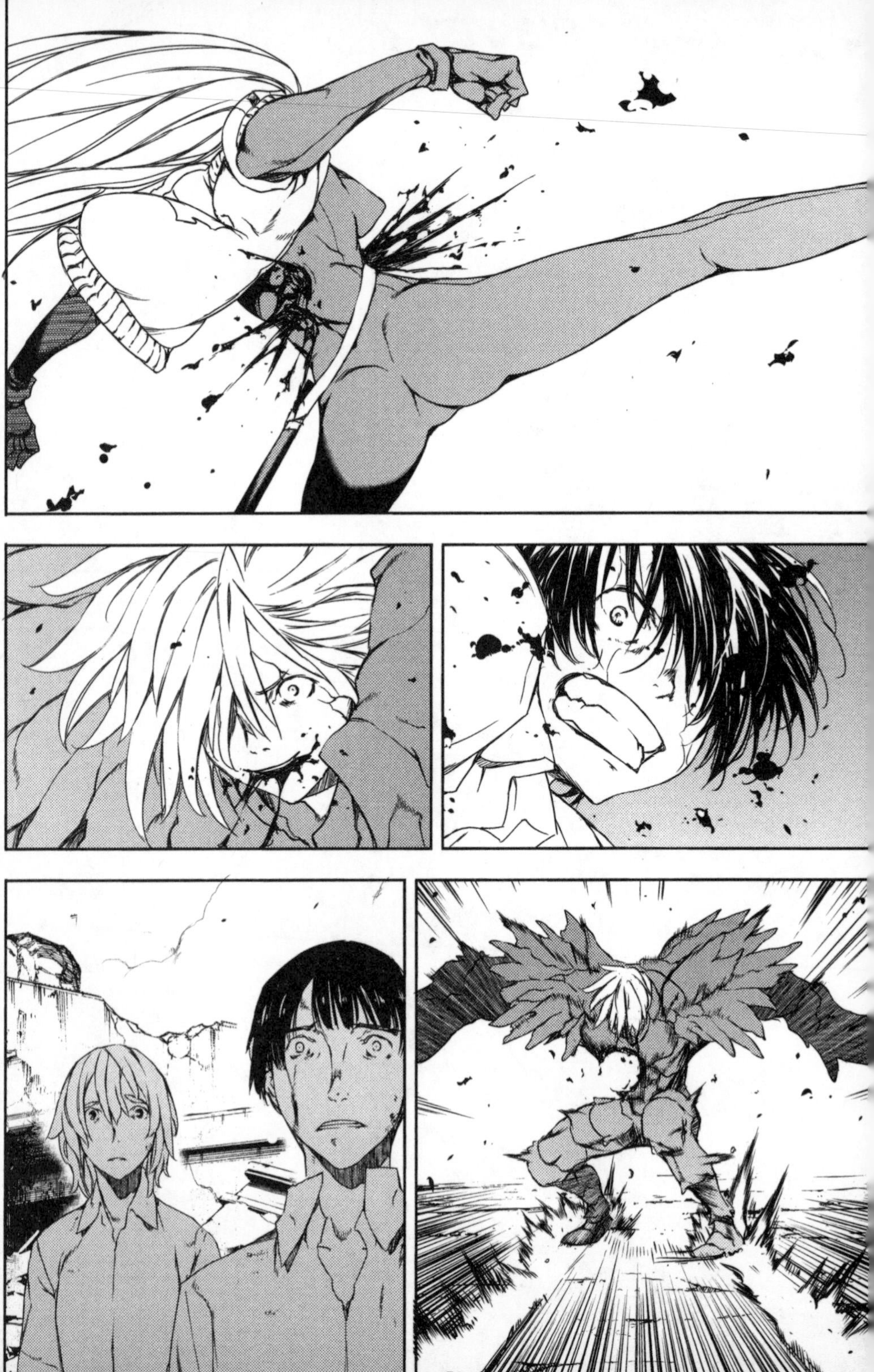

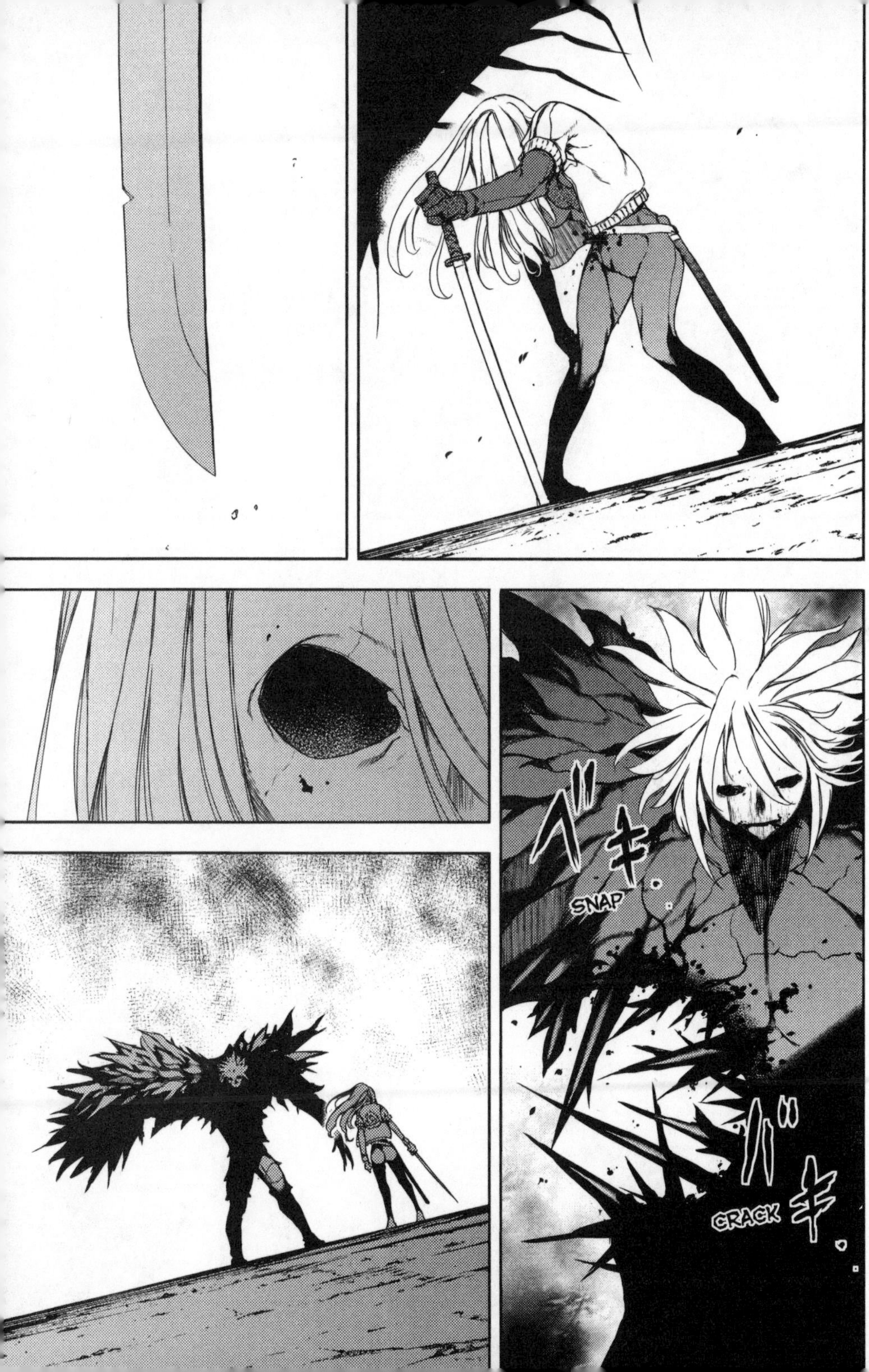

SNAP
CRACK

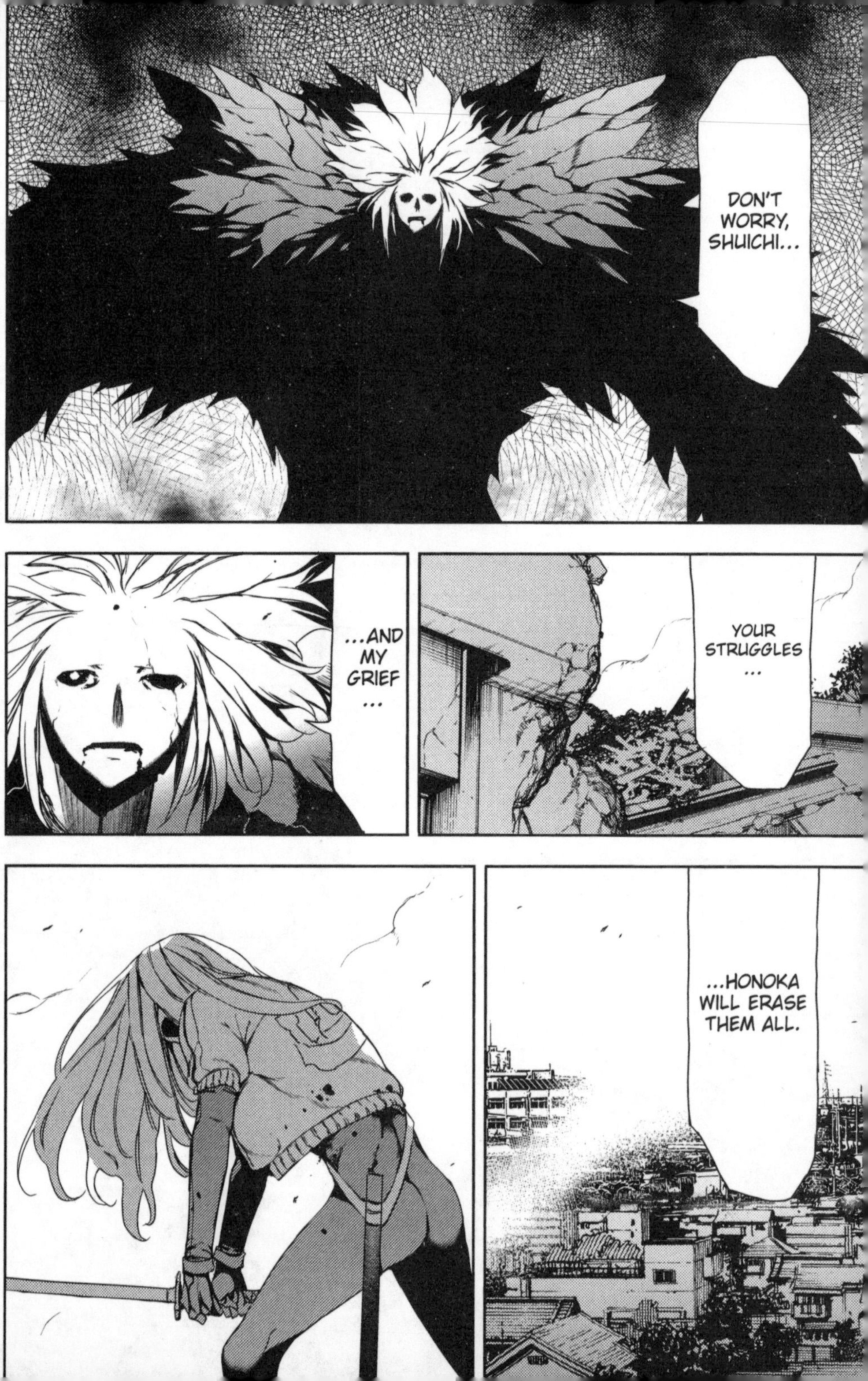
DON'T WORRY, SHUICHI...
YOUR STRUGGLES ...
...AND MY GRIEF ...
...HONOKA WILL ERASE THEM ALL.

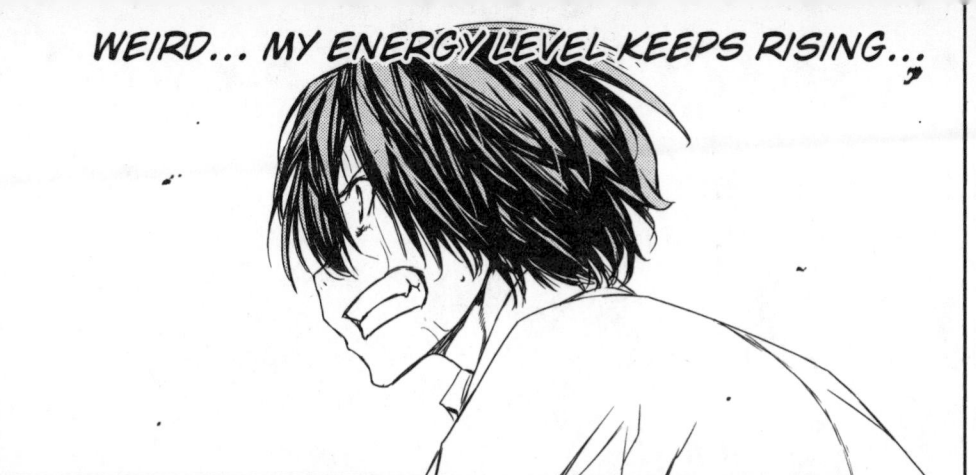

WEIRD... MY ENERGY LEVEL KEEPS RISING...
...BUT MY BODY FEELS HEAVY.
IT'S LIKE I'M IN CLAY.
I CAN'T MOVE FORWARD.
IT'S LIKE TIME STOPPED...BUT ONLY FOR ME...
...NO.

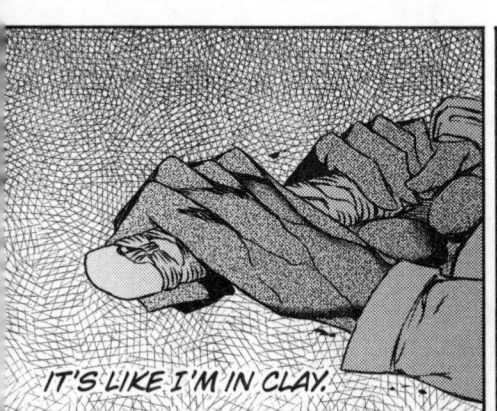

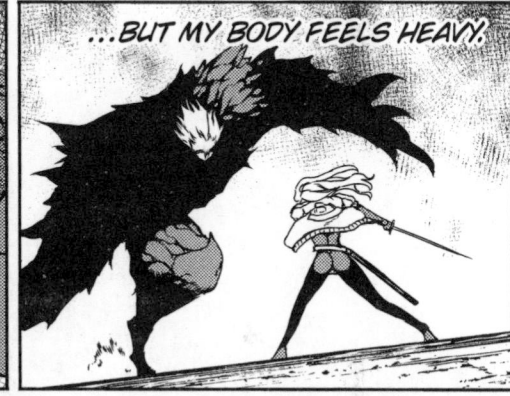

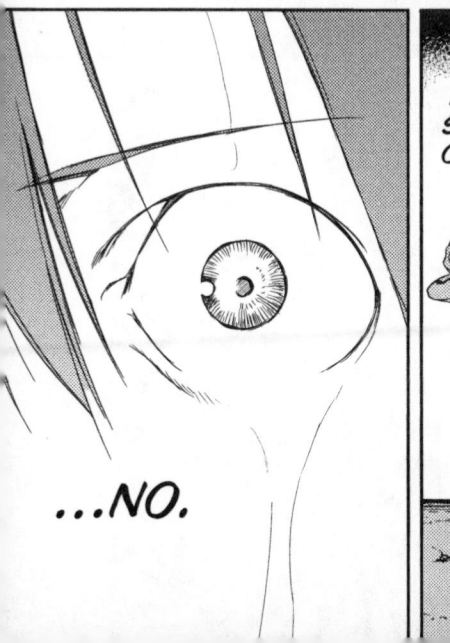

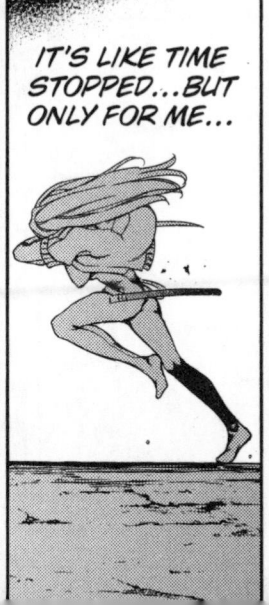

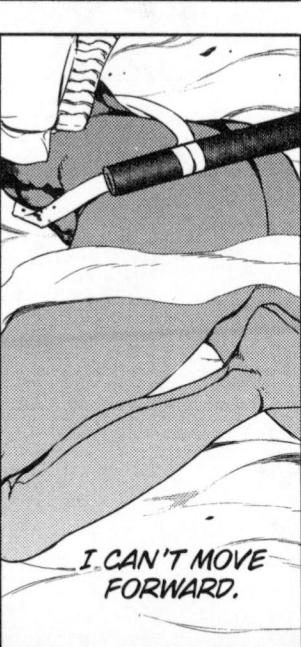

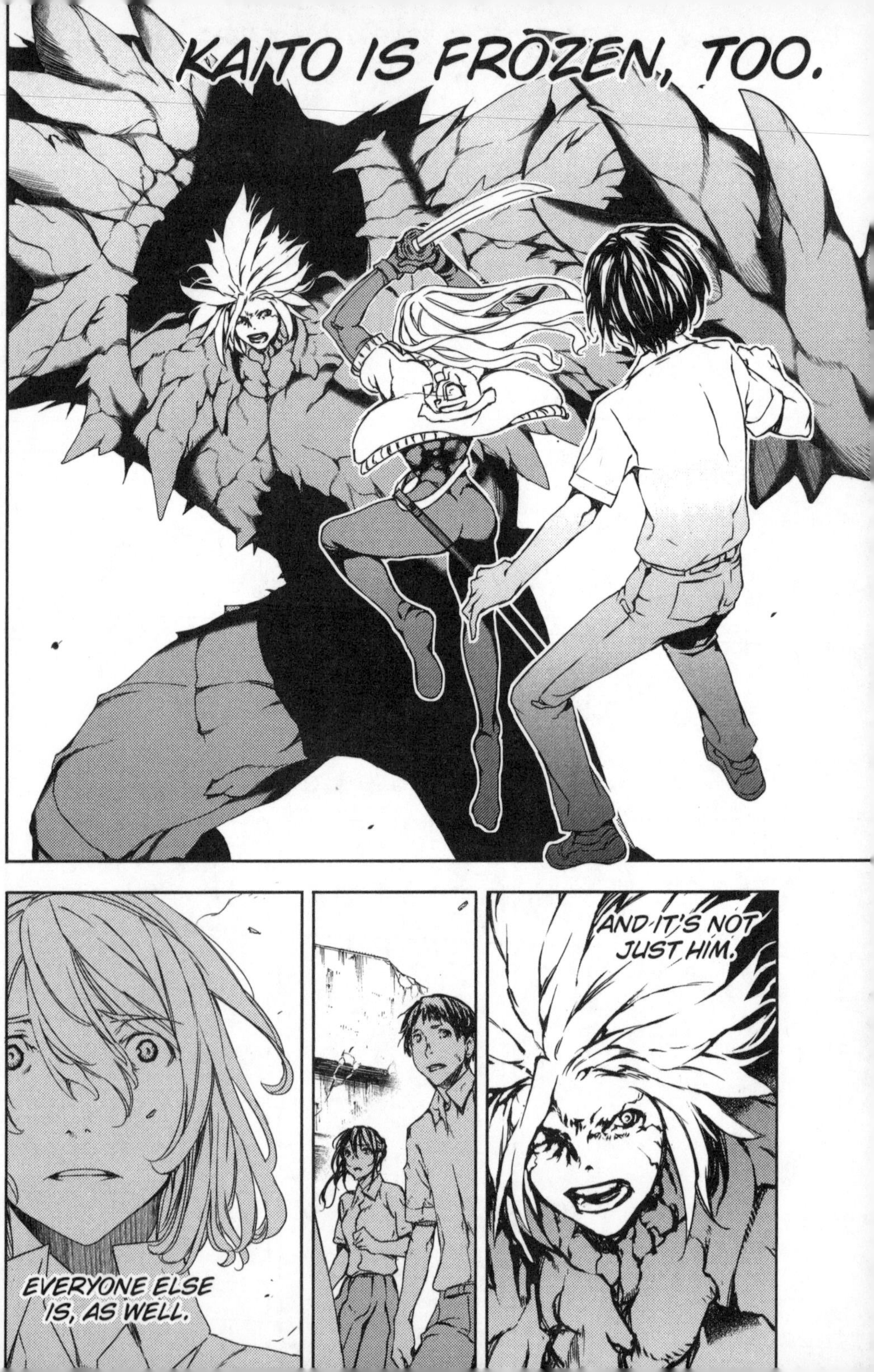
KAITO IS FROZEN, TOO.
AND IT'S NOT JUST HIM.
EVERYONE ELSE IS, AS WELL.

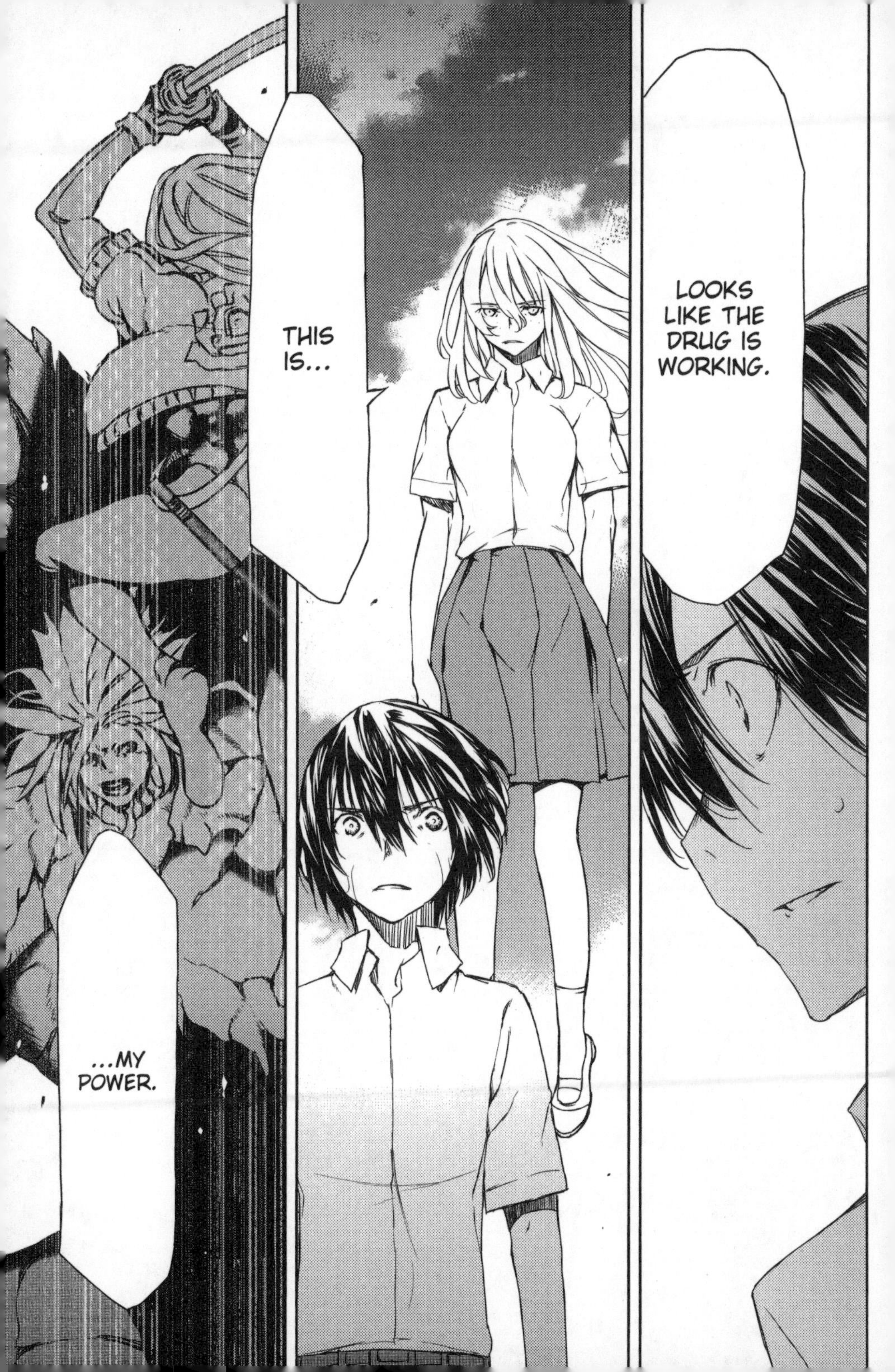
LOOKS LIKE THE DRUG IS WORKING.
THIS IS...
...MY POWER.

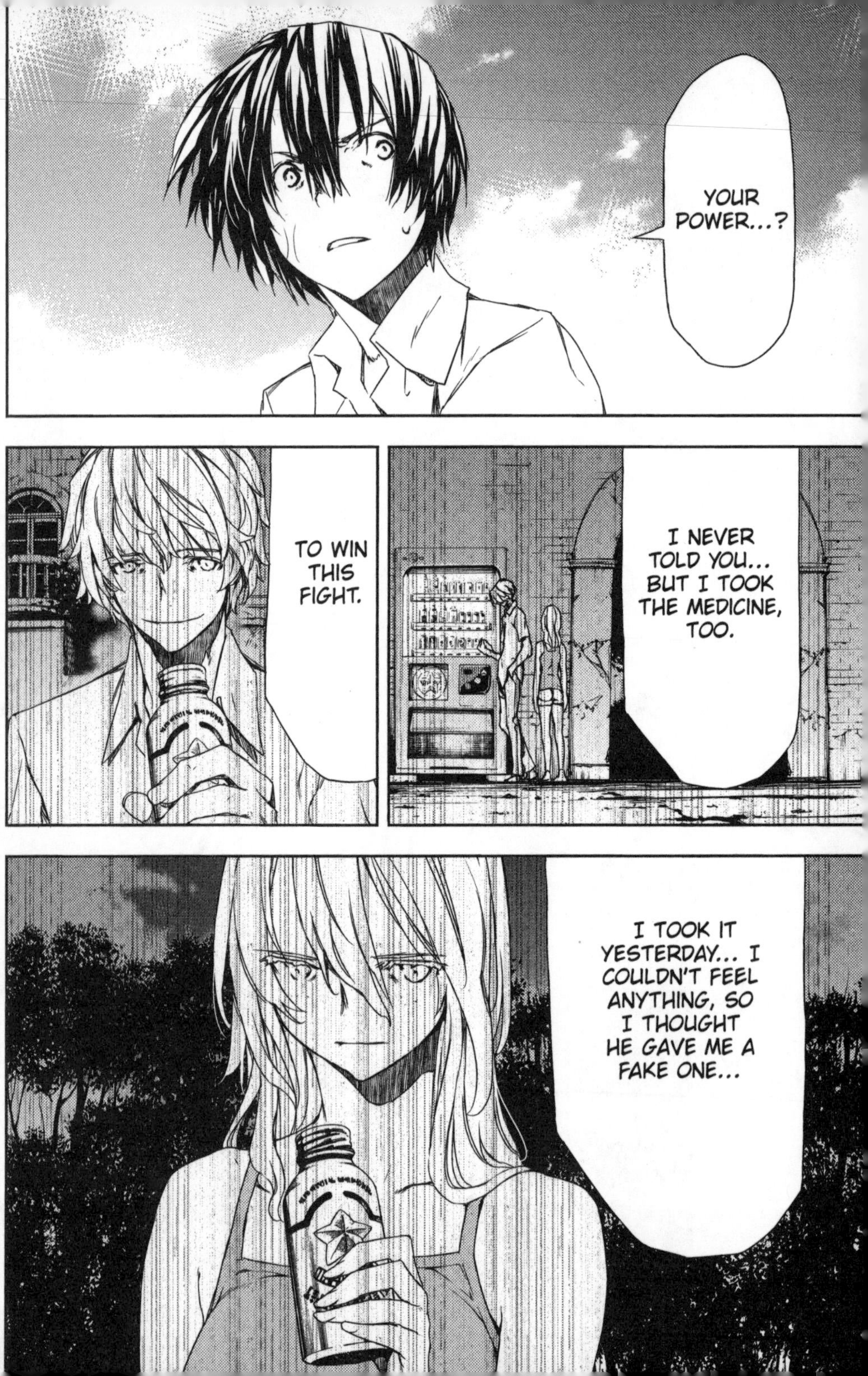
YOUR POWER...?
I NEVER TOLD YOU... BUT I TOOK THE MEDICINE, TOO.
TO WIN THIS FIGHT.
I TOOK IT YESTERDAY... I COULDN'T FEEL ANYTHING, SO I THOUGHT HE GAVE ME A FAKE ONE...

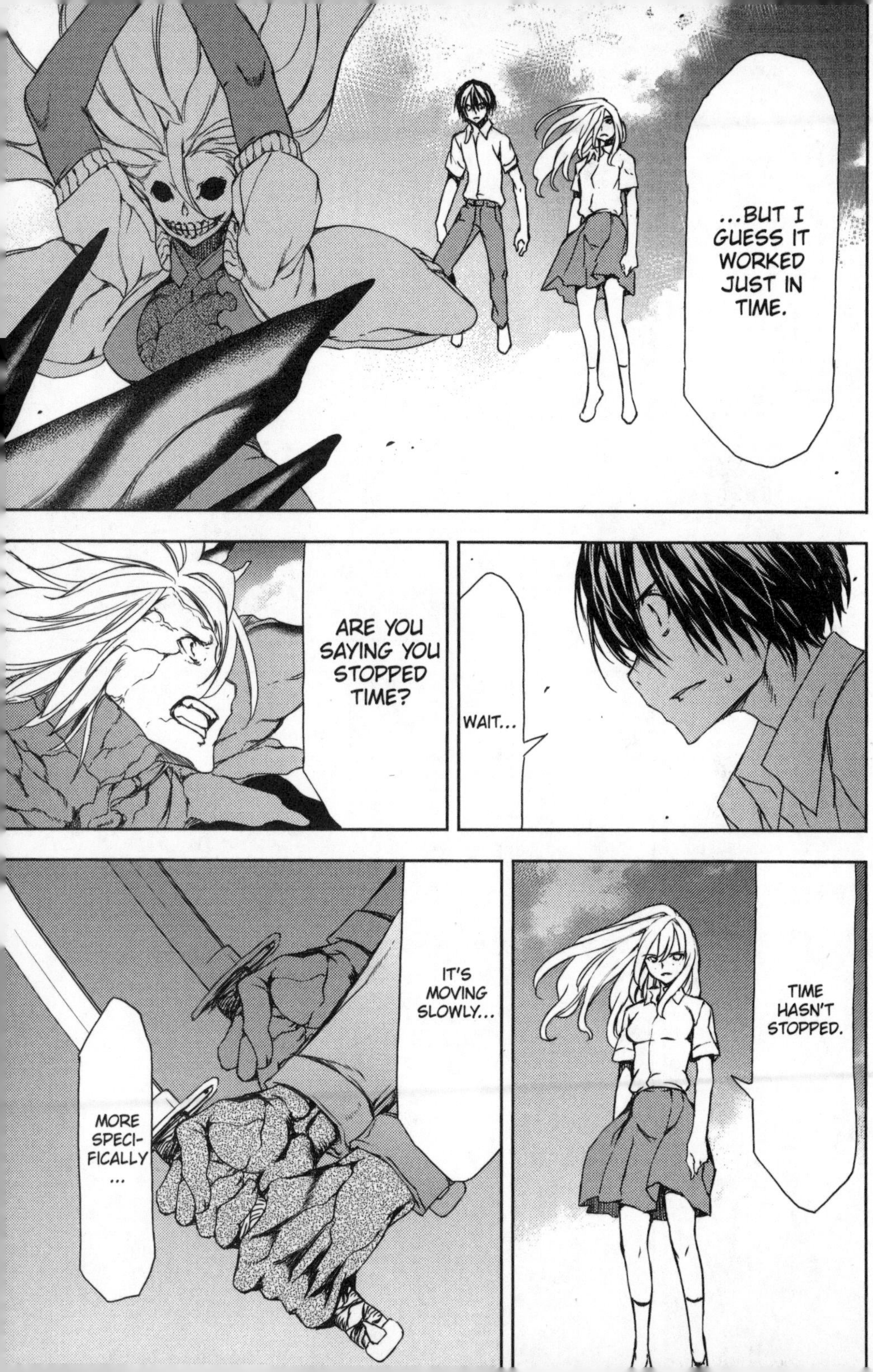
...BUT I GUESS IT WORKED JUST IN TIME.
WAIT...
ARE YOU SAYING YOU STOPPED TIME?
TIME HASN'T STOPPED.
IT'S MOVING SLOWLY...
MORE SPECI-FICALLY ...

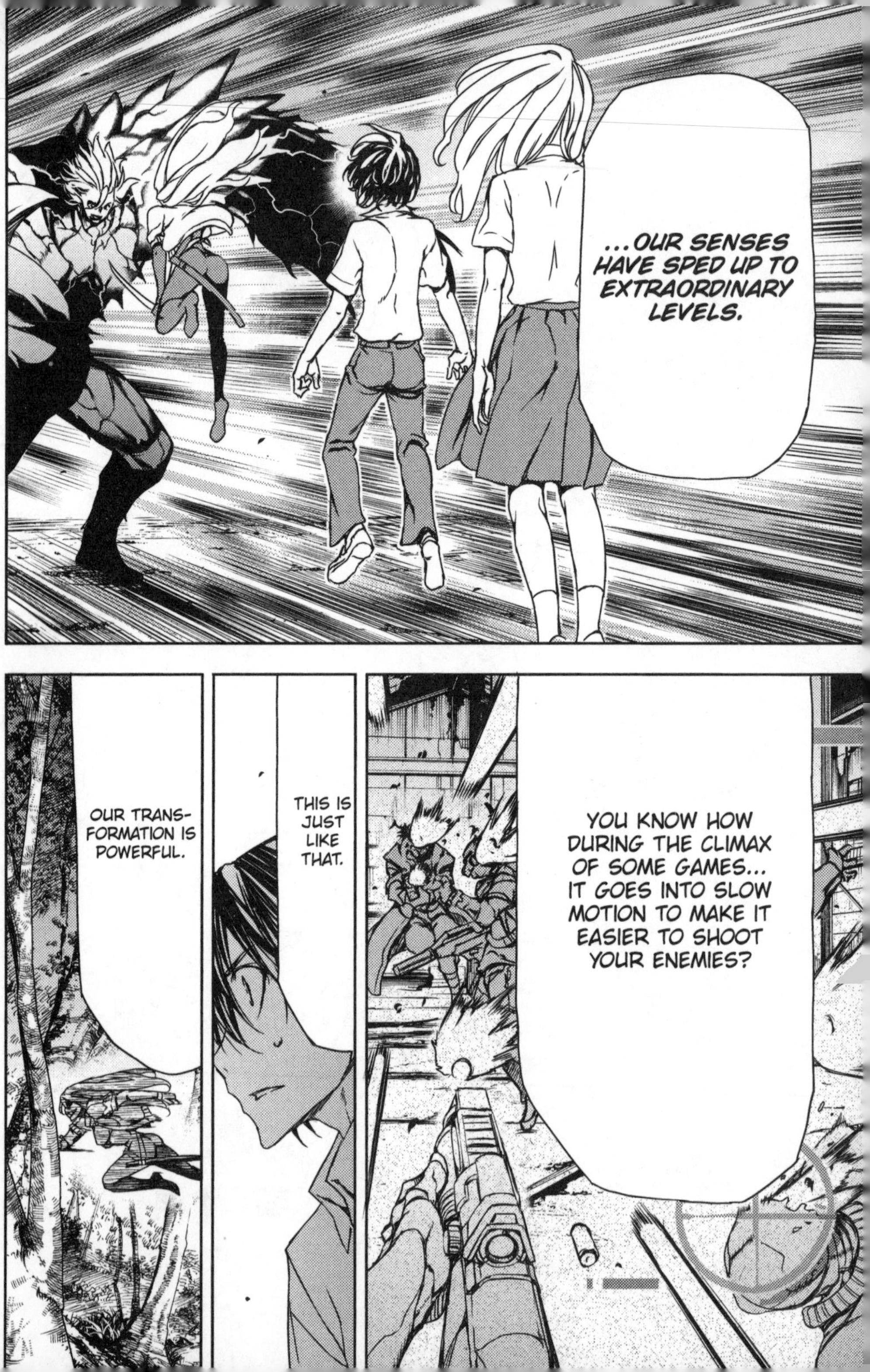
...OUR SENSES HAVE SPED UP TO EXTRAORDINARY LEVELS.
YOU KNOW HOW DURING THE CLIMAX OF SOME GAMES... IT GOES INTO SLOW MOTION TO MAKE IT EASIER TO SHOOT YOUR ENEMIES?
THIS IS JUST LIKE THAT.
OUR TRANS-FORMATION IS POWERFUL.

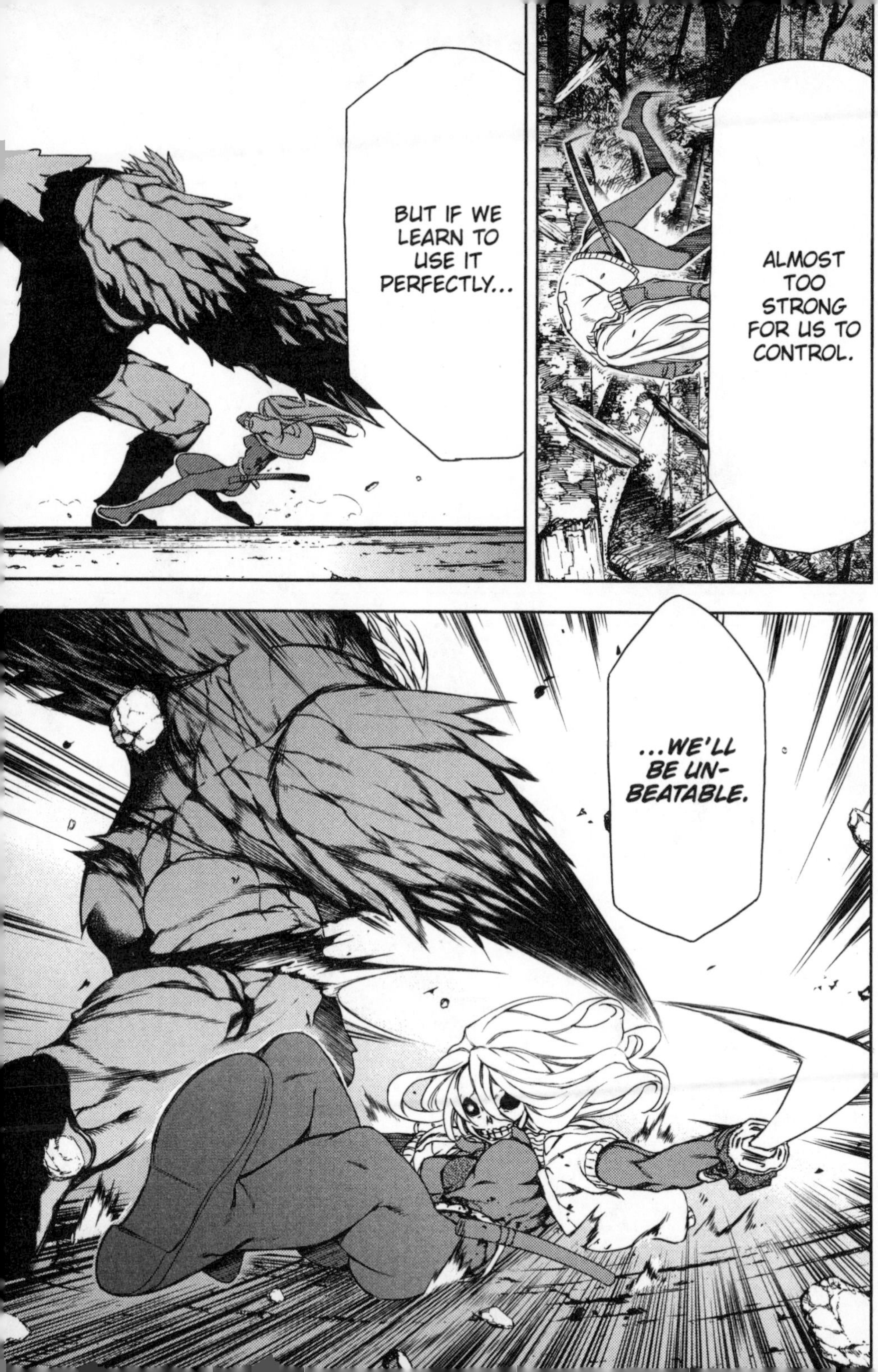
ALMOST TOO STRONG FOR US TO CONTROL.
BUT IF WE LEARN TO USE IT PERFECTLY...
...WE'LL BE UN-
BEATABLE.

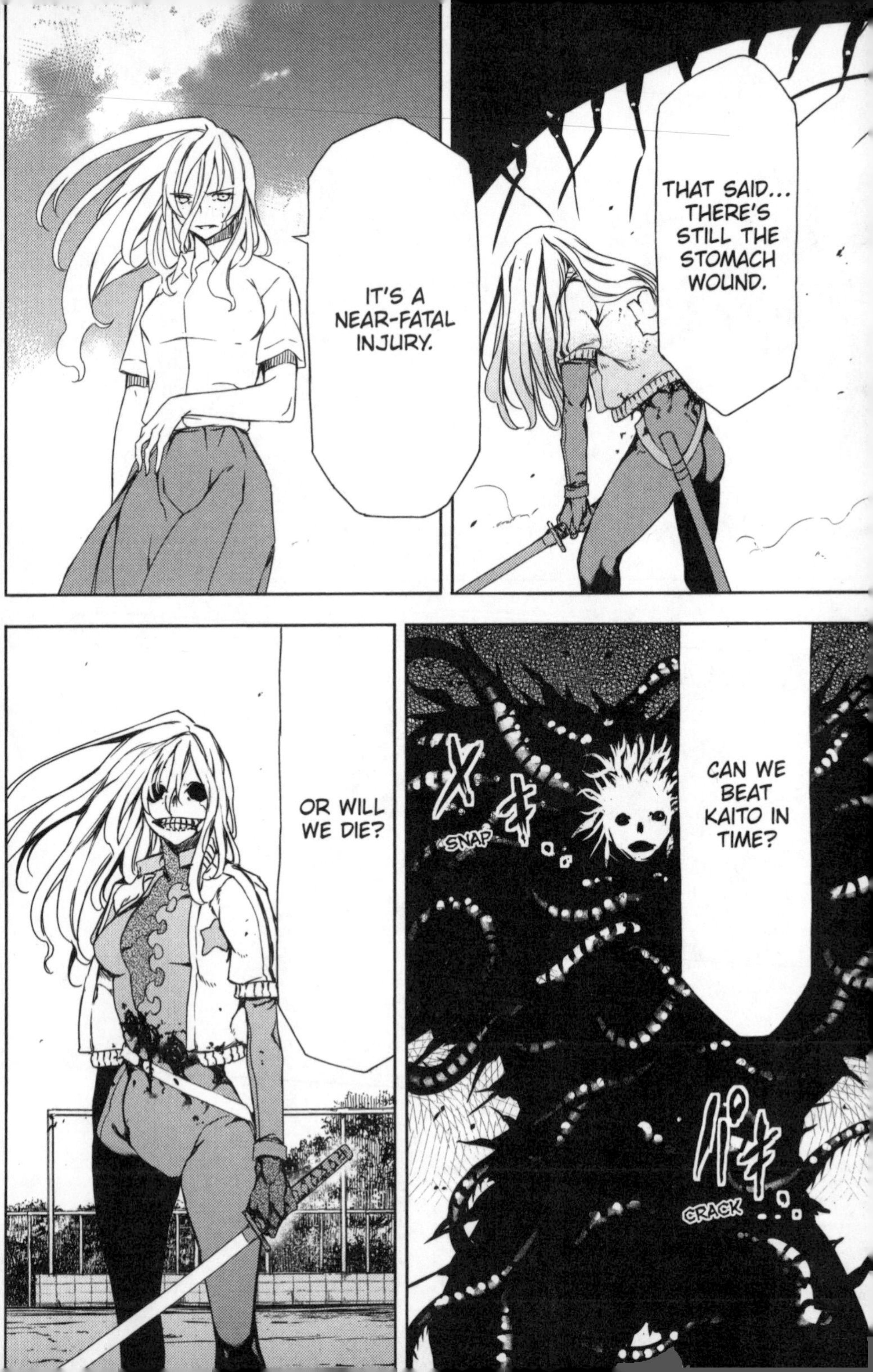
THAT SAID... THERE'S STILL THE STOMACH WOUND.
IT'S A NEAR-FATAL INJURY.
CAN WE BEAT KAITO IN TIME?
メキ
SNAP
パキ
CRACK
OR WILL WE DIE?

WHAT SHOULD WE DO, SHUICHI?

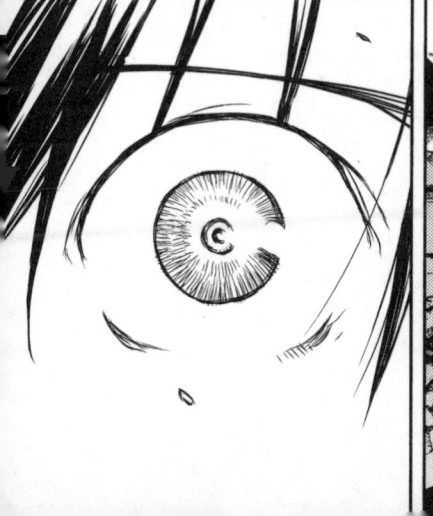

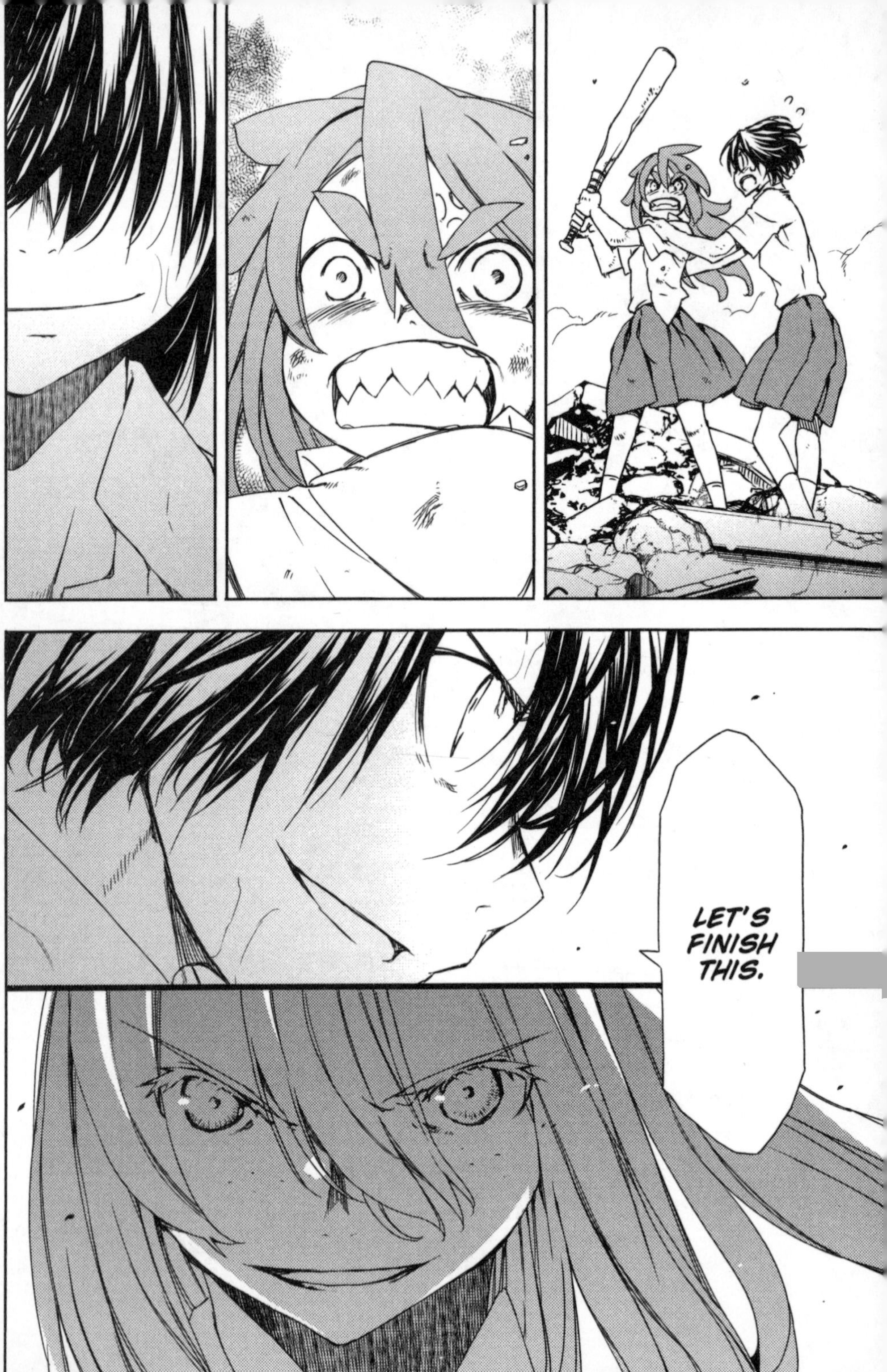
LET'S FINISH THIS.

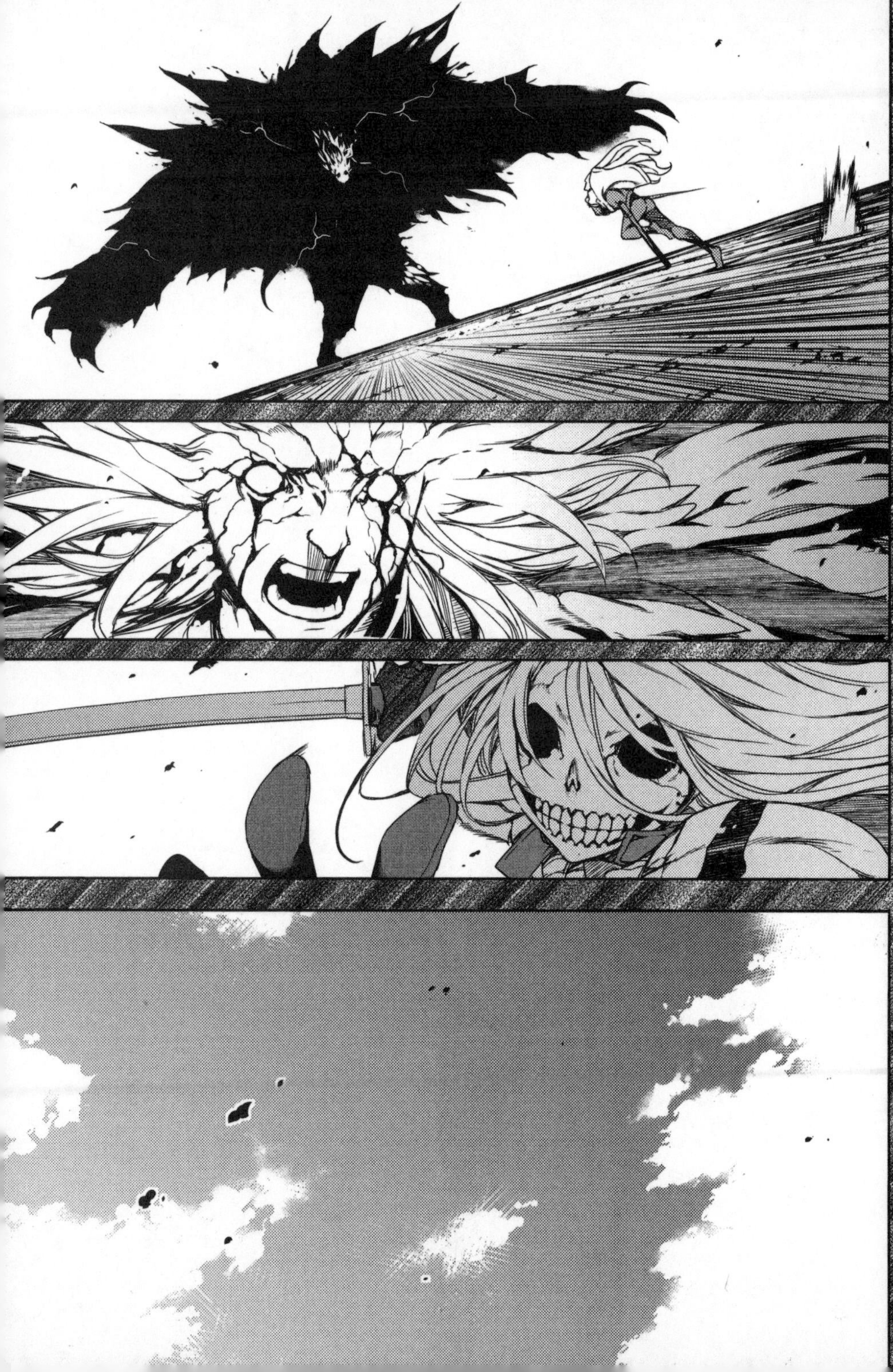

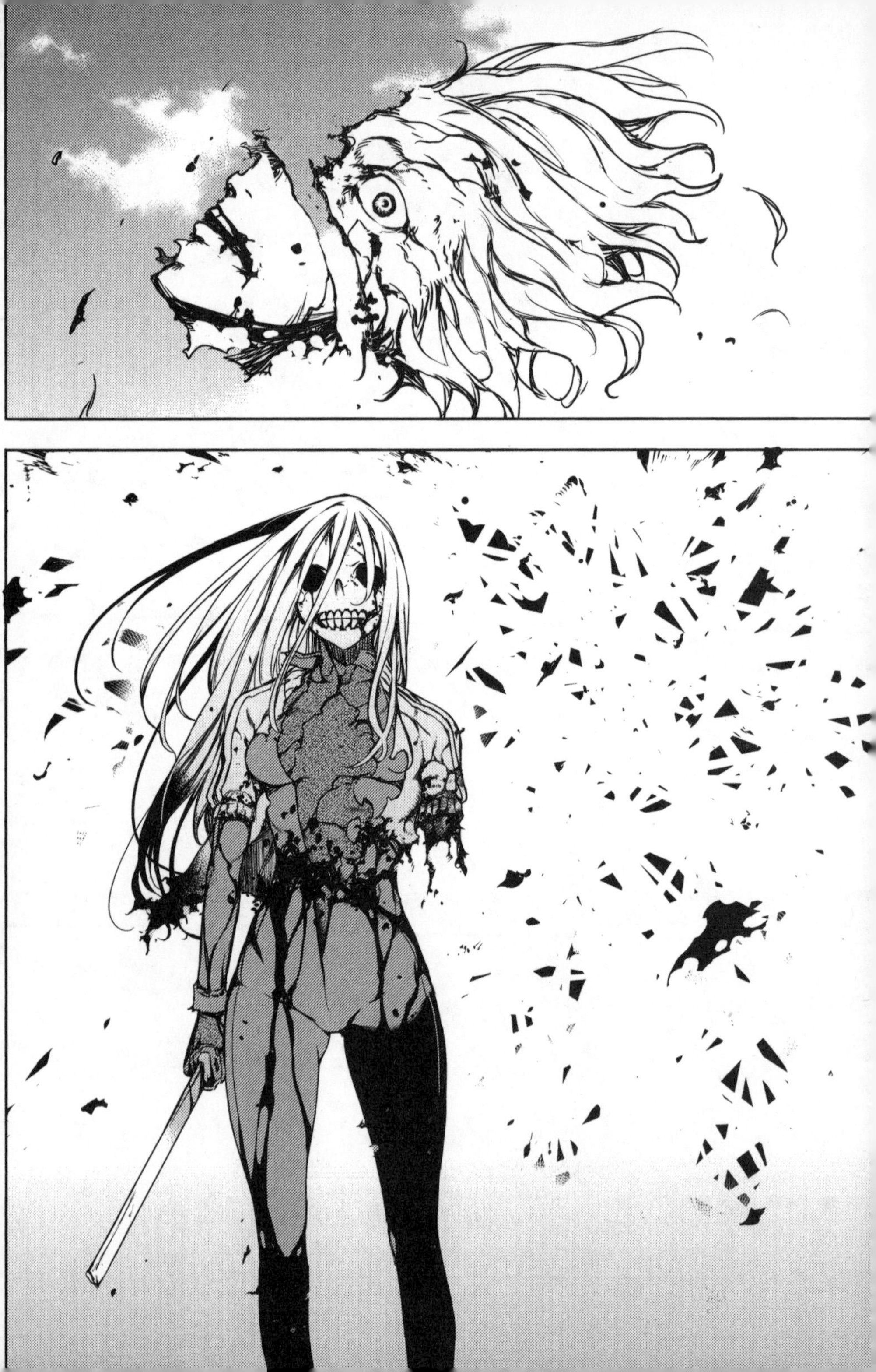

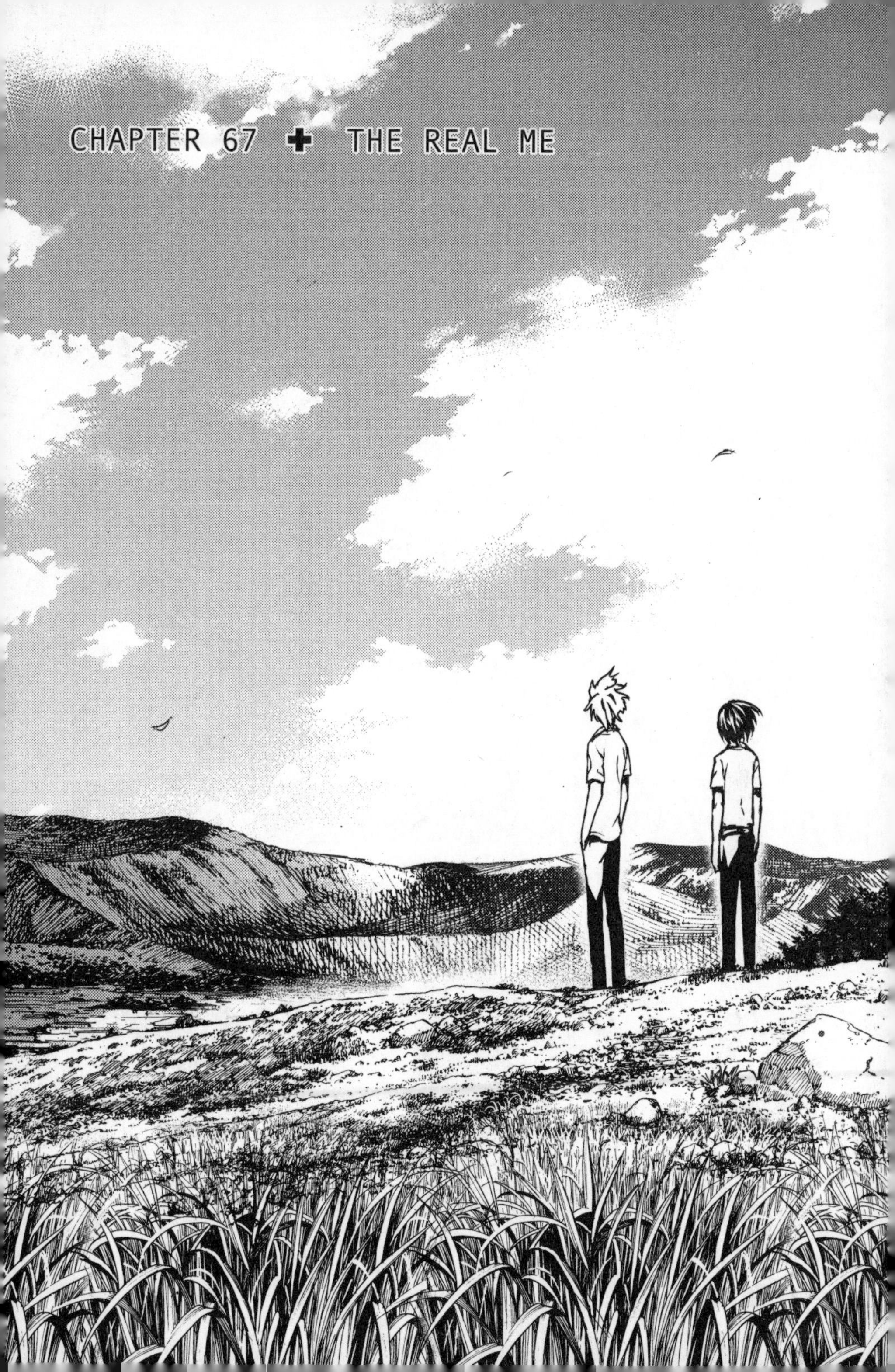
CHAPTER 67 ✚ THE REAL ME

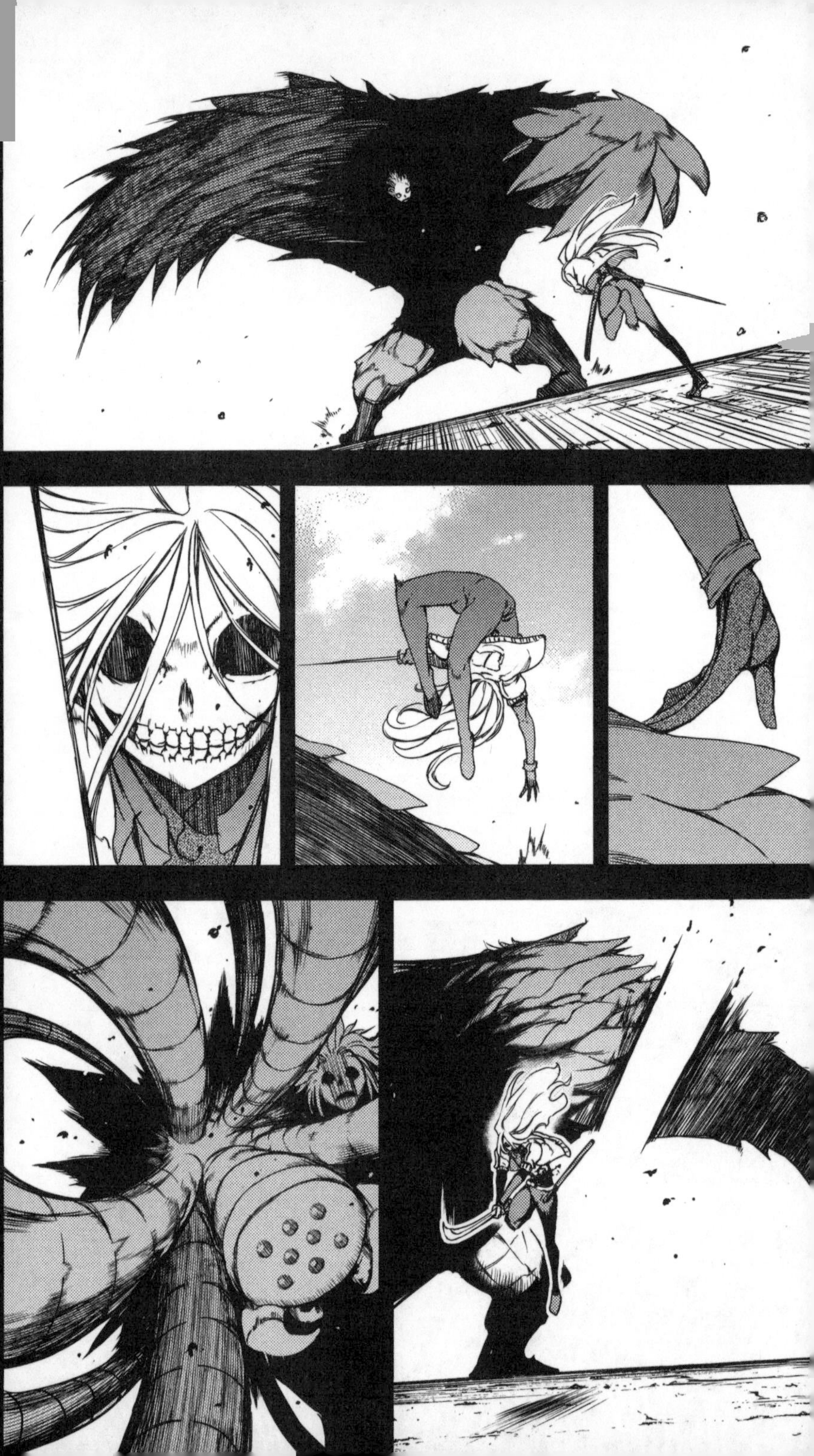

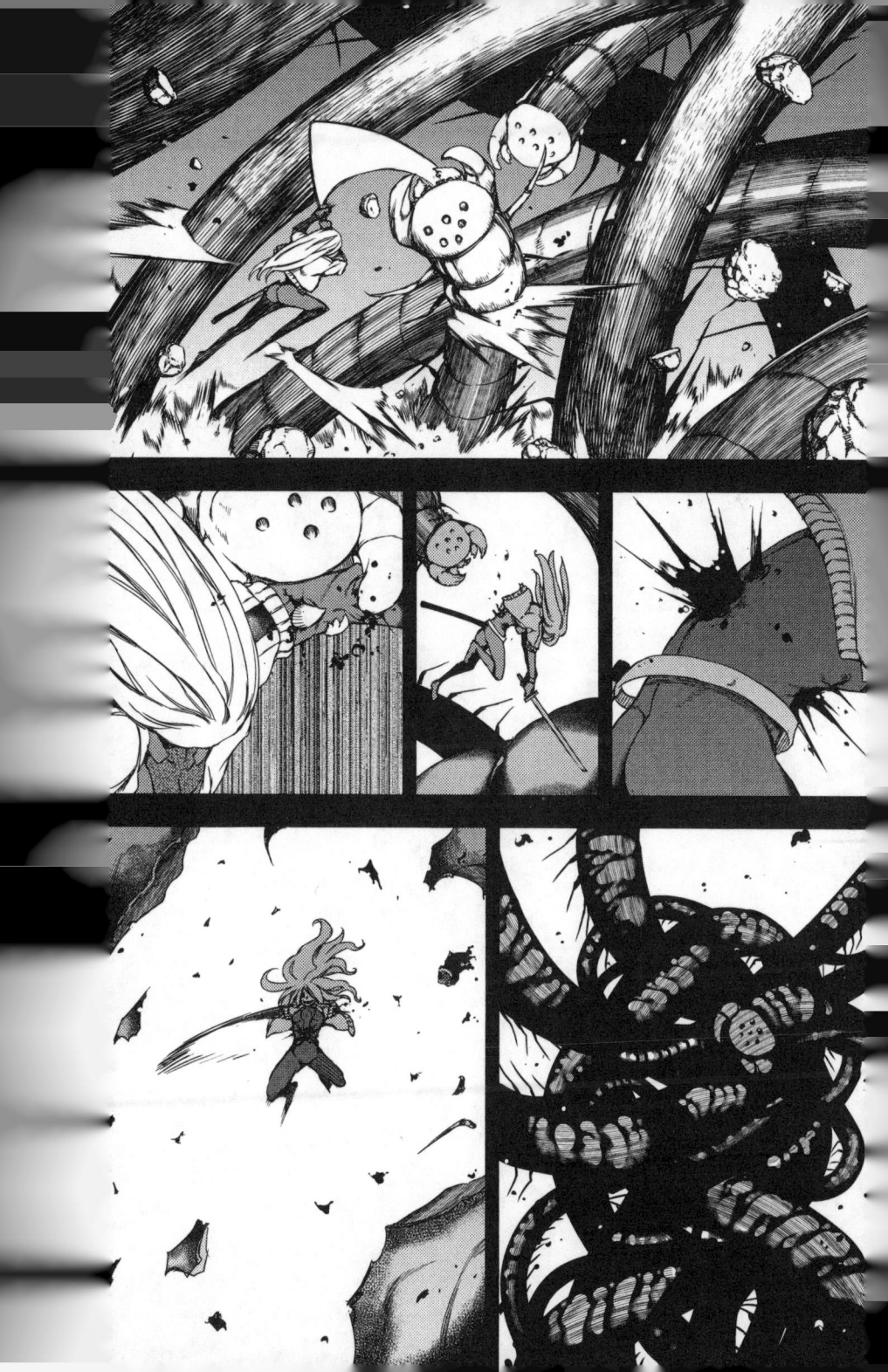

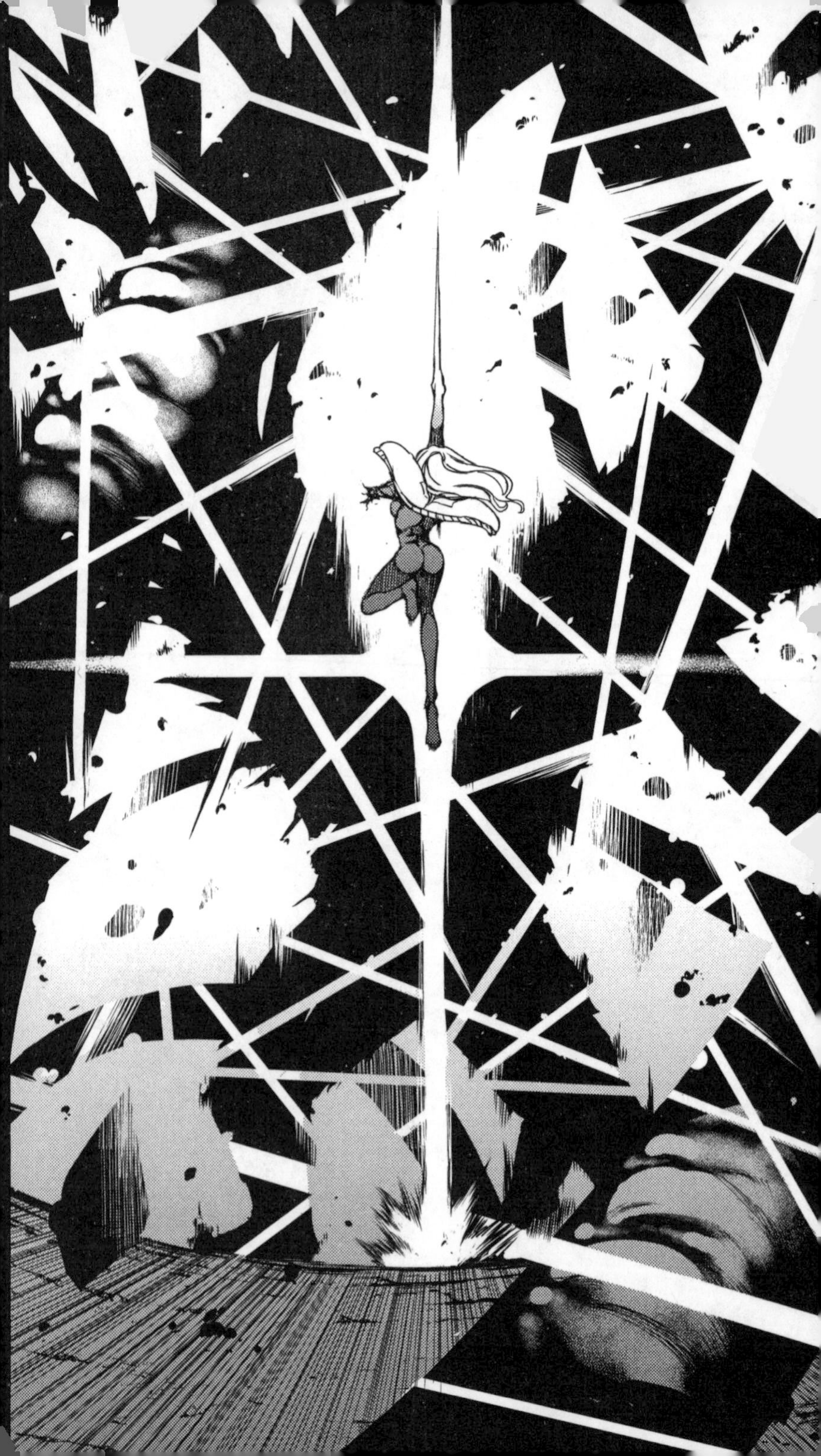

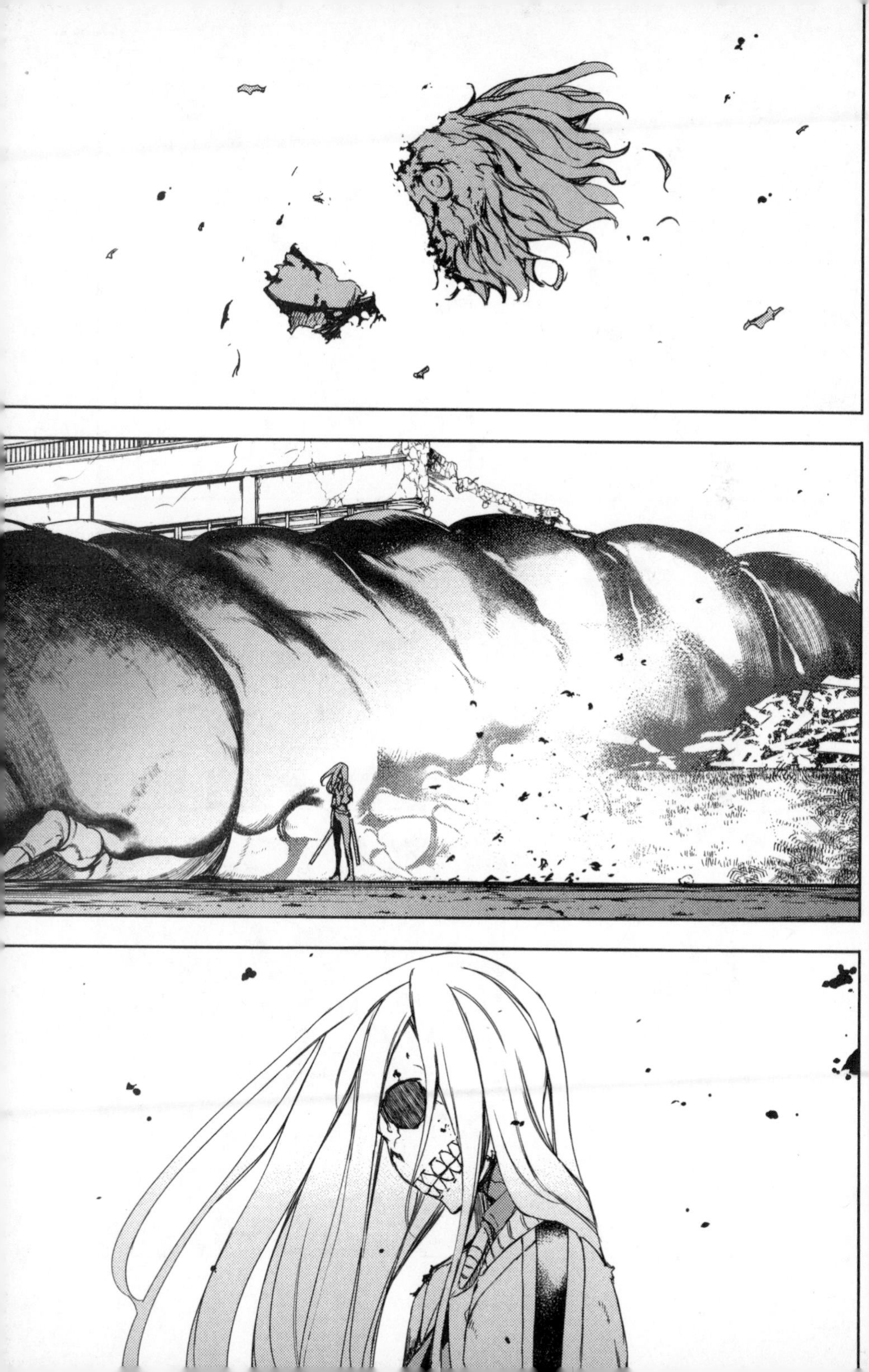

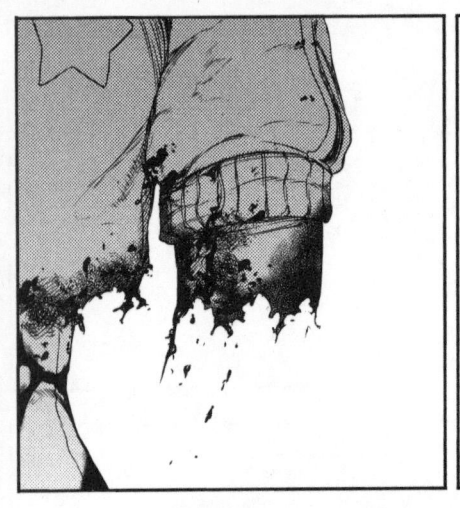

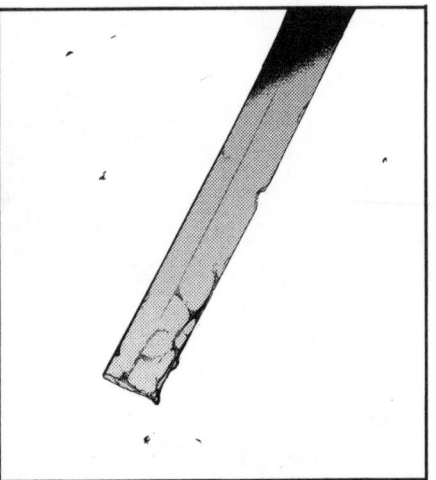

WAIT...

SNAP

CRACK

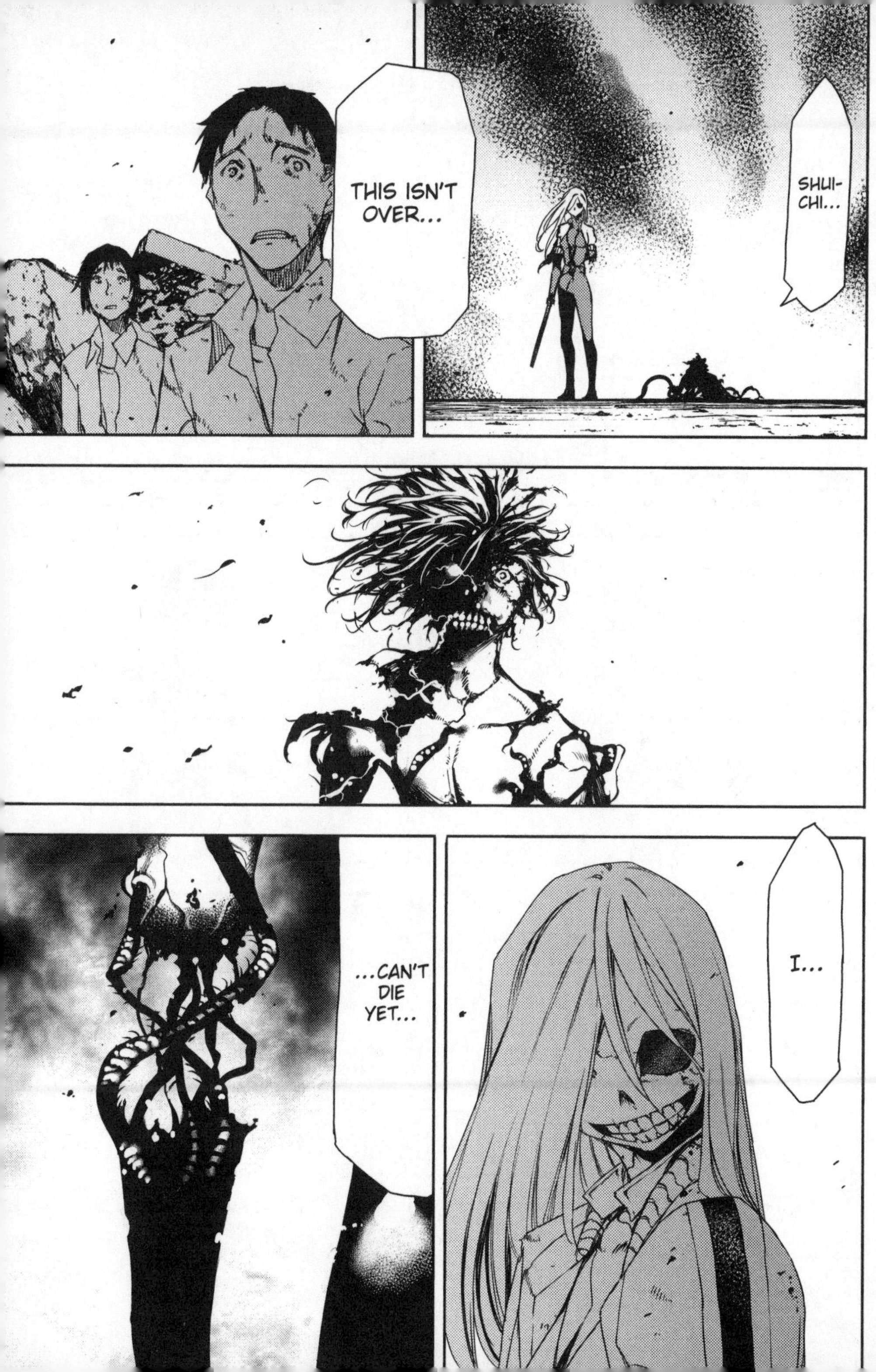
SHUI-CHI...
THIS ISN'T OVER...
I...
...CAN'T DIE YET...

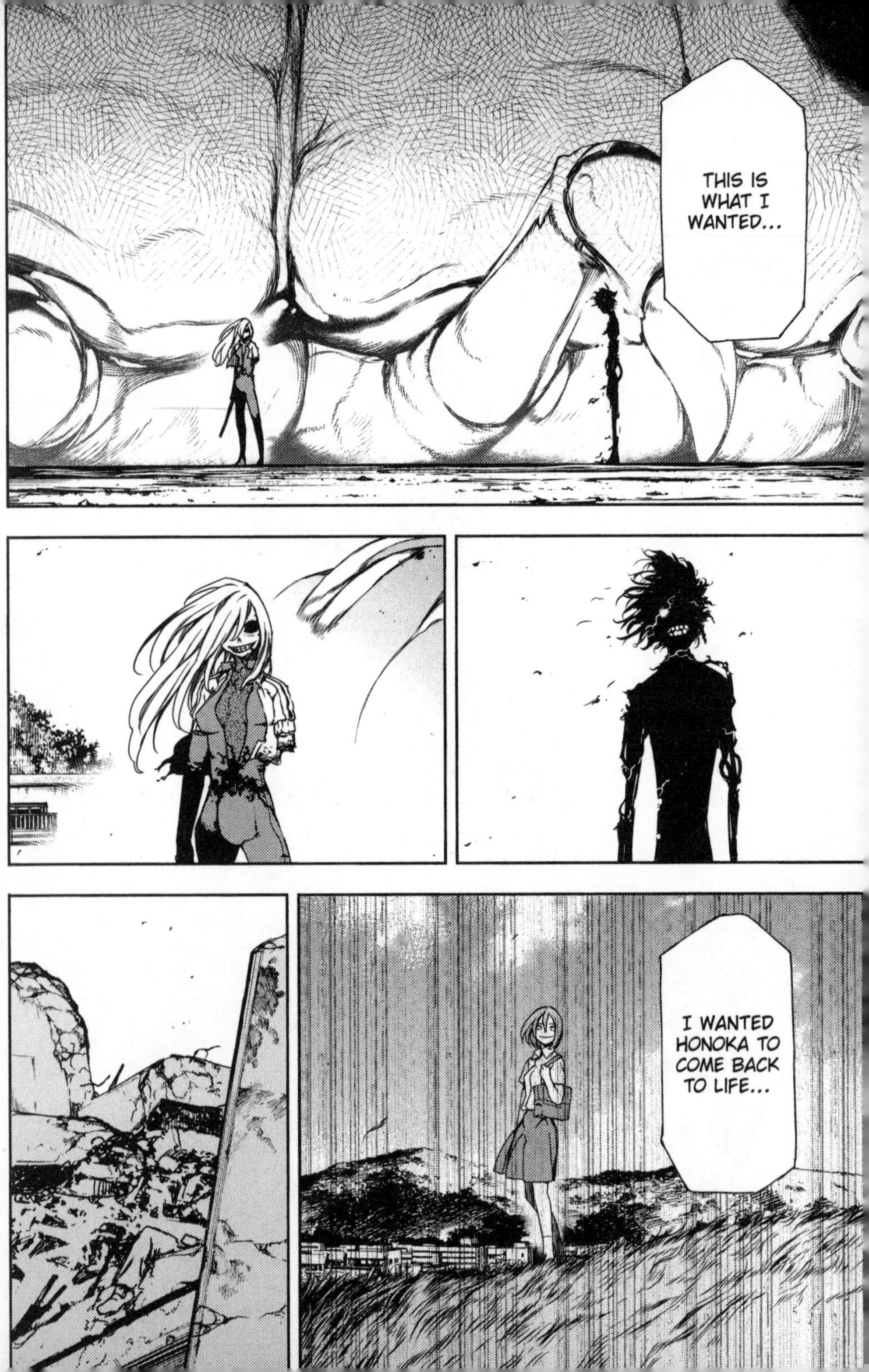
THIS IS WHAT I WANTED...
I WANTED HONOKA TO COME BACK TO LIFE...

NO MATTER THE
CONSEQUENCES.

EVEN IF
THAT MEANT
HELL ON
EARTH.

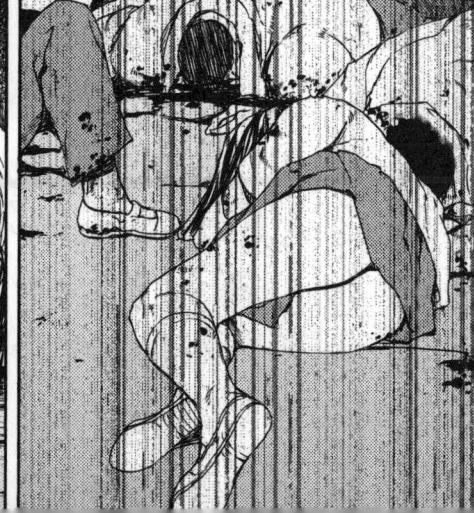

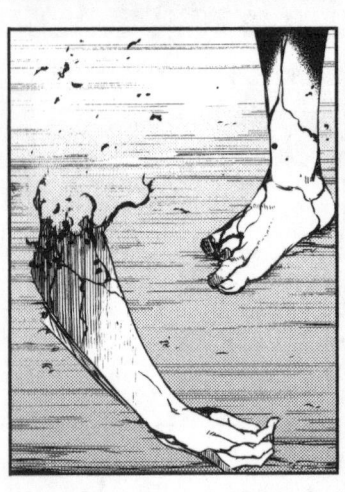

I...
WANTED
THIS...

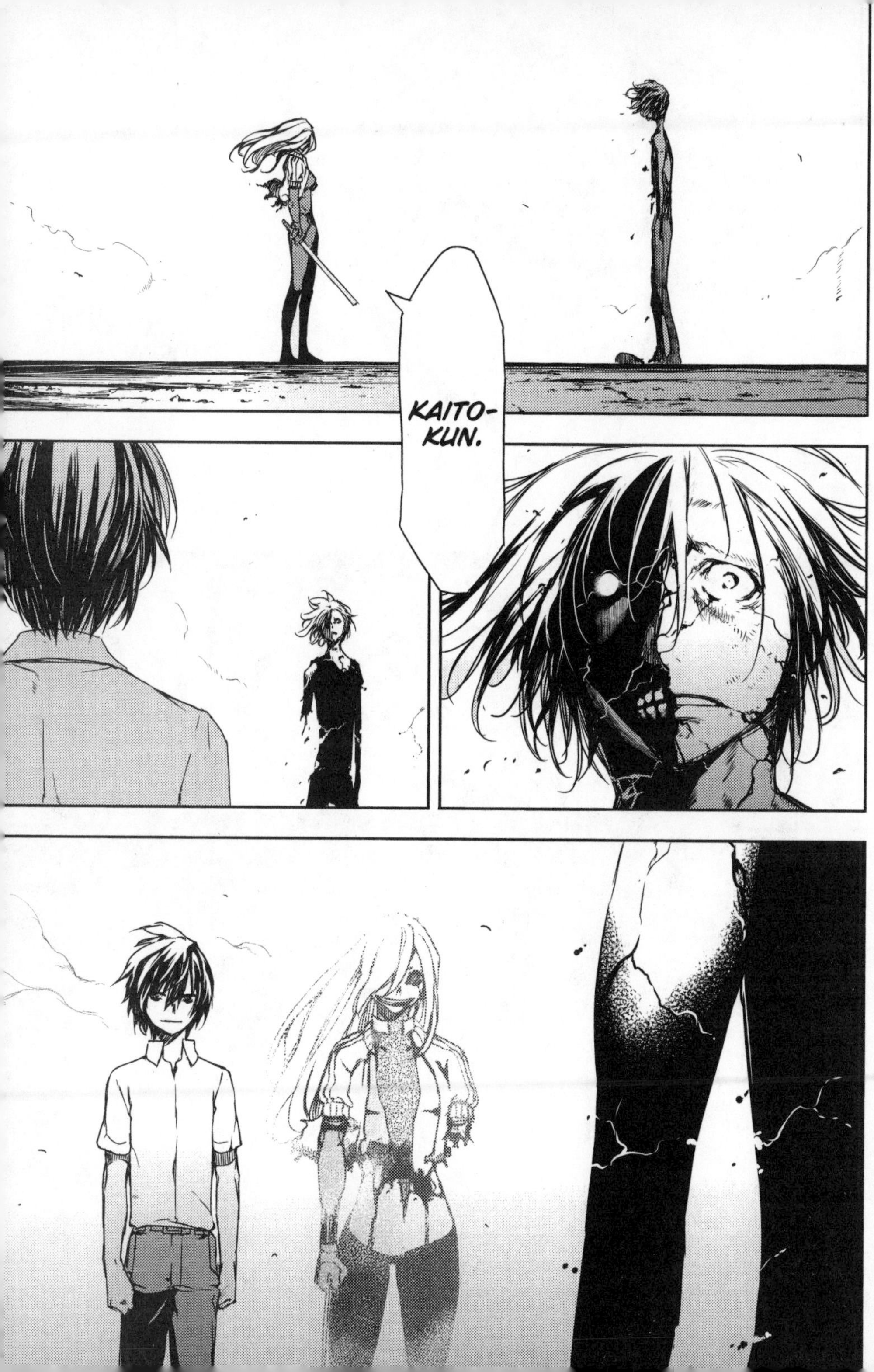
KAITO-KUN.

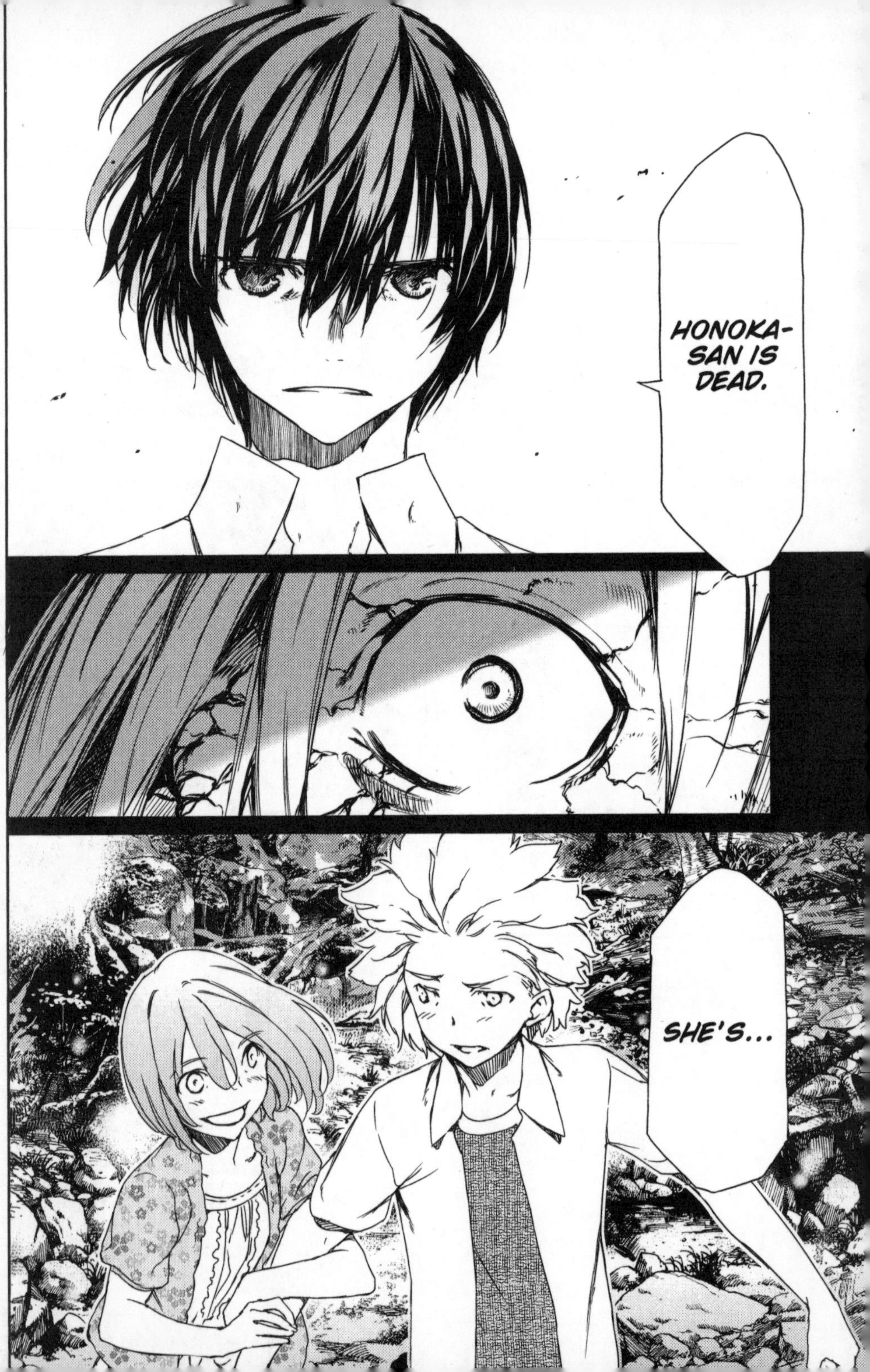
HONOKA-SAN IS DEAD.
SHE'S...

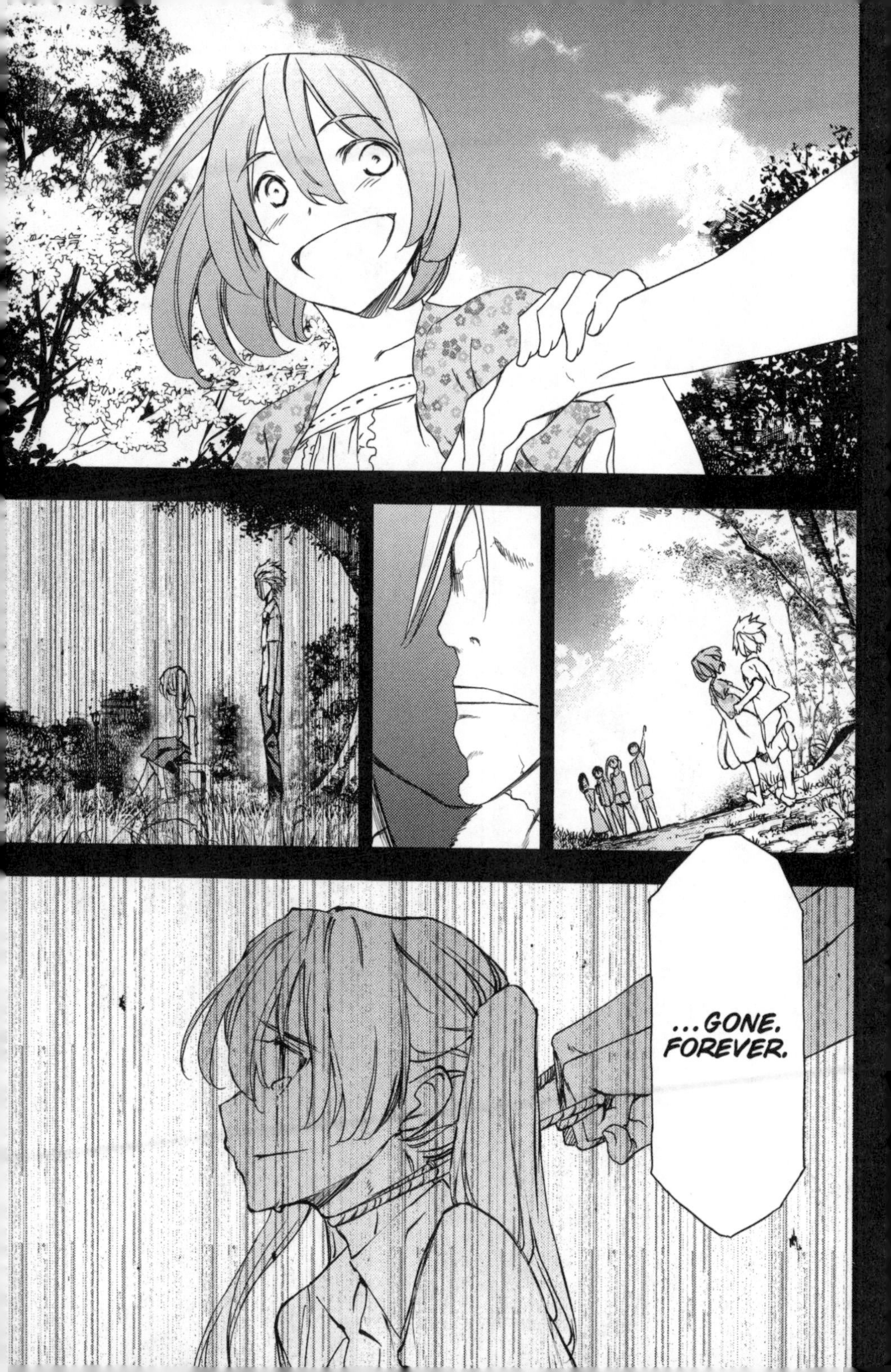
...GONE.
FOREVER.

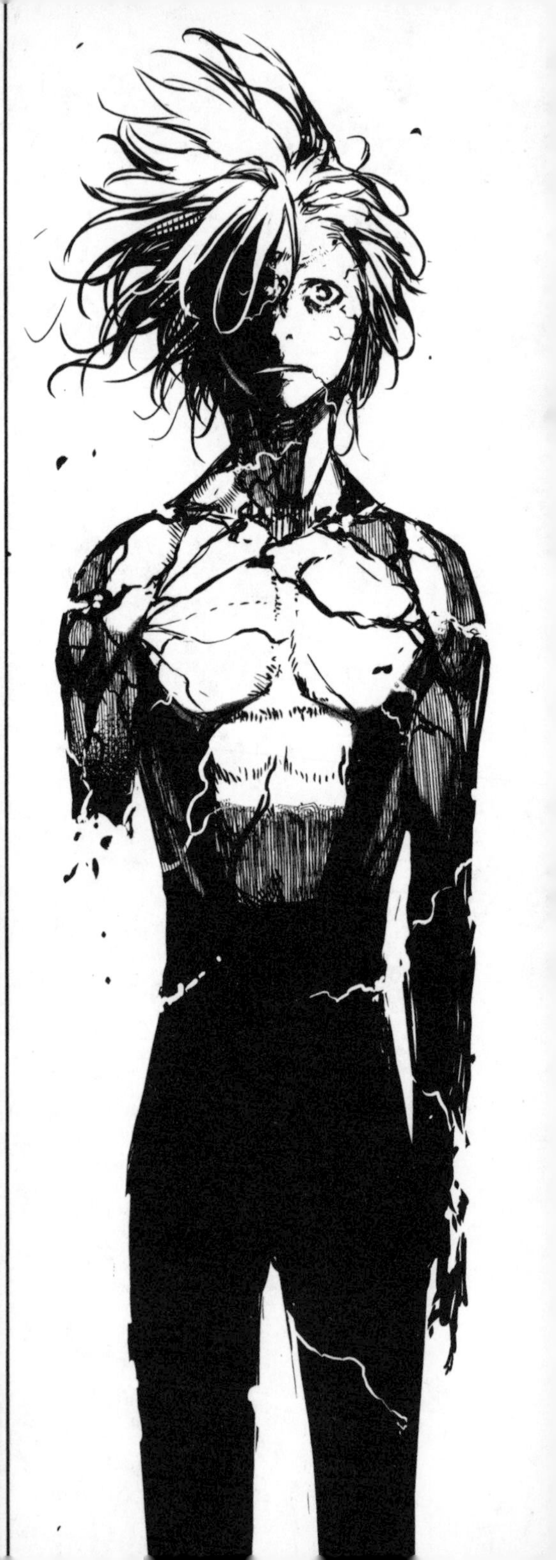
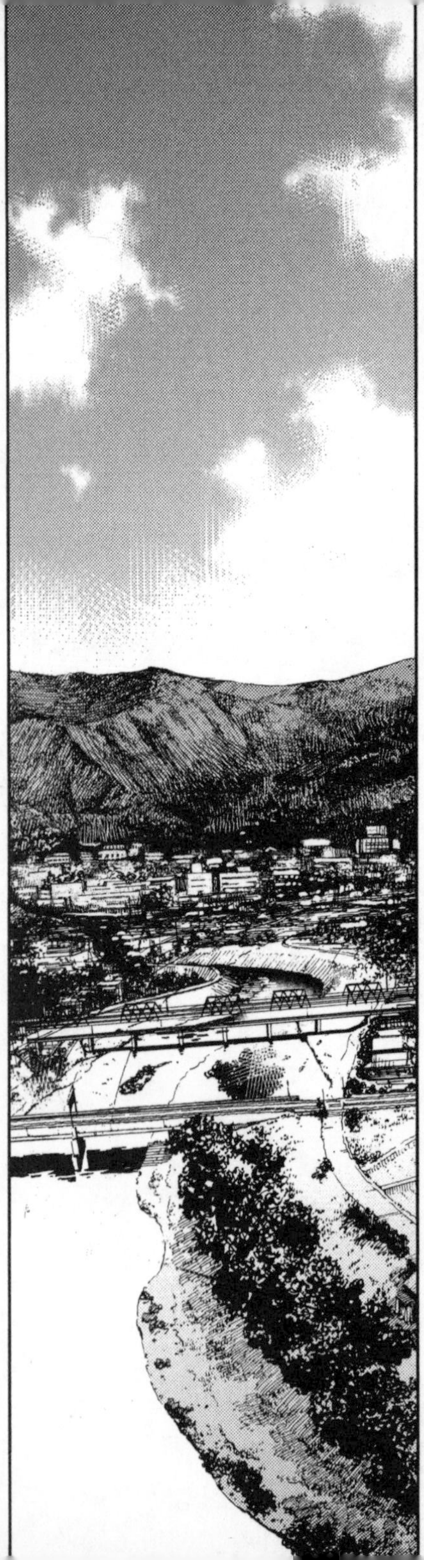

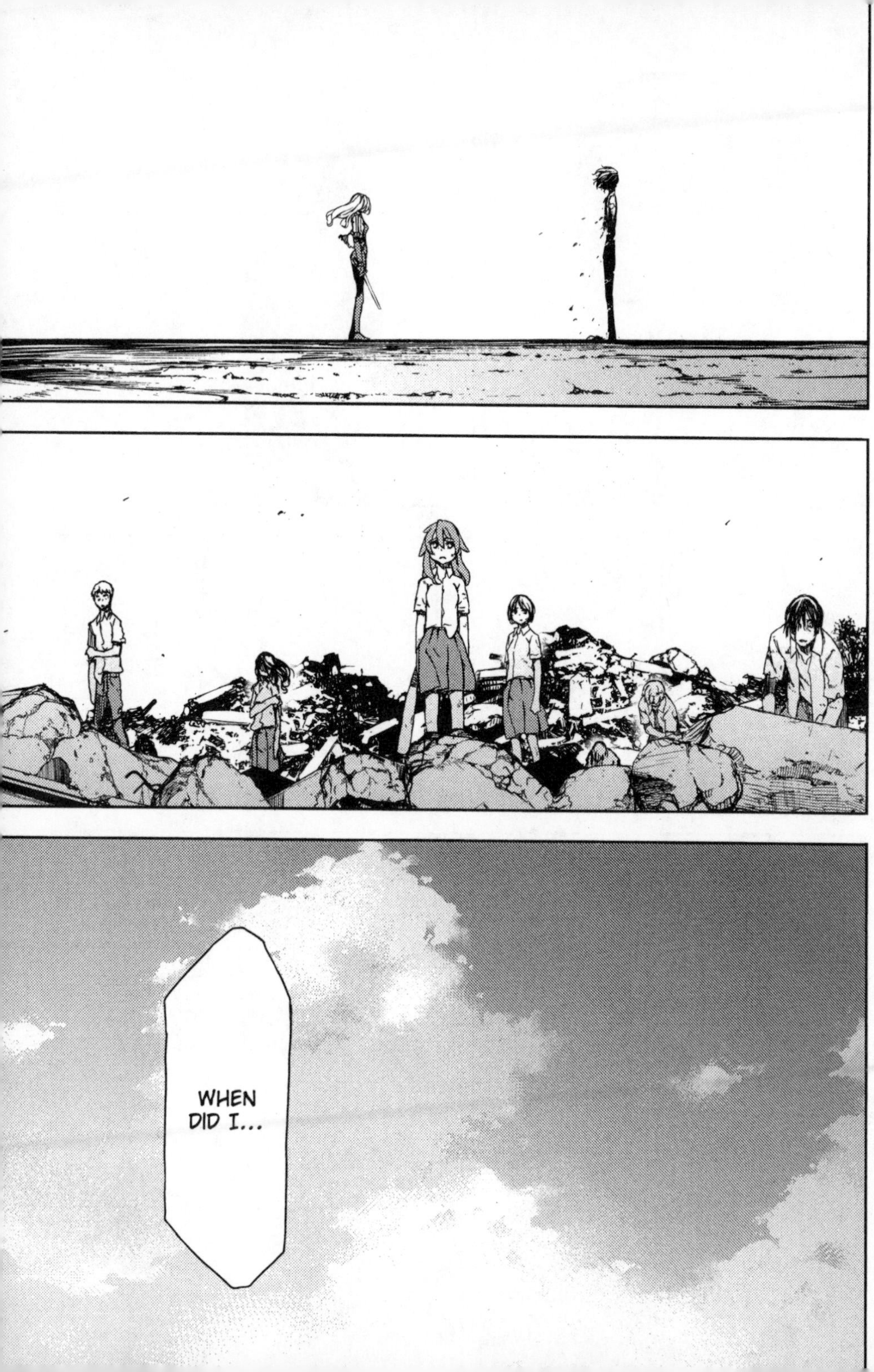
WHEN DID I...

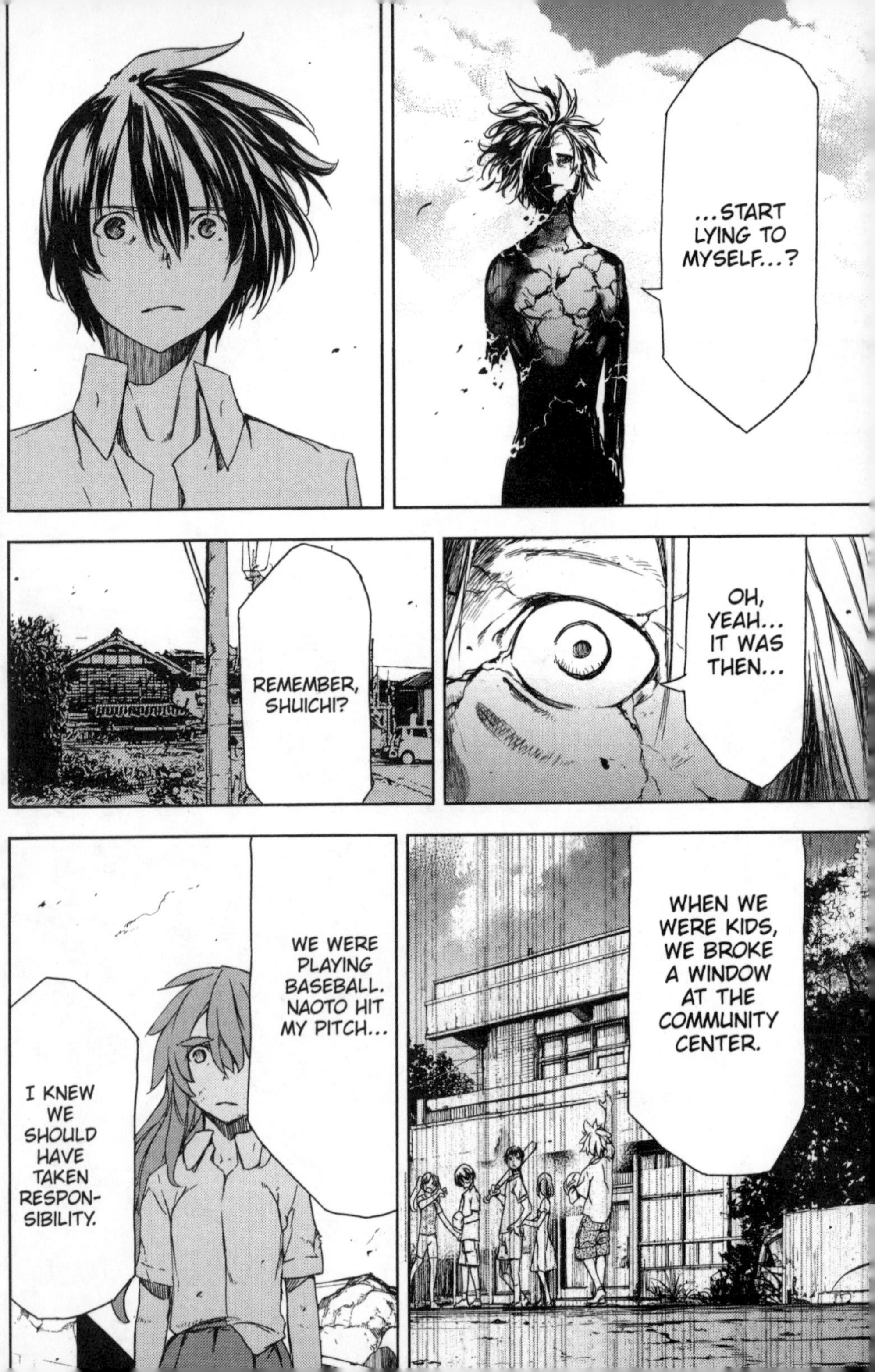
...START LYING TO MYSELF...?
OH, YEAH... IT WAS THEN...
REMEMBER, SHUICHI?
WHEN WE WERE KIDS, WE BROKE A WINDOW AT THE COMMUNITY CENTER.
WE WERE PLAYING BASEBALL. NAOTO HIT MY PITCH...
I KNEW WE SHOULD HAVE TAKEN RESPON-SIBILITY.

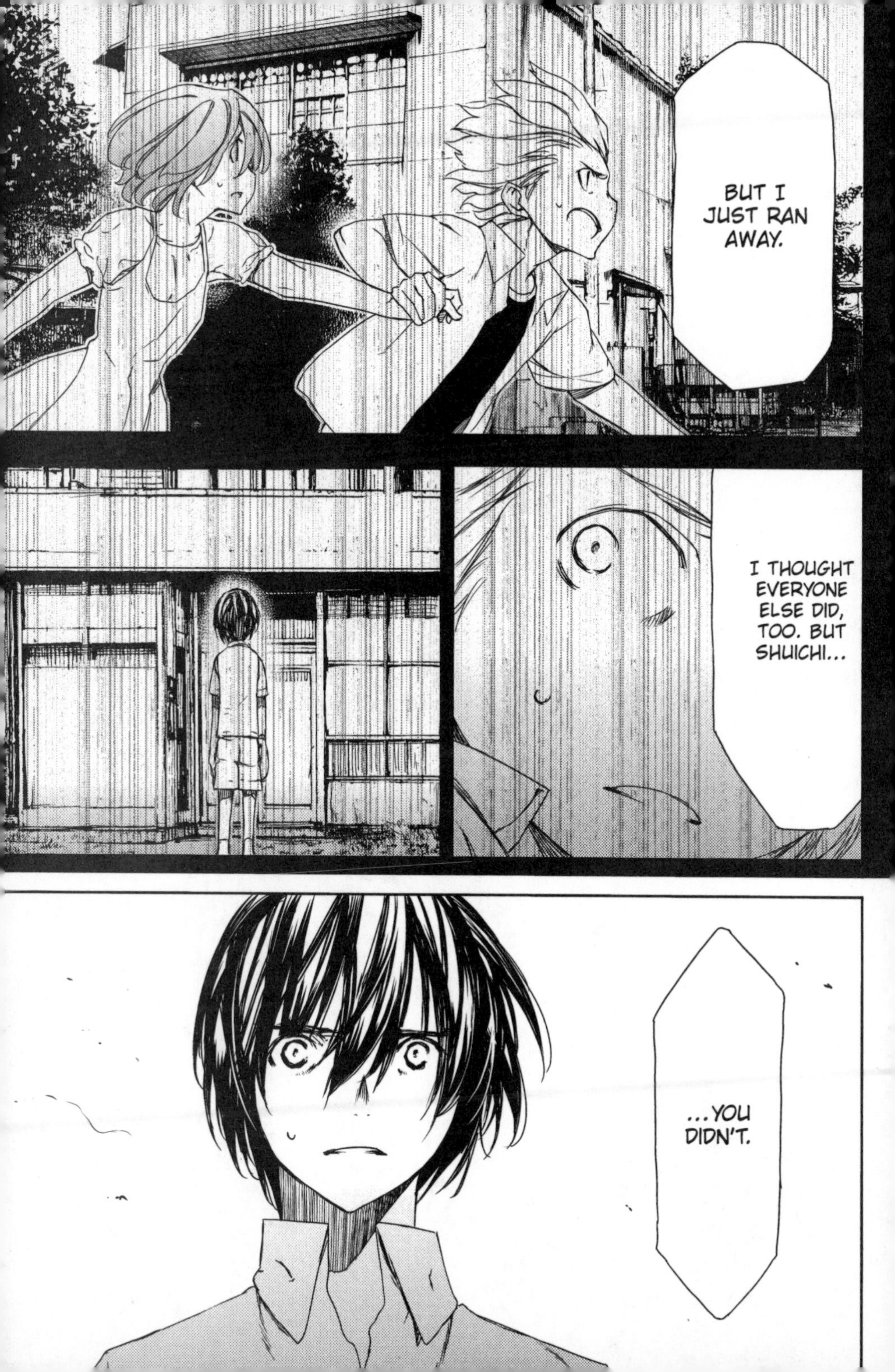
BUT I JUST RAN AWAY.
I THOUGHT EVERYONE ELSE DID, TOO. BUT SHUICHI...
...YOU DIDN'T.

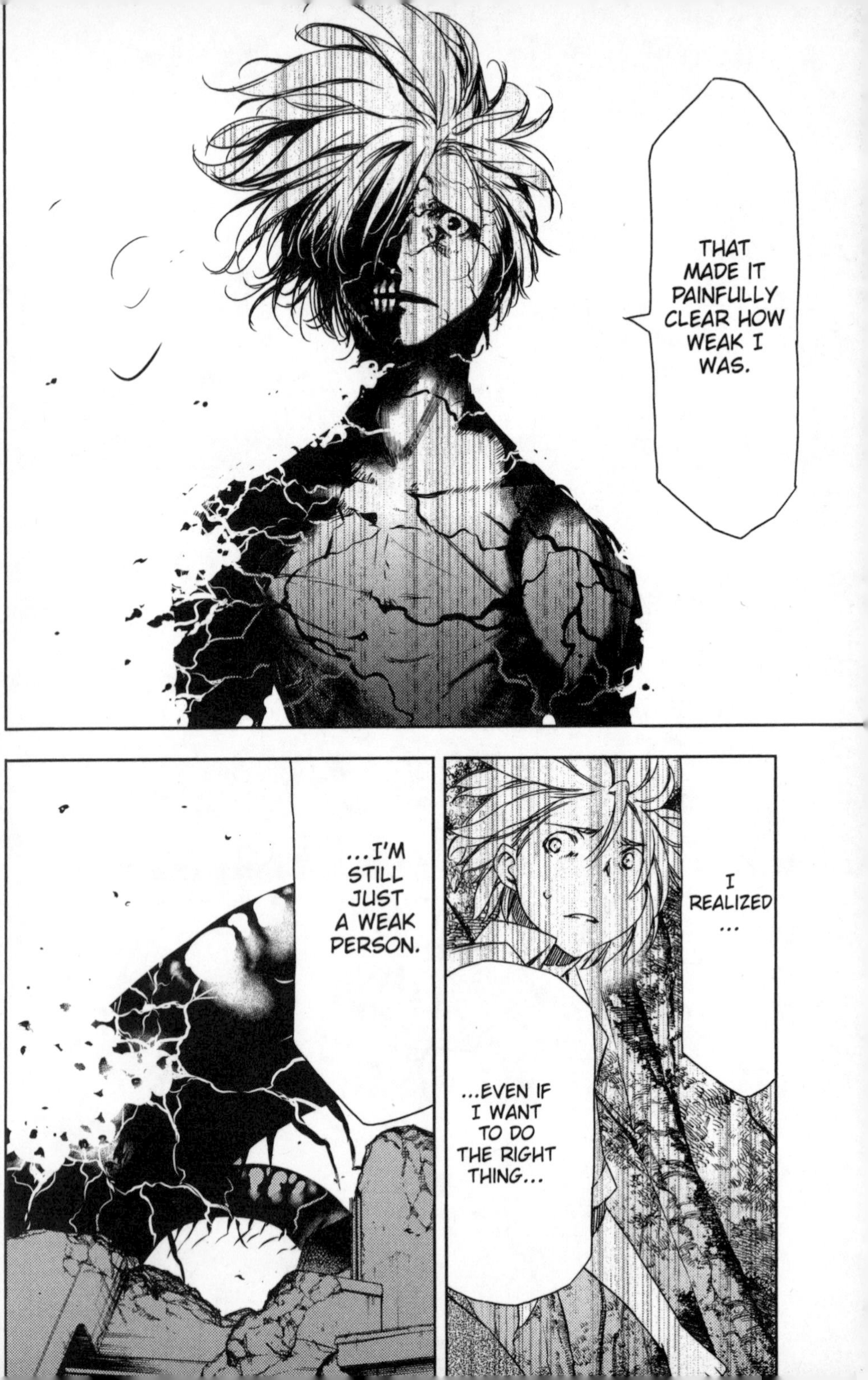
THAT MADE IT PAINFULLY CLEAR HOW WEAK I WAS.
I REALIZED...
...EVEN IF I WANT TO DO THE RIGHT THING...
...I'M STILL JUST A WEAK PERSON.

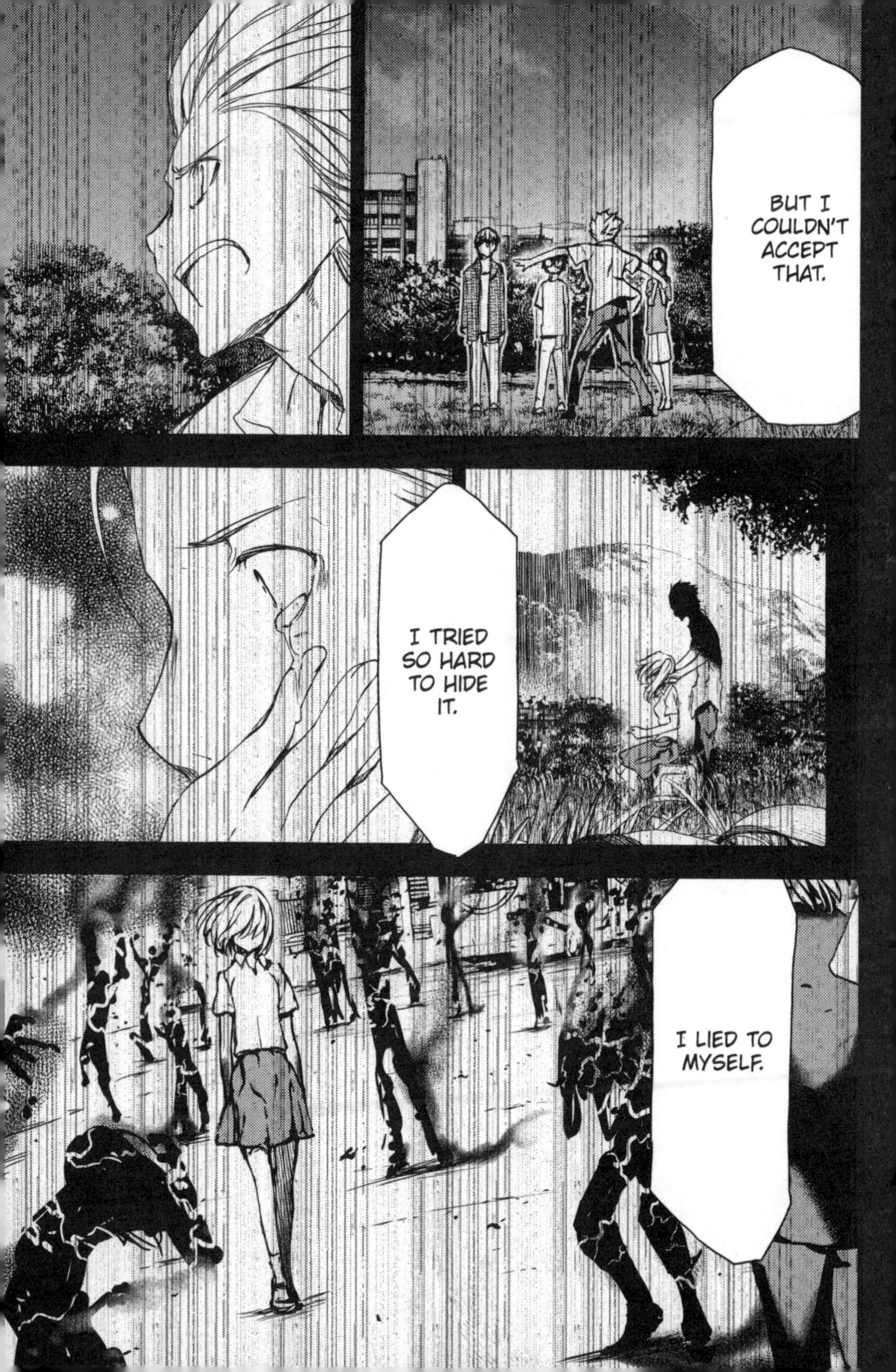
BUT I COULDN'T ACCEPT THAT.
I TRIED SO HARD TO HIDE IT.
I LIED TO MYSELF.

SHUICHI...

I WANT YOU TO BE THE ONE WHO STOPS ME.

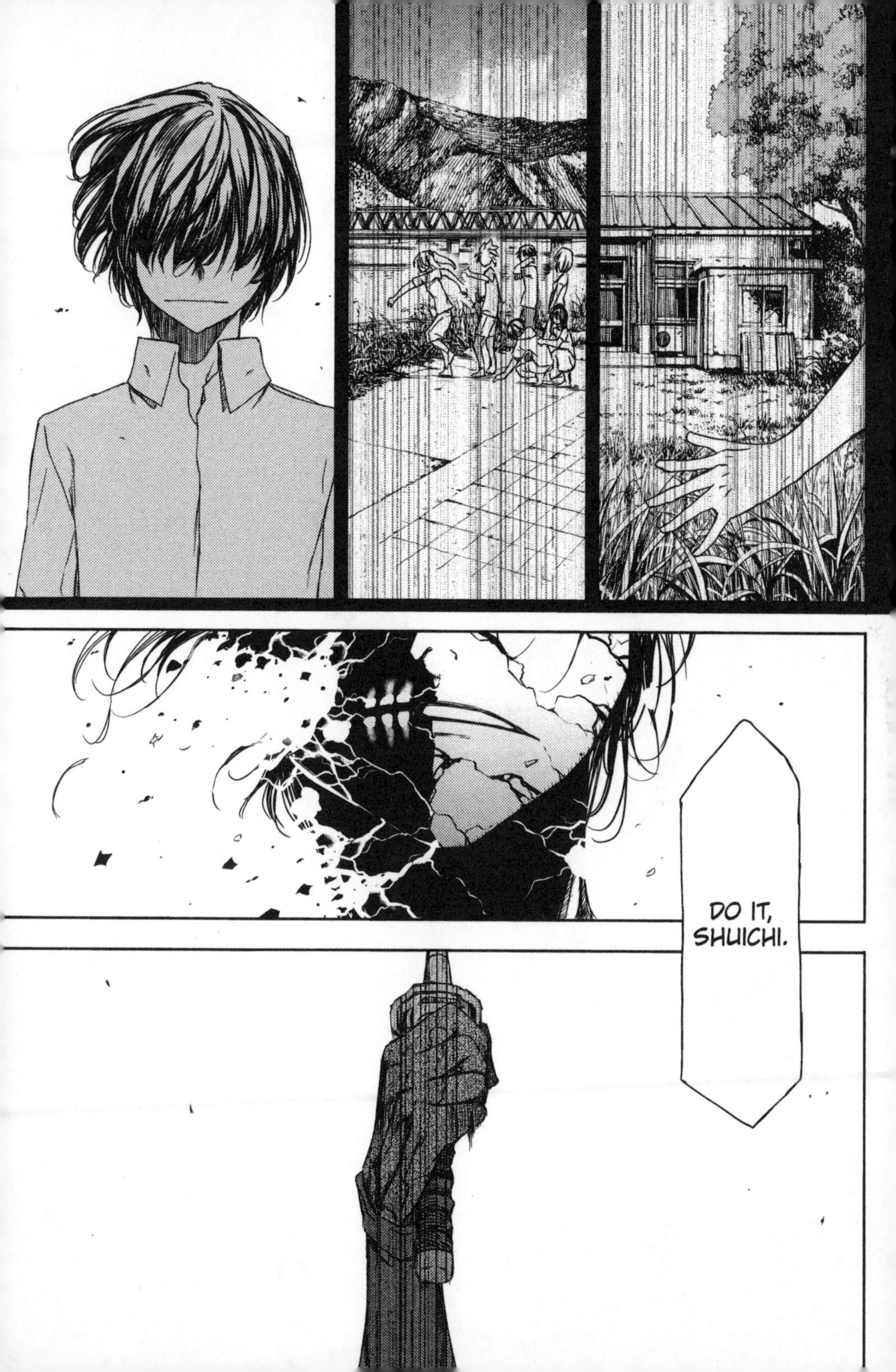
DO IT, SHUICHI.

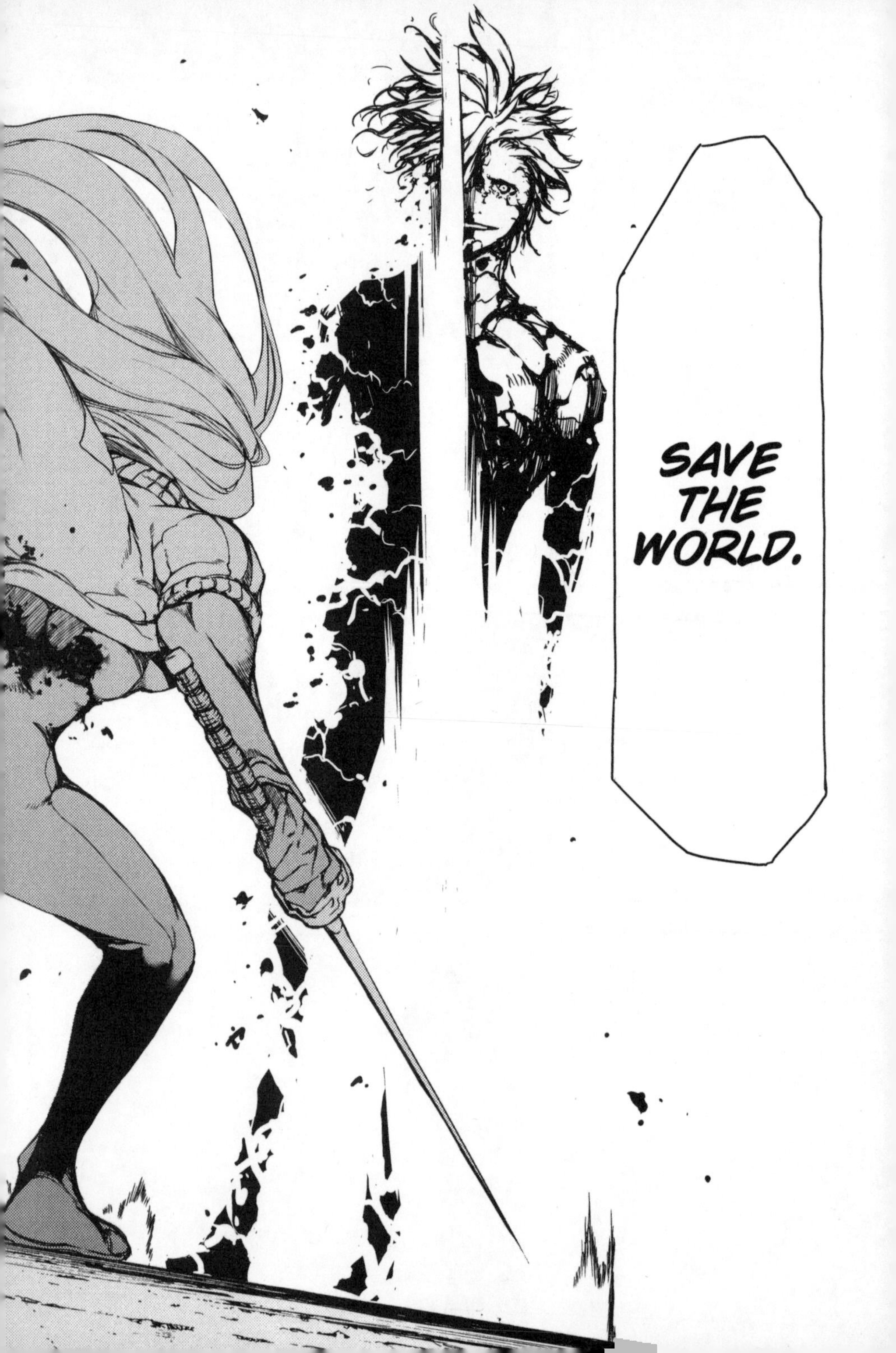
SAVE THE WORLD.

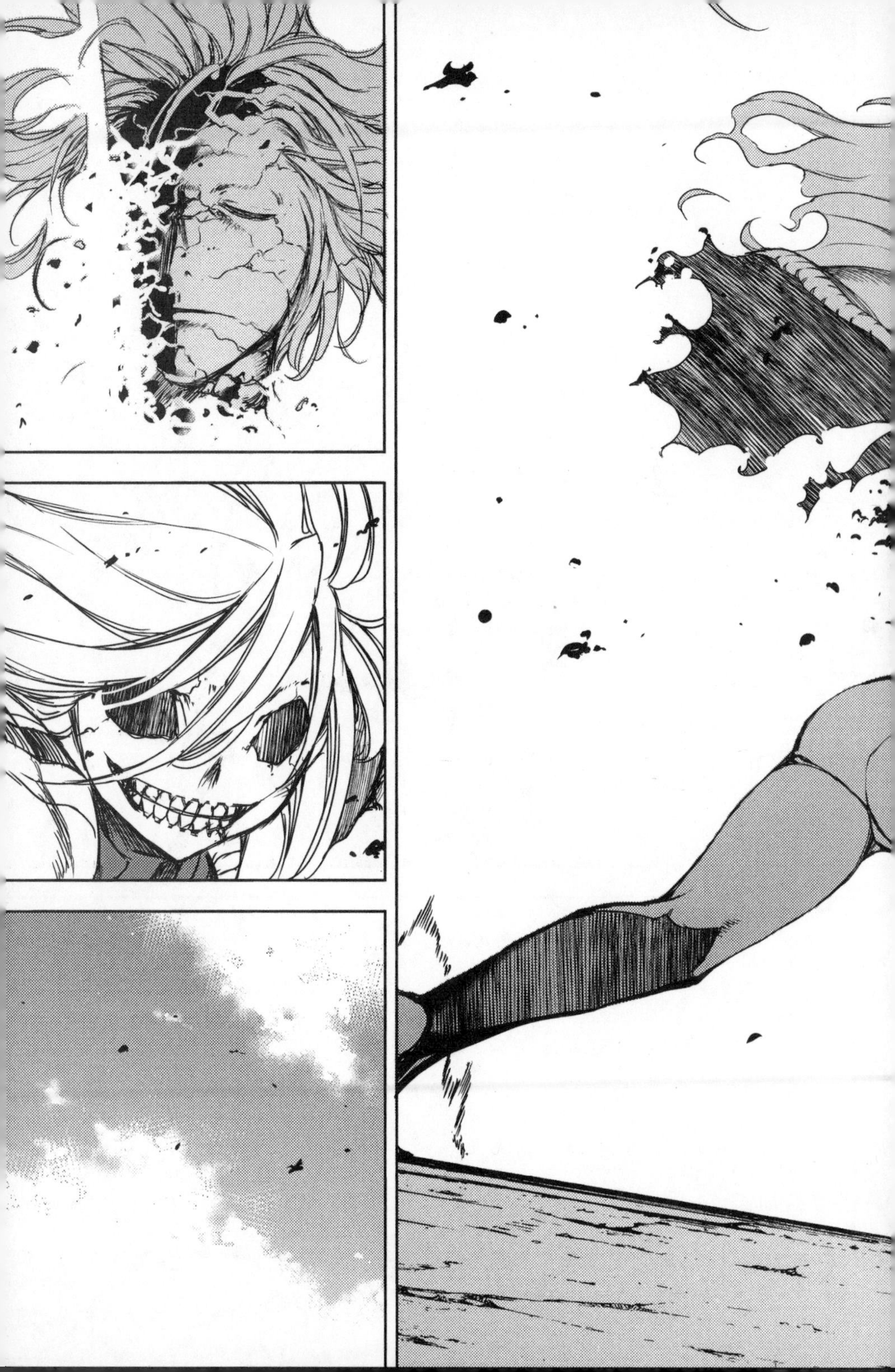

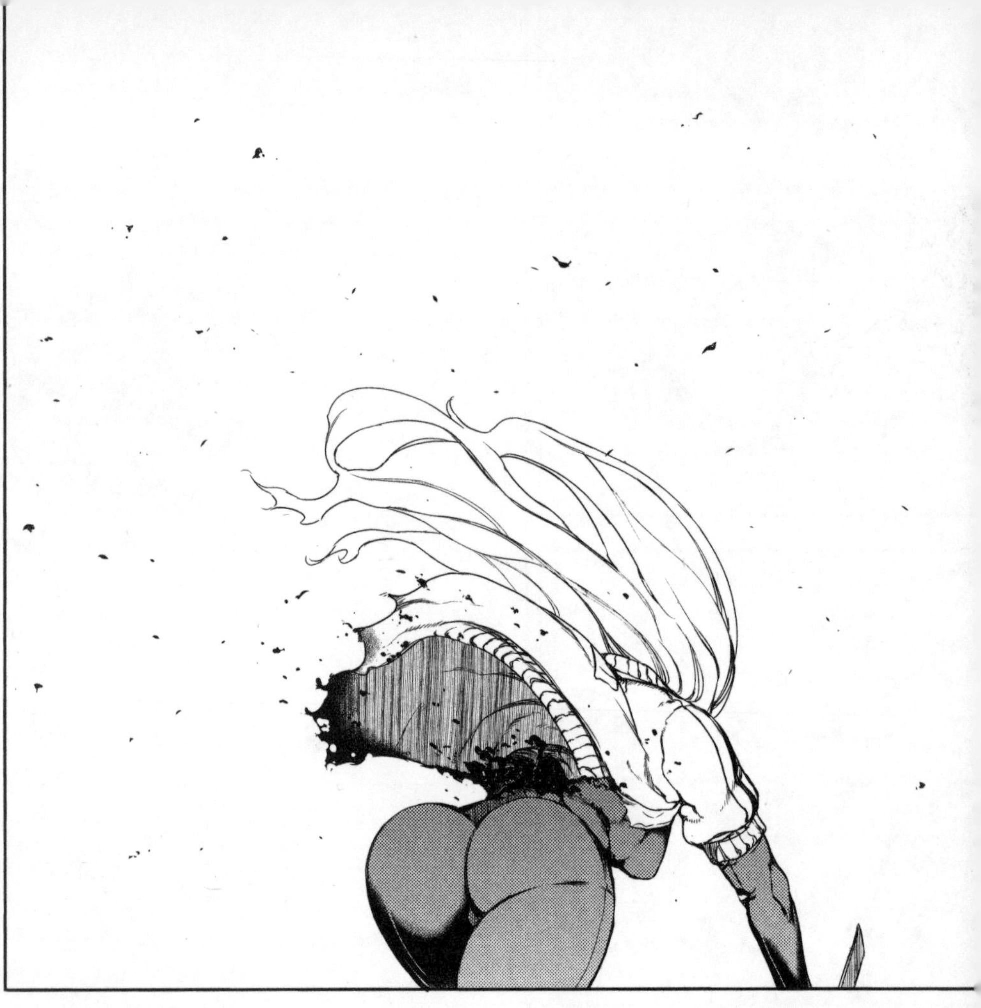
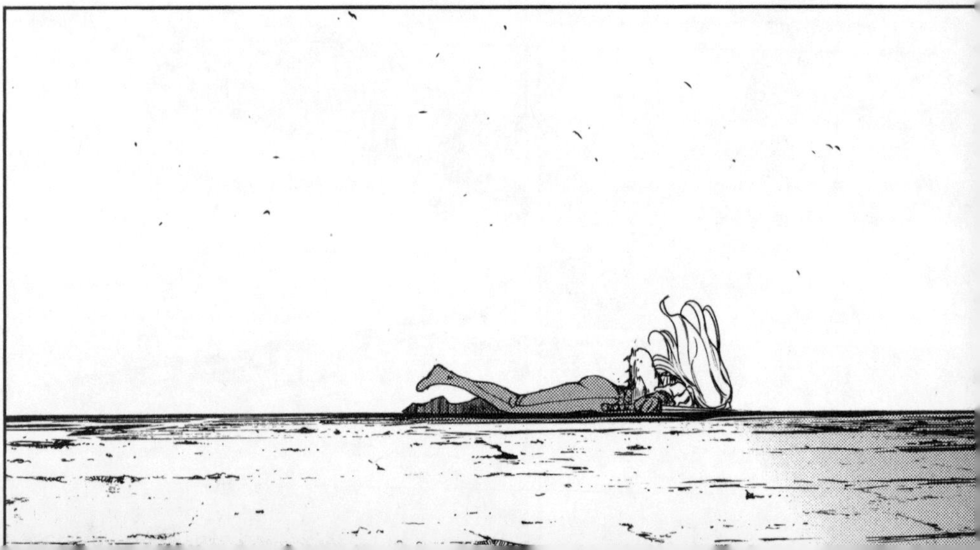

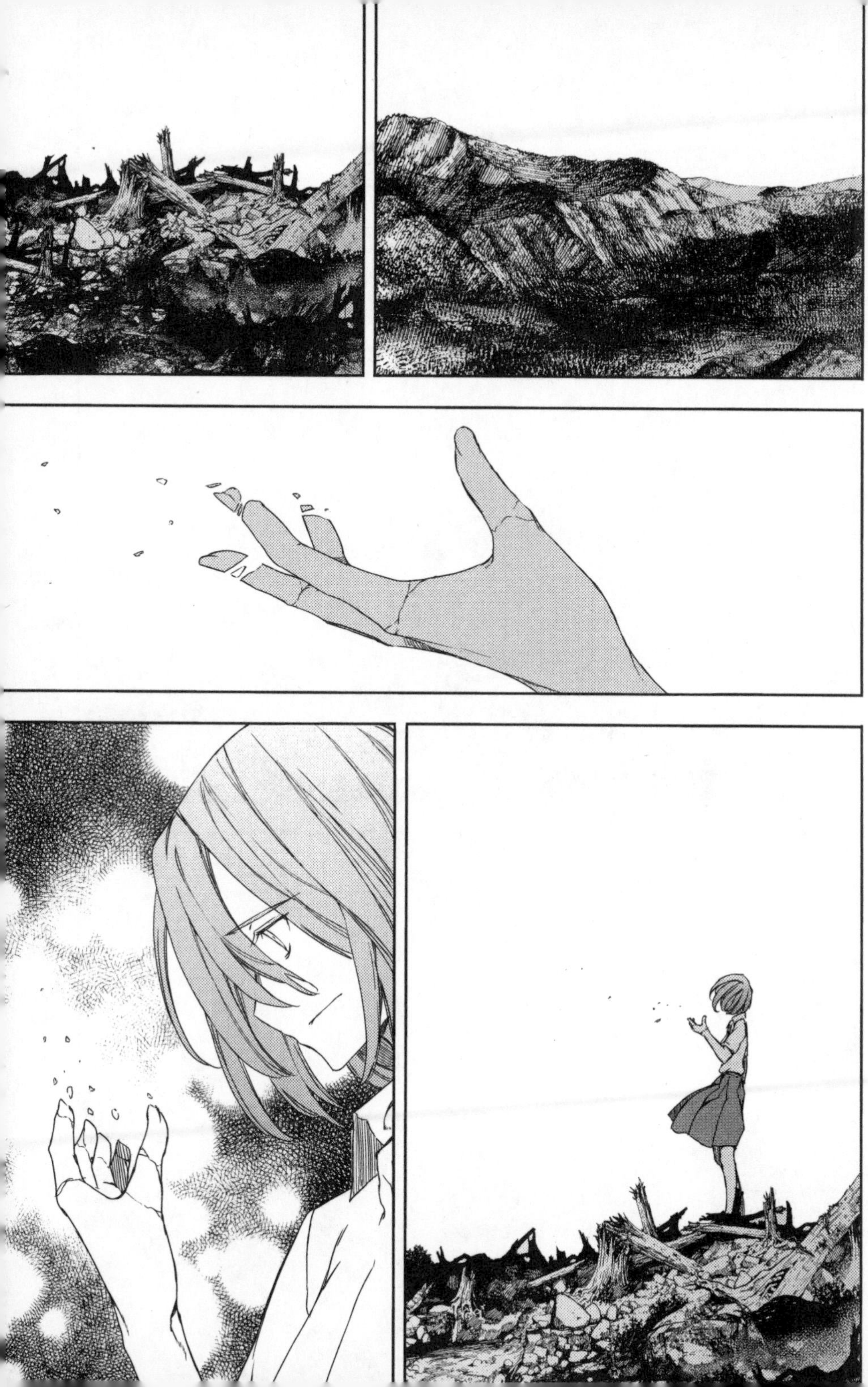

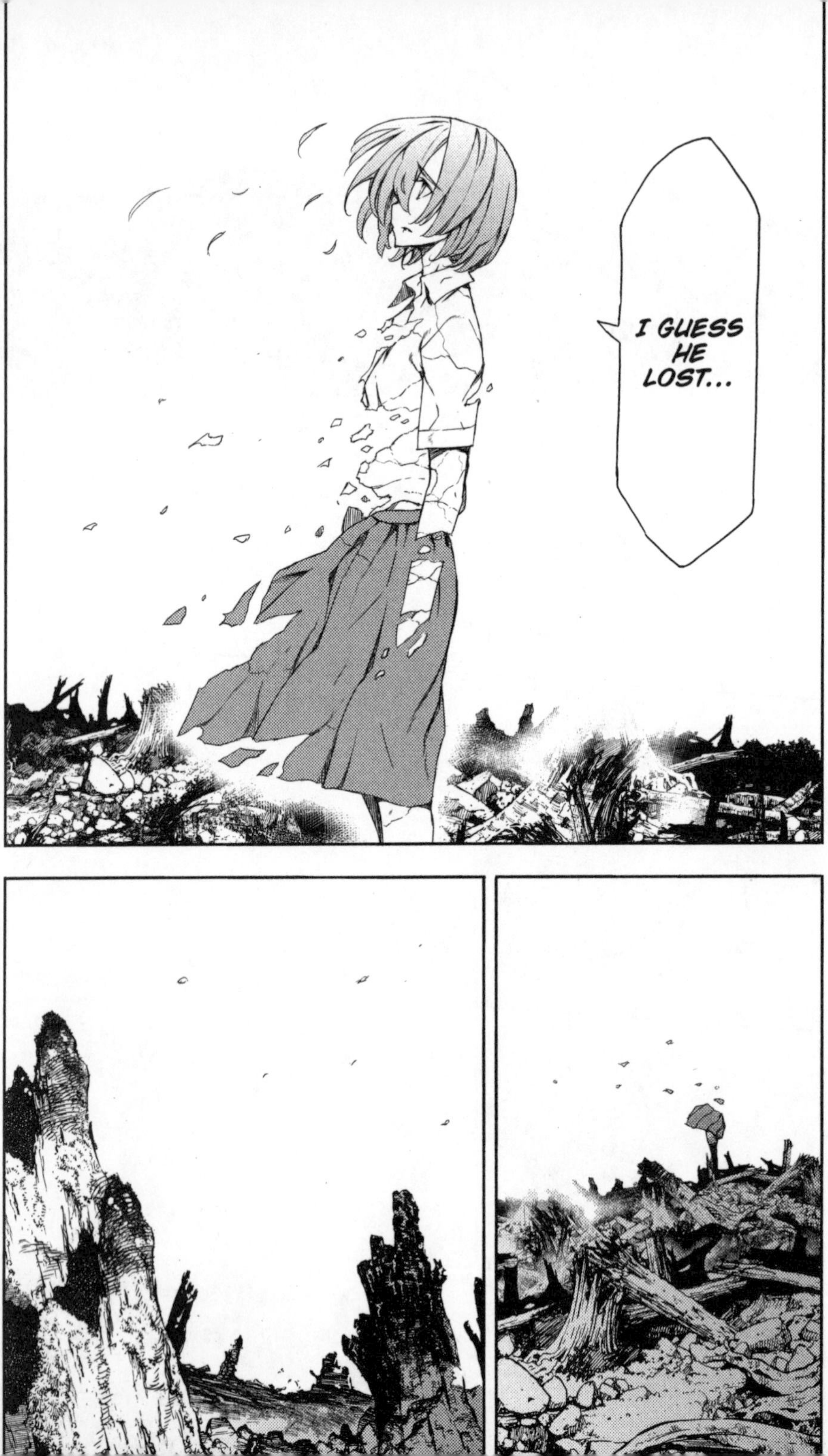
I GUESS HE LOST...

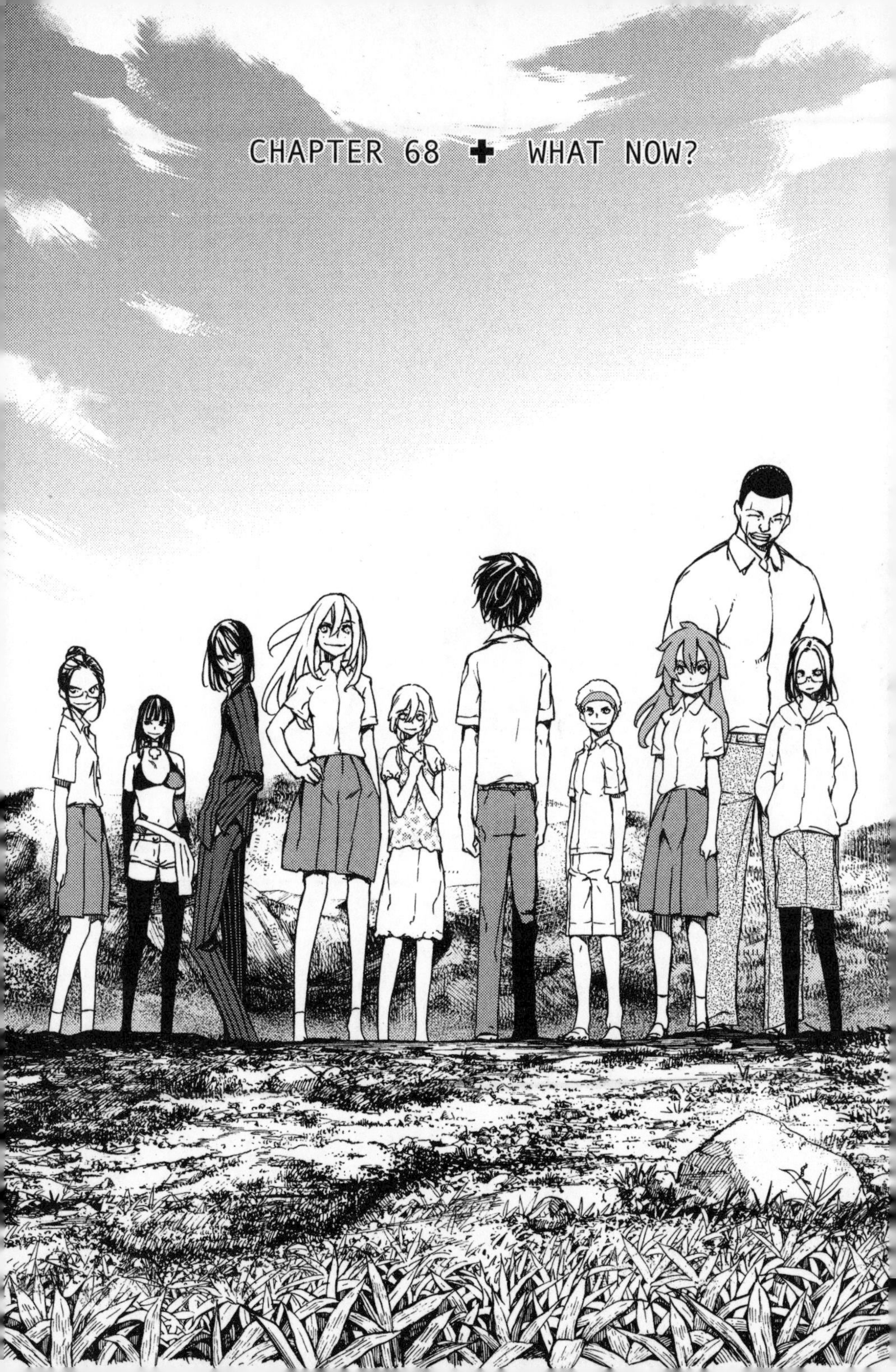
CHAPTER 68 ✚ WHAT NOW?

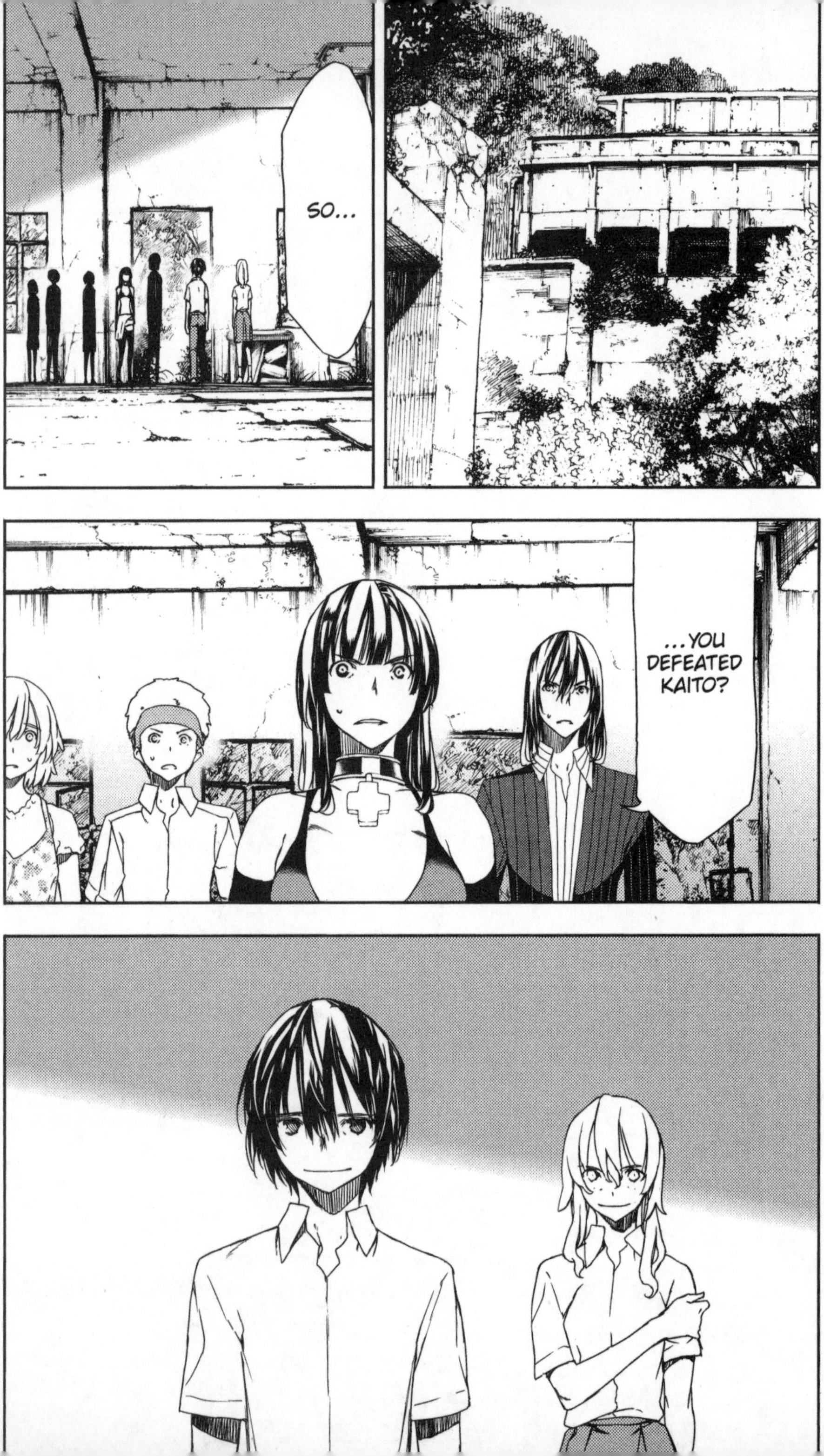
SO...
...YOU DEFEATED KAITO?

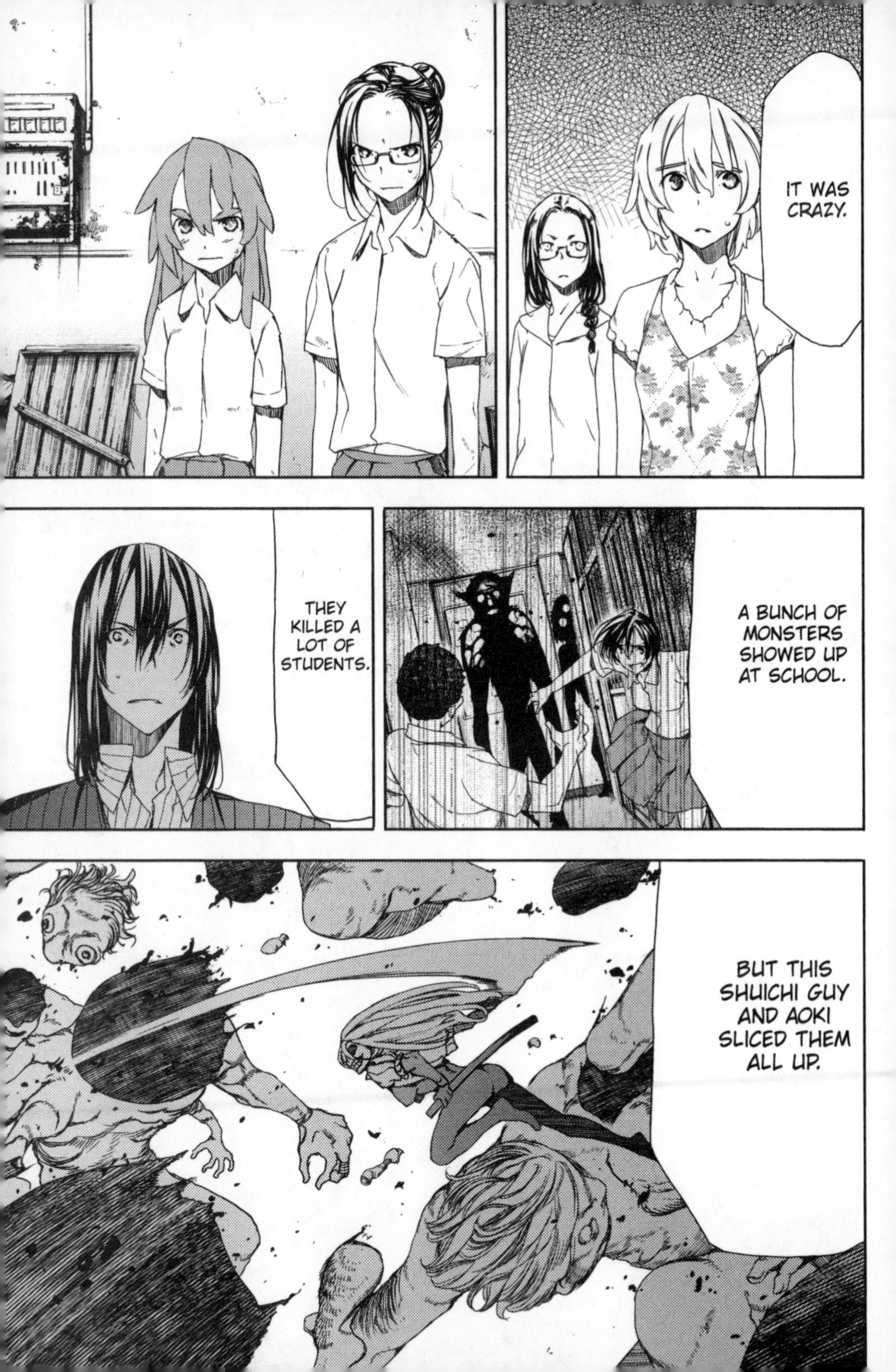
IT WAS CRAZY.
A BUNCH OF MONSTERS SHOWED UP AT SCHOOL.
THEY KILLED A LOT OF STUDENTS.
BUT THIS SHUICHI GUY AND AOKI SLICED THEM ALL UP.

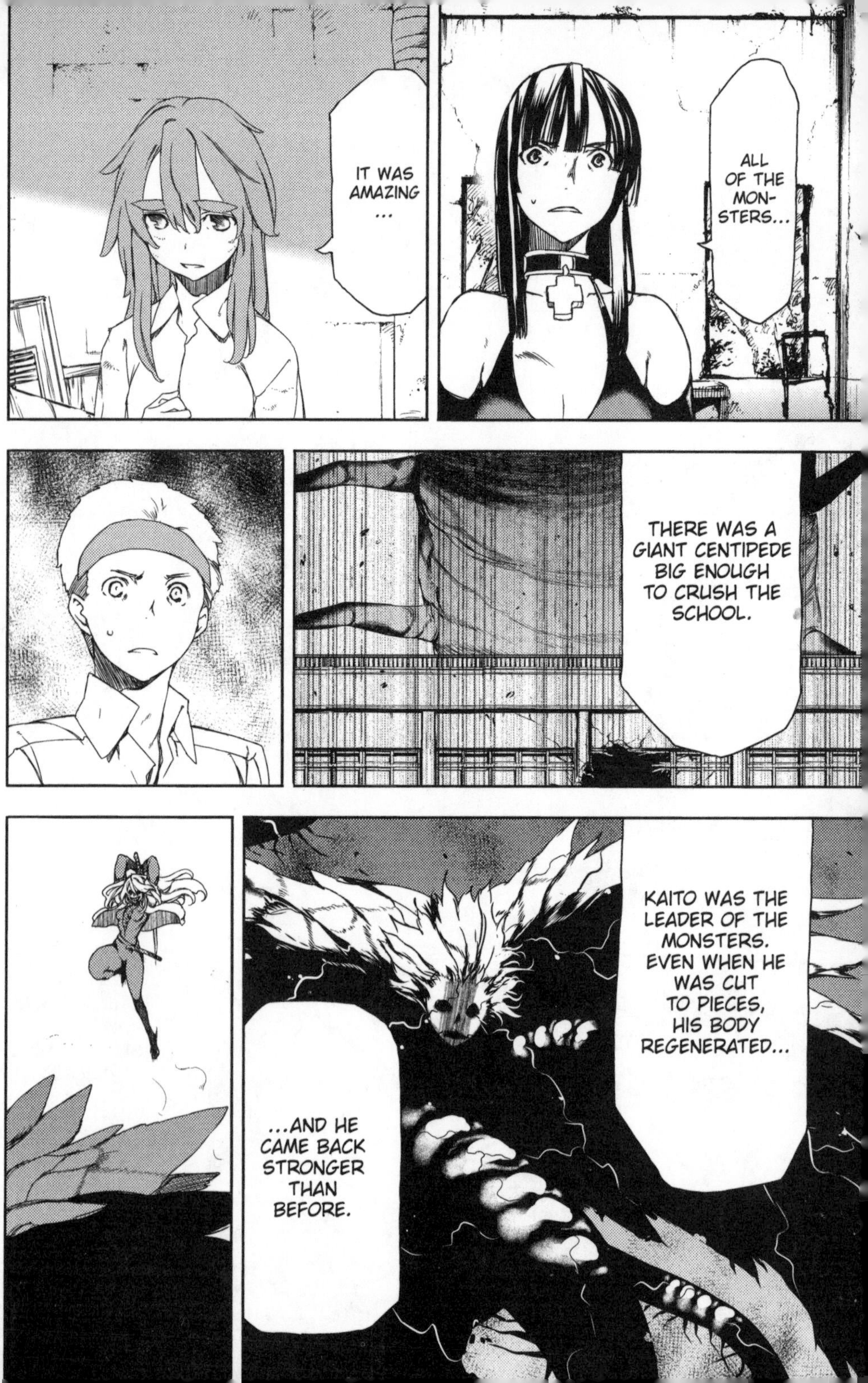
ALL OF THE MON-STERS...
IT WAS AMAZING...
THERE WAS A GIANT CENTIPEDE BIG ENOUGH TO CRUSH THE SCHOOL.
KAITO WAS THE LEADER OF THE MONSTERS. EVEN WHEN HE WAS CUT TO PIECES, HIS BODY REGENERATED...
...AND HE CAME BACK STRONGER THAN BEFORE.

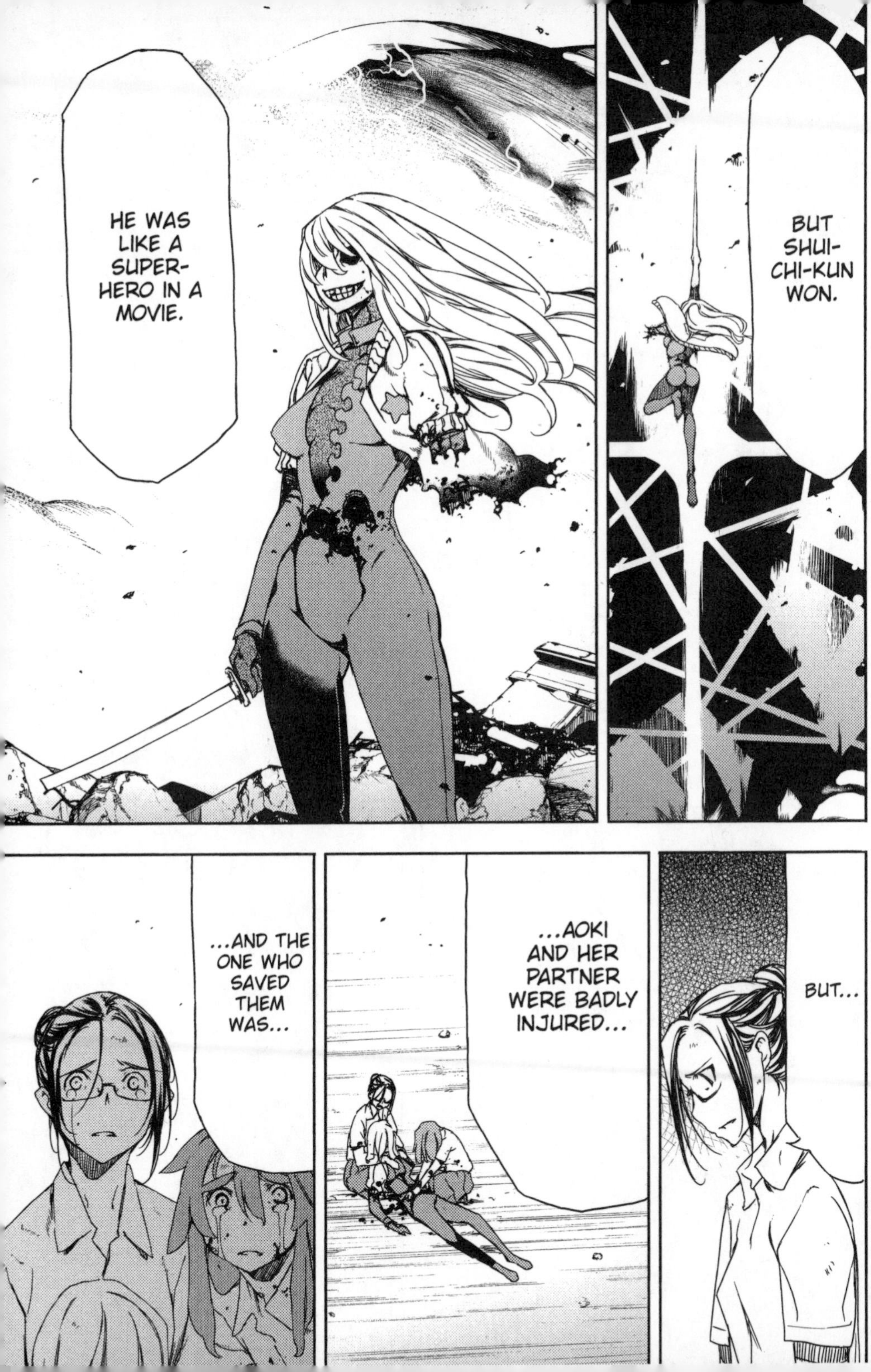
BUT SHUI-CHI-KUN WON.
HE WAS LIKE A SUPER-HERO IN A MOVIE.
BUT...
...AOKI AND HER PARTNER WERE BADLY INJURED...
...AND THE ONE WHO SAVED THEM WAS...

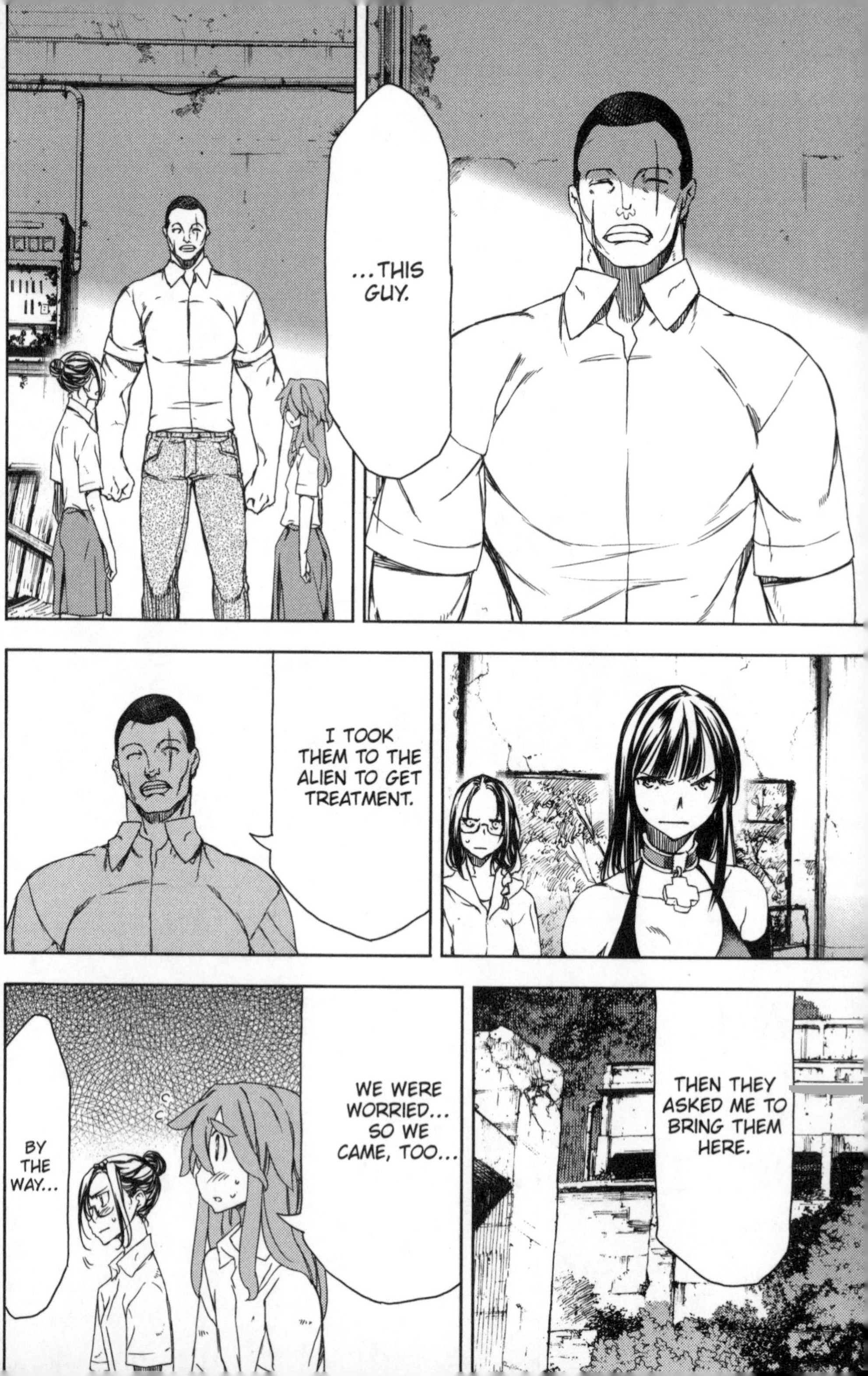
...THIS GUY.
I TOOK THEM TO THE ALIEN TO GET TREATMENT.
THEN THEY ASKED ME TO BRING THEM HERE.
WE WERE WORRIED... SO WE CAME, TOO...
BY THE WAY...

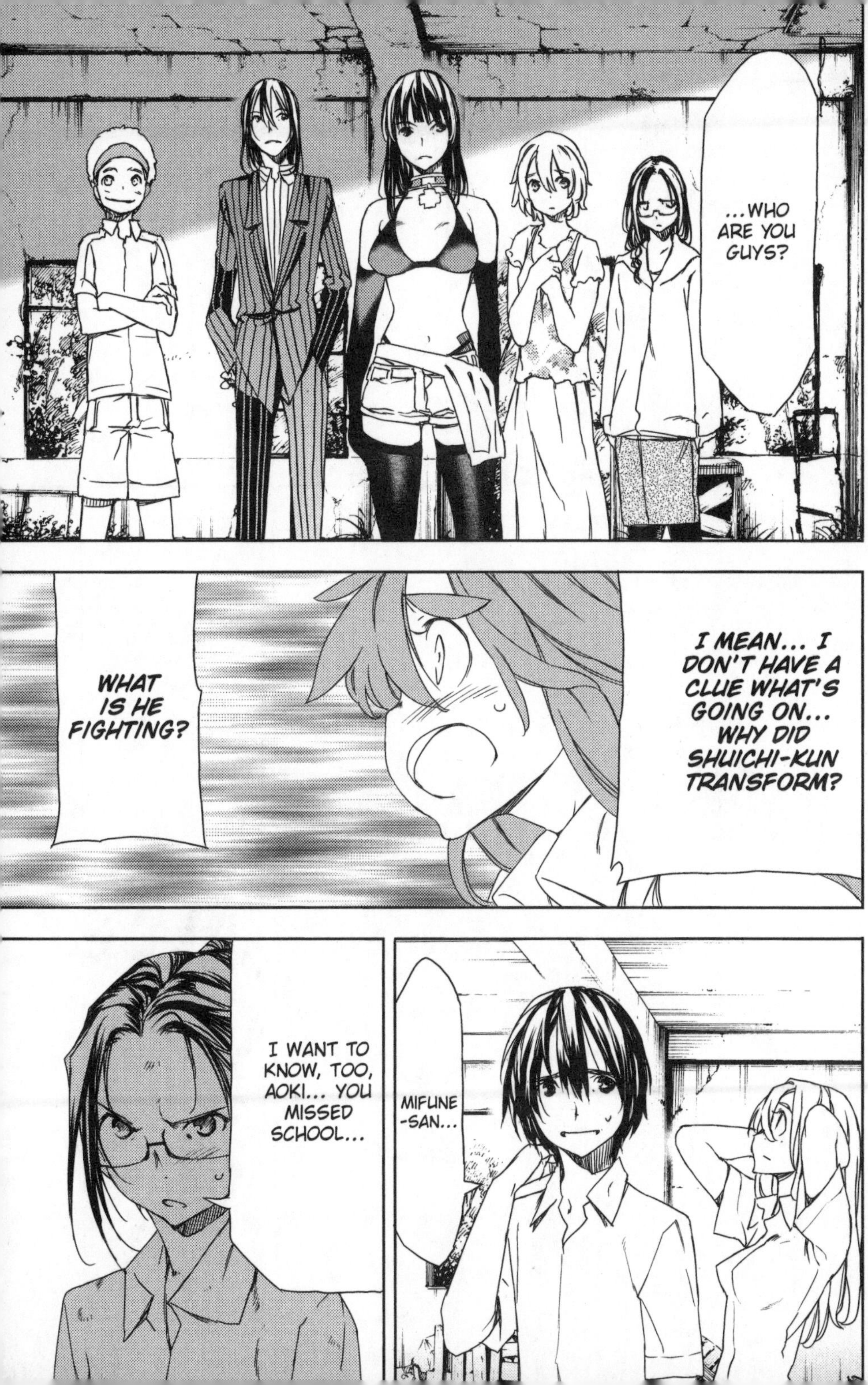
...WHO ARE YOU GUYS?
I MEAN... I DON'T HAVE A CLUE WHAT'S GOING ON... WHY DID SHUICHI-KUN TRANSFORM?
WHAT IS HE FIGHTING?
MIFUNE -SAN...
I WANT TO KNOW, TOO, AOKI... YOU MISSED SCHOOL...

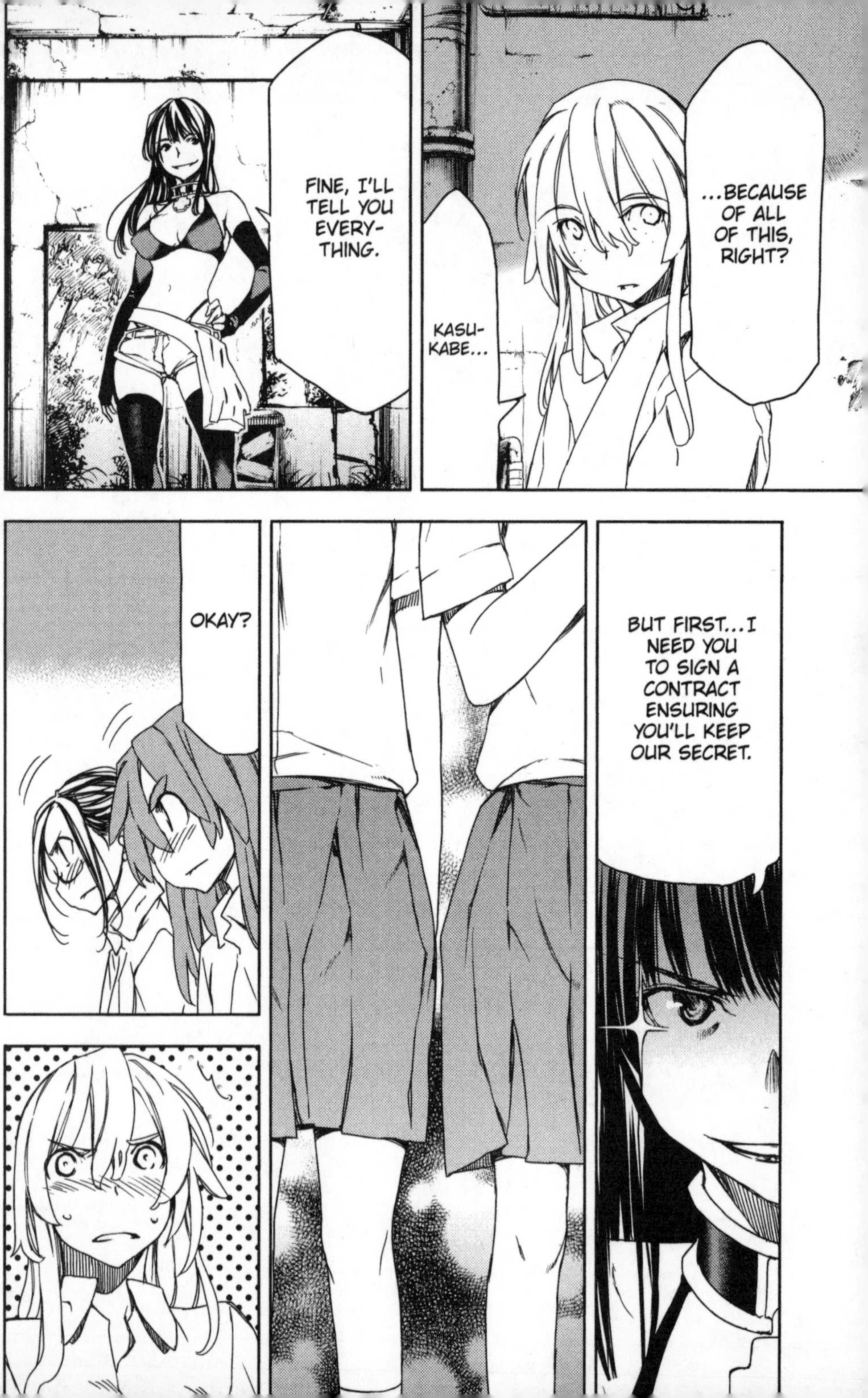
...BECAUSE OF ALL OF THIS, RIGHT?
KASU-KABE...
FINE, I'LL TELL YOU EVERY-THING.
BUT FIRST...I NEED YOU TO SIGN A CONTRACT ENSURING YOU'LL KEEP OUR SECRET.
OKAY?

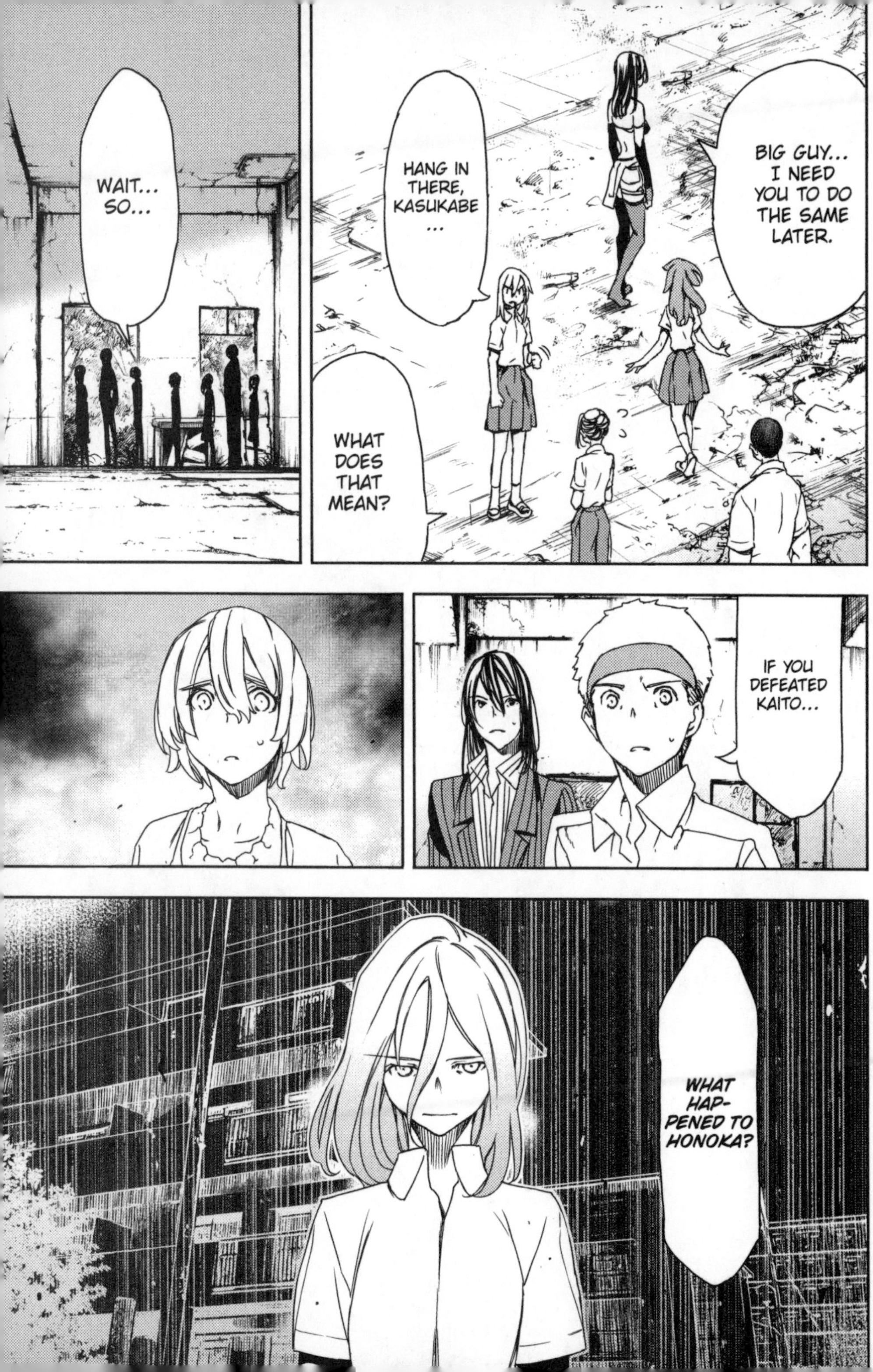
BIG GUY... I NEED YOU TO DO THE SAME LATER.
HANG IN THERE, KASUKABE ...
WHAT DOES THAT MEAN?
WAIT... SO...
IF YOU DEFEATED KAITO...
WHAT HAP-PENED TO HONOKA?

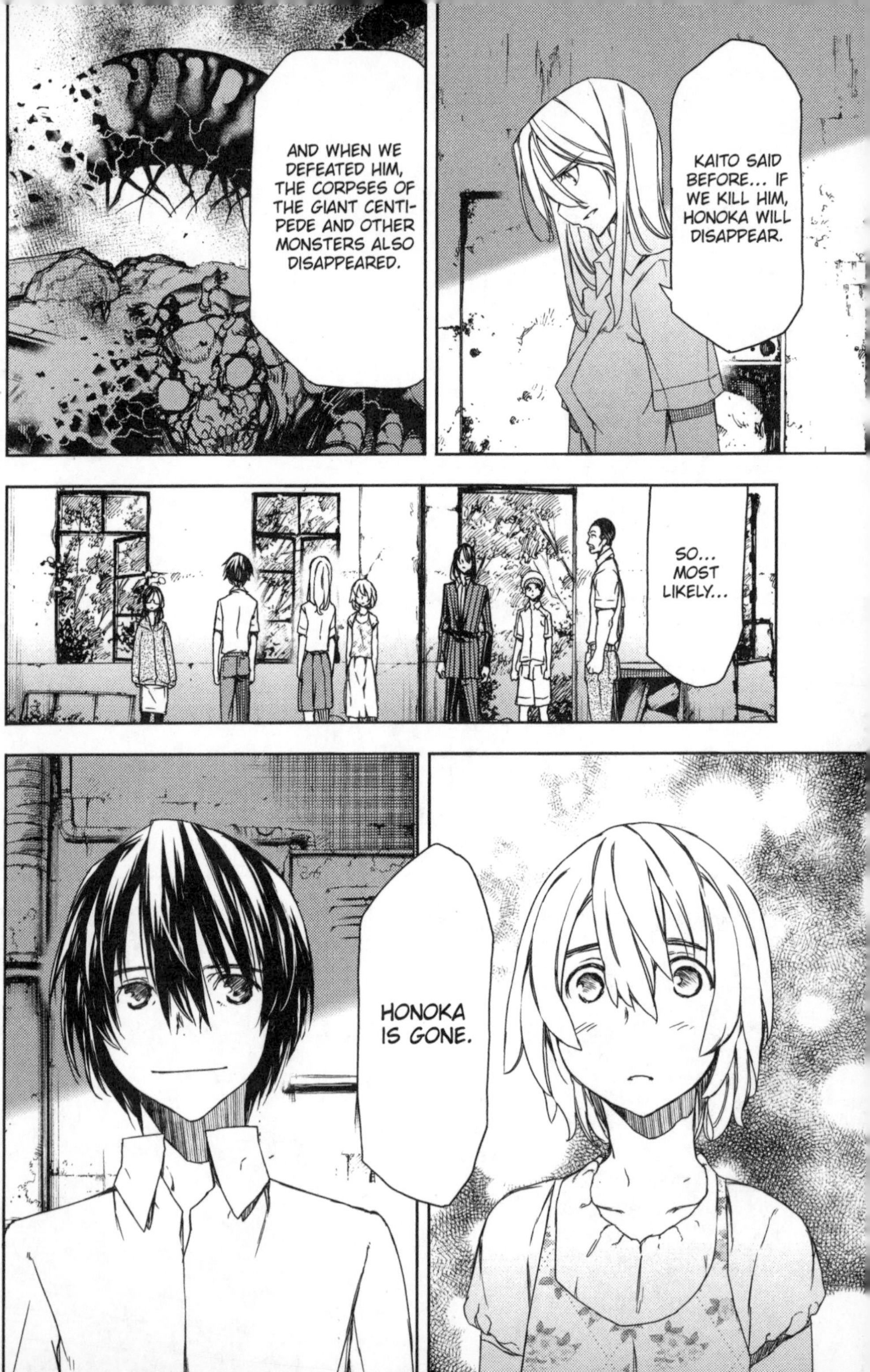
KAITO SAID BEFORE... IF WE KILL HIM, HONOKA WILL DISAPPEAR.
AND WHEN WE DEFEATED HIM, THE CORPSES OF THE GIANT CENTI-PEDE AND OTHER MONSTERS ALSO DISAPPEARED.
SO... MOST LIKELY...
HONOKA IS GONE.

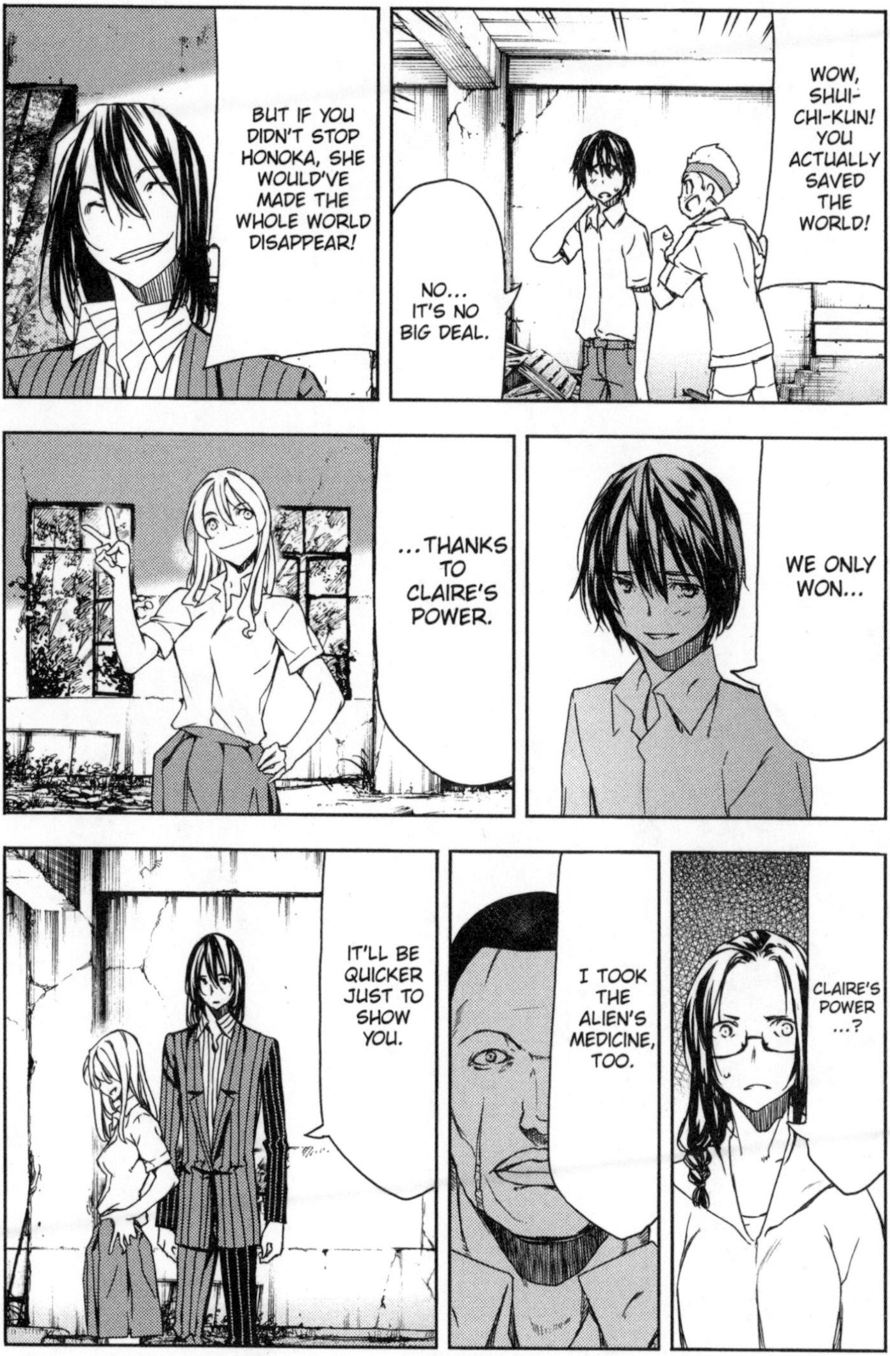
WOW, SHUI-CHI-KUN! YOU ACTUALLY SAVED THE WORLD!
NO... IT'S NO BIG DEAL.
BUT IF YOU DIDN'T STOP HONOKA, SHE WOULD'VE MADE THE WHOLE WORLD DISAPPEAR!
WE ONLY WON...
...THANKS TO CLAIRE'S POWER.
CLAIRE'S POWER ...?
I TOOK THE ALIEN'S MEDICINE, TOO.
IT'LL BE QUICKER JUST TO SHOW YOU.

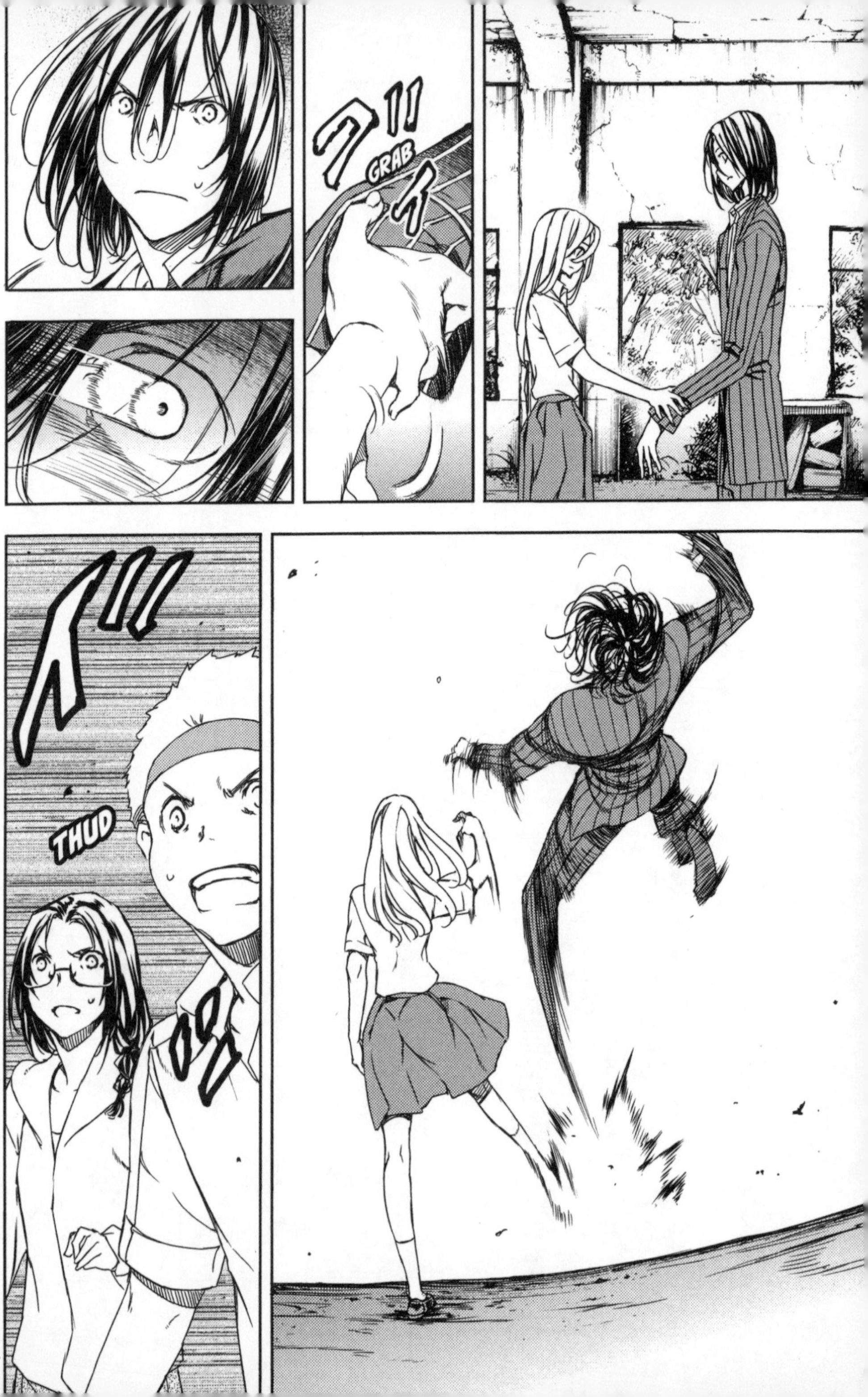
GRAB
THUD

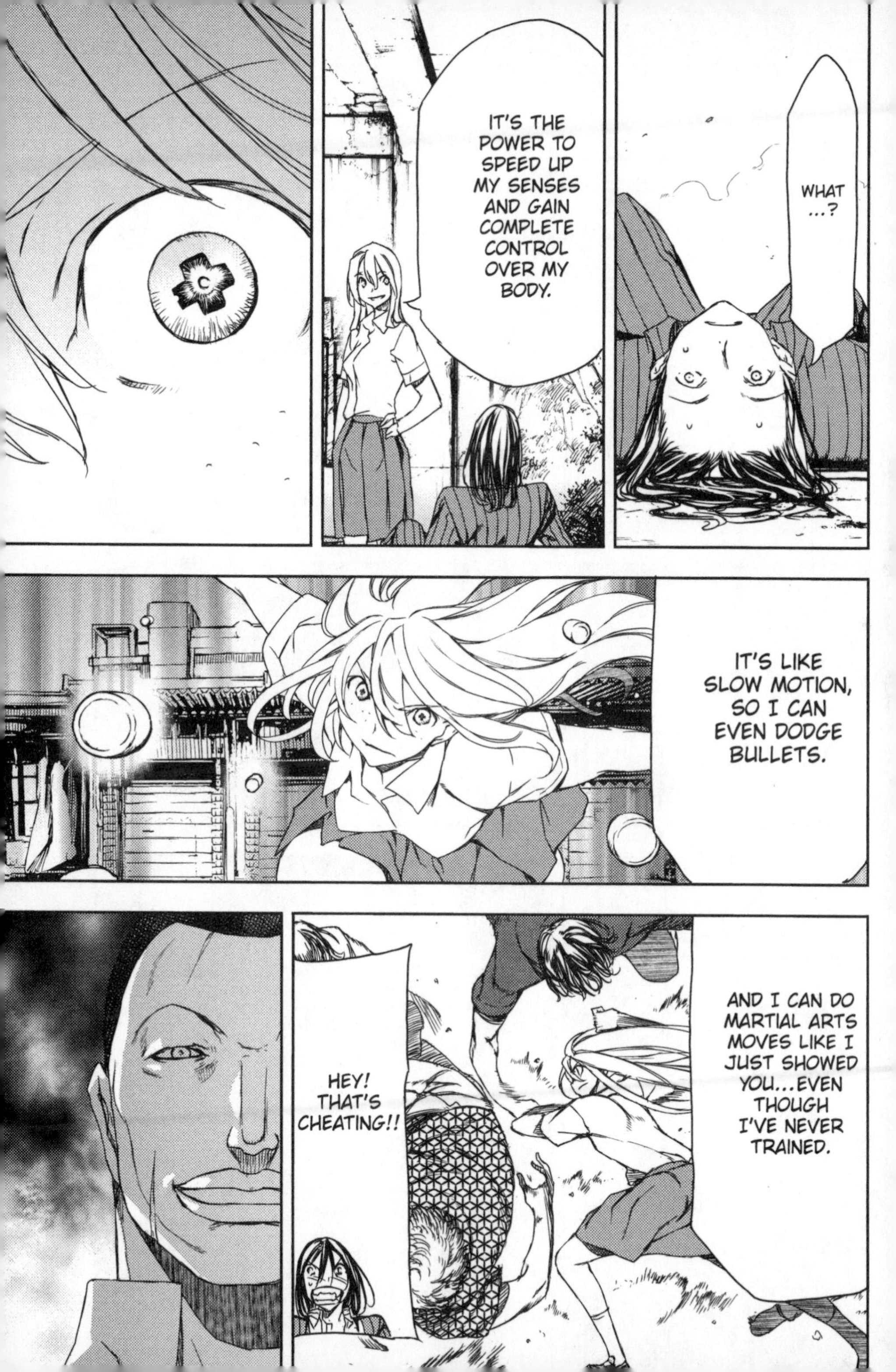
WHAT ...?
IT'S THE POWER TO SPEED UP MY SENSES AND GAIN COMPLETE CONTROL OVER MY BODY.
IT'S LIKE SLOW MOTION, SO I CAN EVEN DODGE BULLETS.
AND I CAN DO MARTIAL ARTS MOVES LIKE I JUST SHOWED YOU...EVEN THOUGH I'VE NEVER TRAINED.
HEY! THAT'S CHEATING!!

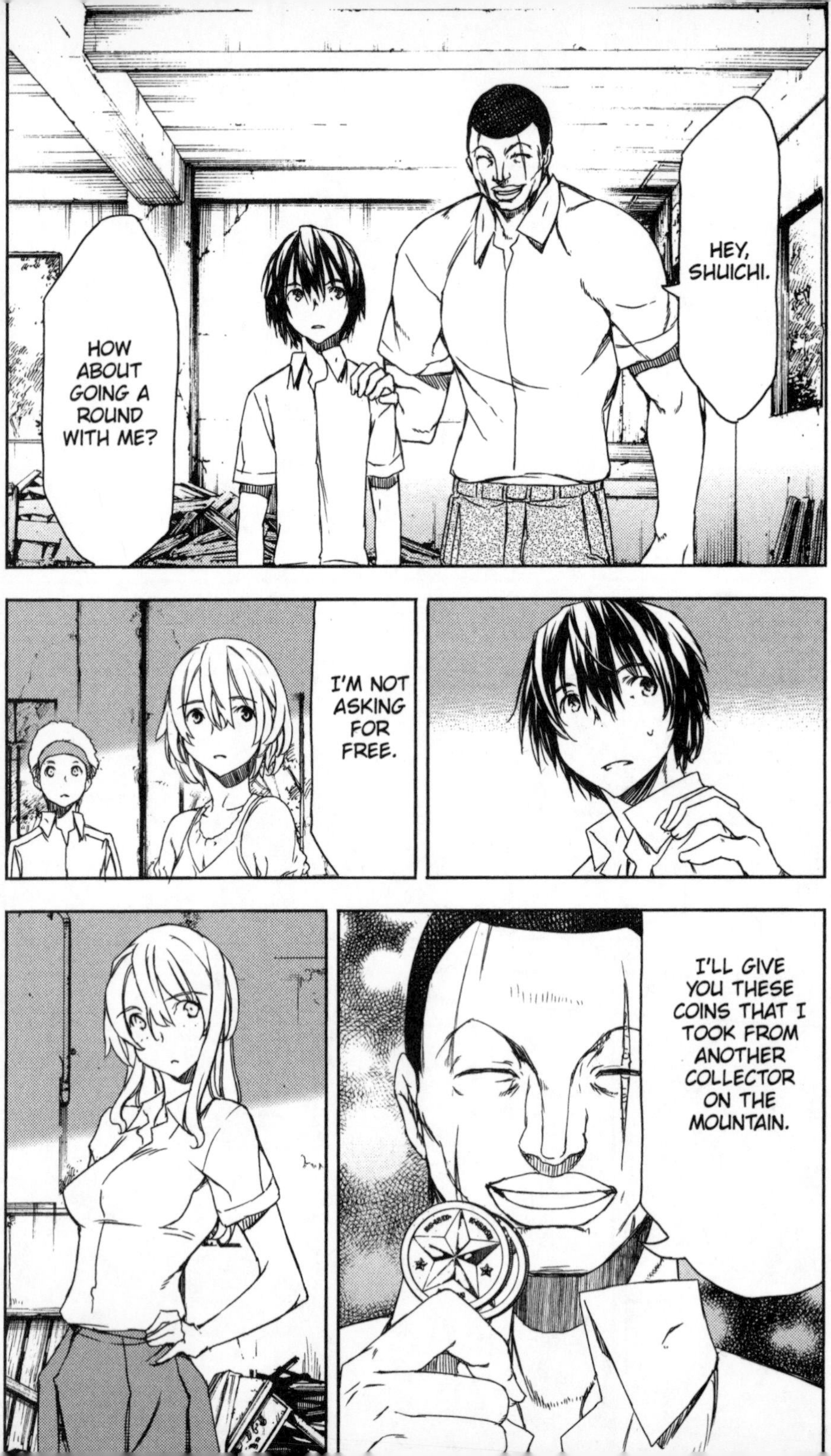
HEY, SHUICHI.
HOW ABOUT GOING A ROUND WITH ME?
I'M NOT ASKING FOR FREE.
I'LL GIVE YOU THESE COINS THAT I TOOK FROM ANOTHER COLLECTOR ON THE MOUNTAIN.

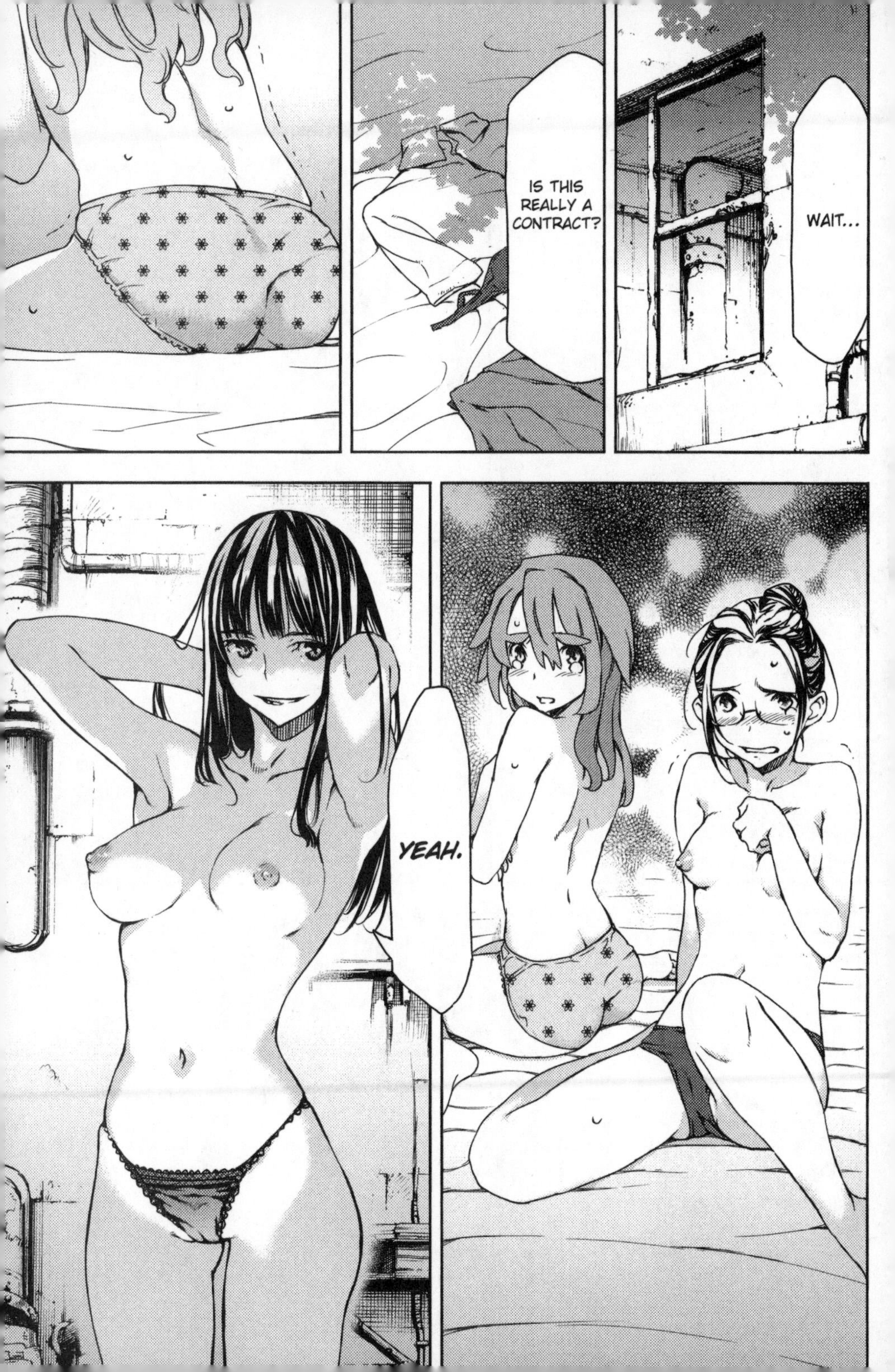
WAIT...
IS THIS REALLY A CONTRACT?
YEAH.

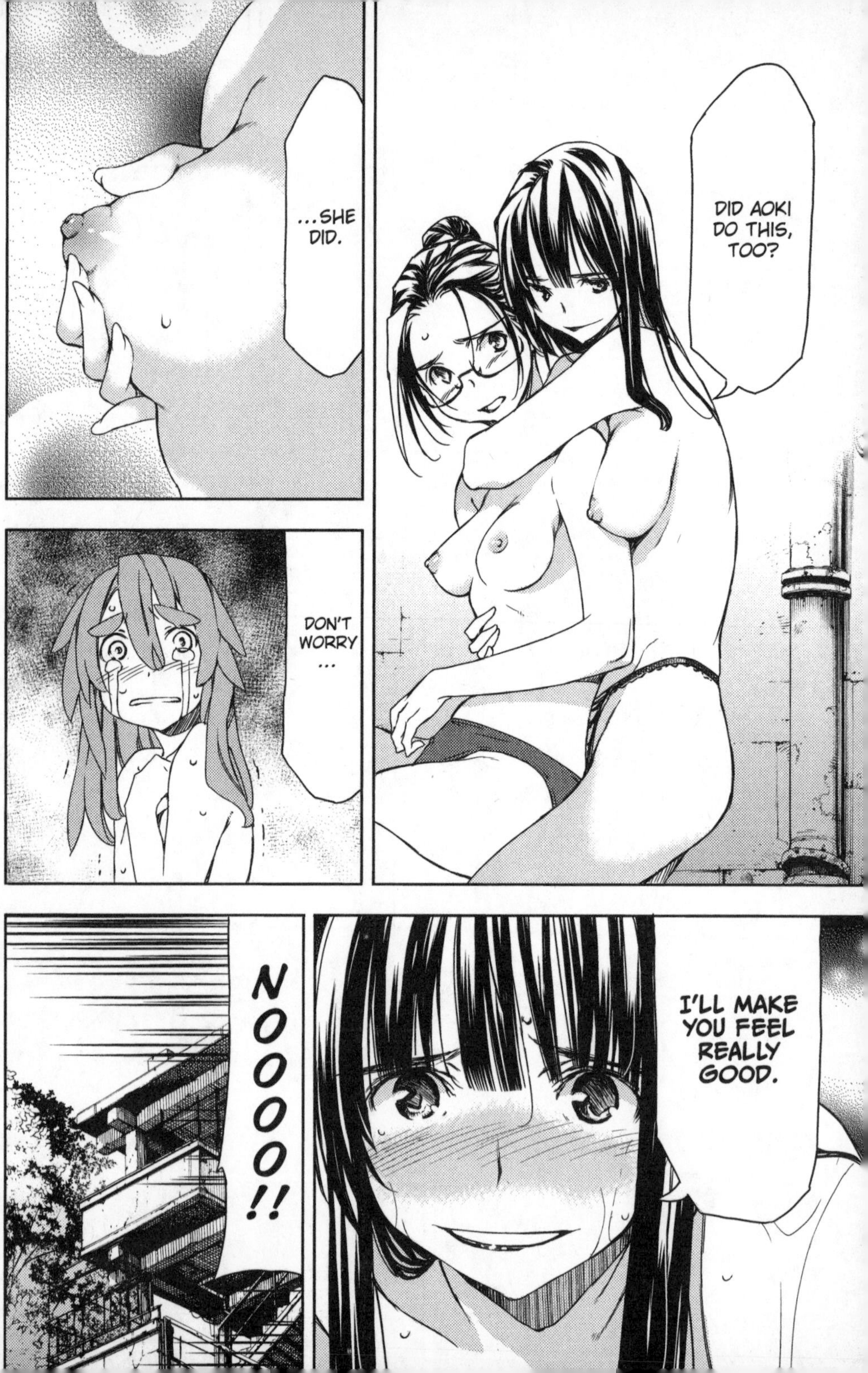
DID AOKI DO THIS, TOO?
...SHE DID.
DON'T WORRY ...
I'LL MAKE YOU FEEL REALLY GOOD.
NOOOOO!!

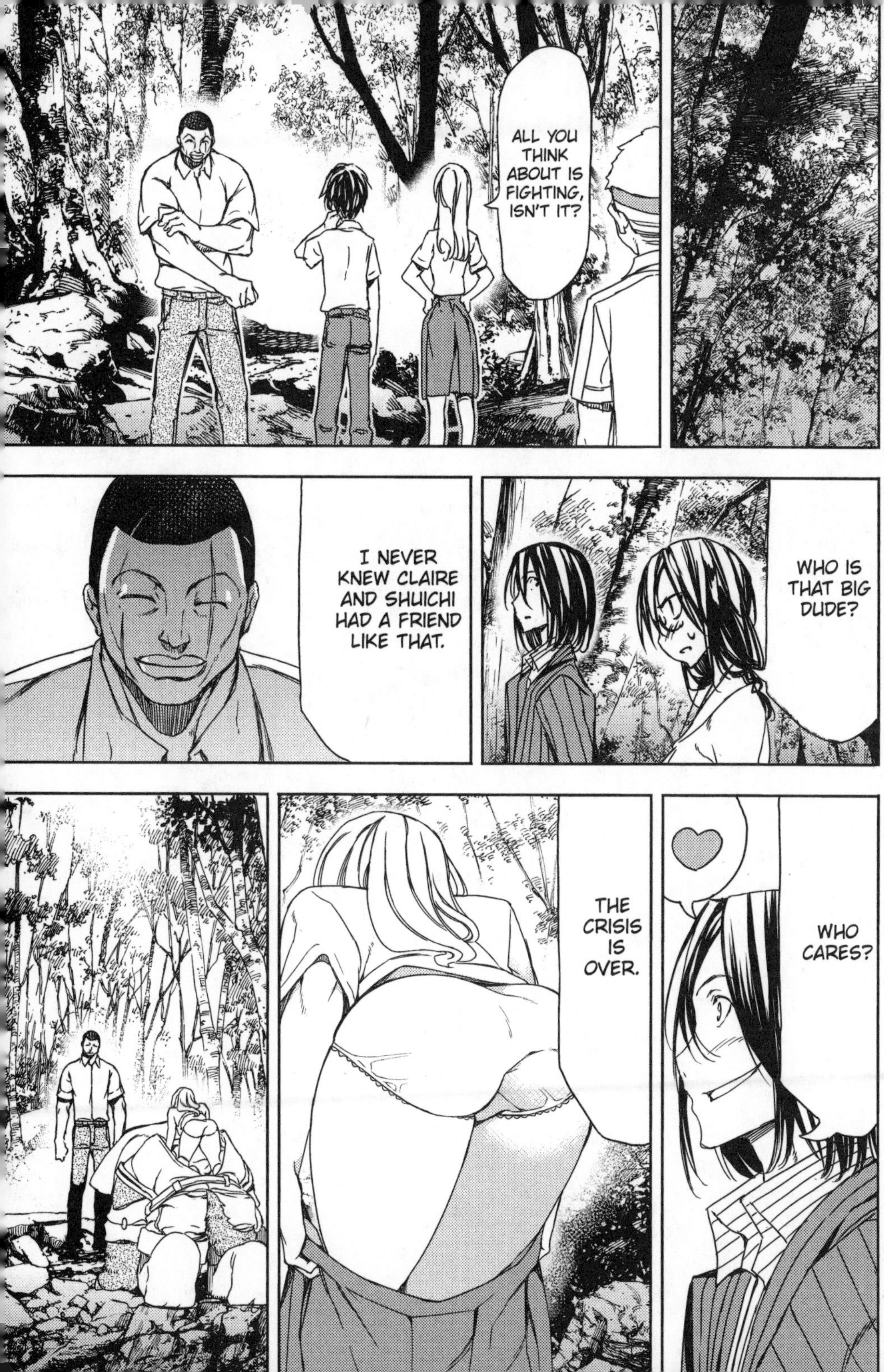
ALL YOU THINK ABOUT IS FIGHTING, ISN'T IT?
WHO IS THAT BIG DUDE?
I NEVER KNEW CLAIRE AND SHUICHI HAD A FRIEND LIKE THAT.
WHO CARES?
THE CRISIS IS OVER.

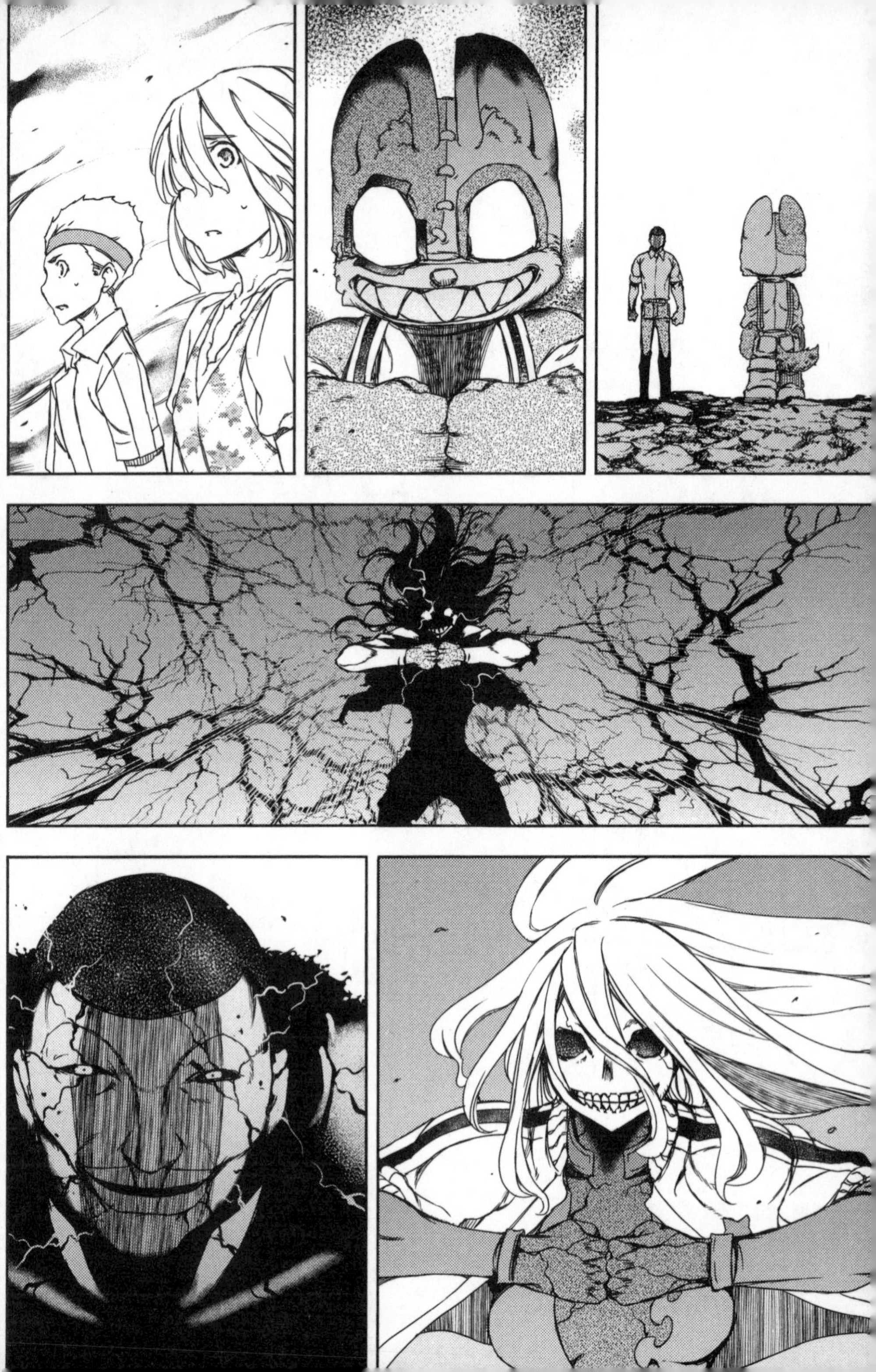

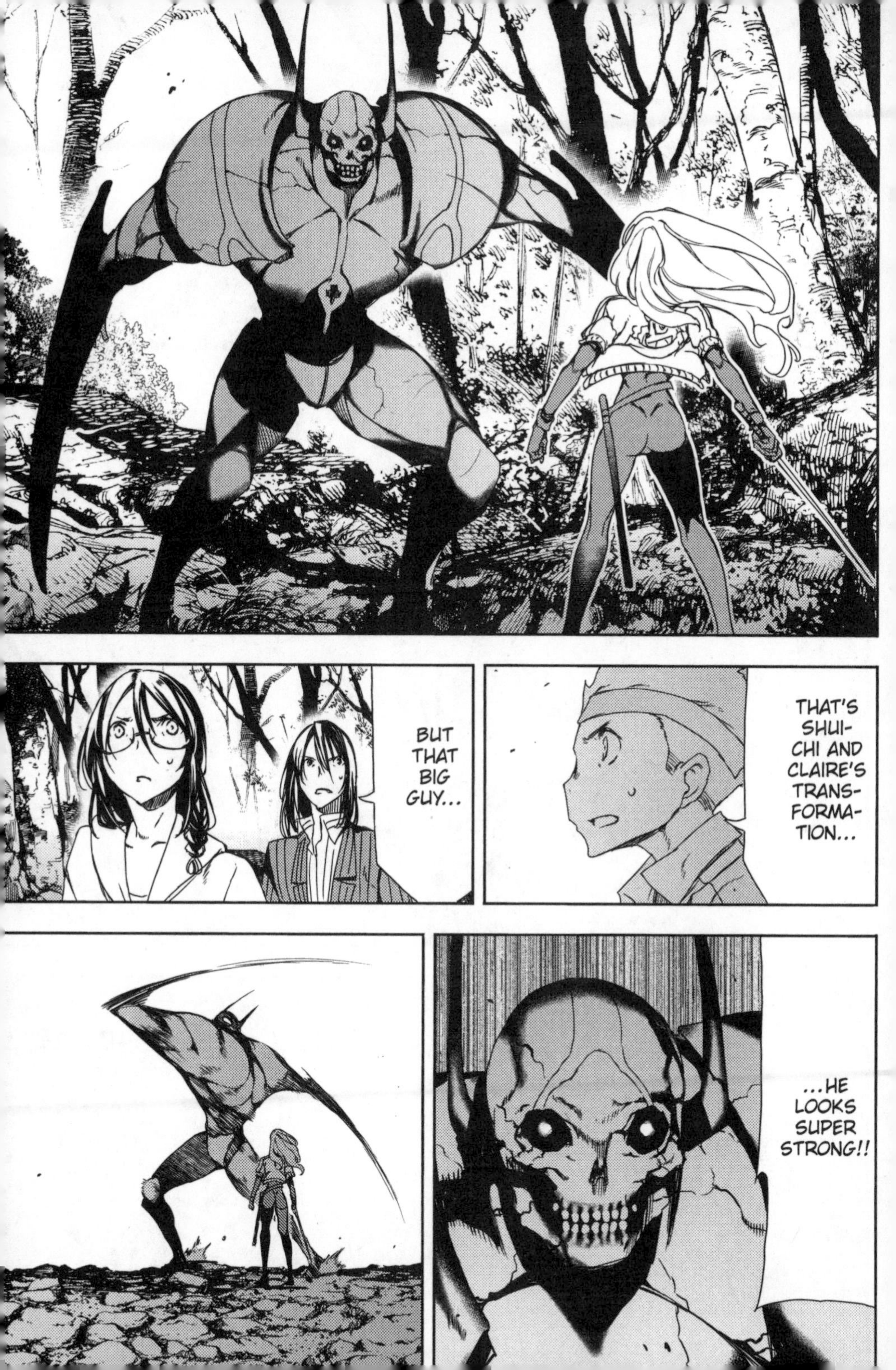
THAT'S SHUI-CHI AND CLAIRE'S TRANS-FORMA-TION...
BUT THAT BIG GUY...
...HE LOOKS SUPER STRONG!!

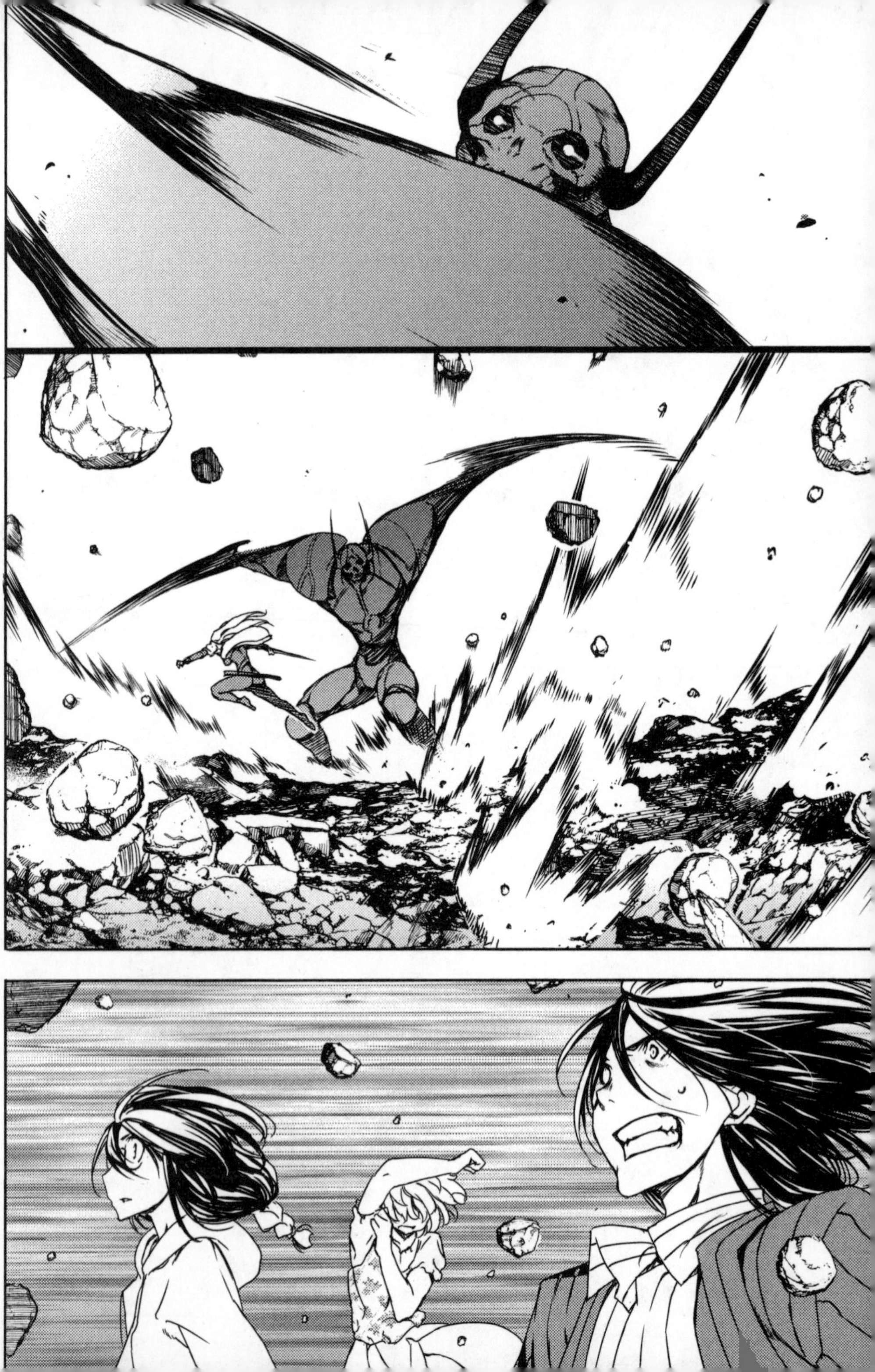

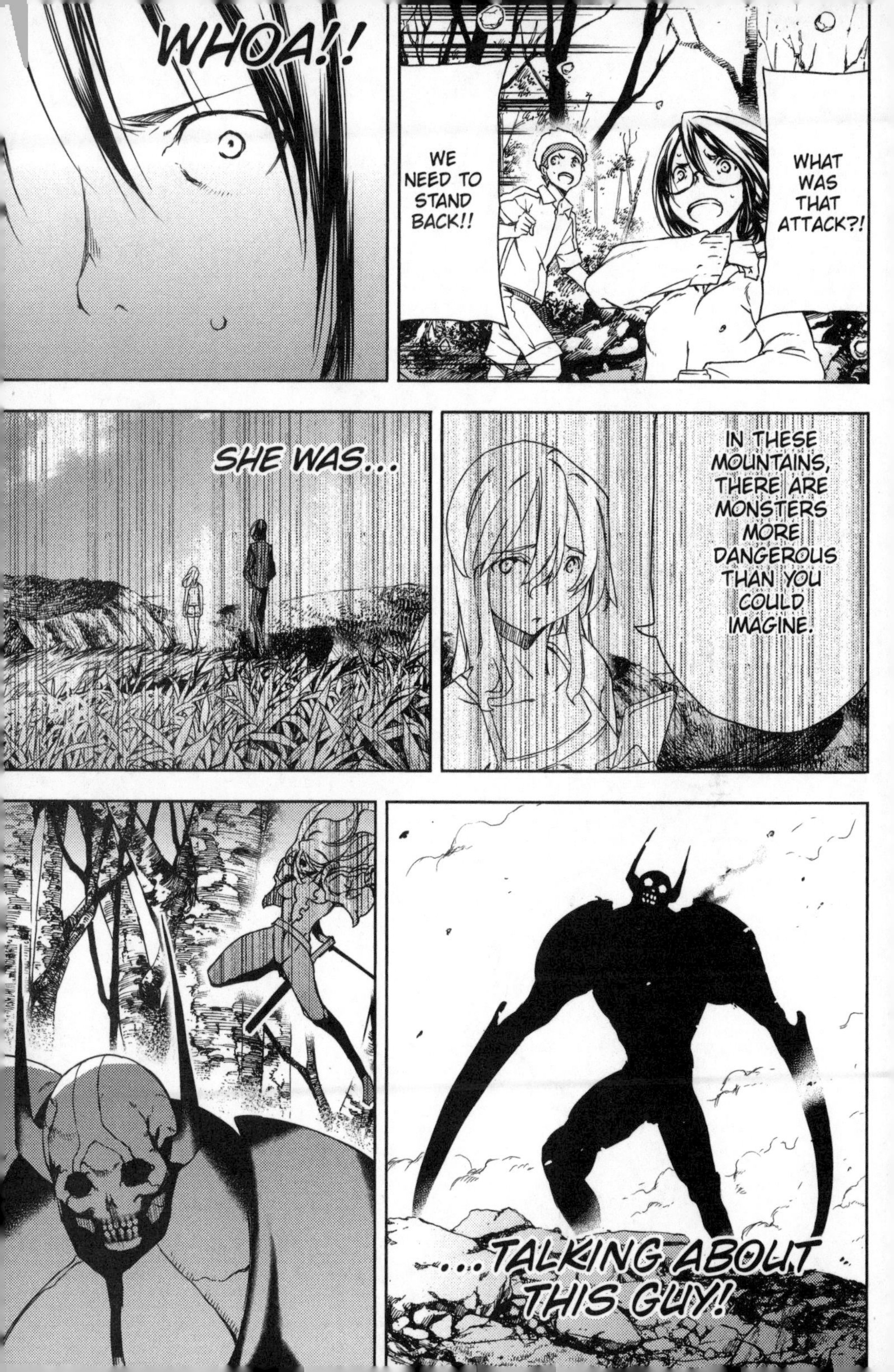
WHAT WAS THAT ATTACK?!
WE NEED TO STAND BACK!!
WHOA!!
IN THESE MOUNTAINS, THERE ARE MONSTERS MORE DANGEROUS THAN YOU COULD IMAGINE.
SHE WAS...
...TALKING ABOUT THIS GUY!

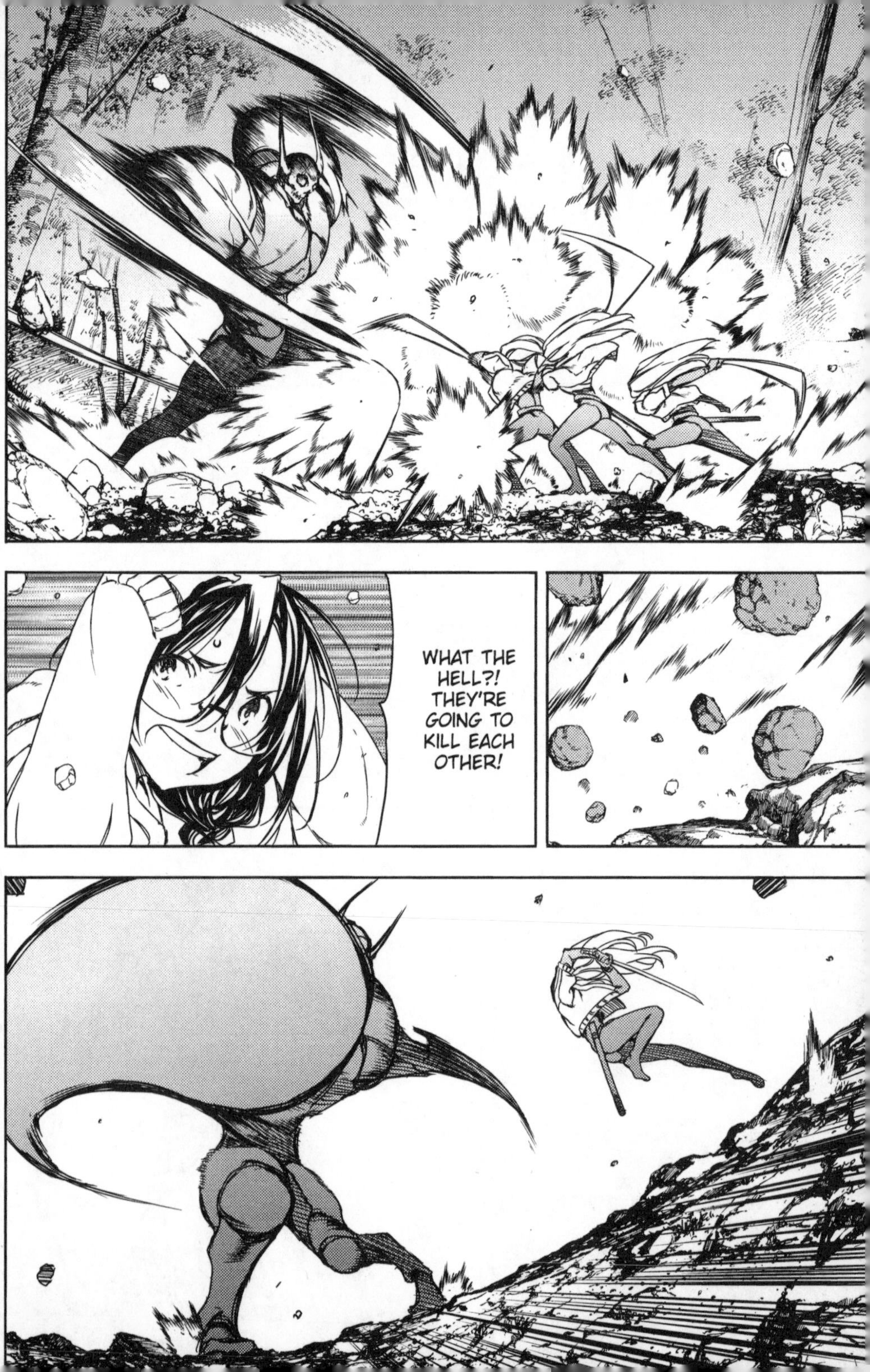
WHAT THE HELL?! THEY'RE GOING TO KILL EACH OTHER!

WHAT...

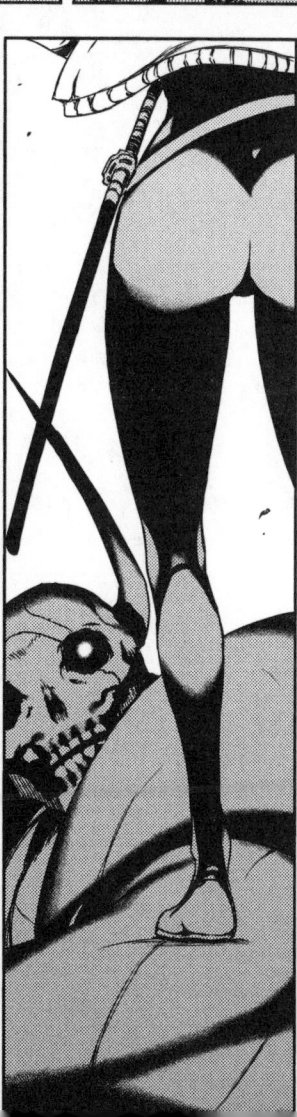

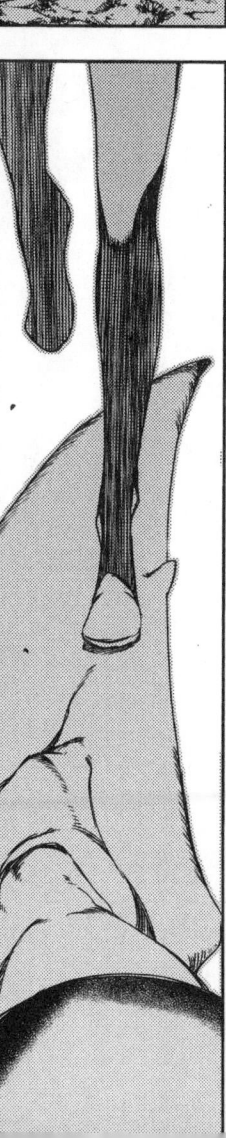

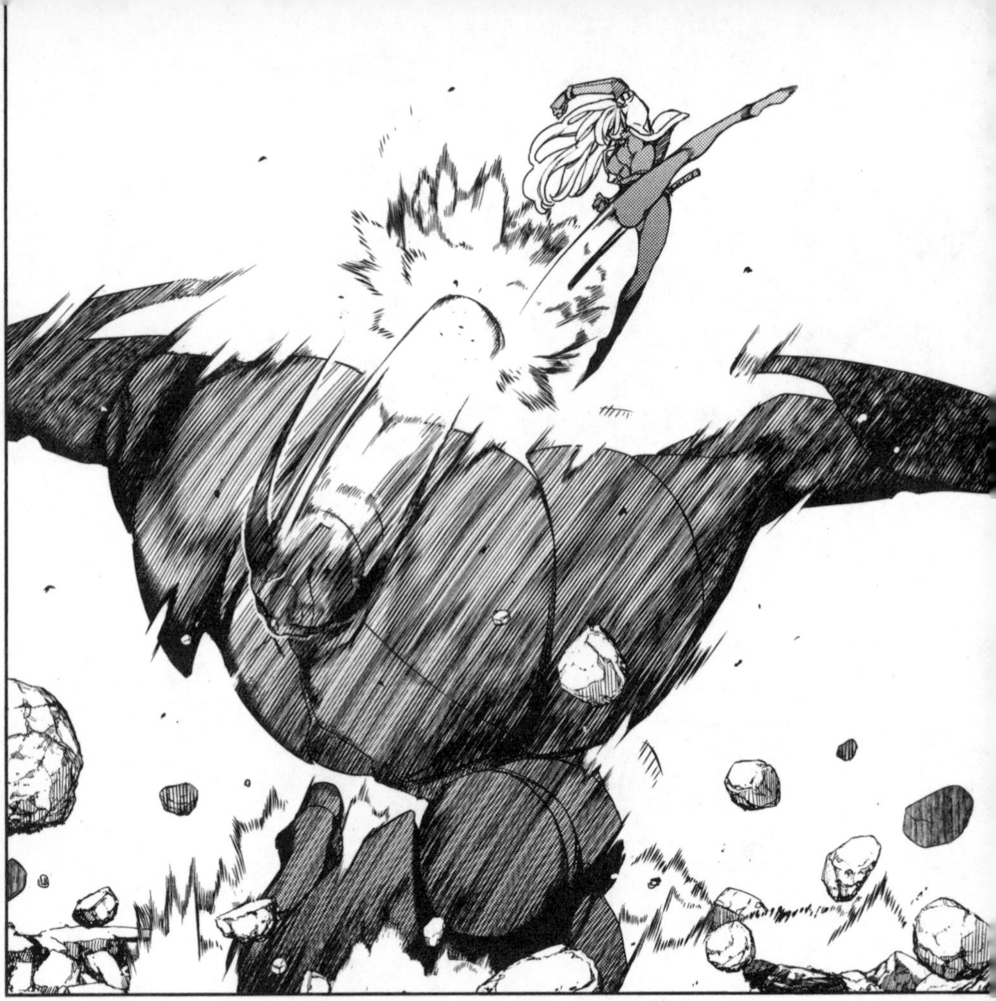
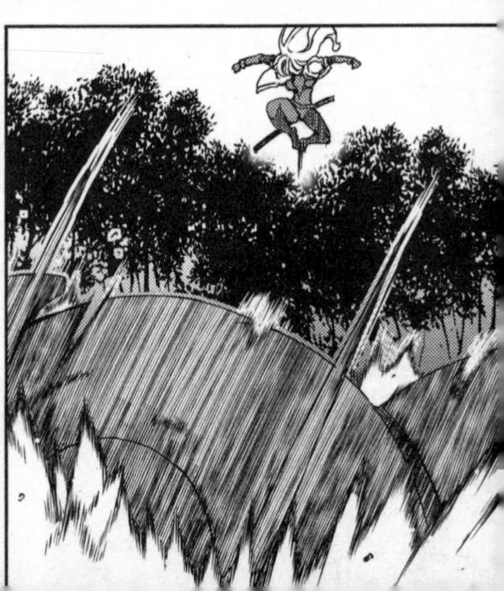
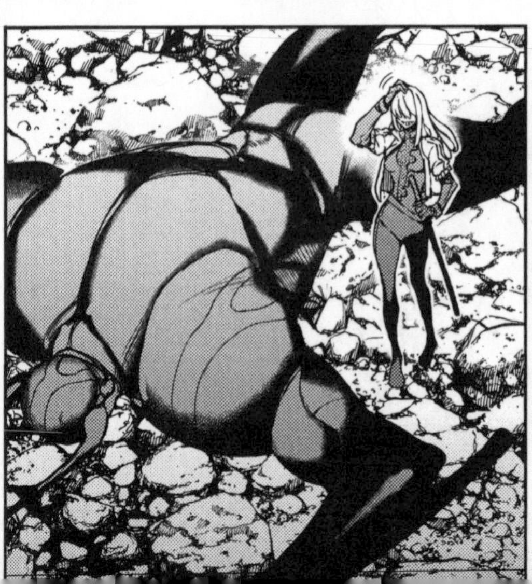

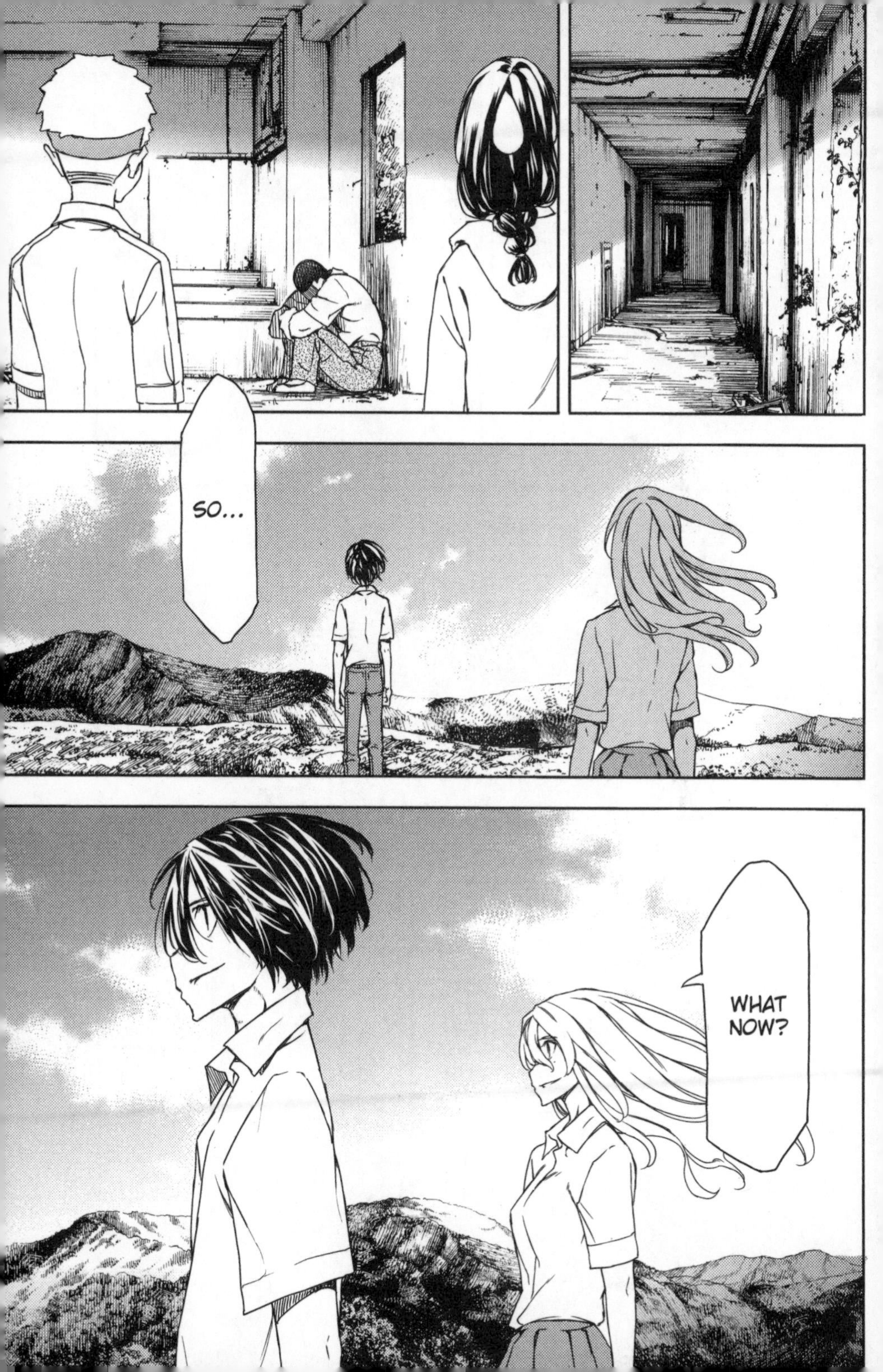
SO...
WHAT NOW?

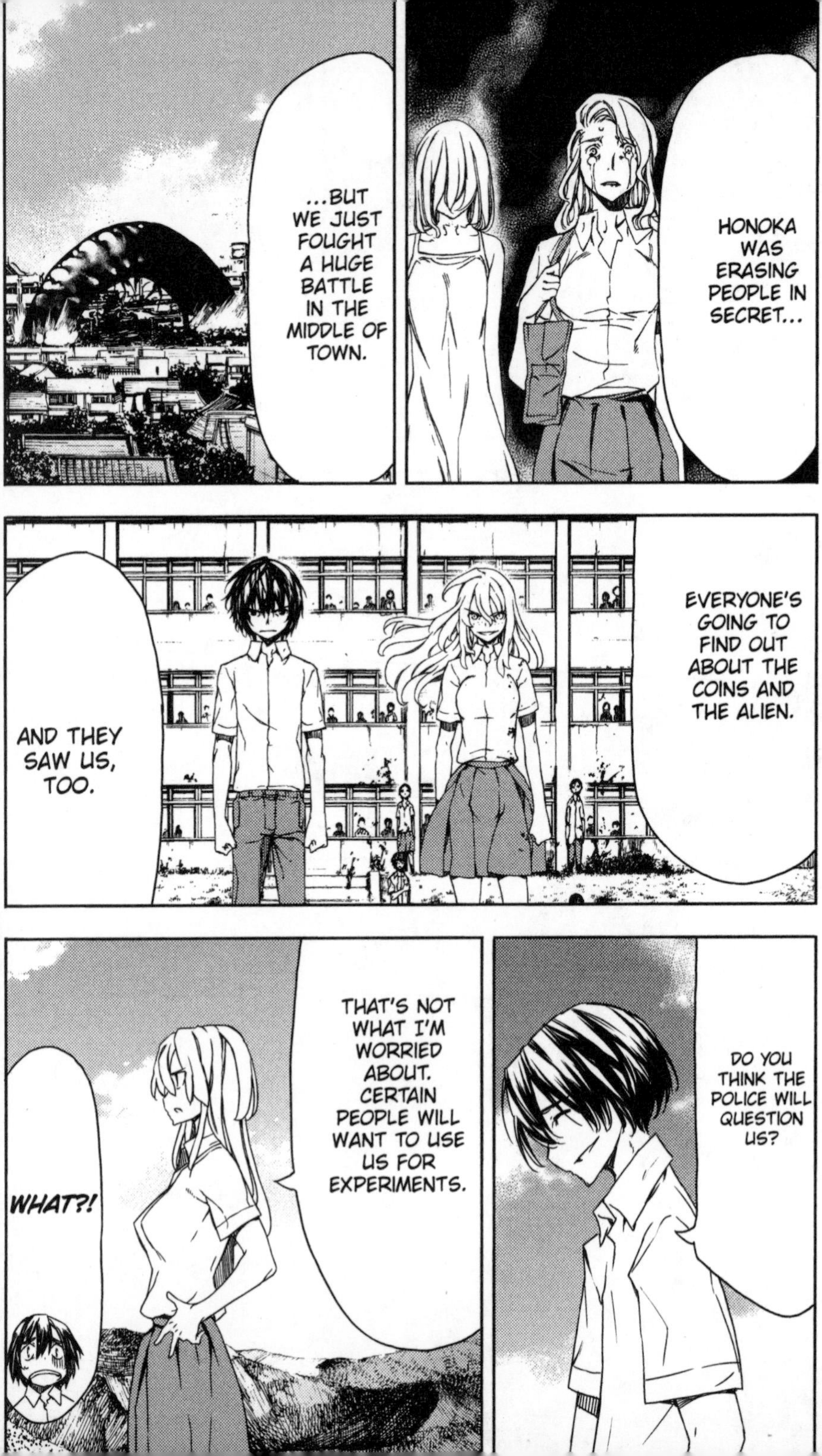
HONOKA WAS ERASING PEOPLE IN SECRET...
...BUT WE JUST FOUGHT A HUGE BATTLE IN THE MIDDLE OF TOWN.
EVERYONE'S GOING TO FIND OUT ABOUT THE COINS AND THE ALIEN.
AND THEY SAW US, TOO.
DO YOU THINK THE POLICE WILL QUESTION US?
THAT'S NOT WHAT I'M WORRIED ABOUT. CERTAIN PEOPLE WILL WANT TO USE US FOR EXPERIMENTS.
WHAT?!

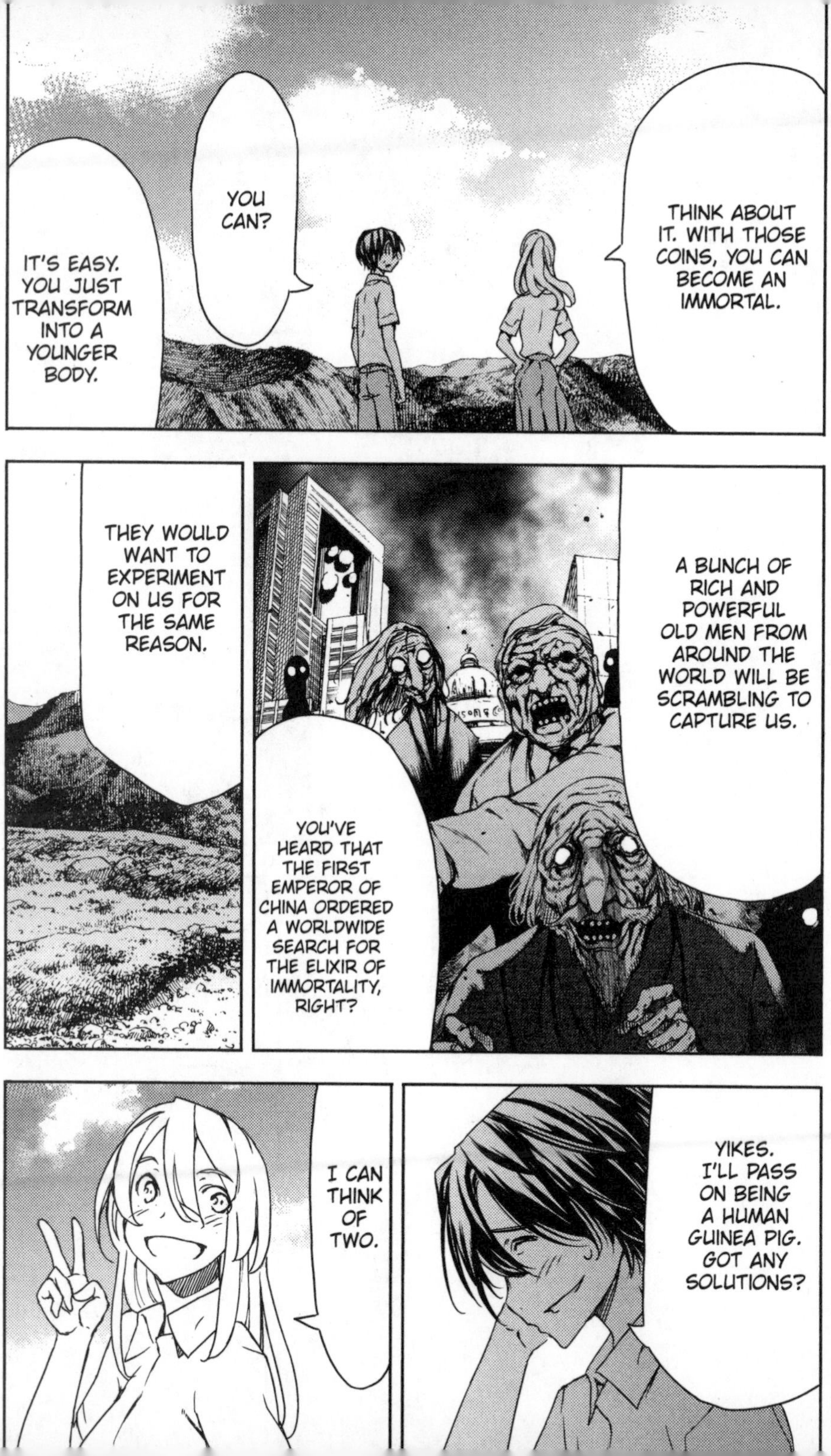
THINK ABOUT IT. WITH THOSE COINS, YOU CAN BECOME AN IMMORTAL.
YOU CAN?
IT'S EASY. YOU JUST TRANSFORM INTO A YOUNGER BODY.
A BUNCH OF RICH AND POWERFUL OLD MEN FROM AROUND THE WORLD WILL BE SCRAMBLING TO CAPTURE US.
YOU'VE HEARD THAT THE FIRST EMPEROR OF CHINA ORDERED A WORLDWIDE SEARCH FOR THE ELIXIR OF IMMORTALITY, RIGHT?
THEY WOULD WANT TO EXPERIMENT ON US FOR THE SAME REASON.
YIKES. I'LL PASS ON BEING A HUMAN GUINEA PIG. GOT ANY SOLUTIONS?
I CAN THINK OF TWO.

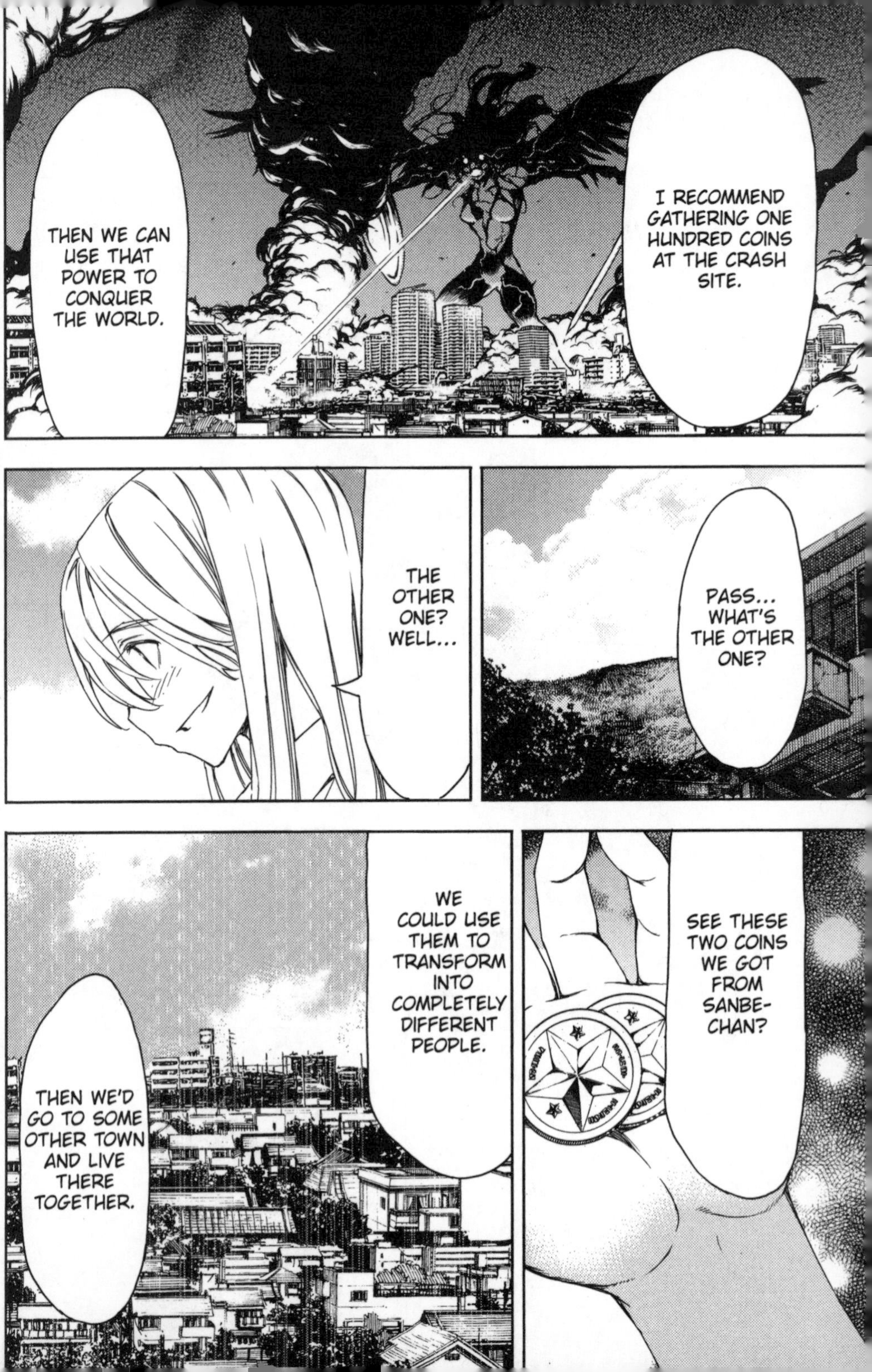
I RECOMMEND GATHERING ONE HUNDRED COINS AT THE CRASH SITE.
THEN WE CAN USE THAT POWER TO CONQUER THE WORLD.
PASS... WHAT'S THE OTHER ONE?
THE OTHER ONE? WELL...
SEE THESE TWO COINS WE GOT FROM SANBE-CHAN?
WE COULD USE THEM TO TRANSFORM INTO COMPLETELY DIFFERENT PEOPLE.
THEN WE'D GO TO SOME OTHER TOWN AND LIVE THERE TOGETHER.

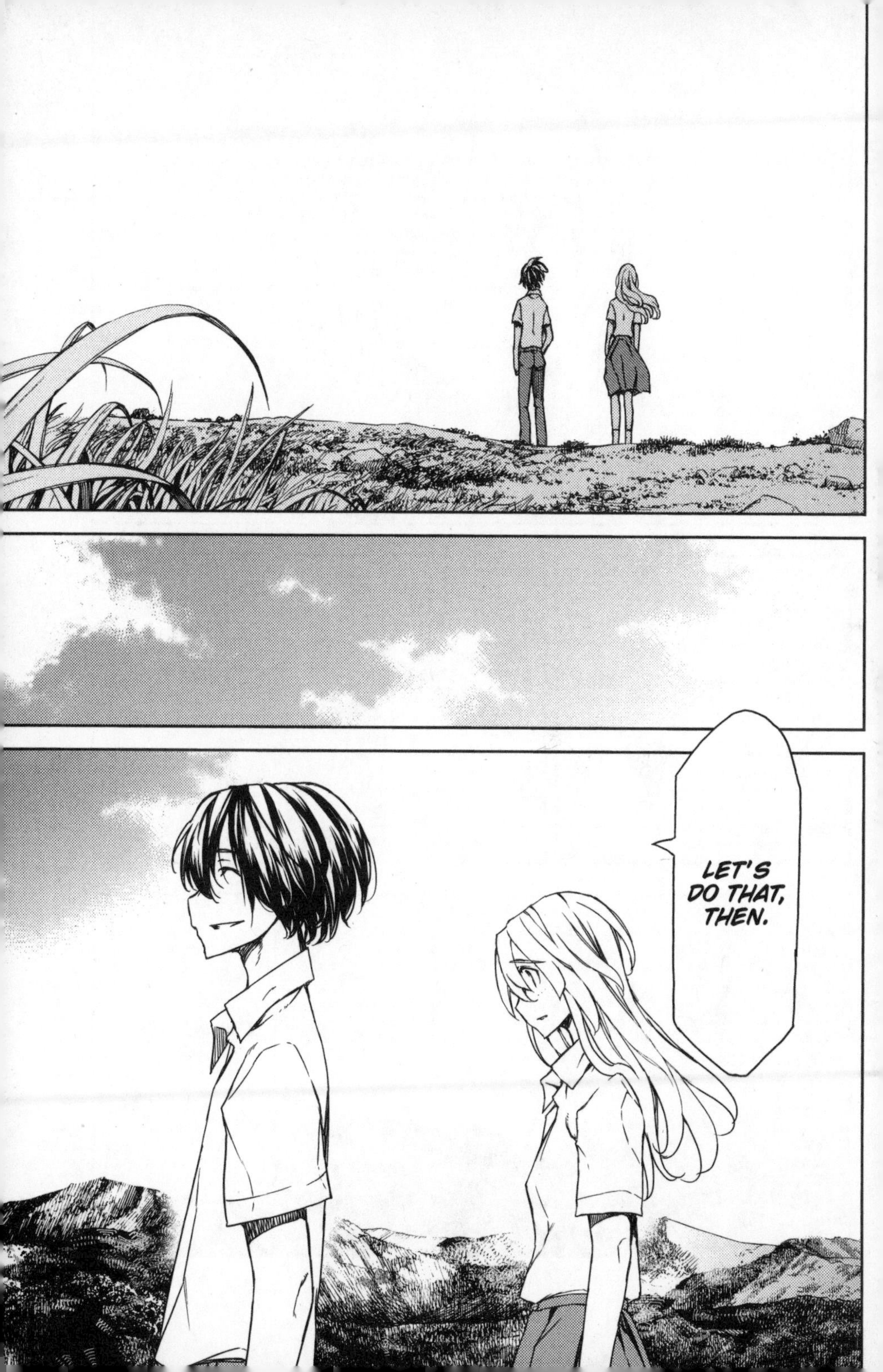
LET'S DO THAT, THEN.

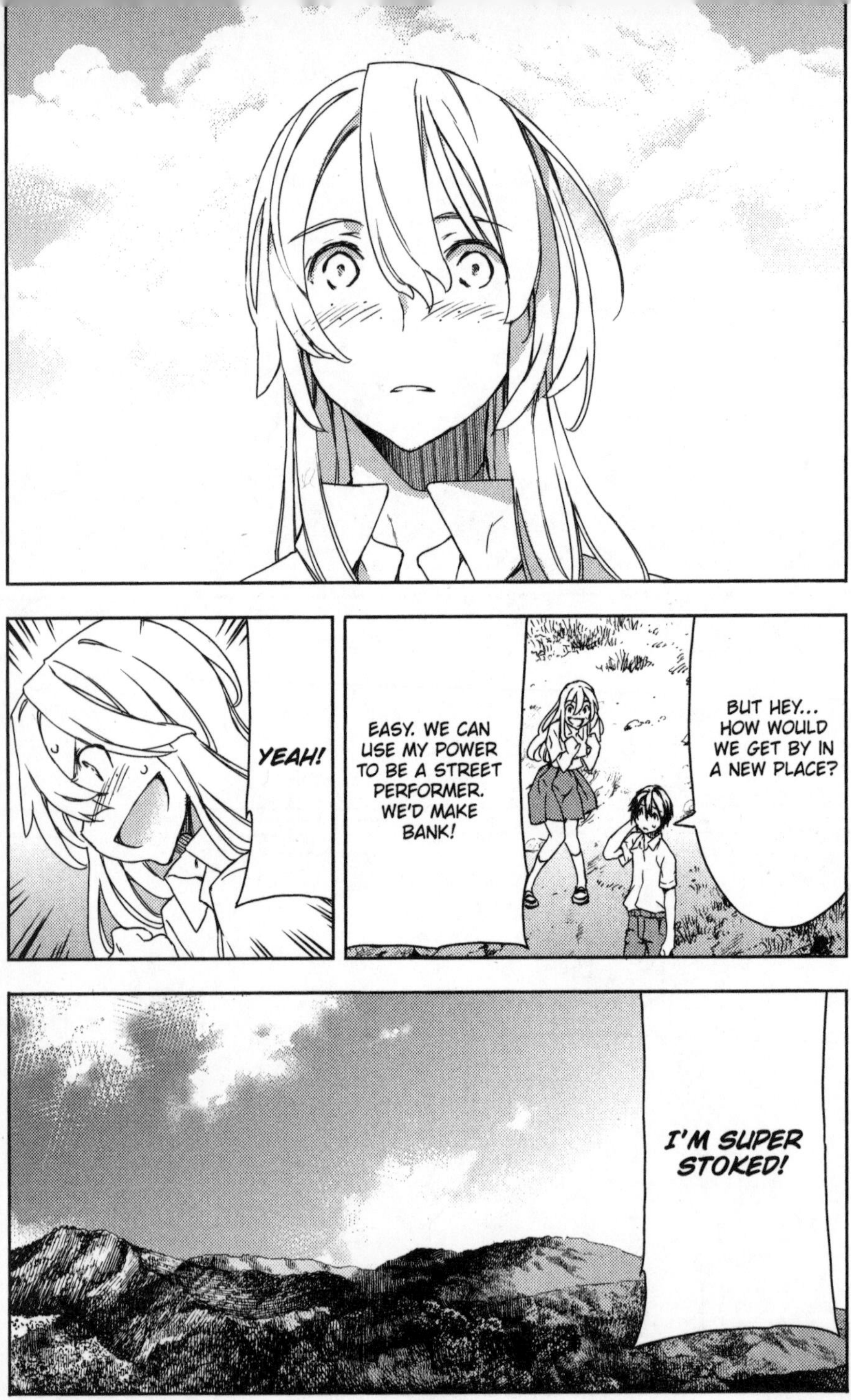
BUT HEY... HOW WOULD WE GET BY IN A NEW PLACE?
EASY. WE CAN USE MY POWER TO BE A STREET PERFORMER. WE'D MAKE BANK!
YEAH!
I'M SUPER STOKED!

CHAPTER 69 ✚ AN OLDER SISTER'S WISH

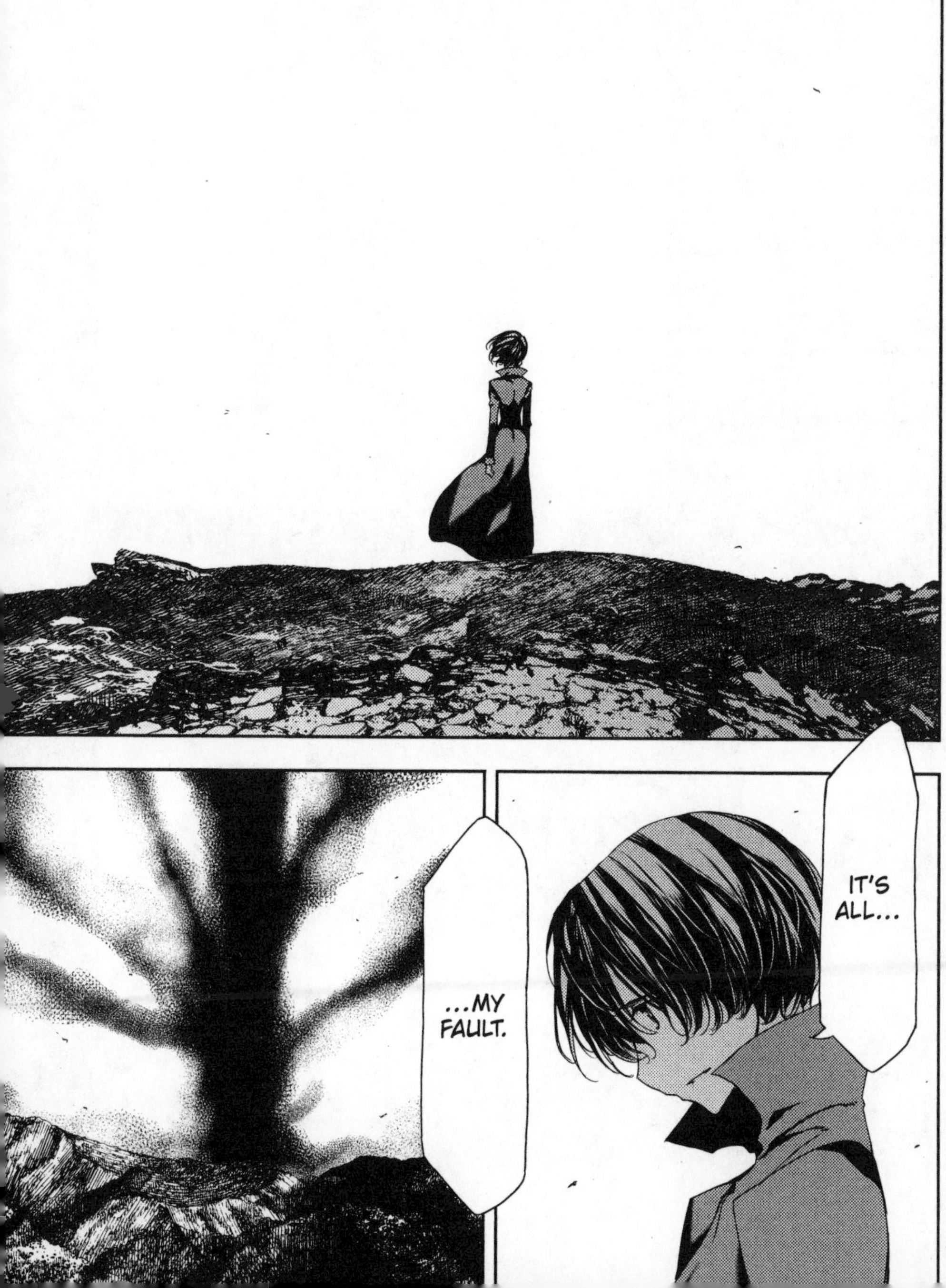
IT'S ALL...
...MY FAULT.

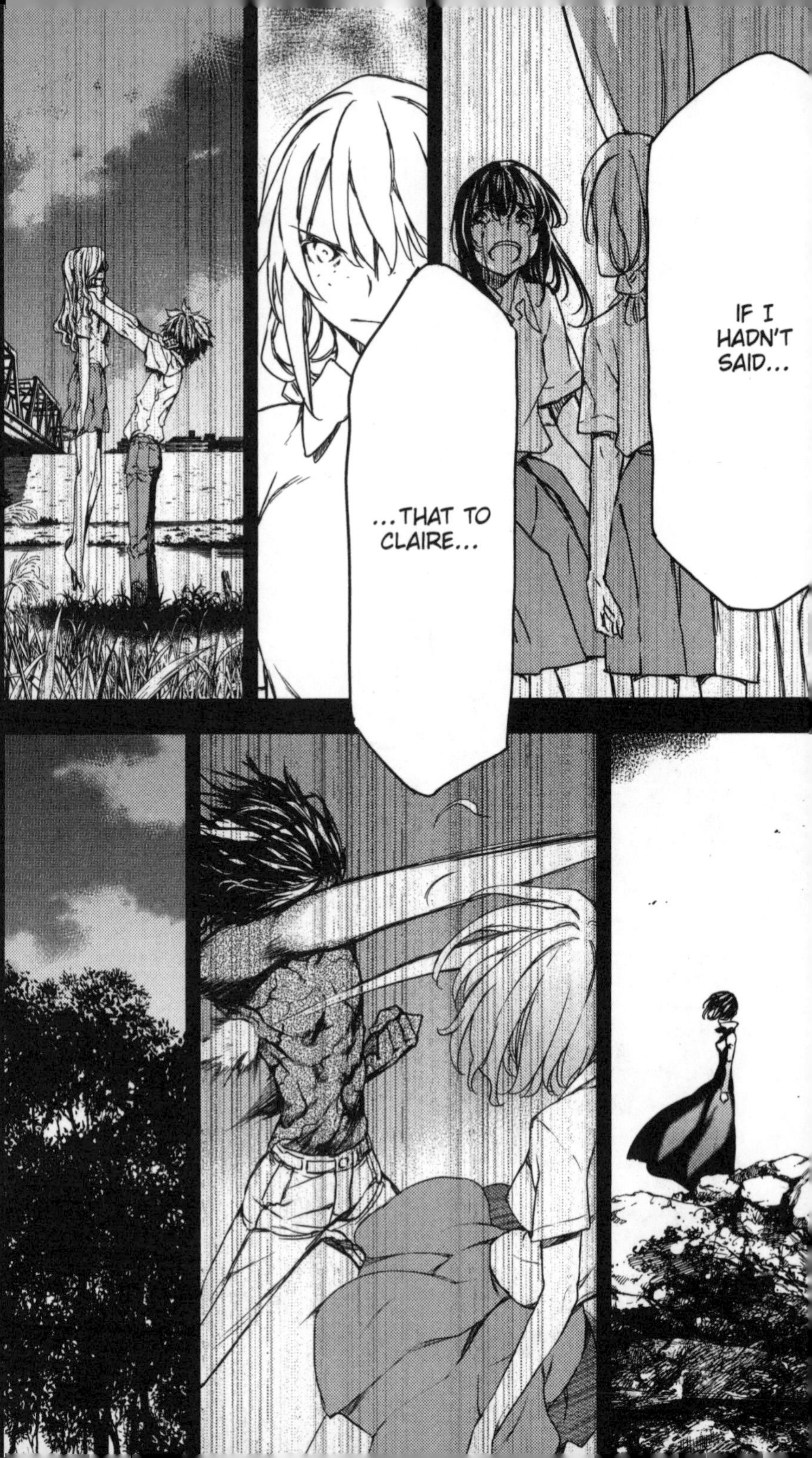
IF I HADN'T SAID...
...THAT TO CLAIRE...

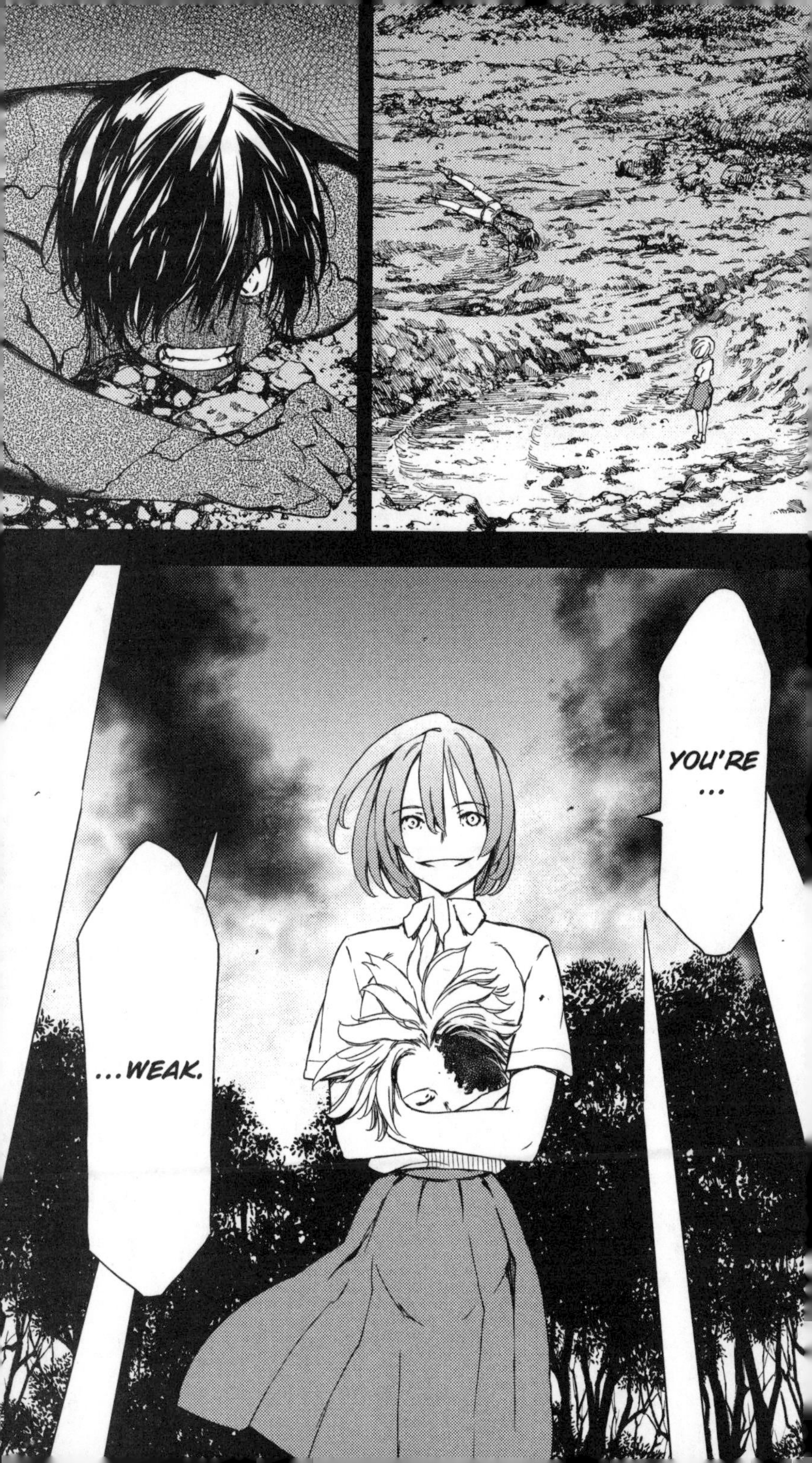
YOU'RE ...
...WEAK.

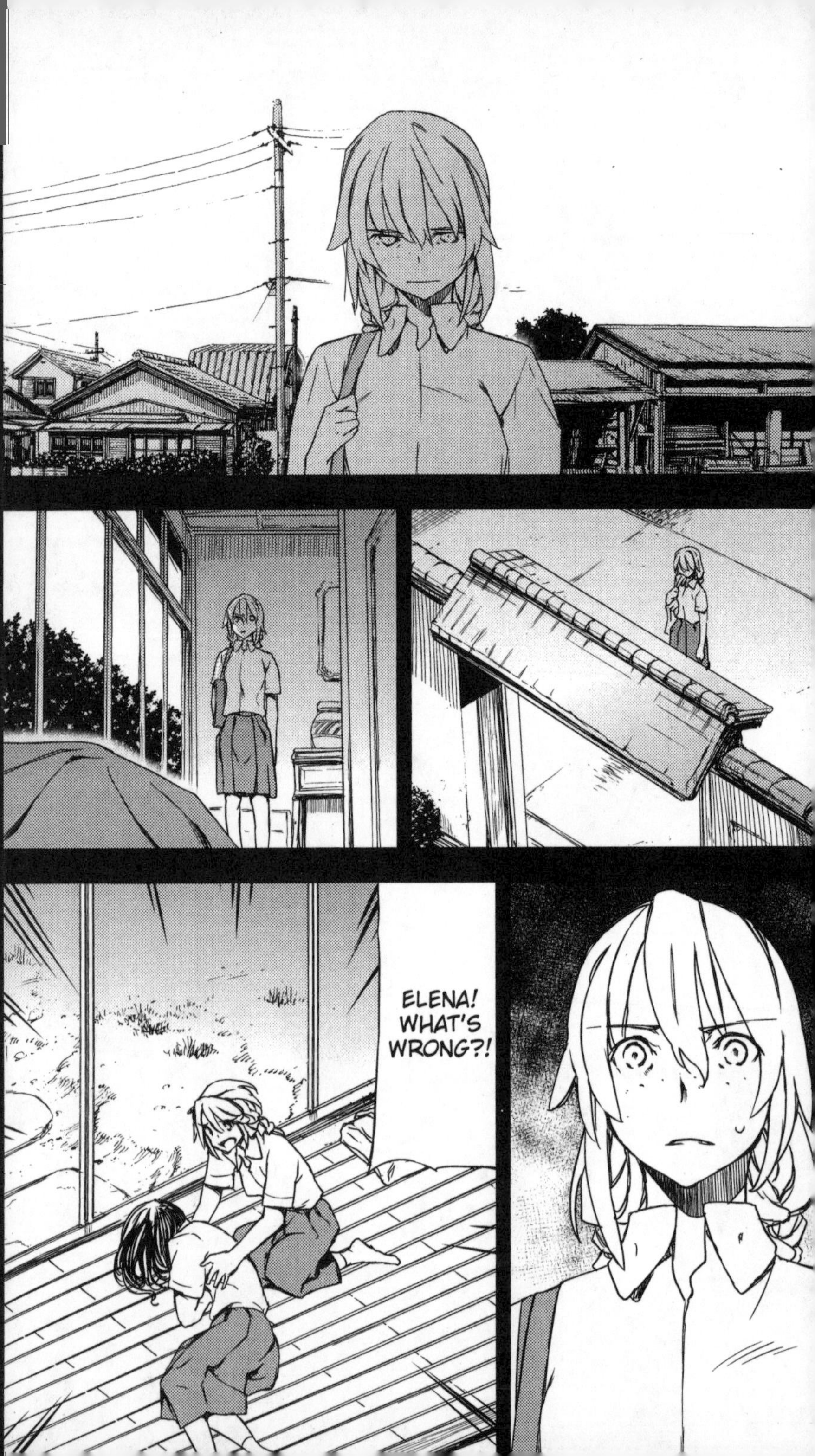
ELENA! WHAT'S WRONG?!

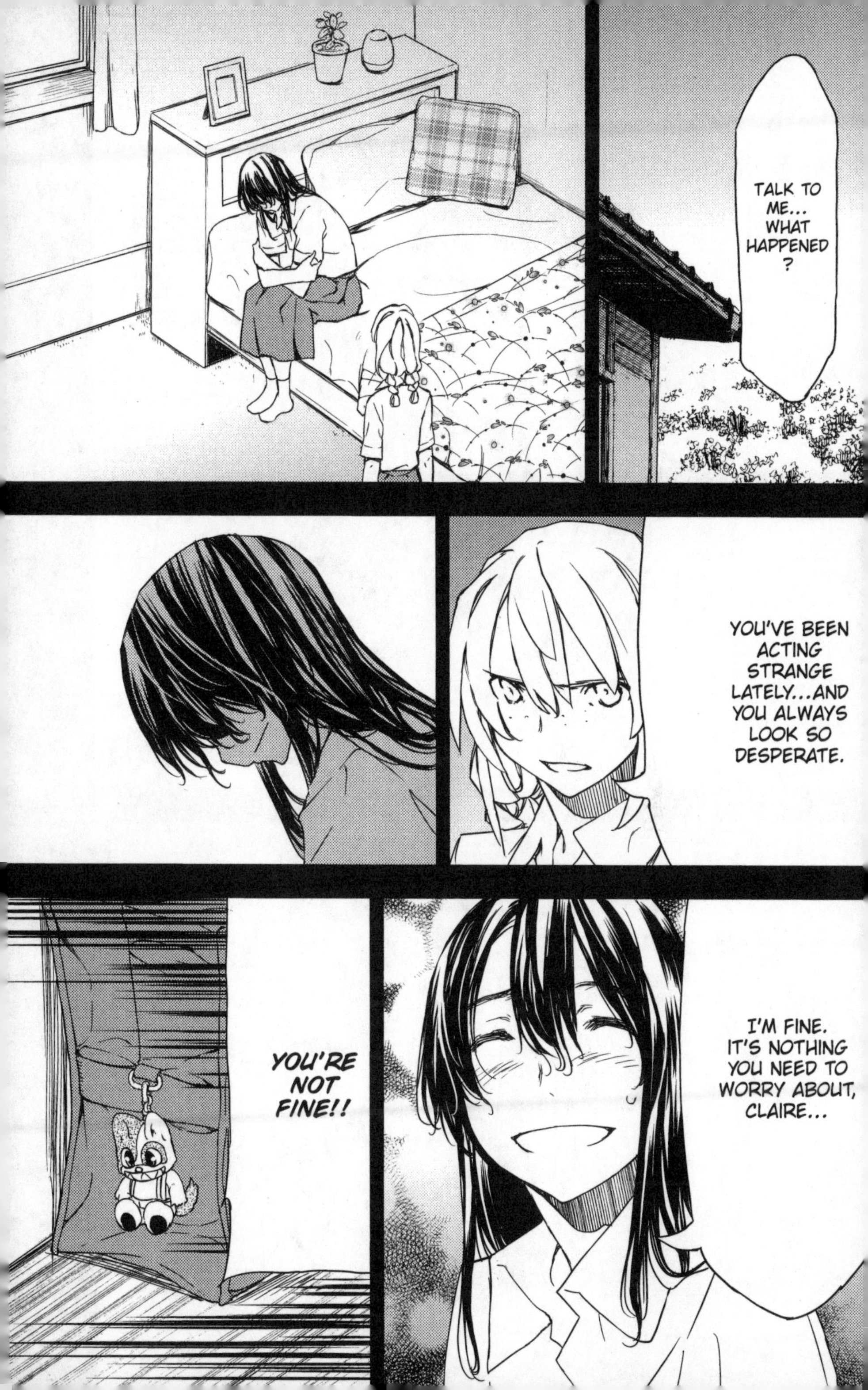
TALK TO ME... WHAT HAPPENED?
YOU'VE BEEN ACTING STRANGE LATELY...AND YOU ALWAYS LOOK SO DESPERATE.
I'M FINE. IT'S NOTHING YOU NEED TO WORRY ABOUT, CLAIRE...
YOU'RE NOT FINE!!

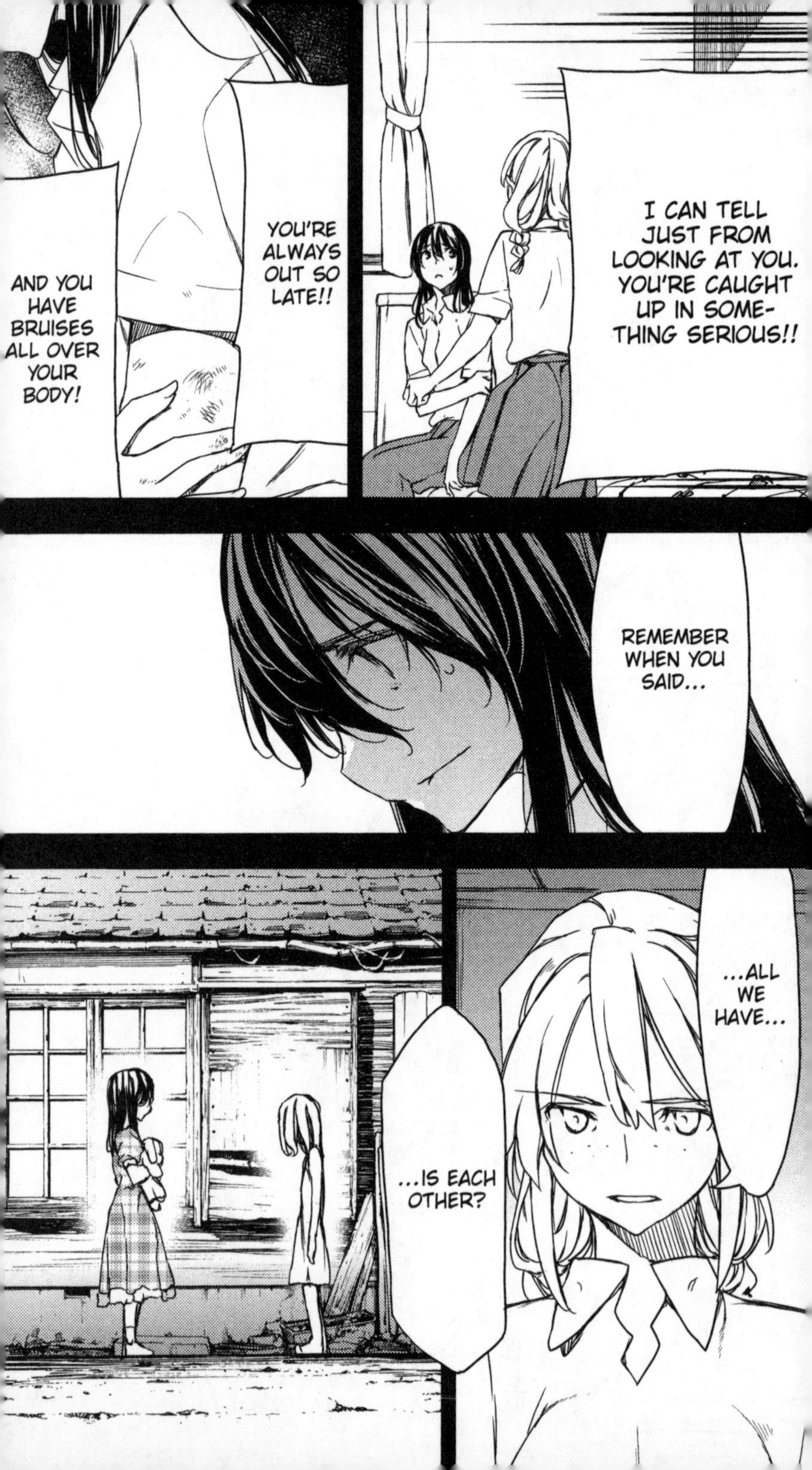
I CAN TELL JUST FROM LOOKING AT YOU. YOU'RE CAUGHT UP IN SOME-THING SERIOUS!!
YOU'RE ALWAYS OUT SO LATE!!
AND YOU HAVE BRUISES ALL OVER YOUR BODY!
REMEMBER WHEN YOU SAID...
...ALL WE HAVE...
...IS EACH OTHER?

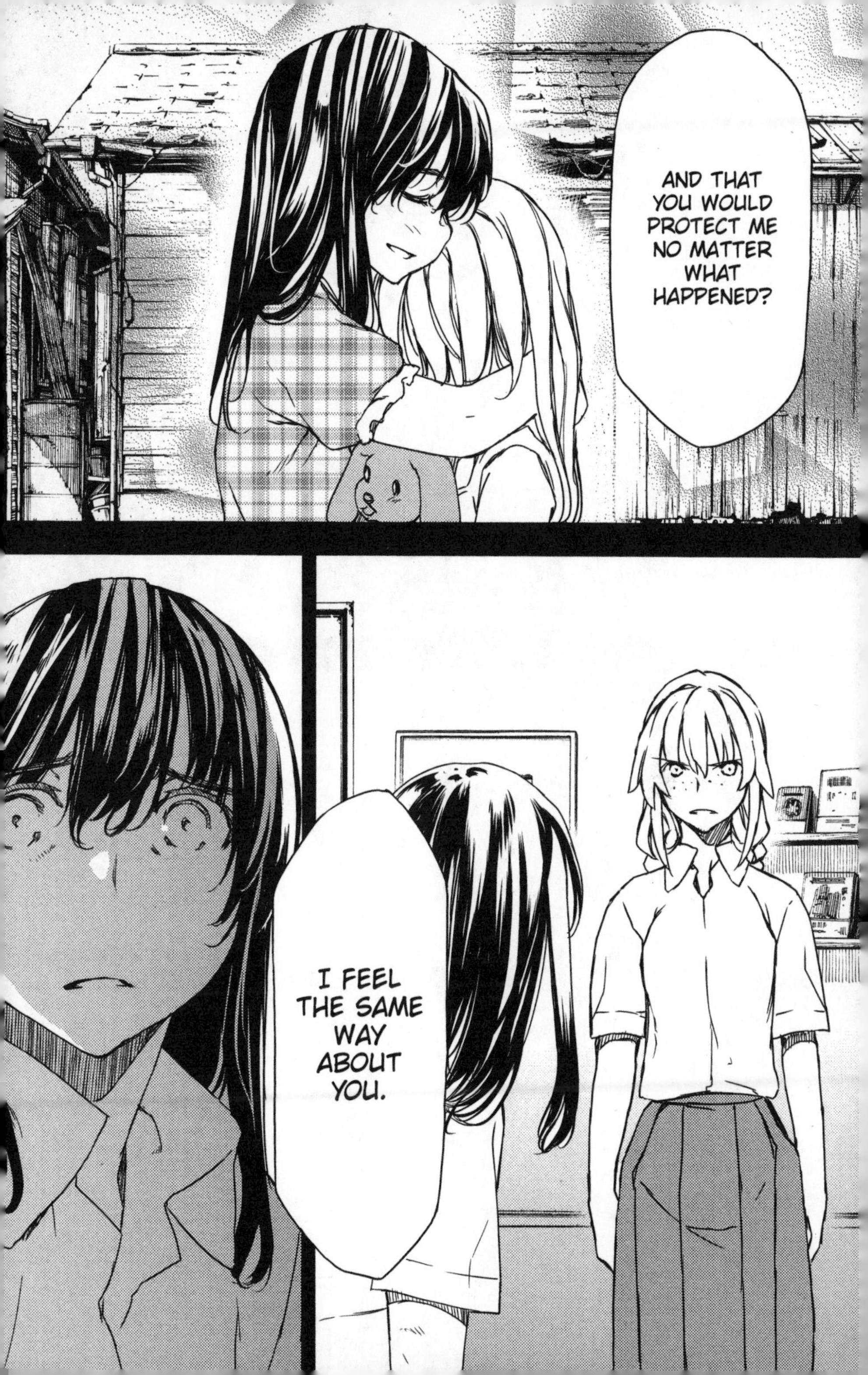
AND THAT YOU WOULD PROTECT ME NO MATTER WHAT HAPPENED?
I FEEL THE SAME WAY ABOUT YOU.

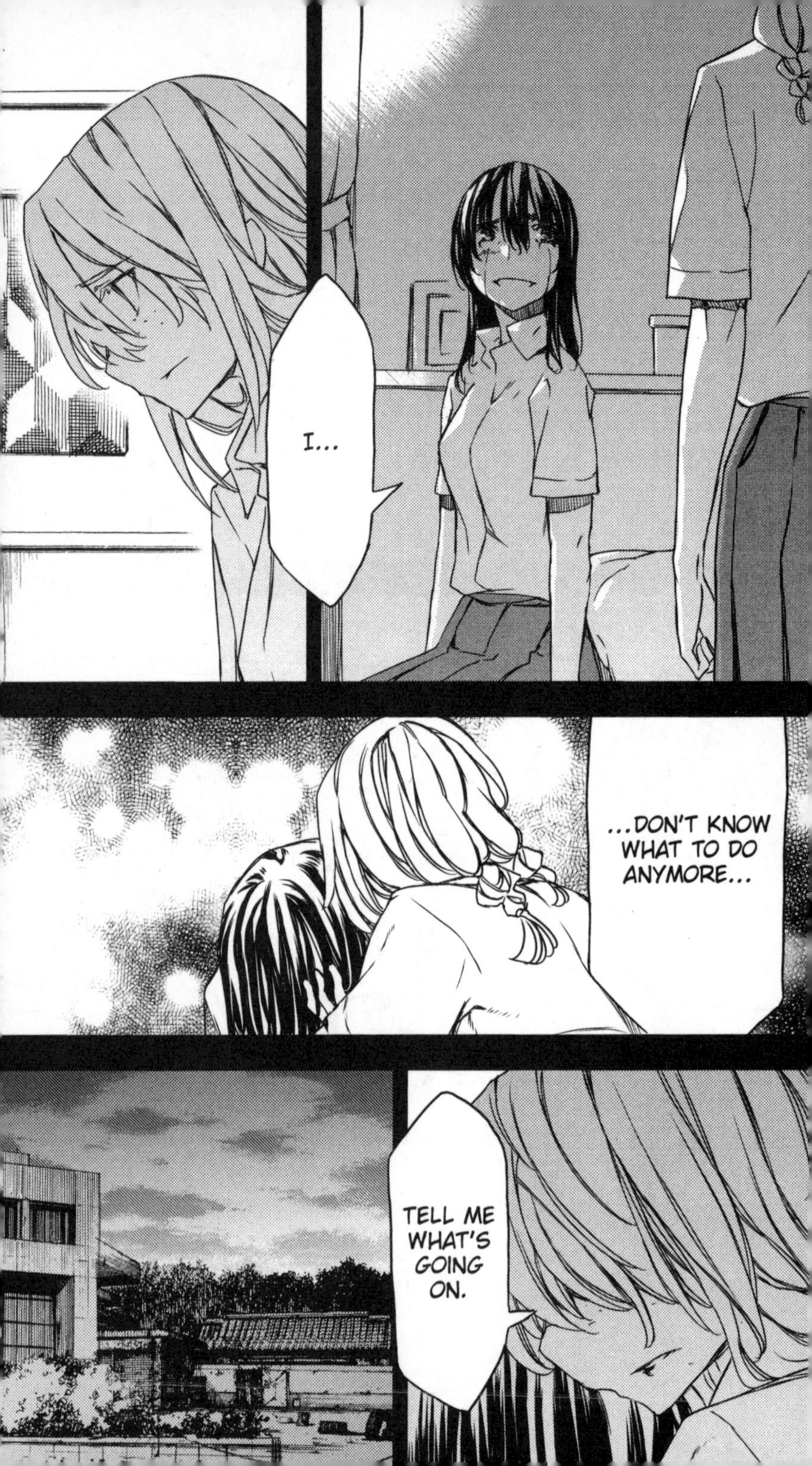
I...
...DON'T KNOW WHAT TO DO ANYMORE...
TELL ME WHAT'S GOING ON.

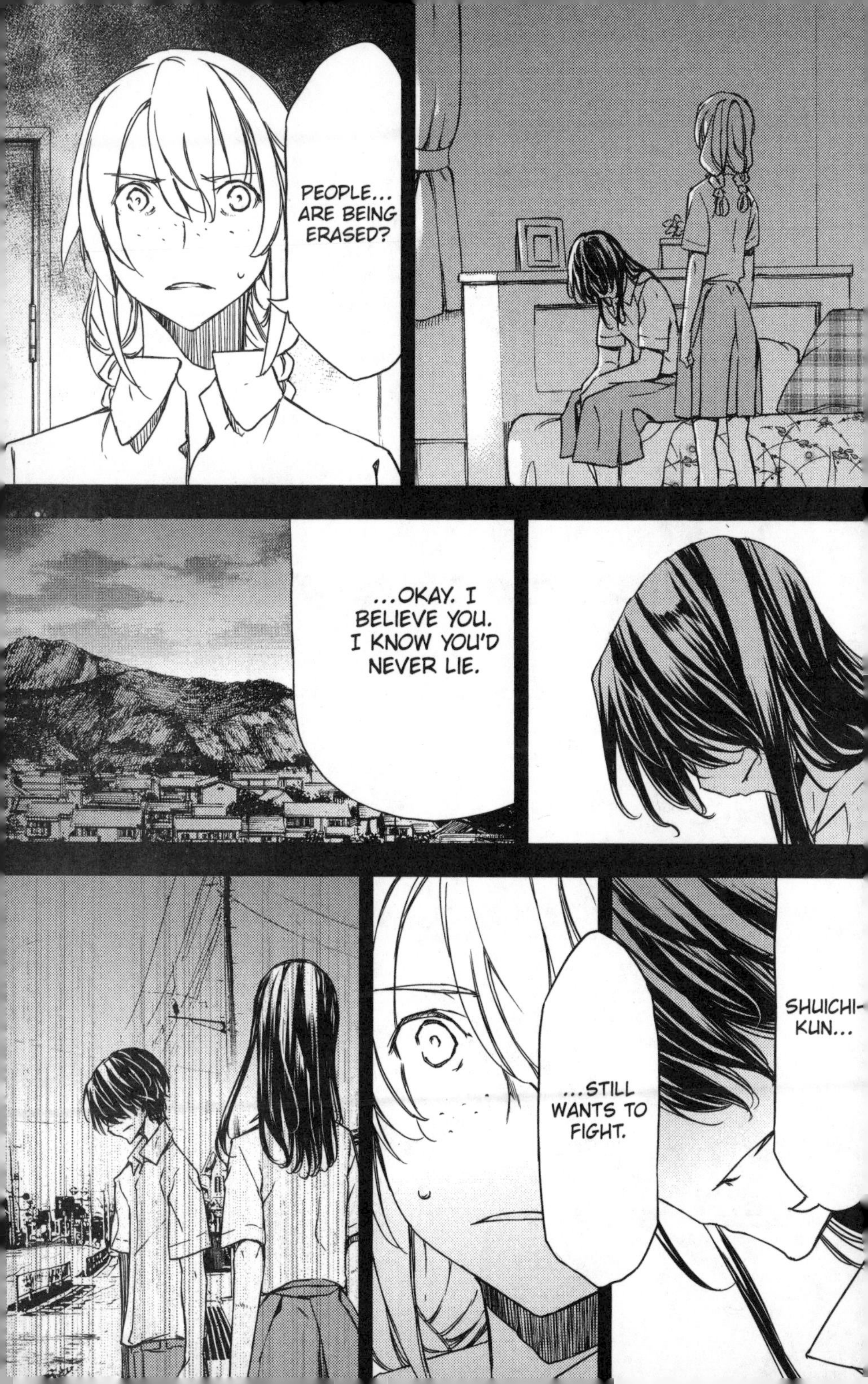
PEOPLE... ARE BEING ERASED?
...OKAY. I BELIEVE YOU. I KNOW YOU'D NEVER LIE.
SHUICHI-KUN...
...STILL WANTS TO FIGHT.

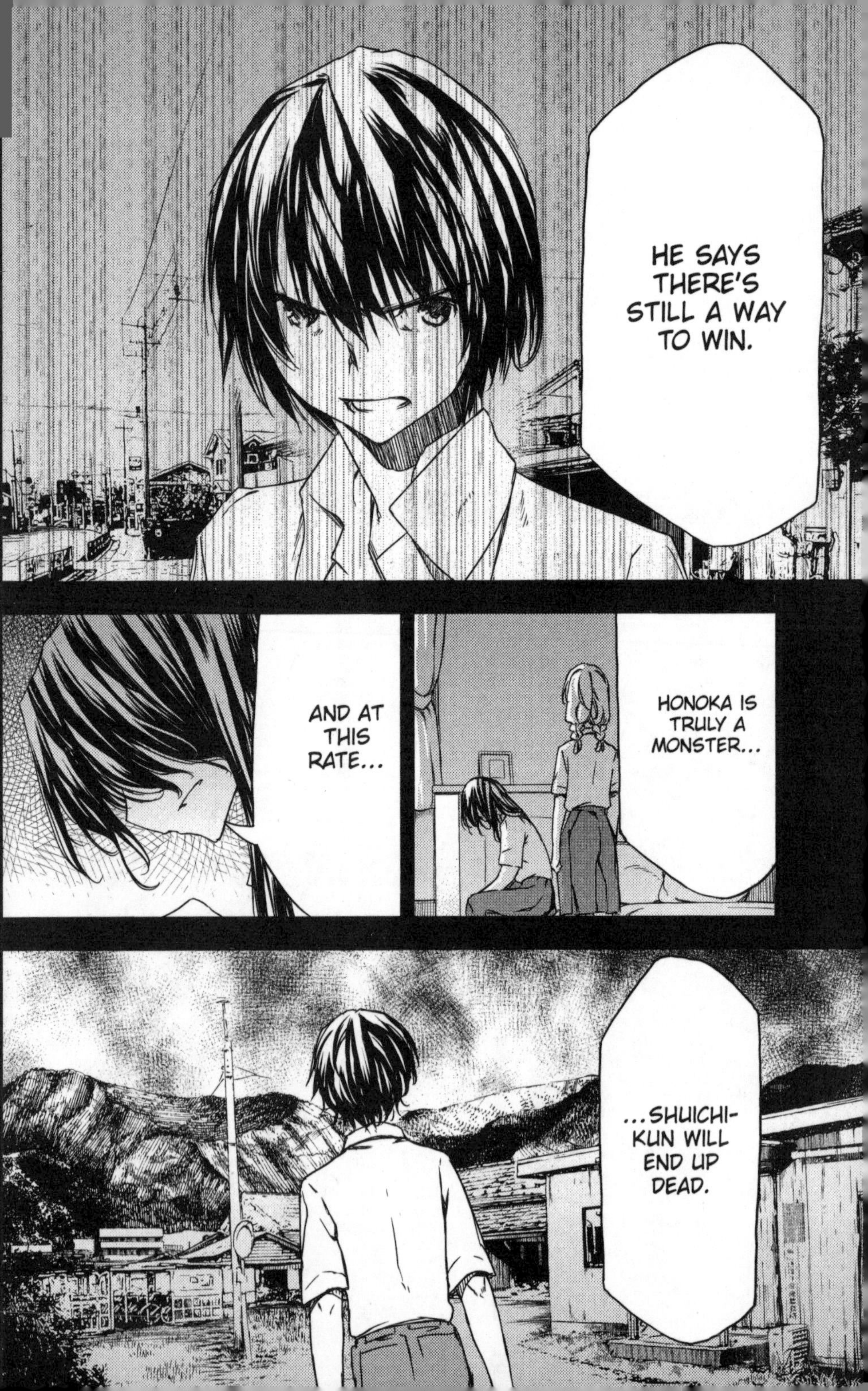
HE SAYS THERE'S STILL A WAY TO WIN.
HONOKA IS TRULY A MONSTER...
AND AT THIS RATE...
...SHUICHI-KUN WILL END UP DEAD.

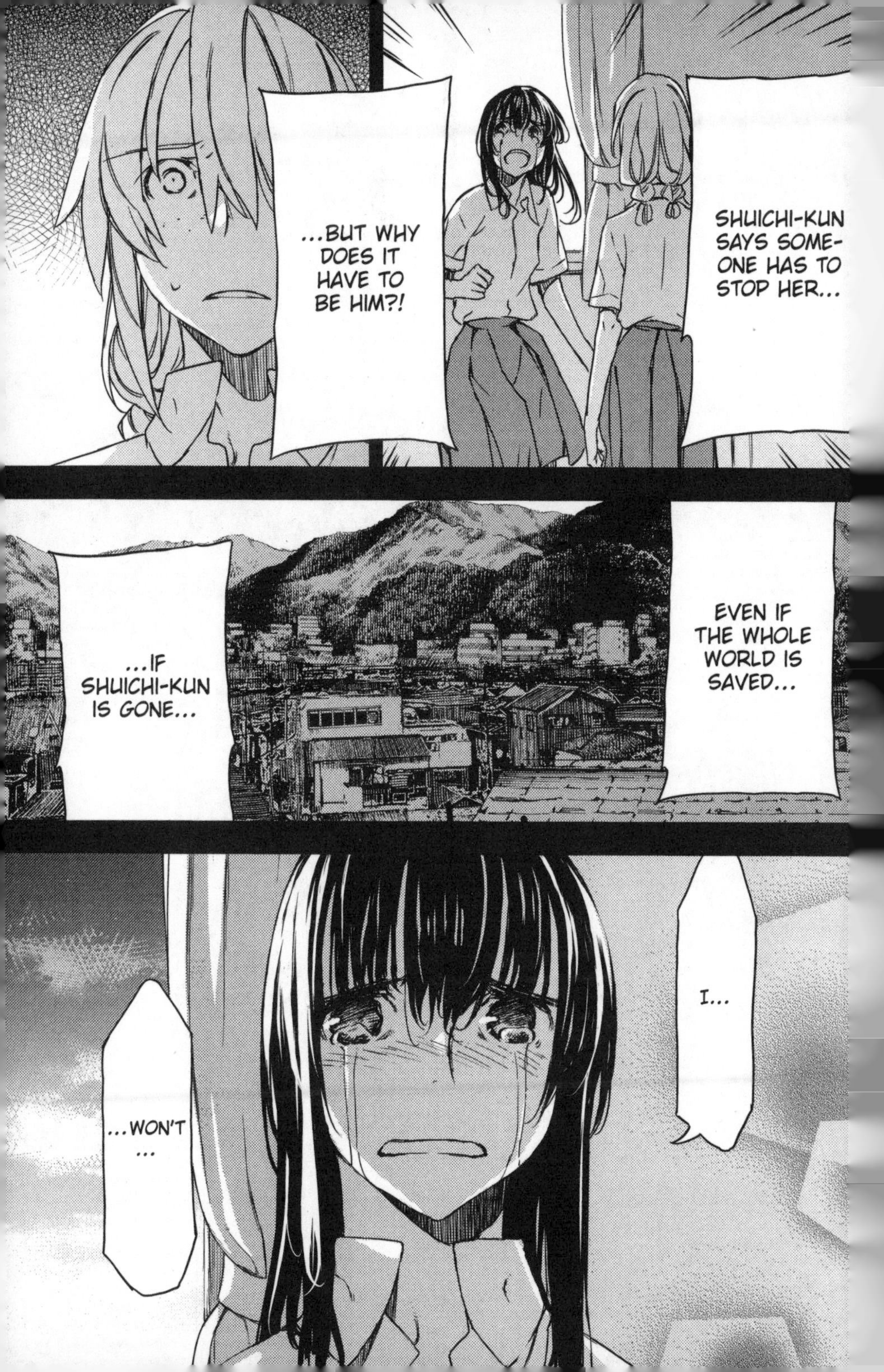
SHUICHI-KUN SAYS SOME-ONE HAS TO STOP HER...
...BUT WHY DOES IT HAVE TO BE HIM?!
EVEN IF THE WHOLE WORLD IS SAVED...
...IF SHUICHI-KUN IS GONE...
I...
...WON'T ...

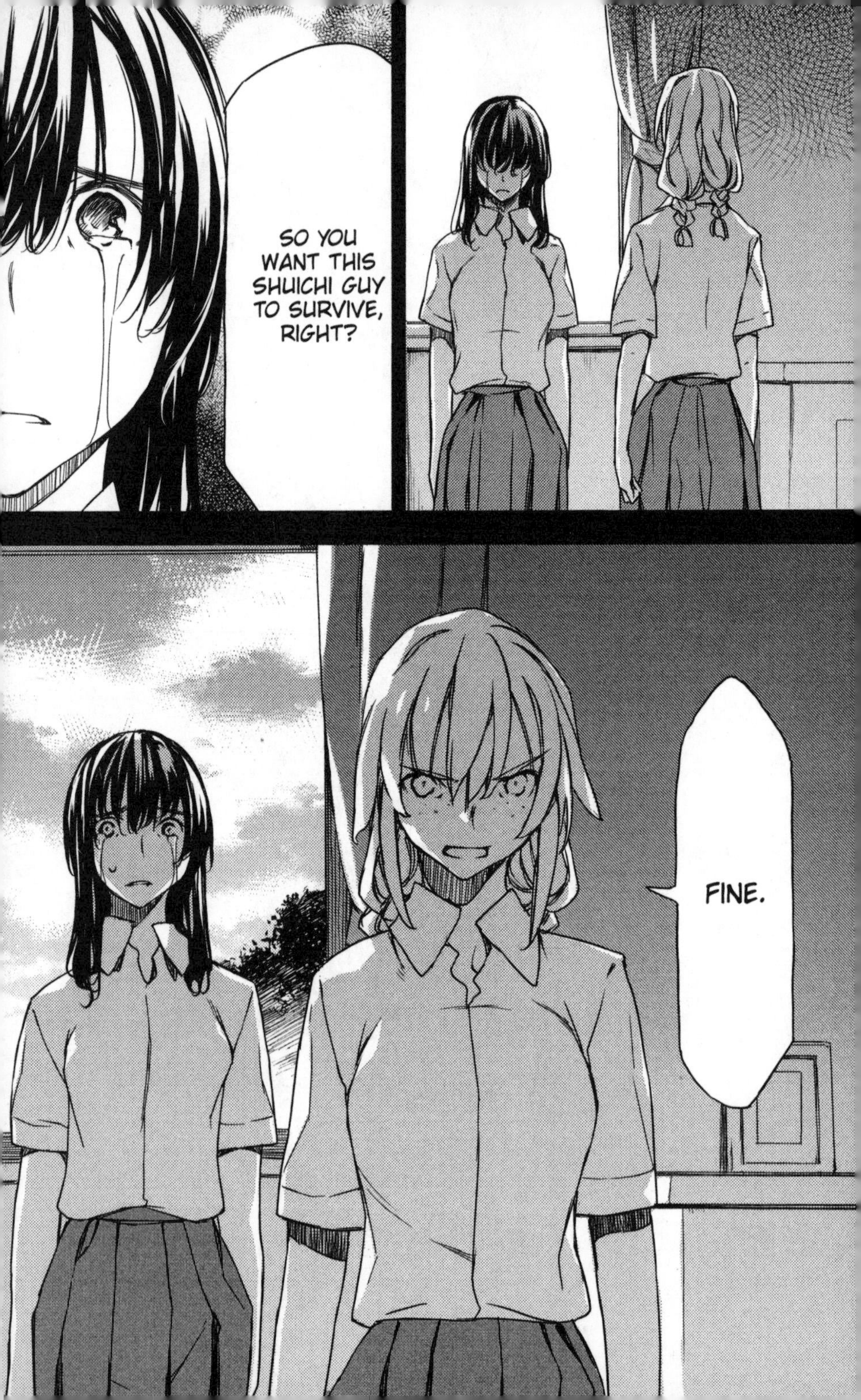
SO YOU WANT THIS SHUICHI GUY TO SURVIVE, RIGHT?
FINE.

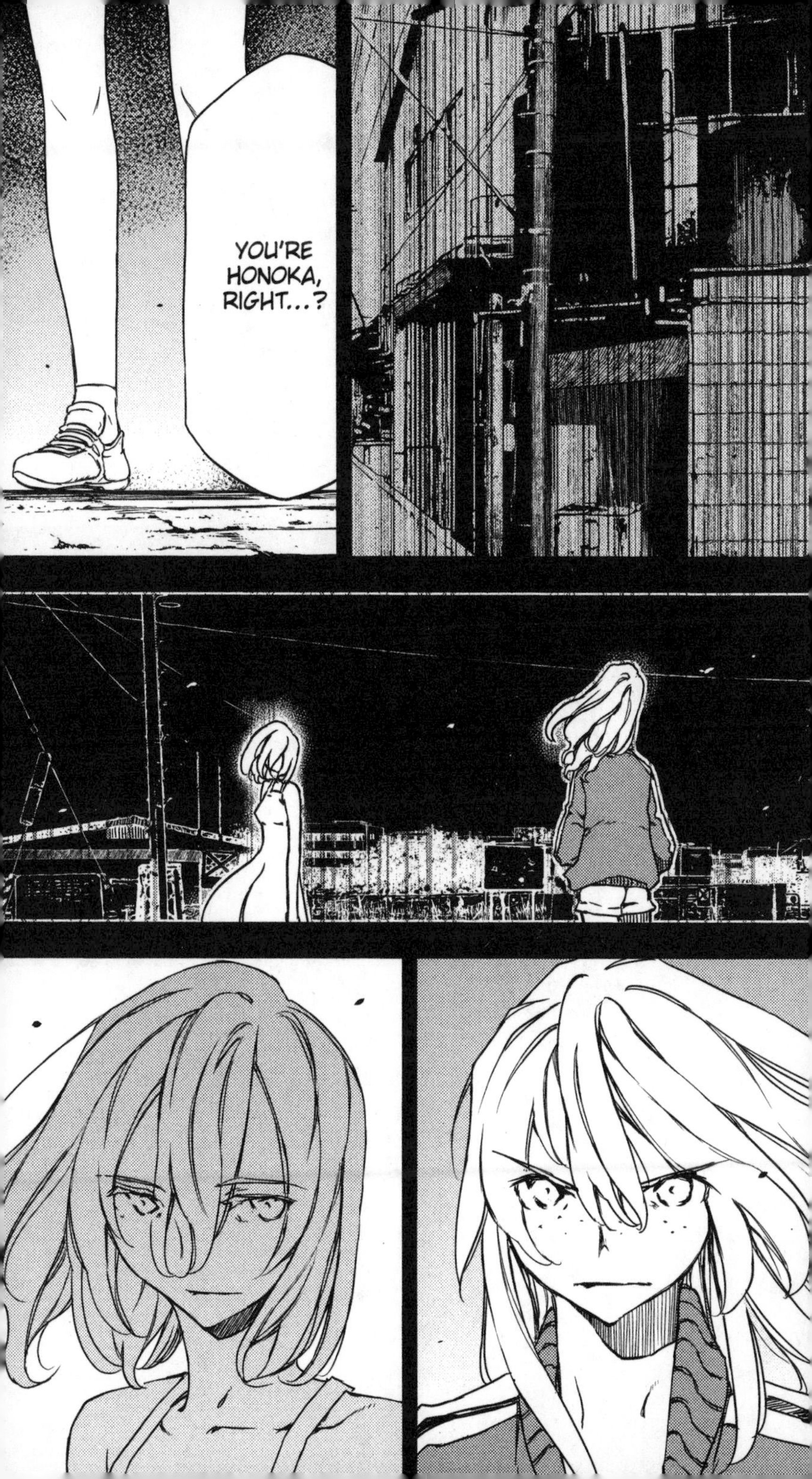
YOU'RE HONOKA, RIGHT...?

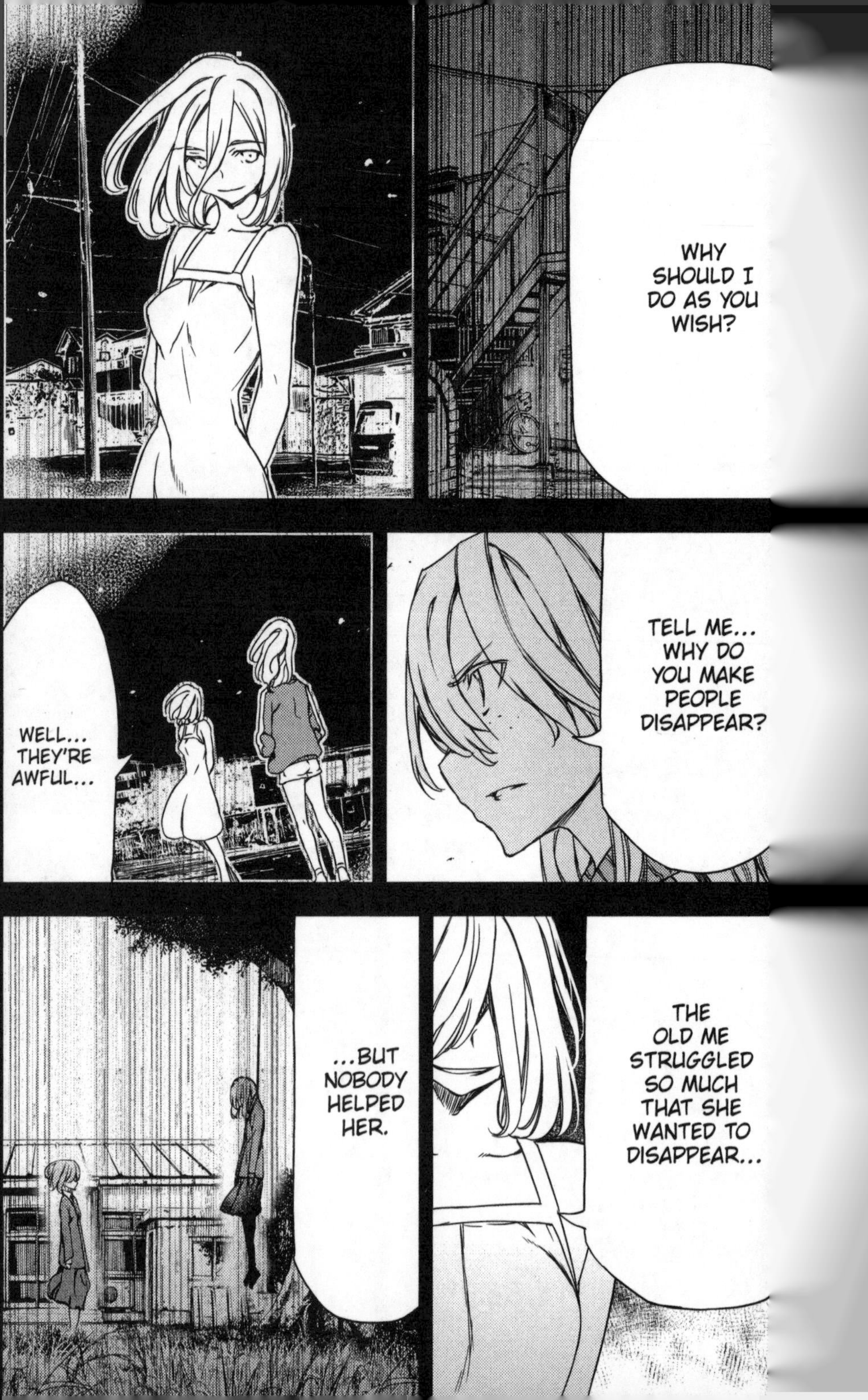
WHY SHOULD I DO AS YOU WISH?
TELL ME... WHY DO YOU MAKE PEOPLE DISAPPEAR?
WELL... THEY'RE AWFUL...
THE OLD ME STRUGGLED SO MUCH THAT SHE WANTED TO DISAPPEAR...
...BUT NOBODY HELPED HER.

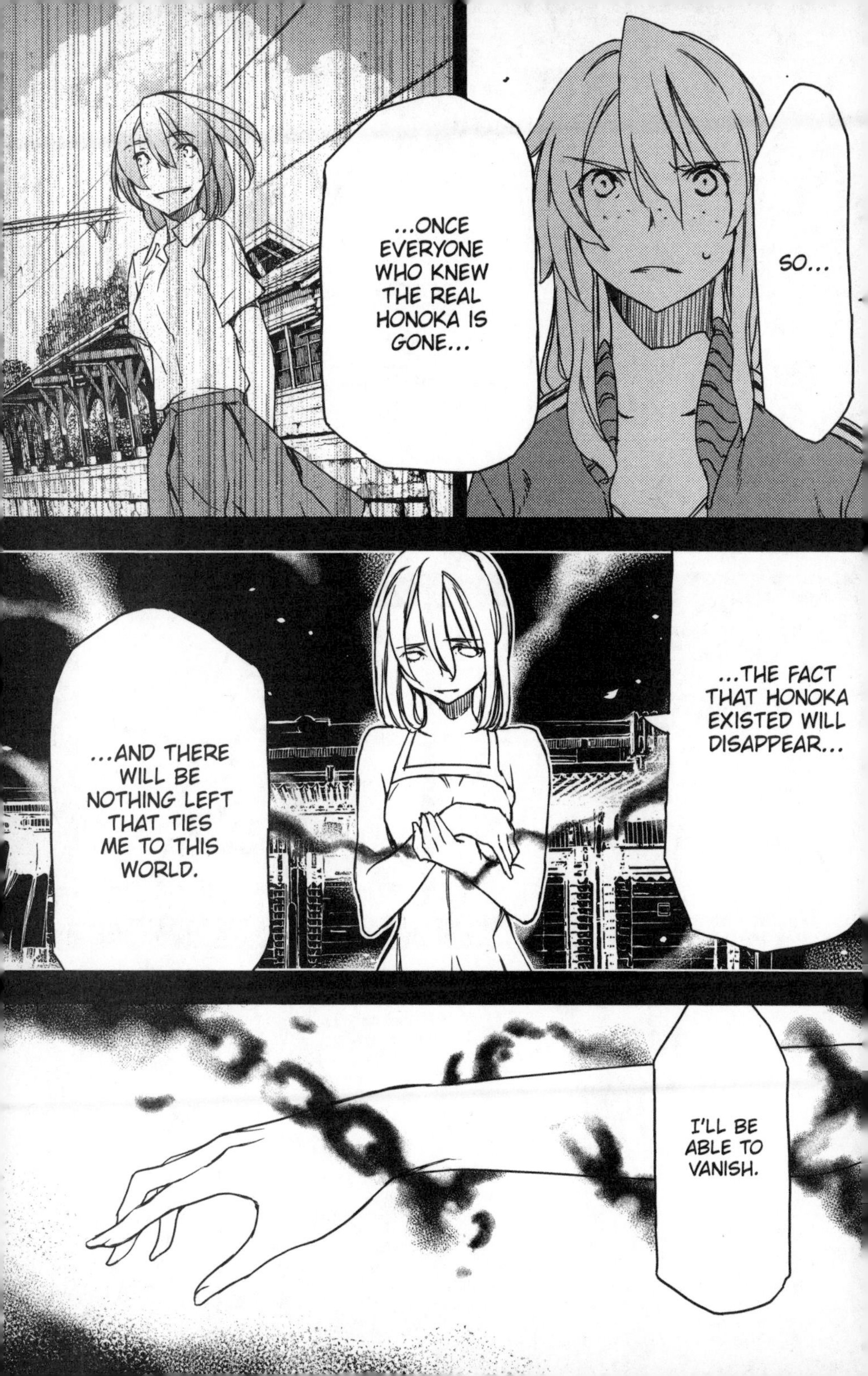
SO...
...ONCE EVERYONE WHO KNEW THE REAL HONOKA IS GONE...
...THE FACT THAT HONOKA EXISTED WILL DISAPPEAR...
...AND THERE WILL BE NOTHING LEFT THAT TIES ME TO THIS WORLD.
I'LL BE ABLE TO VANISH.

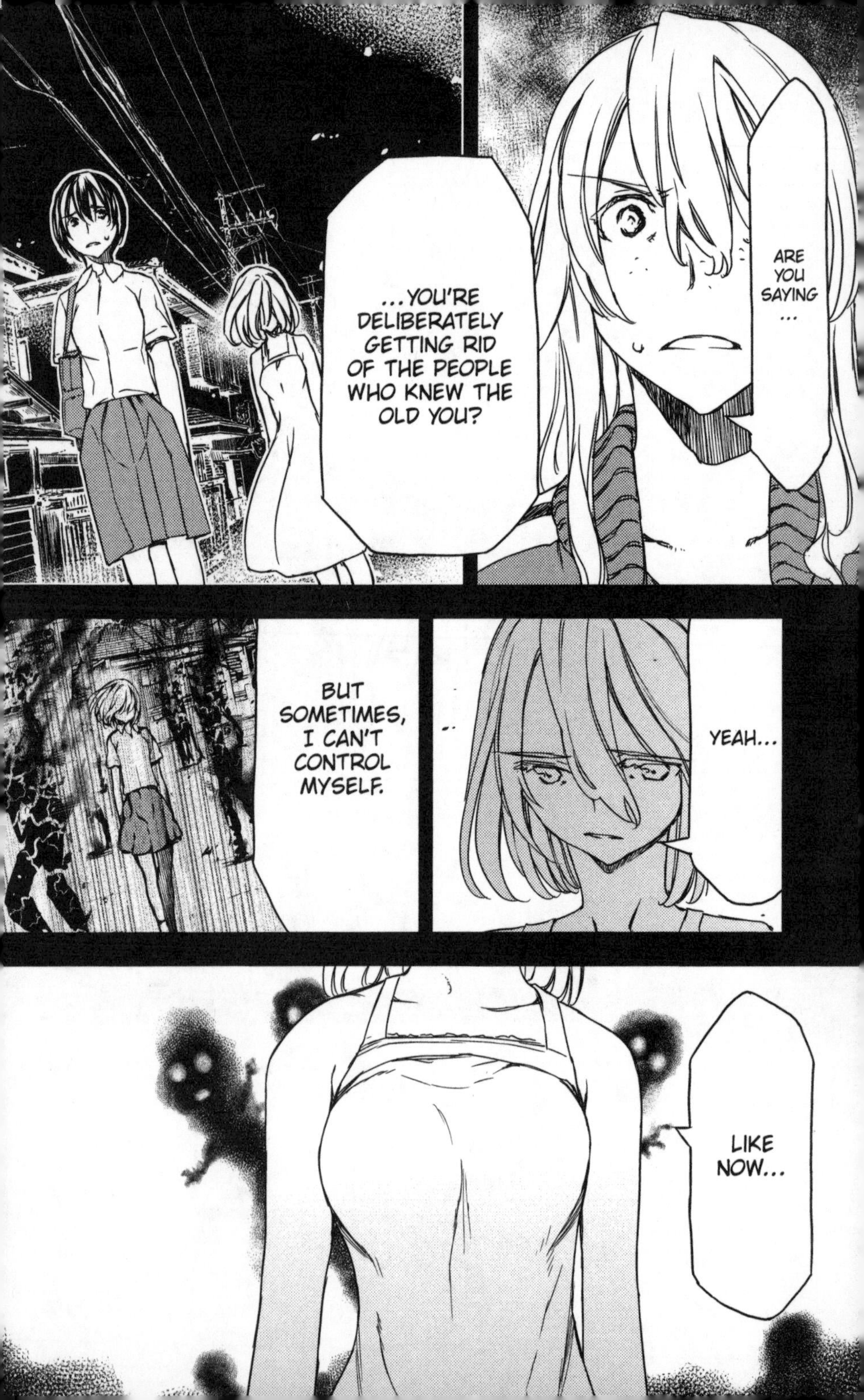
ARE YOU SAYING ...
...YOU'RE DELIBERATELY GETTING RID OF THE PEOPLE WHO KNEW THE OLD YOU?
YEAH...
BUT SOMETIMES, I CAN'T CONTROL MYSELF.
LIKE NOW...

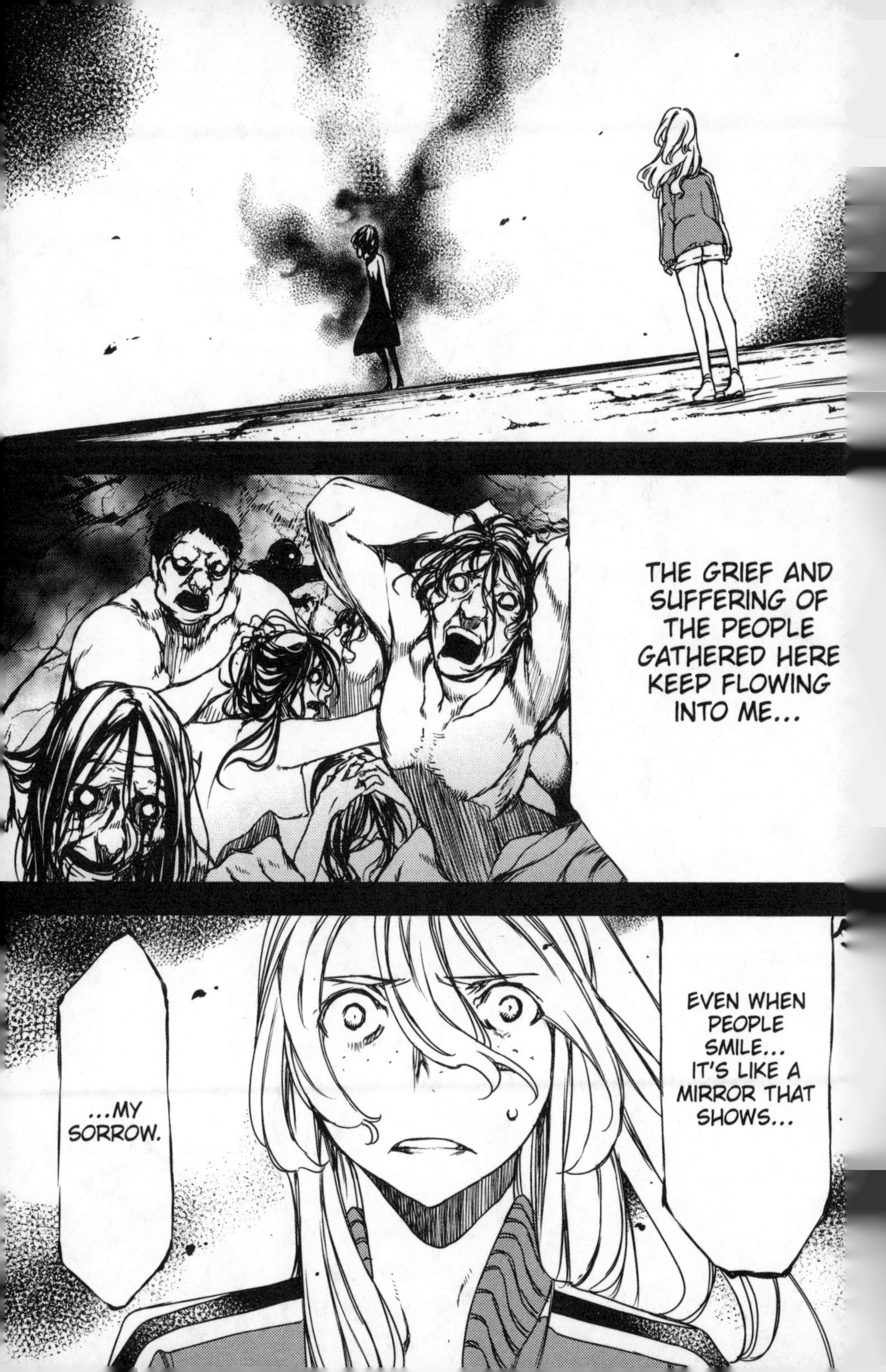
THE GRIEF AND SUFFERING OF THE PEOPLE GATHERED HERE KEEP FLOWING INTO ME...
EVEN WHEN PEOPLE SMILE... IT'S LIKE A MIRROR THAT SHOWS...
...MY SORROW.

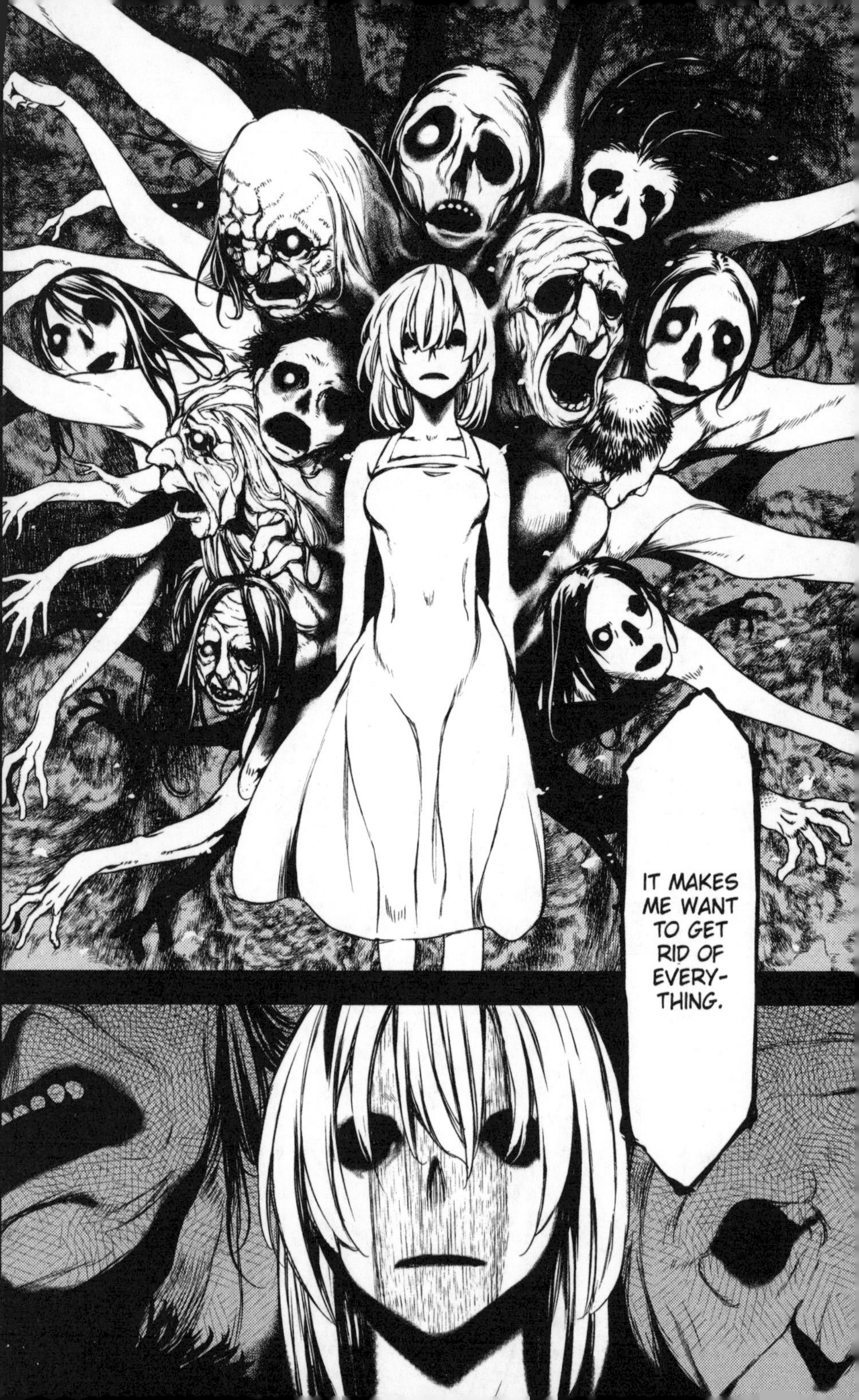
IT MAKES ME WANT TO GET RID OF EVERY-THING.

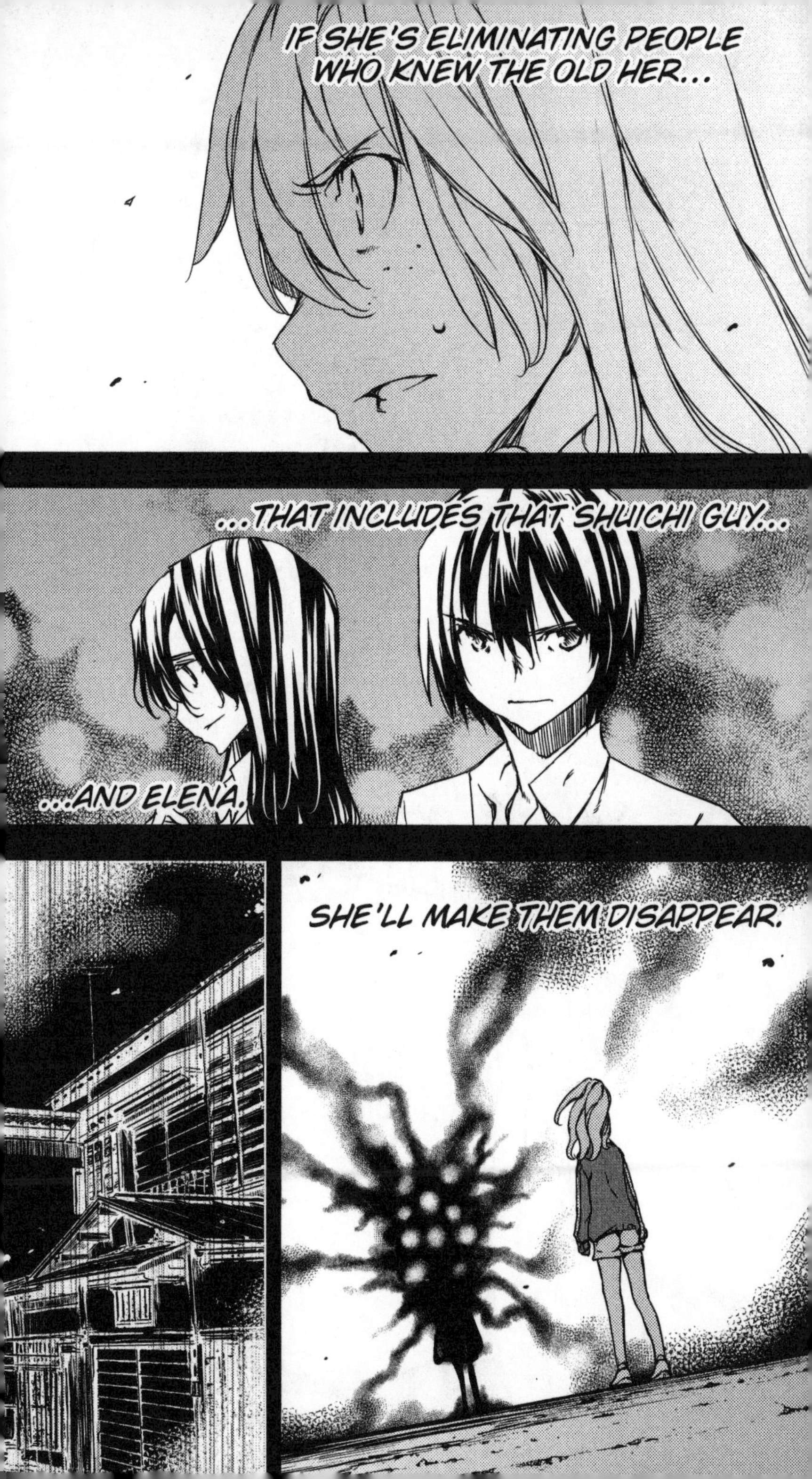
IF SHE'S ELIMINATING PEOPLE WHO KNEW THE OLD HER...
...THAT INCLUDES THAT SHUICHI GUY...
...AND ELENA.
SHE'LL MAKE THEM DISAPPEAR.

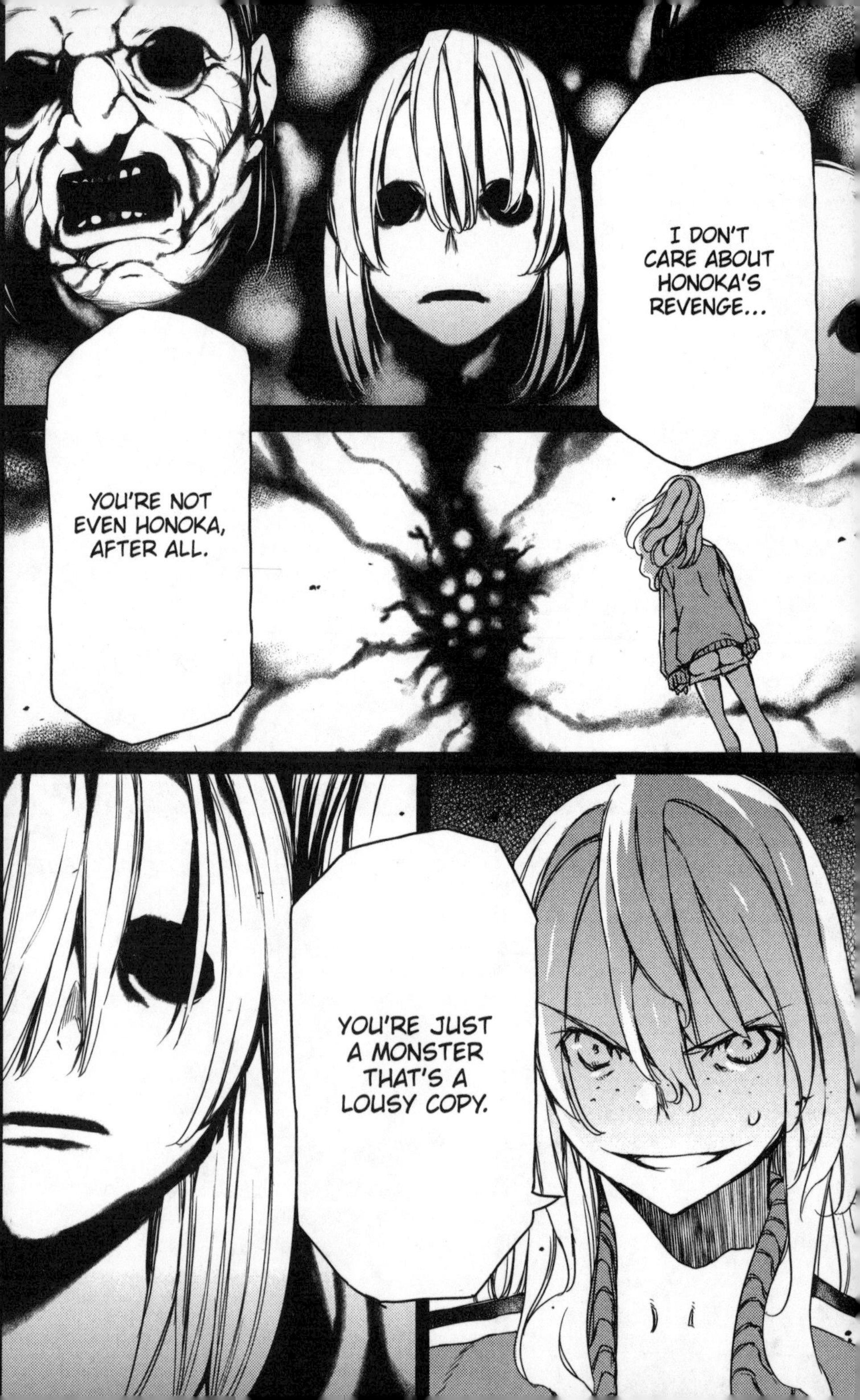
I DON'T CARE ABOUT HONOKA'S REVENGE...
YOU'RE NOT EVEN HONOKA, AFTER ALL.
YOU'RE JUST A MONSTER THAT'S A LOUSY COPY.

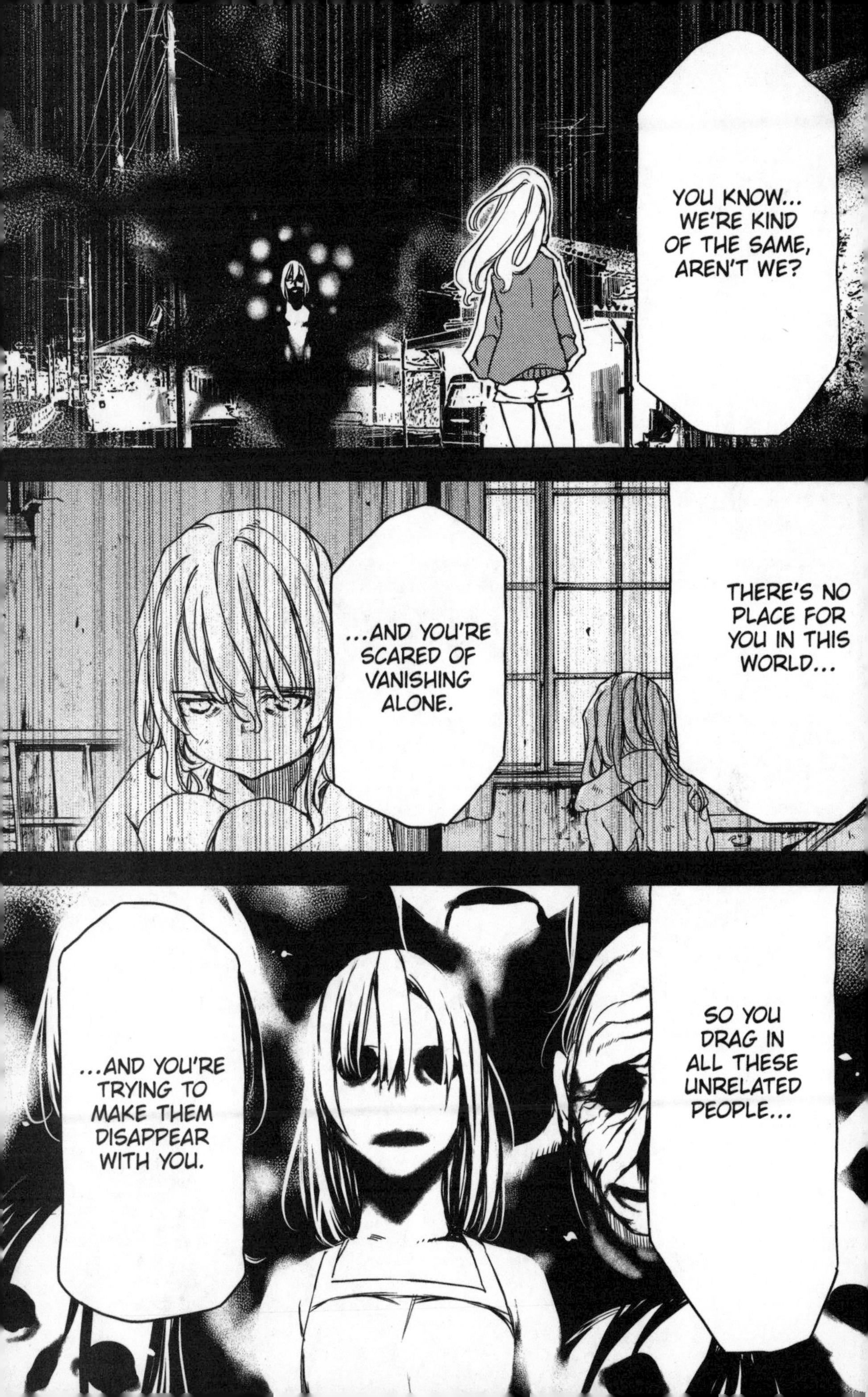
YOU KNOW... WE'RE KIND OF THE SAME, AREN'T WE?
THERE'S NO PLACE FOR YOU IN THIS WORLD...
...AND YOU'RE SCARED OF VANISHING ALONE.
SO YOU DRAG IN ALL THESE UNRELATED PEOPLE...
...AND YOU'RE TRYING TO MAKE THEM DISAPPEAR WITH YOU.

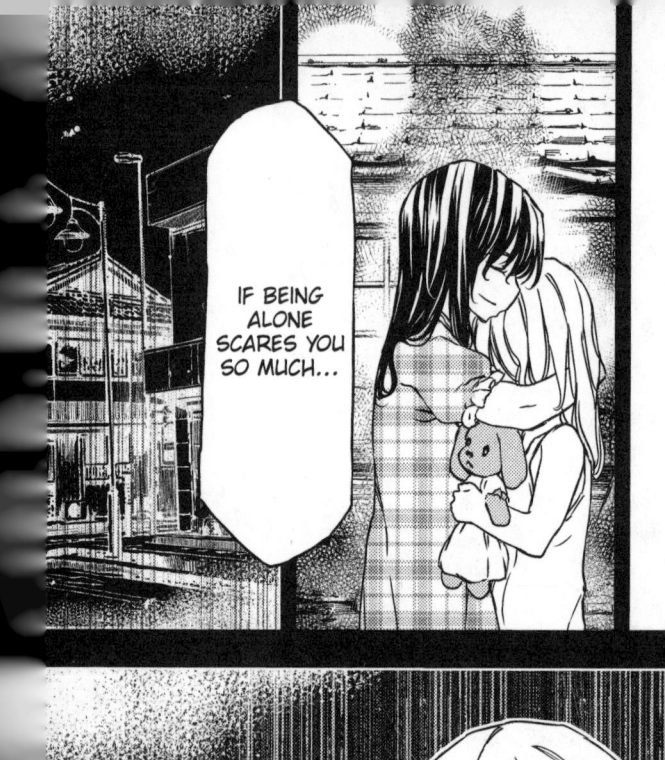

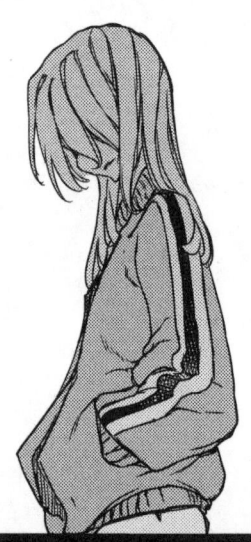

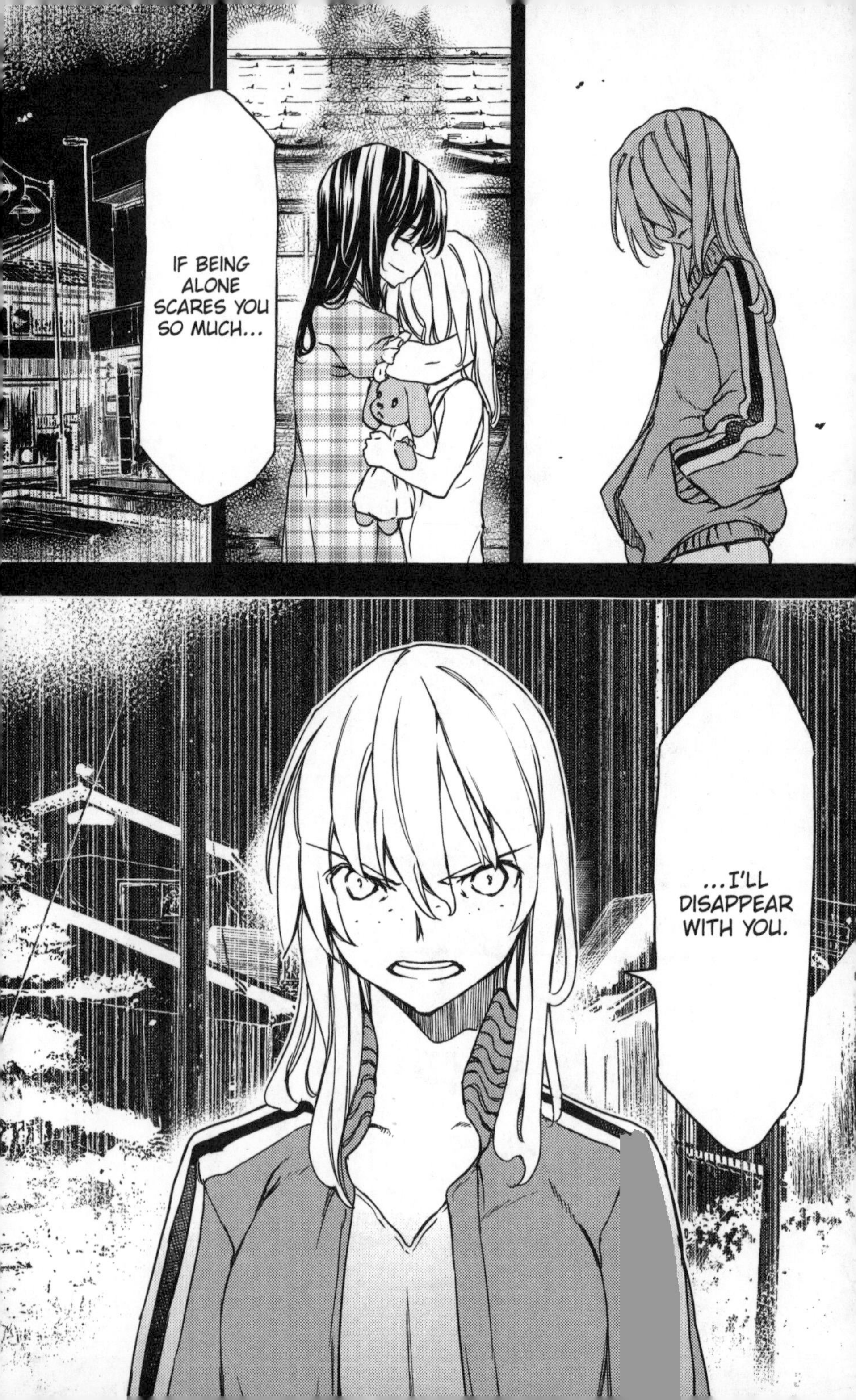
IF BEING ALONE SCARES YOU SO MUCH...
...I'LL DISAPPEAR WITH YOU.

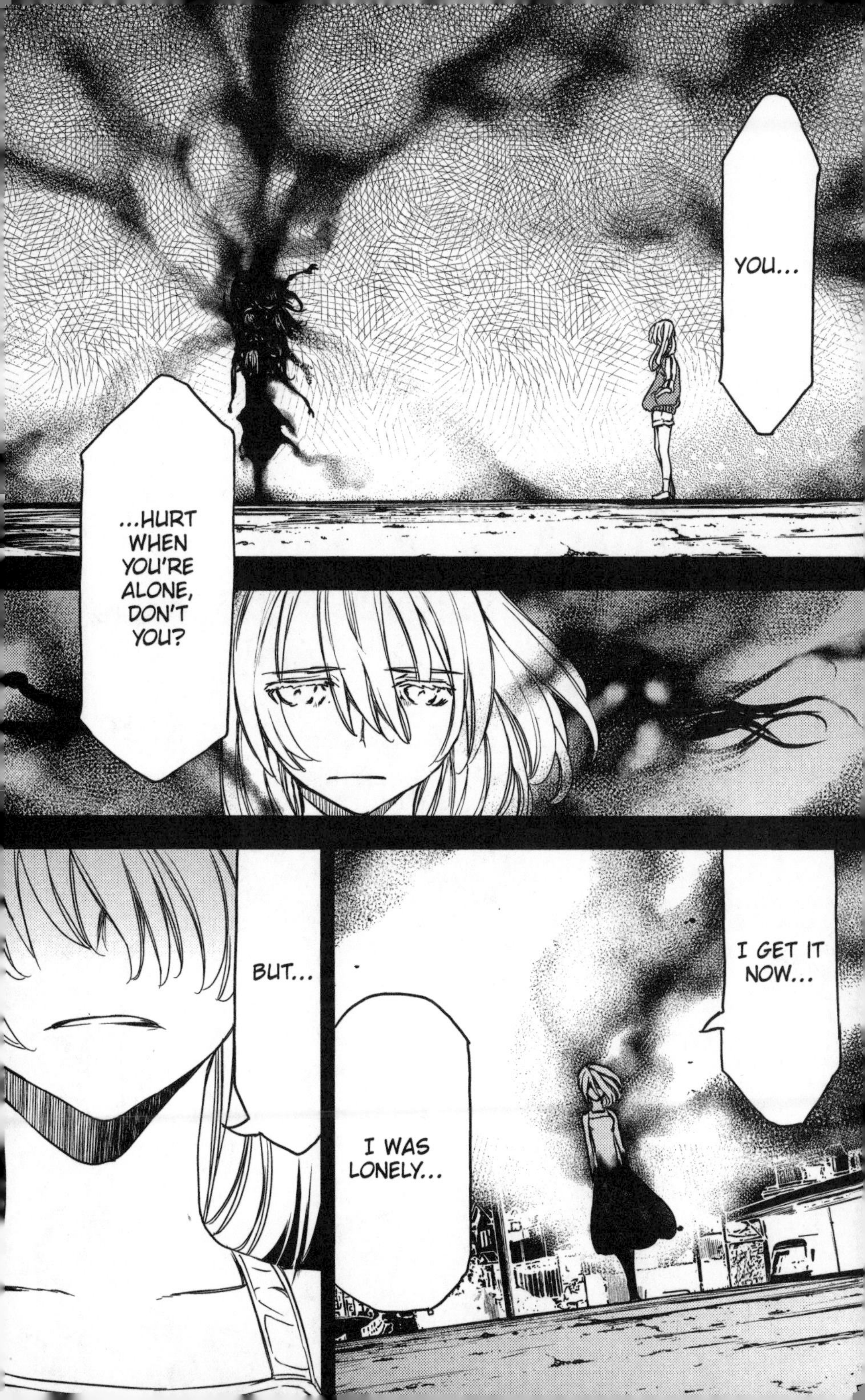
YOU...
...HURT WHEN YOU'RE ALONE, DON'T YOU?
I GET IT NOW...
I WAS LONELY...
BUT...

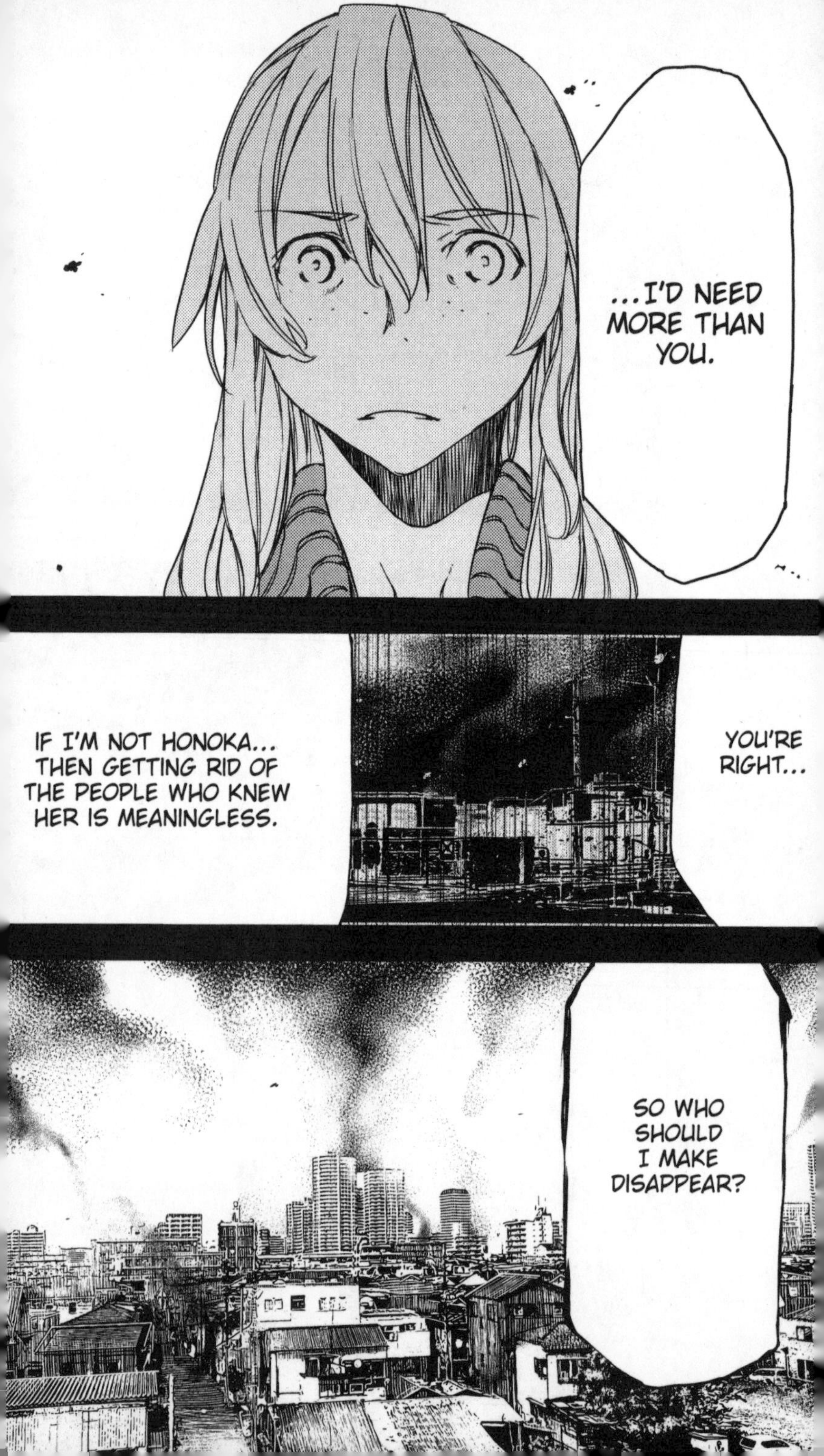
...I'D NEED MORE THAN YOU.
YOU'RE RIGHT...
IF I'M NOT HONOKA... THEN GETTING RID OF THE PEOPLE WHO KNEW HER IS MEANINGLESS.
SO WHO SHOULD I MAKE DISAPPEAR?

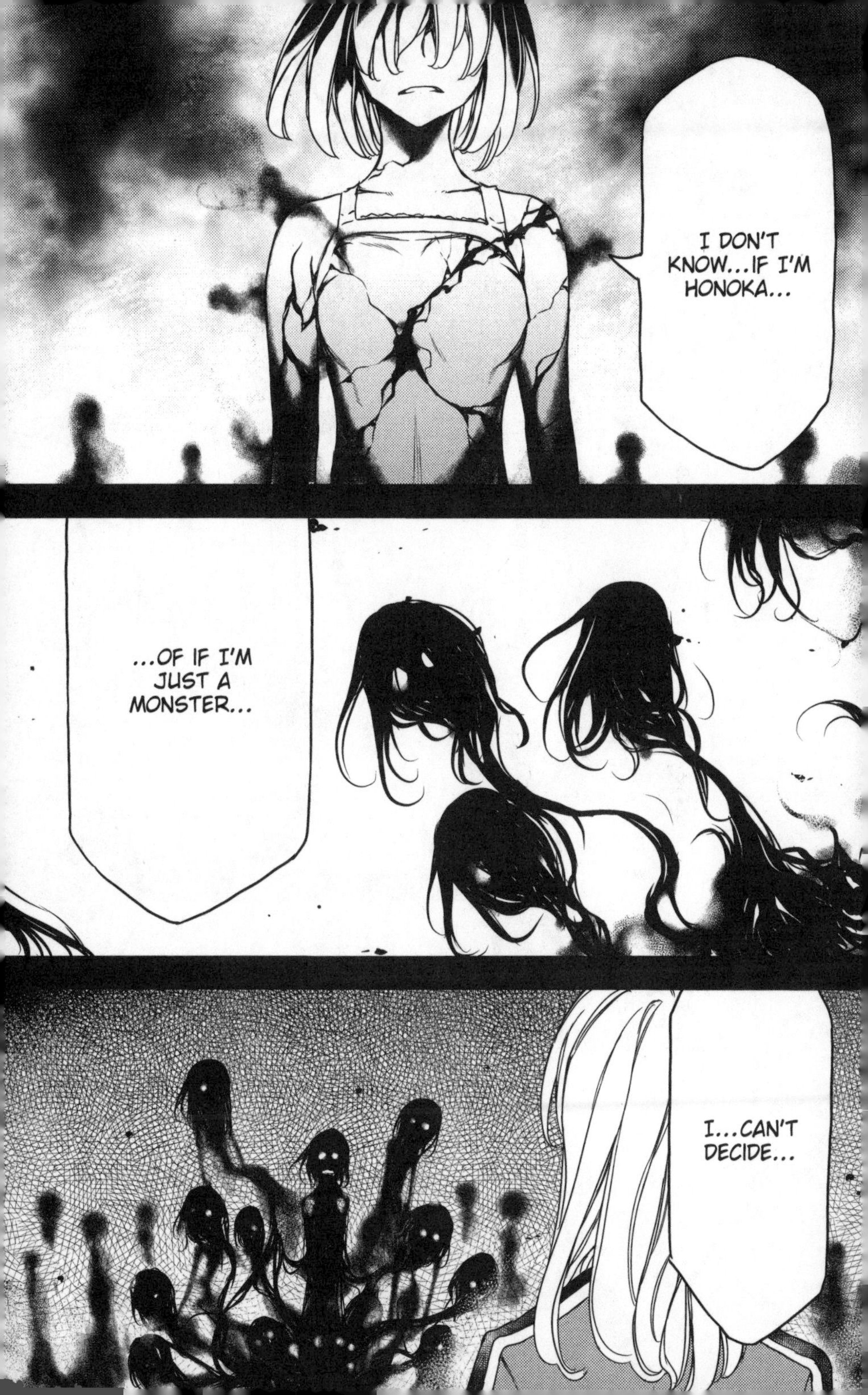
I DON'T KNOW...IF I'M HONOKA...
...OF IF I'M JUST A MONSTER...
I...CAN'T DECIDE...

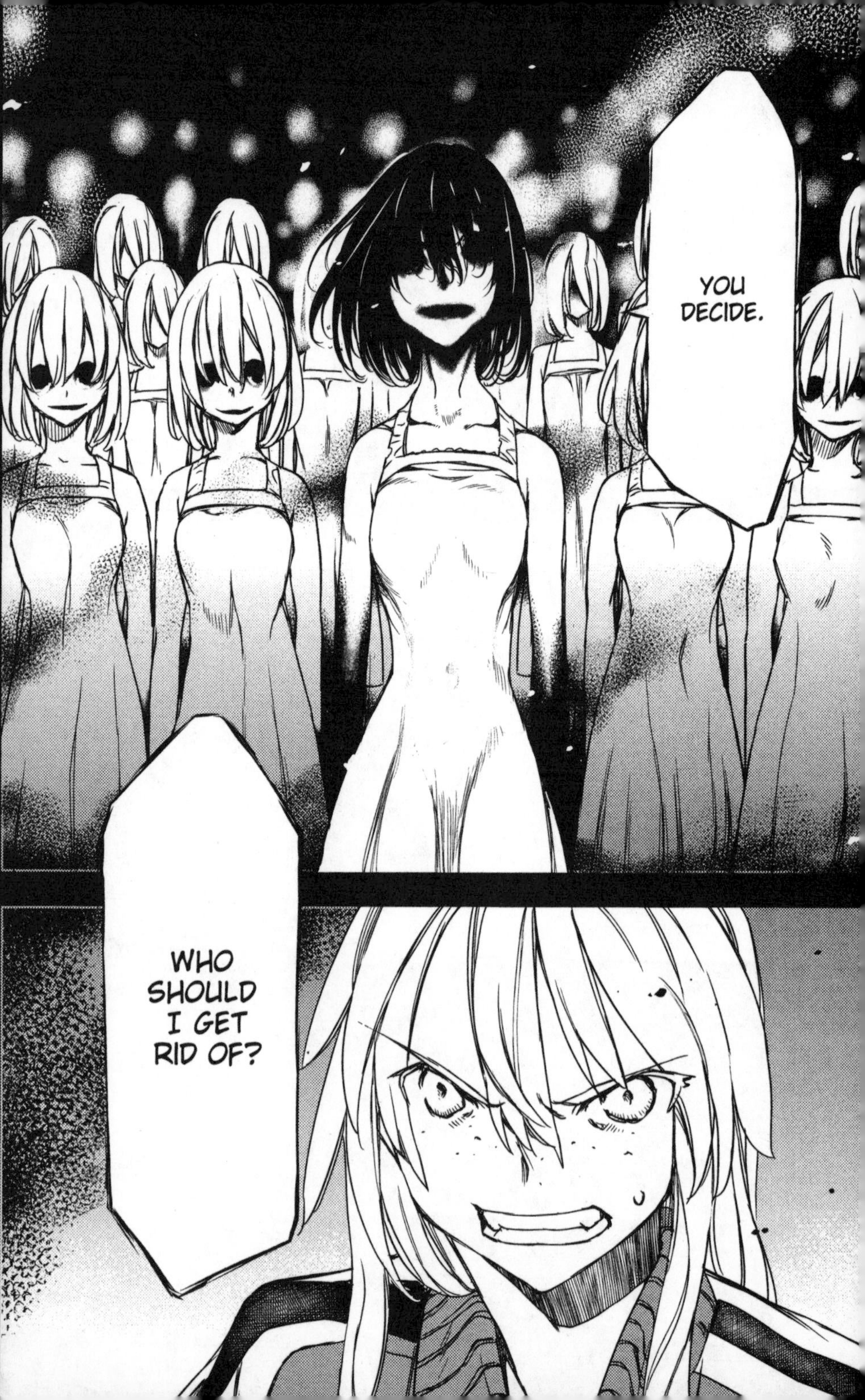
YOU DECIDE.
WHO SHOULD I GET RID OF?

CHAPTER 70 ✚ THE STRONGEST LITTLE SISTER

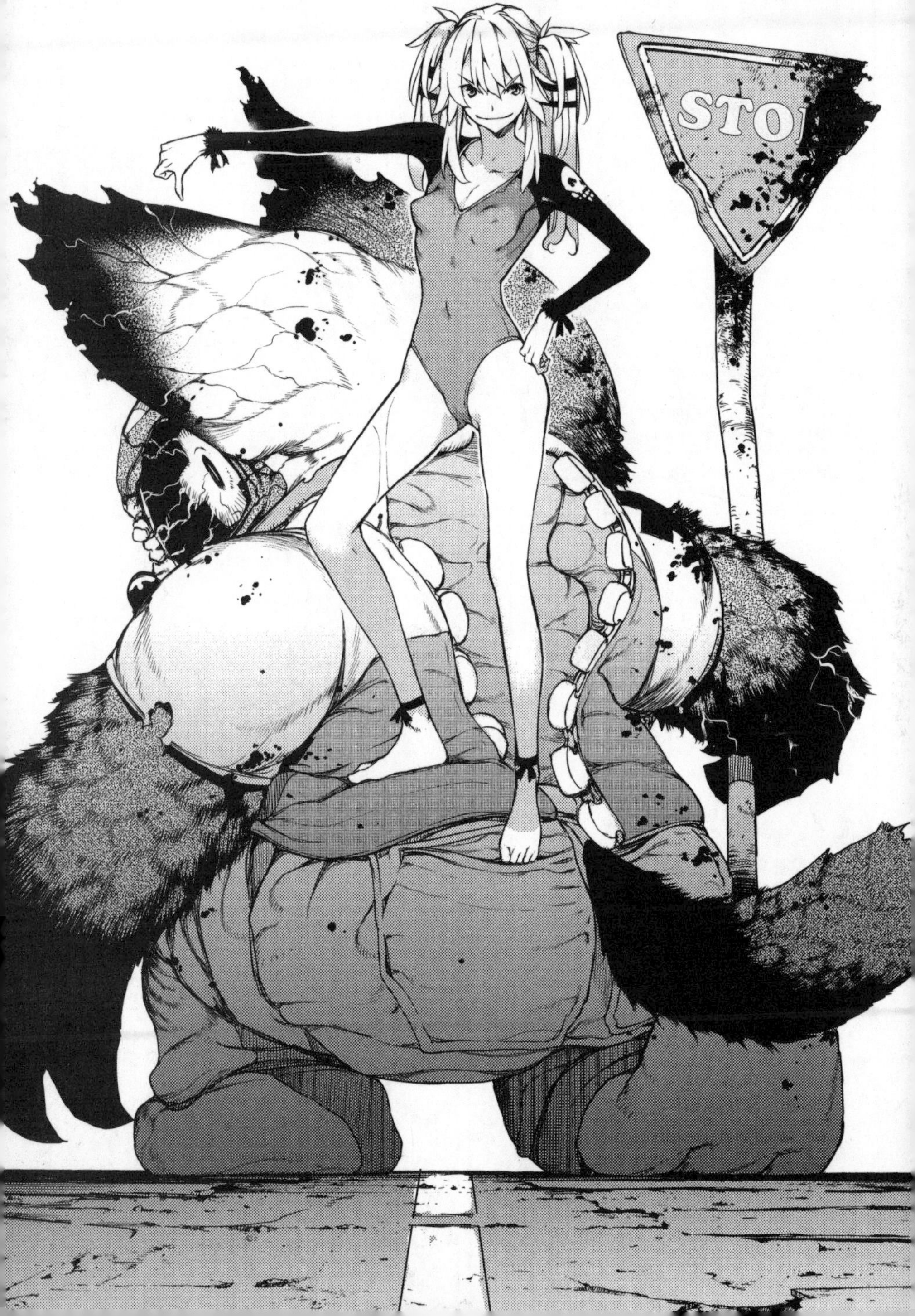
STO

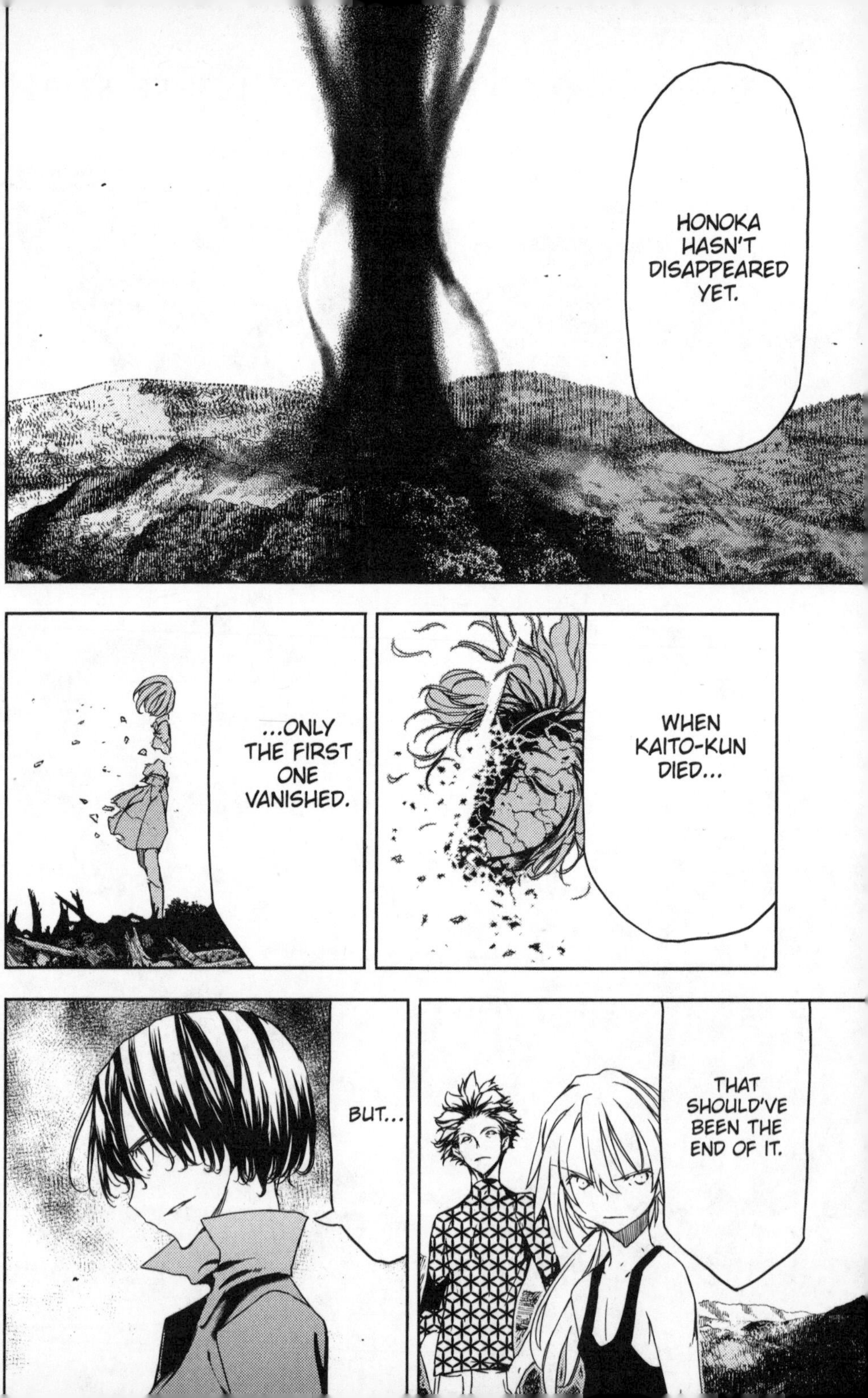
HONOKA HASN'T DISAPPEARED YET.
WHEN KAITO-KUN DIED...
...ONLY THE FIRST ONE VANISHED.
THAT SHOULD'VE BEEN THE END OF IT.
BUT...

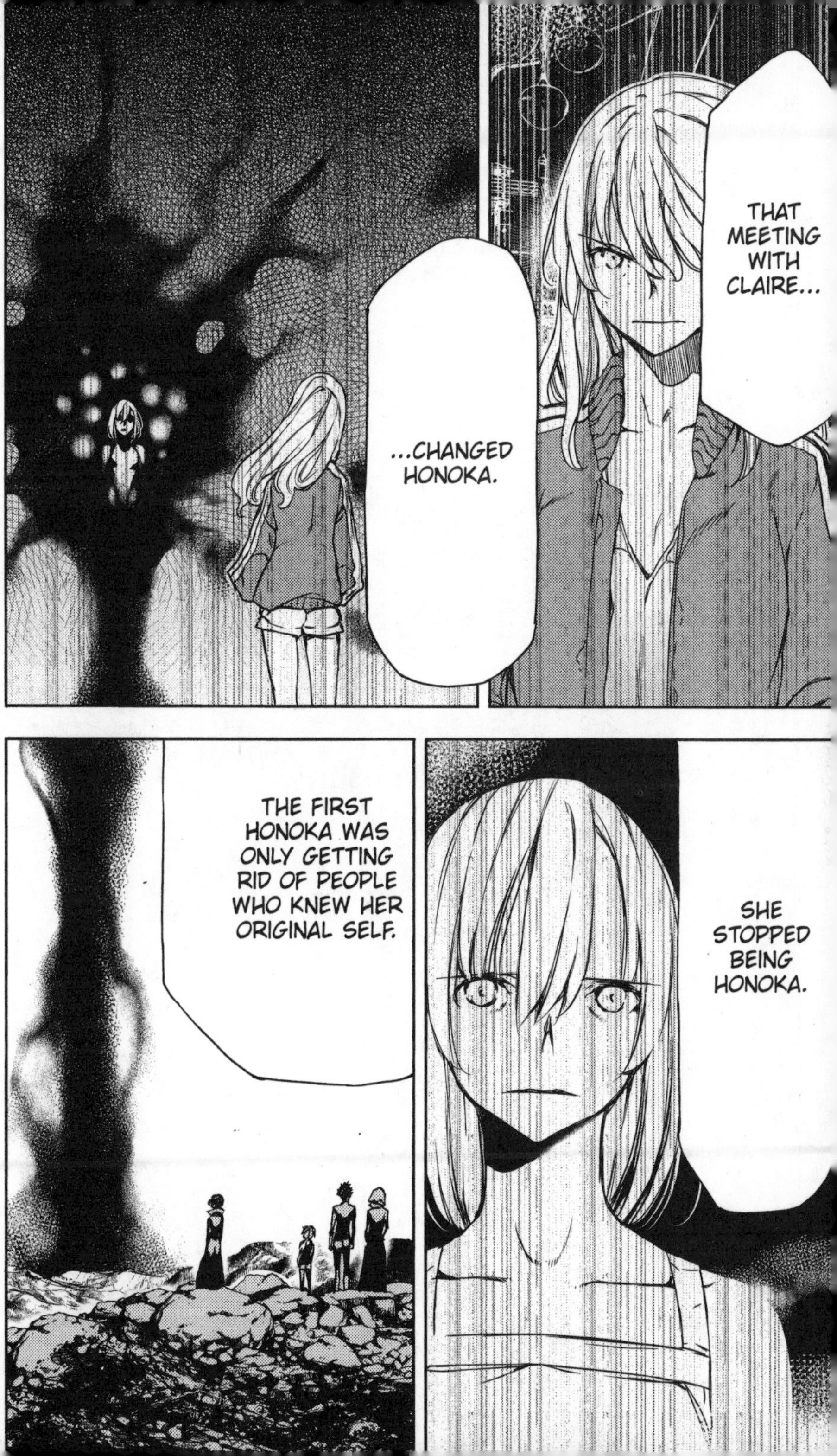
THAT MEETING WITH CLAIRE...
...CHANGED HONOKA.
SHE STOPPED BEING HONOKA.
THE FIRST HONOKA WAS ONLY GETTING RID OF PEOPLE WHO KNEW HER ORIGINAL SELF.

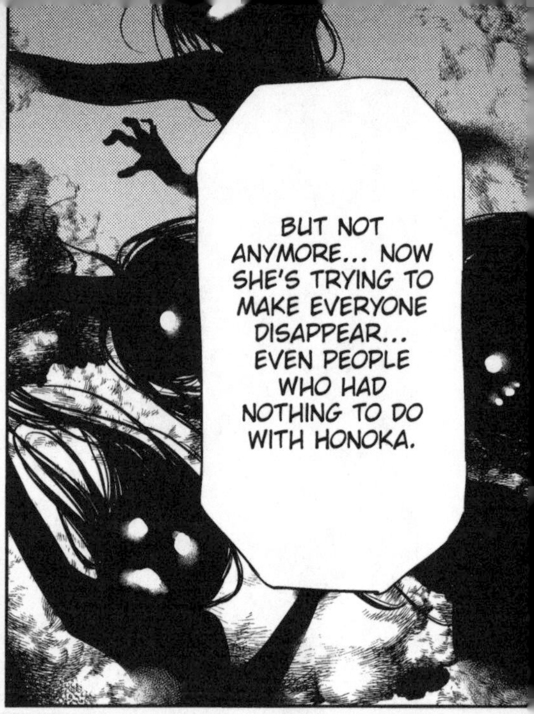
BUT NOT ANYMORE... NOW SHE'S TRYING TO MAKE EVERYONE DISAPPEAR... EVEN PEOPLE WHO HAD NOTHING TO DO WITH HONOKA.

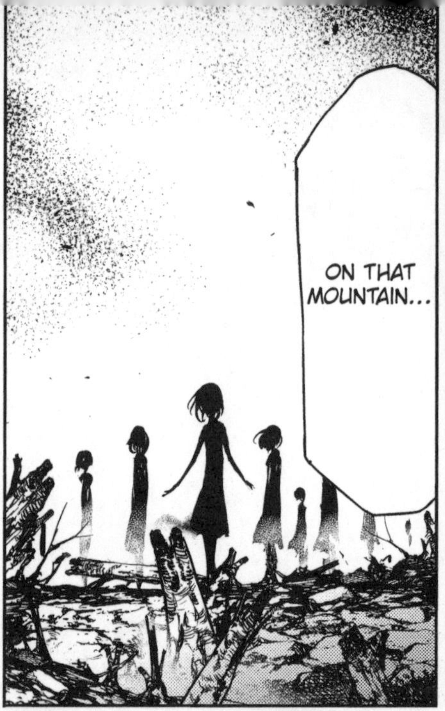
ON THAT MOUNTAIN...

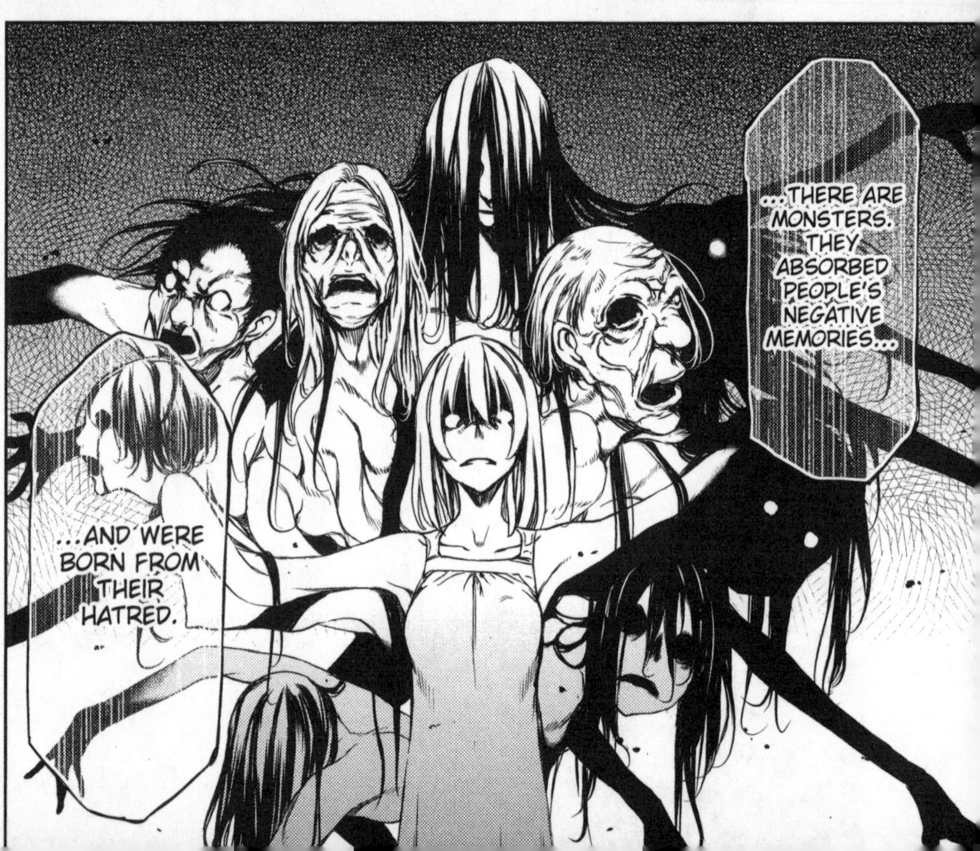
...THERE ARE MONSTERS. THEY ABSORBED PEOPLE'S NEGATIVE MEMORIES...
...AND WERE BORN FROM THEIR HATRED.

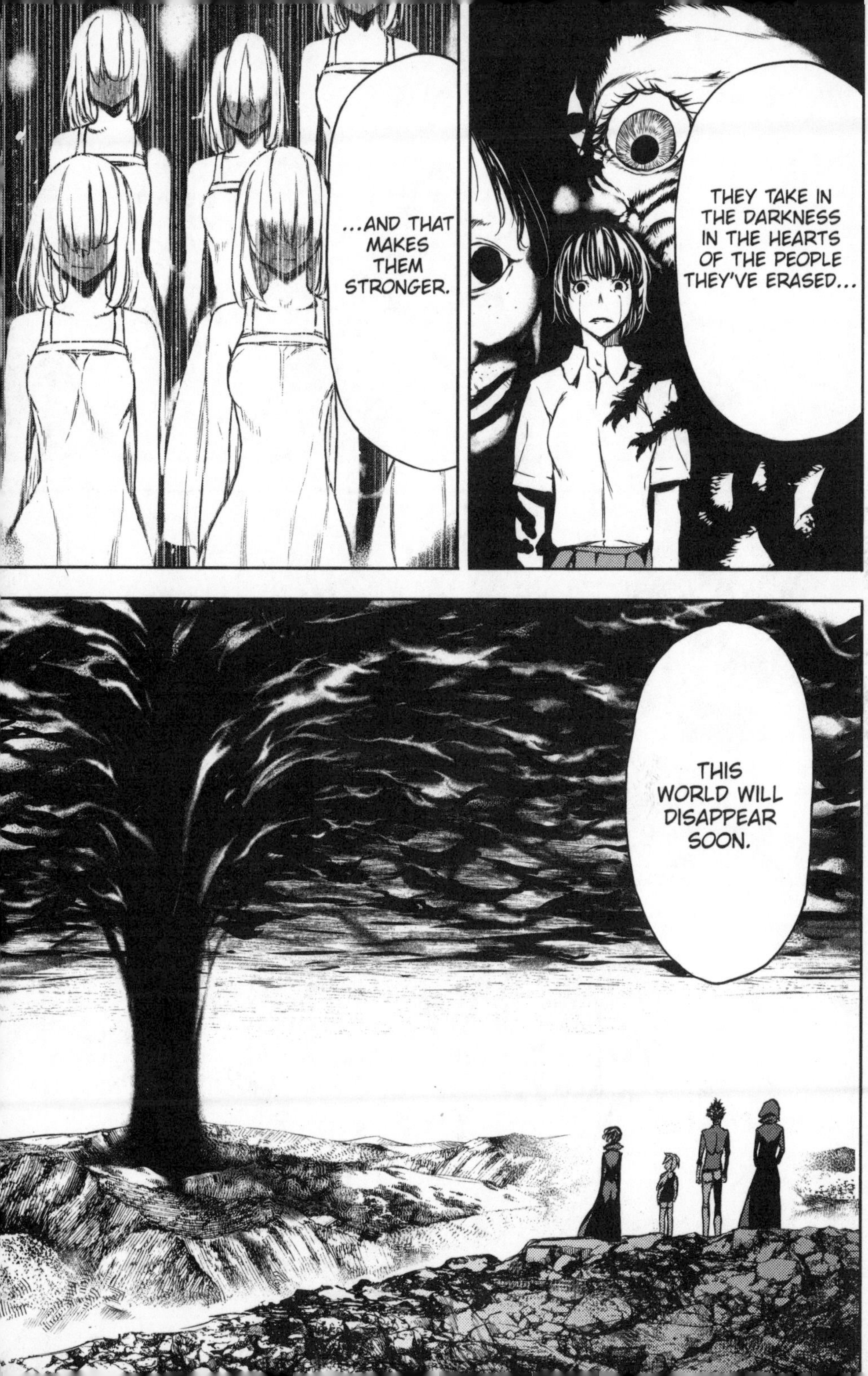
THEY TAKE IN THE DARKNESS IN THE HEARTS OF THE PEOPLE THEY'VE ERASED...
...AND THAT MAKES THEM STRONGER.
THIS WORLD WILL DISAPPEAR SOON.

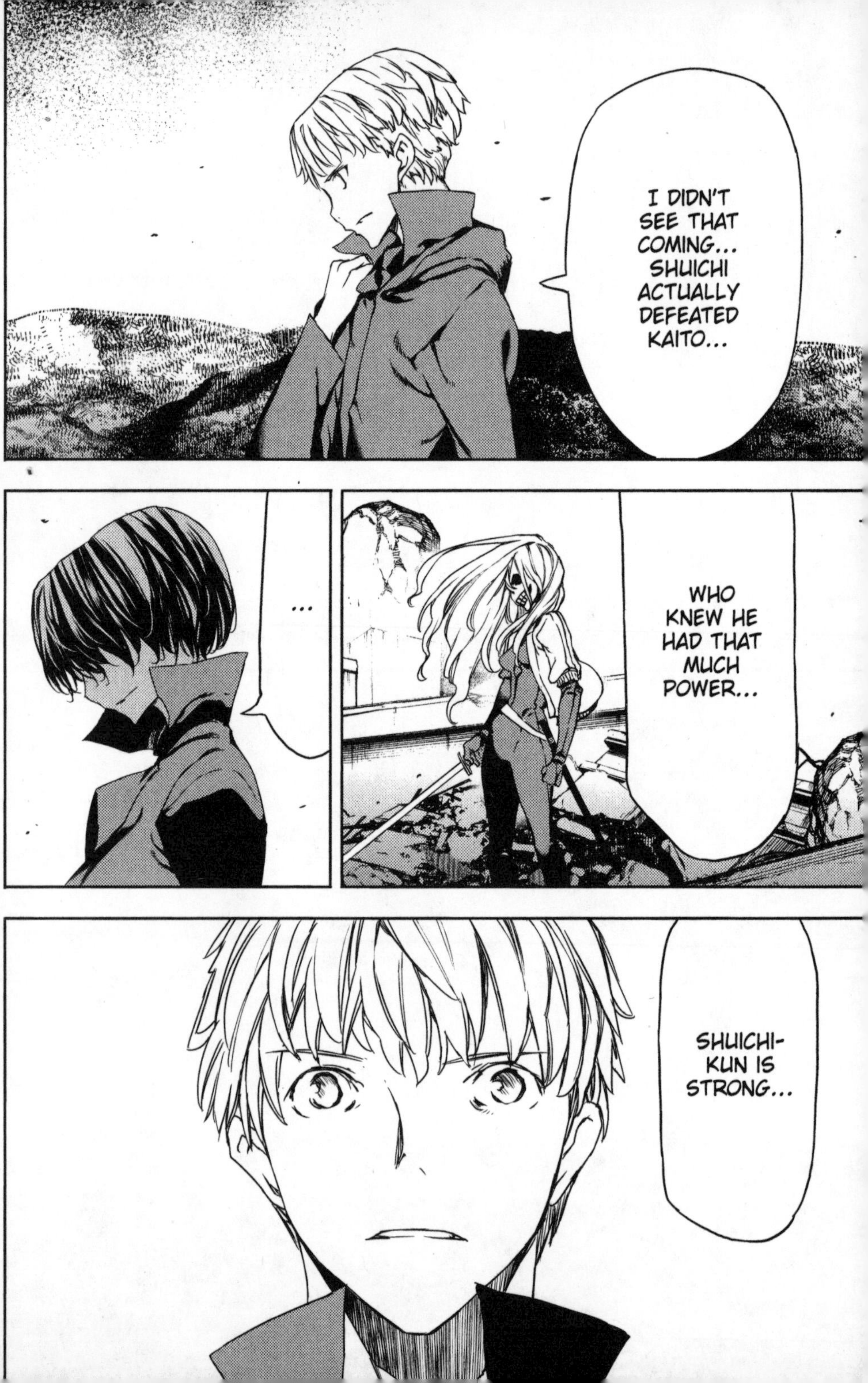
I DIDN'T SEE THAT COMING... SHUICHI ACTUALLY DEFEATED KAITO...
WHO KNEW HE HAD THAT MUCH POWER...
...
SHUICHI-KUN IS STRONG...

MUCH STRONGER THAN YOU THINK...

BUT HE'S TOO KIND.

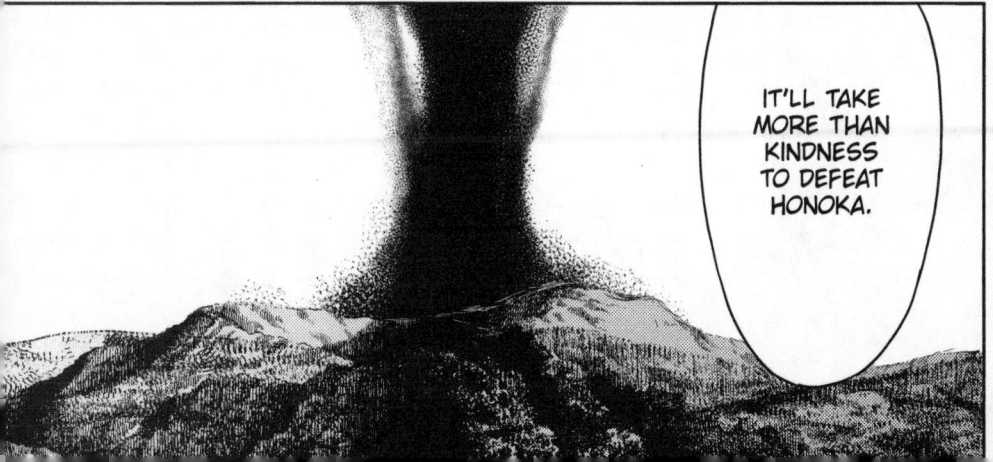

IT'LL TAKE MORE THAN KINDNESS TO DEFEAT HONOKA.

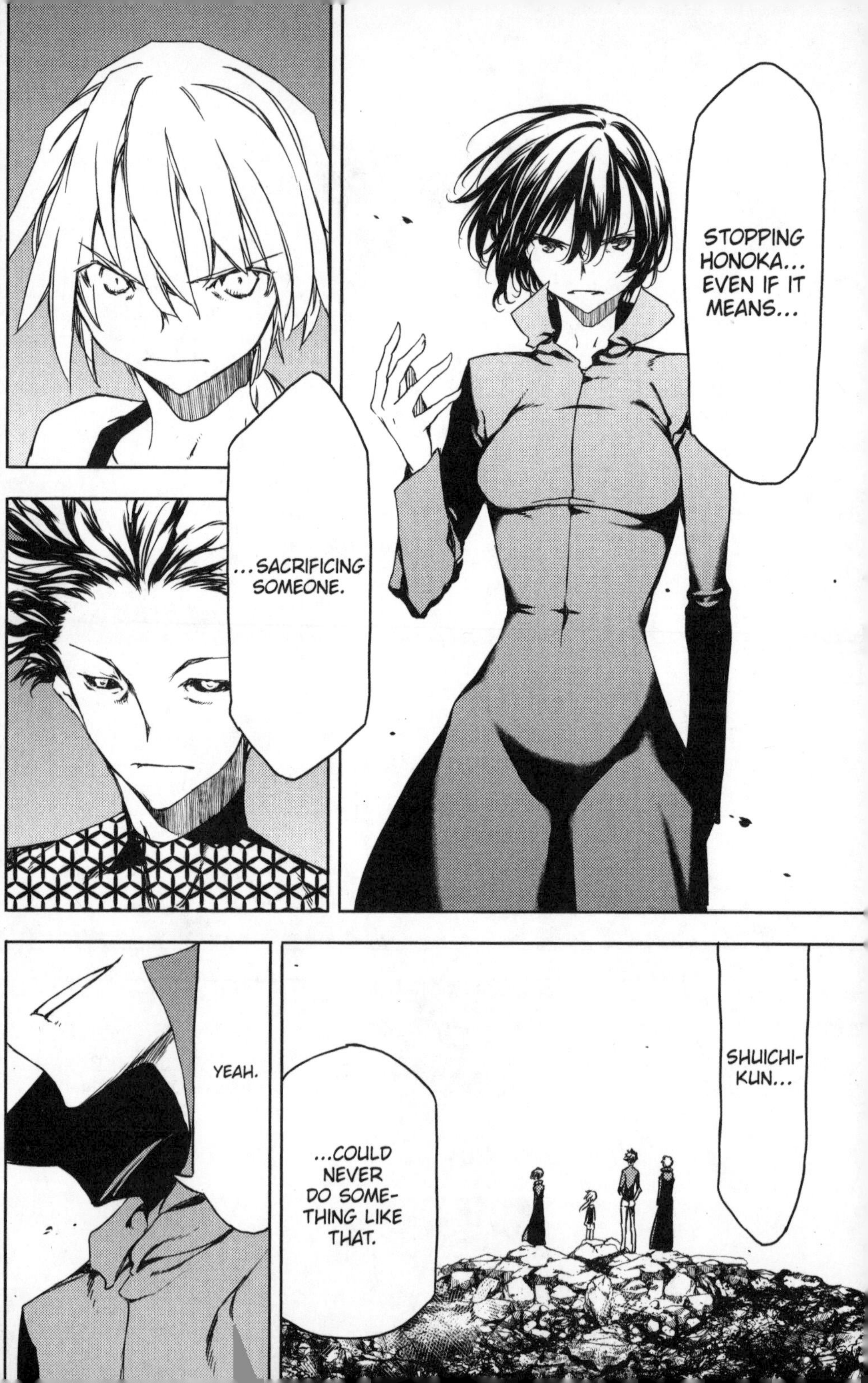
STOPPING HONOKA... EVEN IF IT MEANS...
...SACRIFICING SOMEONE.
SHUICHI-KUN...
...COULD NEVER DO SOME-THING LIKE THAT.
YEAH.

I WANT SHUICHI TO STAY ALIVE, TOO.

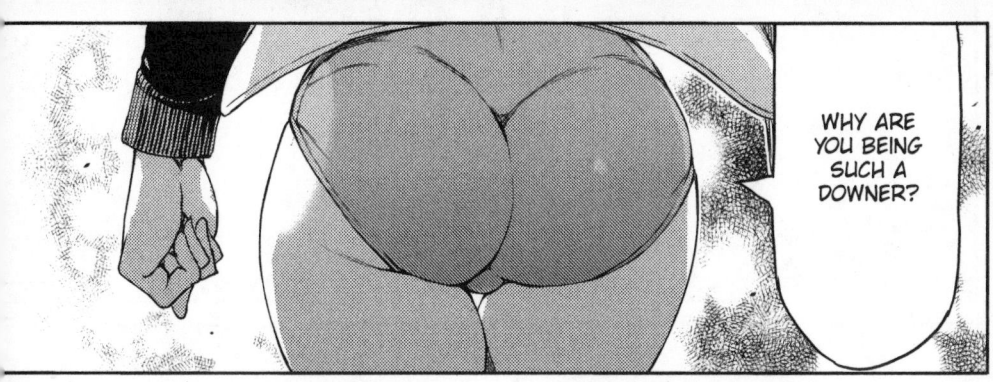

WHY ARE YOU BEING SUCH A DOWNER?

'CUZ ...

NOBODY'S GOING TO DIE.

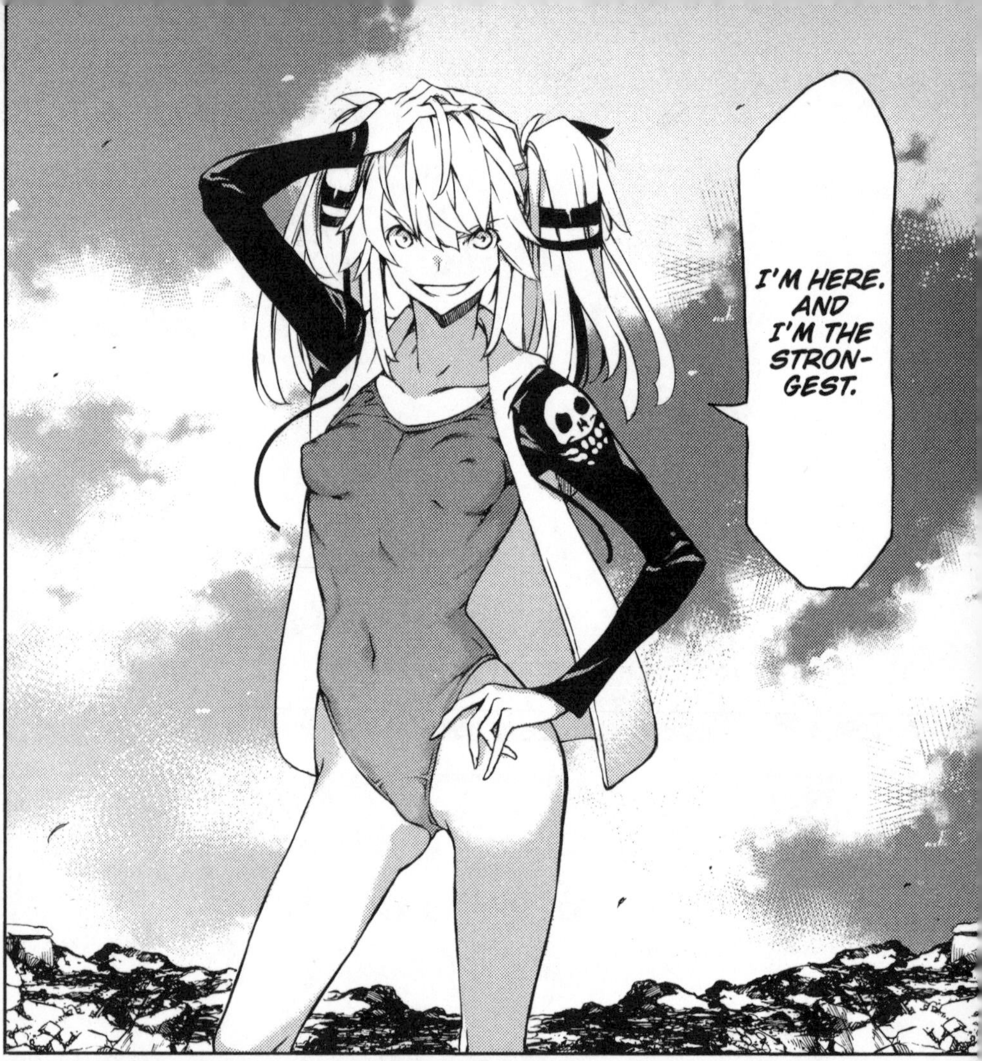
I'M HERE. AND I'M THE STRONG-GEST.
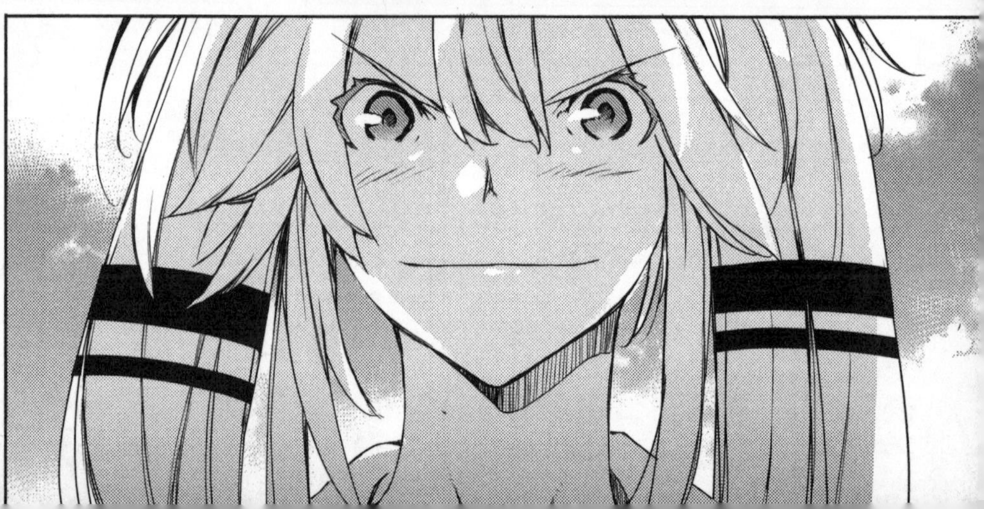

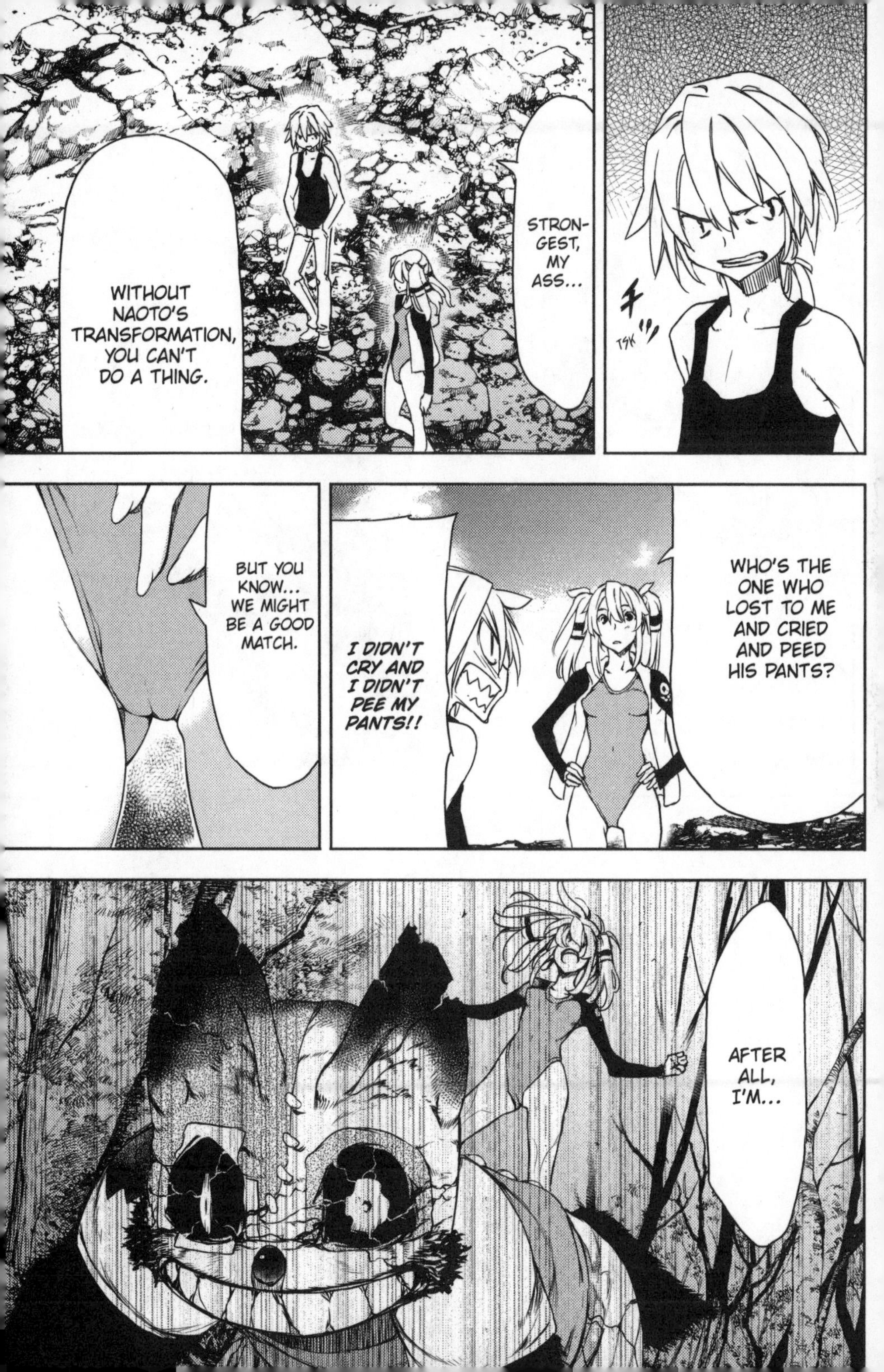
TSK
STRON-GEST, MY ASS...
WITHOUT NAOTO'S TRANSFORMATION, YOU CAN'T DO A THING.
WHO'S THE ONE WHO LOST TO ME AND CRIED AND PEED HIS PANTS?
I DIDN'T CRY AND I DIDN'T PEE MY PANTS!!
BUT YOU KNOW... WE MIGHT BE A GOOD MATCH.
AFTER ALL, I'M...

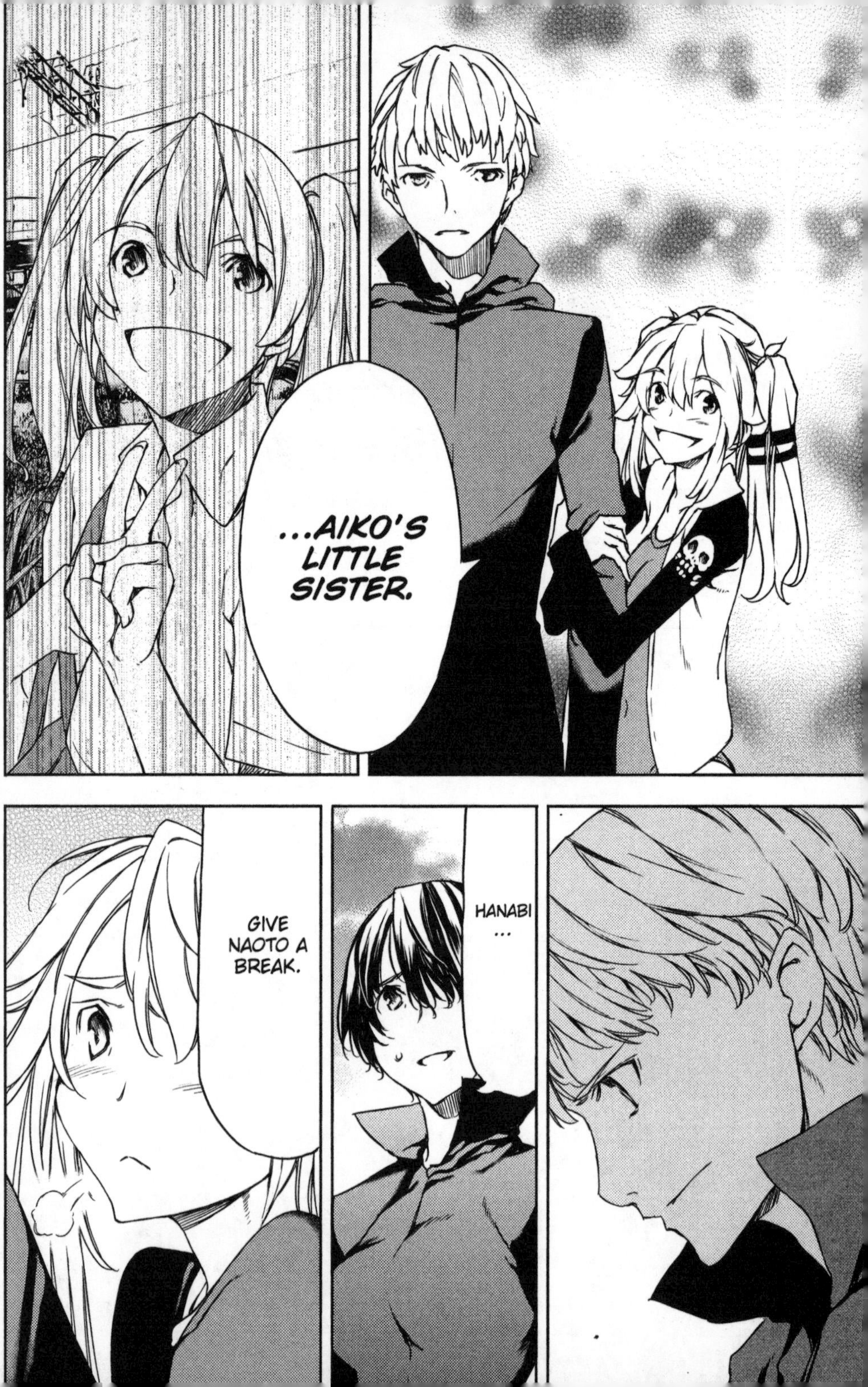
...AIKO'S LITTLE SISTER.
HANABI ...
GIVE NAOTO A BREAK.

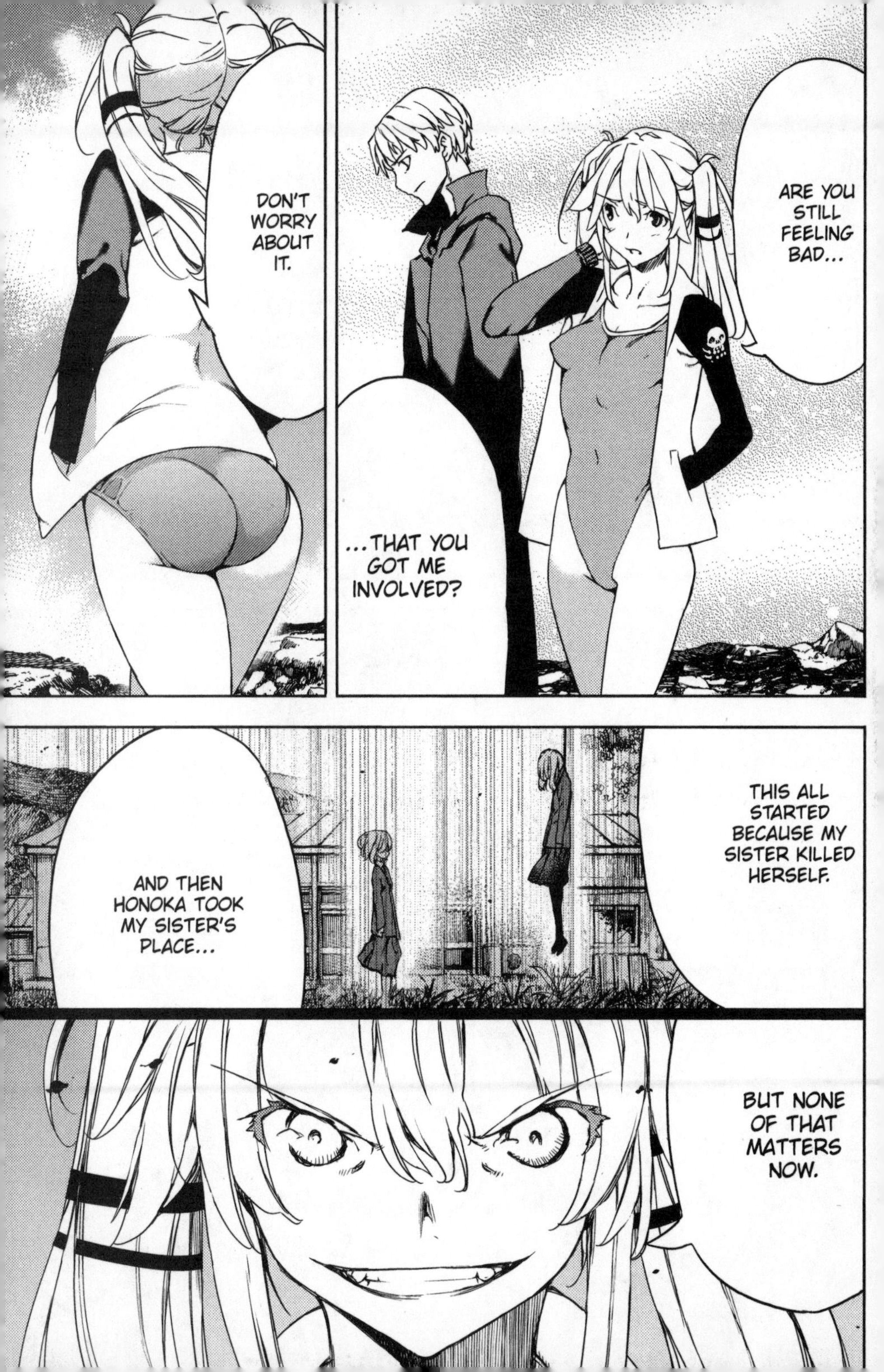
ARE YOU STILL FEELING BAD...
...THAT YOU GOT ME INVOLVED?
DON'T WORRY ABOUT IT.
THIS ALL STARTED BECAUSE MY SISTER KILLED HERSELF.
AND THEN HONOKA TOOK MY SISTER'S PLACE...
BUT NONE OF THAT MATTERS NOW.

EITHER WAY...IF WE DON'T DEFEAT HONOKA, THIS WORLD IS GOING TO DISAPPEAR.
SO WHETHER WE JUST LET HER ERASE US...
...OR WE DIE FIGHTING... IT'S ALL THE SAME.
WE DON'T NEED THAT SHUICHI GUY'S HELP.

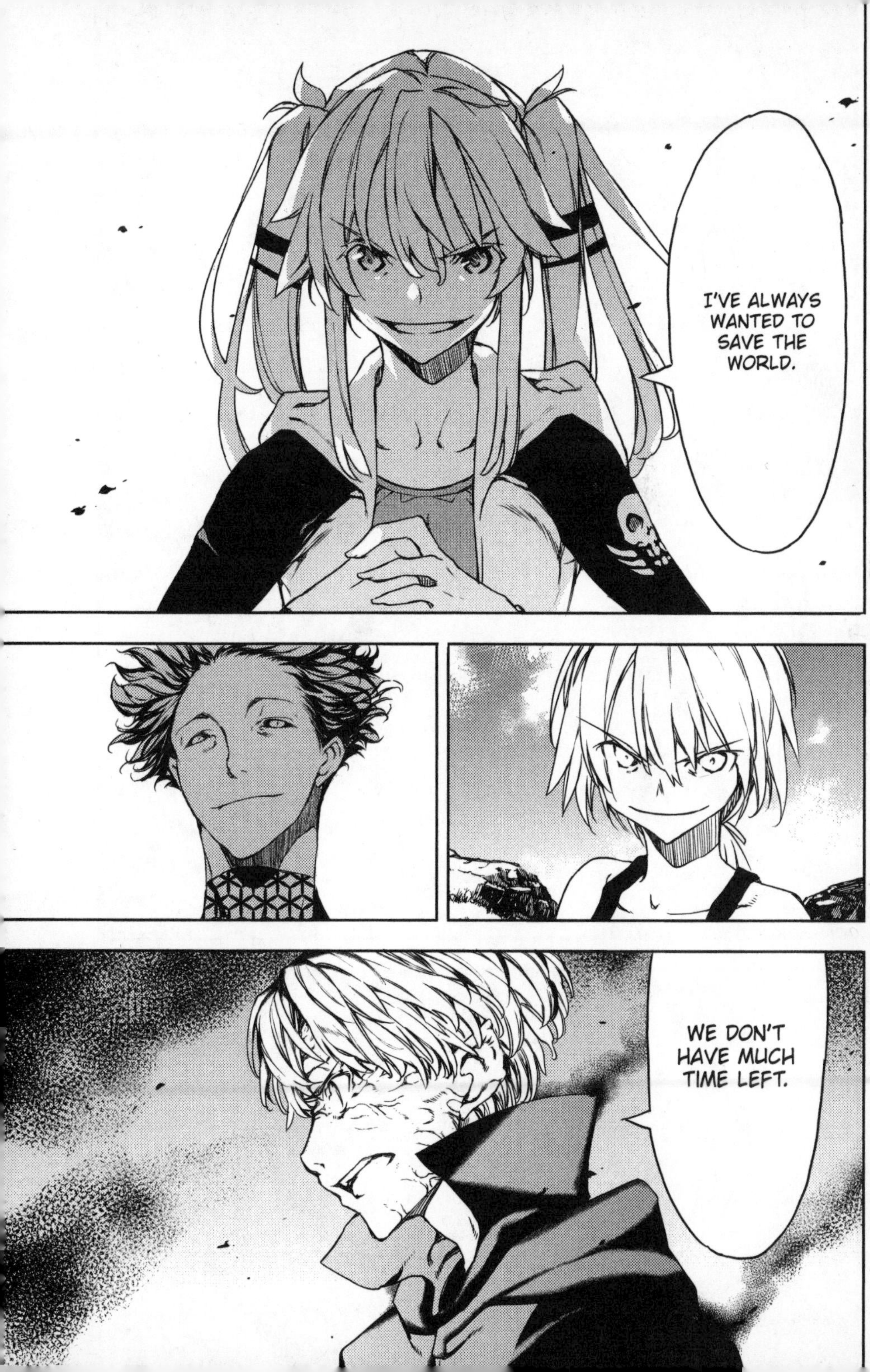
I'VE ALWAYS WANTED TO SAVE THE WORLD.
WE DON'T HAVE MUCH TIME LEFT.

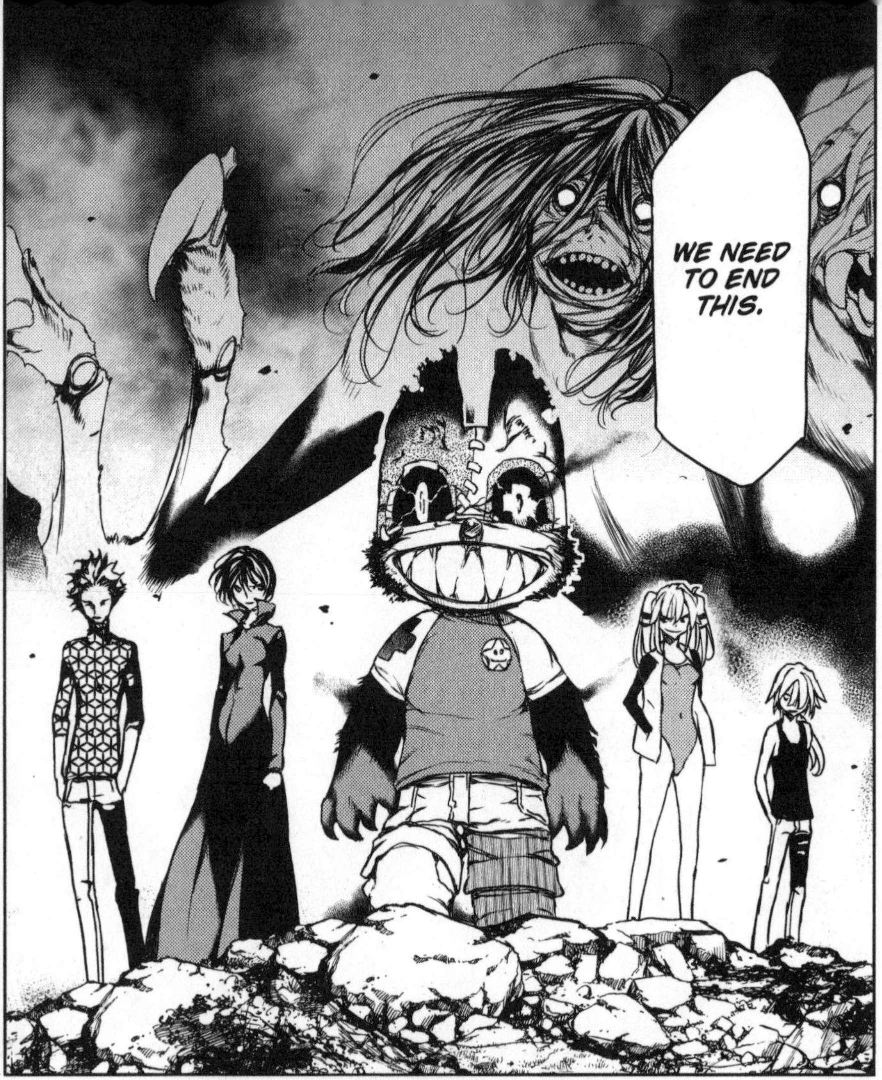
WE NEED TO END THIS.
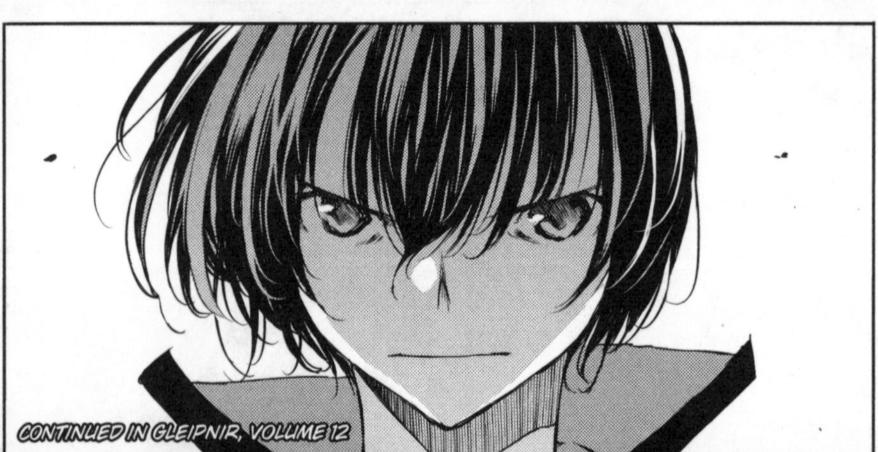
CONTINUED IN GLEIPNIR, VOLUME 12

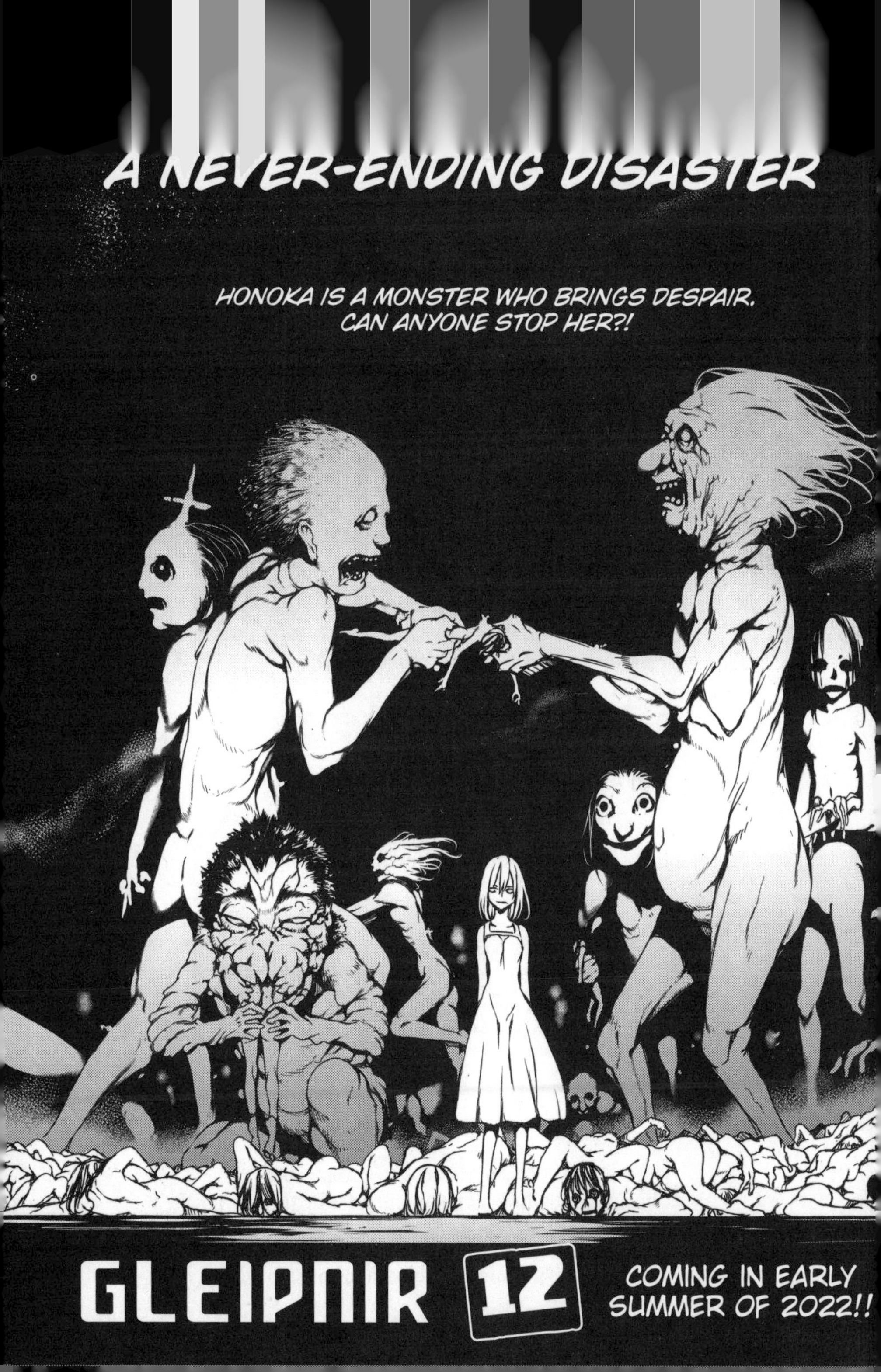
A NEVER-ENDING DISASTER
HONOKA IS A MONSTER WHO BRINGS DESPAIR. CAN ANYONE STOP HER?!
GLEIPNIR 12
COMING IN EARLY SUMMER OF 2022!!

A Kodansha Comics Trade Paperback Original
Gleipnir 11 copyright © 2021 Sun Takeda
English translation copyright © 2022 Sun Takeda

Published in the United States by Kodansha Comics, an imprint of Kodansha USA Publishing, LLC, New York.

Publication rights for this English edition arranged through Kodansha Ltd., Tokyo.

First published in Japan in 2021 by Kodansha Ltd., Tokyo.
as *Gureipuniiru*, volume 11.

ISBN 978-1-64651-397-0

Printed in the United States of America.

www.kodansha.us

9 8 7 6 5 4 3 2 1
Translation: Iyasu Adair Nagata
Lettering: Daniel Lee
Editing: Jordan Blanco
Kodansha Comics edition cover design by Phil Balsman

Publisher: Kiichiro Sugawara

Director of publishing services: Ben Applegate
Director of publishing operations: Dave Barrett
Associate director, publishing operations: Stephen Pakula
Publishing services managing editors: Madison Salters, Alanna Ruse
Production managers: Emi Lotto, Angela Zurlo